THE
MEDICI GIRAFFE

THE
MEDICI GIRAFFE

AND OTHER TALES OF
EXOTIC ANIMALS AND POWER

MARINA BELOZERSKAYA

LITTLE, BROWN AND COMPANY

New York   Boston   London

Little, Brown and Company
Hachette Book Group USA
1271 Avenue of the Americas, New York, NY 10020
Visit our Web site at www.HachetteBookGroupUSA.com

Copyright acknowledgments appear on page 388.

First Edition: August 2006

Library of Congress Cataloging-in-Publication Data

Belozerskaya, Marina.
    The Medici giraffe : and other tales of exotic animals and power / Marina
Belozerskaya. — 1st ed.
        p.   cm.
    ISBN-13: 978-0-316-52565-7
    ISBN-10: 0-316-52565-0
    1. Wild animals as pets — History.   2. Wild animals collecting — History.
3. Exotic animals — History.   4. Human-animal relationships — History.
5. Diplomatic gifts — History.   I. Title.

SF411.35.B45 2006
636 — dc22   2006009659

10   9   8   7   6   5   4   3   2   1

Q-FF

Printed in the United States of America

Book design by JoAnne Metsch

TO AUDREY,
MY FOUR-LEGGED MUSE

CONTENTS

ILLUSTRATIONS

CHAPTER 1: Silver phalera depicting a war elephant. Hellenistic period.
Courtesy of The State Hermitage Museum, St. Petersburg

CHAPTER 2: Mosaic showing an elephant being loaded onto a ship. Found at a Roman villa at Veii (Italy), second century AD (?). Badisches Landesmuseum Karlsruhe.
Photograph by Kenneth Lapatin

CHAPTER 3: Giorgio Vasari, *Homage to Lorenzo Il Magnifico*. Sala di Lorenzo, Palazzo Vecchio, Florence.
Courtesy of Scala / Art Resource, New York

CHAPTER 4: Aztec juggler drawn by Christoph Weiditz in his *Das Trachtenbuch des Christoph Weiditz von seinen Reisen nach Spanien (1529) und den Niederlanden (1531/32)*, Nürnberg, Germanisches Nationalmuseum Handschrift 22474. After Theodor Hampe's fascimile of this volume, Berlin und Leipzig: Verlag von Walter De Gruyter & Co., 1927.
Photograph by Kenneth Lapatin

CHAPTER 5: Frontispiece from Benedetto Ceruti and Andrea Chiocco, *Musaeum Francesci Calceolari junioris*

Veronensis (Verona, 1622), illustrating the natural history collection founded by Francesco Calzolari, a contemporary of Rudolf.

Courtesy of Getty Research Institute, Special Collections

CHAPTER 6: Title page emblem showing Josephine's park at Malmaison in François Péron's *Voyage de decouvertes aux terres Australes* (Paris, 1807–1816), call number Oc 128.06.5*.

By permission of the Houghton Library, Harvard University

CHAPTER 7: William Randolph Hearst seated in front of a fountain with his dachshund Helen.

© Hearst Castle® / CA State Parks

INTRODUCTION

A few years ago I read Silvio Bedini's *The Pope's Elephant,* a fascinating account of a white elephant named Hanno that the king of Portugal, Emmanuel I, sent to Pope Leo X in 1516 to cajole the pontiff into granting him a trade monopoly in the Spice Islands. The story captured my imagination. Animals as diplomatic gifts, I thought; how clever, how perfect. The more I considered it, and paid attention, the more I noticed exotic beasts peeking from the margins of history. Yet if they were such effective and memorable presents, why did they so seldom appear in history books?

In our age of easy travel and global media, exotic animals still delight but rarely truly astonish us. We are superficially familiar with a great variety of them and tend to take them for granted. For much of history, when fauna from distant lands was scarce and communication slow, strange beasts could be potent, marvelous, and terrifying.

Mesopotamian kings, who received foreign beasts as tribute, for example, laid out splendid parks called *paradeisoi,* in which they kept their exotic stock. These royal preserves provided the model for the Garden of Eden, the biblical paradise where God created all the animals before sculpting man.

The very difficulty of finding rare beasts made them impressive diplomatic gifts. Seeking to climb higher and higher in society, the Medici married into the French royal family in 1533.

During the wedding Pope Clement VII, who arranged the union of his kinswoman Catherine de' Medici to Henry II, exchanged a series of lavish gifts with his French in-laws. He gave them splendid objects of gold and precious stones, a unicorn's horn, and a tapestry replicating Leonardo's *Last Supper*. The king of France reciprocated with a live lion. For millennia people have endowed lions with regal connotations, so the animal was a flattering gift to the Medici, who had risen to the papal throne from humble merchant beginnings.

The Chinese emperor Xian Zong Zhu Jianshen, however, was presented with so many lions that when an embassy from Sultan Ahmid, the Timurid ruler of Samarkand, arrived at his court in the 1480s with two more of these beasts, the emperor protested. Quite contrary to the Confucian tradition of graciously accepting gifts from vassals, he declared that lions were useless animals, too expensive to keep and not even fit to harness in front of his carriage. He had had enough of them.

Akbar the Great, the Mughal emperor of India in the sixteenth century, meanwhile, treated his exotic pets with such care and esteem that he ordered his personal doctors to look after his tigers, cheetahs, and deer, as well as his army of five thousand elephants. And he invited the populace at large to visit his animals, urging them, "Meet your brothers, take them to your hearts and respect them."

In coming across such stories, I found that what people thought about exotic animals and how they treated them in different times and places is most revealing. As the anthropologist Claude Lévi-Strauss remarked, societies accord animals special status not because they are "good to eat," but because they are "good to think."

As I began gathering examples of animal collecting, I realized that I did not want to write an encyclopedic account of all the zoos ever kept. (For those who want such a study, I recommend

Gustav Loisel's three-volume *Histoire des ménageries de l'antiquité a nos jours,* published in Paris in 1912.) Instead, I decided to concentrate on a smaller number of collectors whose preoccupations with exotic creatures and treatment of them somehow reflected the mentality and aspirations of their age. I focused my investigation on princes, because through much of history only the rich and powerful had the means to acquire and maintain large groups of rare beasts. Zoos as we know them — public institutions created for educating and diverting the masses — grew out of royal collections only in the nineteenth century. Before that, menageries were privately owned and privately enjoyed, even if — as in the case of Montezuma's vast assortment of animals, birds, and human oddities from across the Aztec Empire — they could be something of a state institution. Besides, I was less interested in zoological organizations shaped by committees than in the individuals who felt compelled for one reason or another to expend enormous resources on tracking down, capturing, transporting, and maintaining wild animals from distant lands.

This book, therefore, consists of a chain of stories that begins in ancient Alexandria and ends at the National Zoo in Washington, D.C. The first story looks at how elephants helped Ptolemy Philadelphos build his kingdom and usher in the golden age of Alexandria. The next one witnesses Pompey the Great gathering hundreds of rare beasts from the territories he conquered and slaughtering them in a public spectacle to assert Rome's mastery over the world and his over Rome. In the Renaissance, the Medici, eager to present themselves as true princes, used exotic animals to boost their image: Cosimo de' Medici staged animal combats in the ancient style, while his grandson Lorenzo the Magnificent imported an unusual beast to shore up his authority in a moment of political crisis.

The story of the vast zoological complex of the Aztec king Montezuma, and of the Spanish conquistadors' response to it (and to the Aztecs themselves), considers the ambiguous and slippery boundary between "humans" and "animals." Rudolf II's collection in seventeenth-century Prague reveals how in that age of renewed fascination with natural history, animals were thought to hold a key to the universe. At the turn of the nineteenth century, the nationalistic urge to advance science led a French captain, Nicolas Baudin, on a perilous voyage to Australia. One of the chief beneficiaries of this spectacular and catastrophic expedition was Josephine Bonaparte, who hoped to use her menagerie to stake out a position independent of Napoleon.

In the early twentieth century, William Randolph Hearst cared passionately about his zoo at San Simeon, in part out of a boyish delight in four-legged creatures, but also out of concern for animal well-being, a preoccupation gaining momentum at that time. Finally, the stories of the giant pandas presented to the United States by the Chinese government demonstrate that the tradition of animal gifts at the highest levels of international diplomacy continues into the present. At the same time, the pandas have come to symbolize an international commitment to the preservation of a highly endangered species — even as they bring into relief our overwhelming modern tendency to anthropomorphize wild animals, as we do so often with our pets.

Each of these stories has its own theme: how menageries served the practical needs of empire building, reflected the wonder of God's creation, or spurred exploration and science. But running through the whole book are larger questions: Why have exotic animals exercised such a pull on people in so many eras and cultures? Why have they been counted among the most advantageous diplomatic gifts, the most cherished royal treasures, and the most impressive symbols of power and learning? How did they make or break rulers and help to shape the definition of what it means to be civilized?

Animals provide us with a useful mirror. From the slaughter of foreign beasts in Roman arenas to our own efforts to perpetuate endangered species in modern zoos and animal preserves, we can see a panorama of human ambitions and ideals, accomplishments and failings. In telling the following stories, I hope to show that the way we perceive and treat animals illuminates our own values, concerns, and aspirations. By pondering the relationships we have had with them across the centuries, we may discover something about ourselves.

THE
MEDICI GIRAFFE

ONE

ELEPHANTS FOR A KINGDOM

By the great bulk of their bodies, the terror inspired by their trumpeting, and the strangeness of their shape, elephants in battle throw into confusion both men and horses.

VEGETIUS,
A Summary of Military Matters

In 275 BC Alexandria was the largest city in the classical world, surpassing in many eyes all others in wealth and beauty. Its grand public buildings had been constructed at enormous expense from limestone and imported marble. Its wide avenues were cooled by refreshing sea breezes. Its gardens flowered year-round with lush vegetation that astonished visitors from harsher climates. An unrivaled center of trade, Alexandria brimmed with goods and people from all over, and its Museum and Library attracted men of learning from around the Mediterranean.

But when Ptolemy Philadelphos ascended the throne of Egypt there on January 7, 282 BC, the city was still a young and relatively modest settlement, its future as uncertain as that of the twenty-five-year-old king. Alexandria had been founded by Alexander the Great only a generation earlier — yet another domineering gesture as he swept through the East to destroy the Persian Empire and make the world his own. When Alexander died in 323 BC, both the city and the kingdom of Egypt were claimed by one of his generals, Ptolemy. As Alexander's successors squabbled over their dead leader's legacy and tried to grab chunks of territory off one another's plates, it was far from certain whether Ptolemy would manage to hold on to Egypt. His son Ptolemy Philadelphos inherited the kingdom, as well as these ongoing disputes. Would the new king be able to retain his father's bequest, or would he squander it in seemingly endless conflicts?

Of all the threats Ptolemy Philadelphos faced, the most difficult was the contest over Coele-Syria (southern Syria) with Antiochos I, the son of another of Alexander's generals, Seleukos. Coele-Syria was in those days the end point of the great trade routes stretching from the East. Caravans loaded with Arabian and Indian gems, spices, and especially frankincense and myrrh — indispensable to religious rituals throughout the ancient world and prized for their medicinal and cosmetic benefits — terminated their thousand-mile journeys in Coele-Syria. From the province's ports, these precious goods were shipped all over the Mediterranean. The region also grew cedar, a highly prized and durable wood that resisted rot and insects, took a good polish, and had a close, straight grain that made it easy to work. Because the trees grew exceptionally tall and straight, cedars of Lebanon were particularly desirable for building temples and ships. For the Ptolemies, who relied on a strong navy to defend their Mediterranean frontier, cedar was a crucial resource.

The Ptolemies and the Seleukids had equal entitlement to Coele-Syria. All the territories they claimed had been up for grabs after Alexander's death, and the one who was most assertive, opportunistic, or ruthless got to hold on to his spoils. The problem for Ptolemy Philadelphos was his military imbalance vis-à-vis Antiochos — namely, his shortage of elephants.

For centuries elephants had been used as war machines in India and the Persian Empire, but the Greeks encountered this military technology only during Alexander's eastern campaign. After his death, elephants became indispensable to his successors in their struggles with one another. Unfortunately for Ptolemy Philadelphos, he had but a small contingent of these giants and no way of obtaining more, while his enemy Antiochos possessed them by the hundreds and controlled the access routes to Asia, the source of all elephants at that time. To wrest control over Coele-Syria from Antiochos and to preserve his kingdom, Ptolemy Philadelphos desperately needed to find his own supply of elephants. Little did he know when he began this quest that while elephants themselves would prove inconsequential to his military maneuvers, his search for them would turn his newly inherited kingdom into a lasting dynastic power and Alexandria into a jewel of the ancient world.

HOW DID THE Hellenistic kingdoms in the time between Alexander's death and the ascent of Rome come to hinge on elephants?

Alexander and his army first came across this astounding animal machinery during their assault on the Persian Empire. At the Battle of Gaugamela (in modern Iraq) in 331 BC, Darius, the king of Persia, met his Greek enemy with a phalanx of fifteen elephants. Flapping their ears, trumpeting, and stomping the ground with their treelike feet, the giant beasts were terrifying to the uninitiated. They threw soldiers and horses into panic, trampled them underfoot, and wreaked havoc on the battlefield. Being a superb strategist, Alexander managed to outmaneuver these living tanks and to win the battle. Still, he grasped the tactical usefulness of elephant warriors and determined to assemble his own animal troops.

Alexander captured Darius's animals at Gaugamela, took others in subsequent battles, and demanded elephants as tribute from the rulers whose territories he traversed on his unstoppable march east. Eventually he herded along such a vast elephant contingent — in addition to his regular troops, horses, military machinery, and camp followers — that he began to give away some of these beasts as special gifts to foreign allies. Unfortunately, he was moving so swiftly from one region to another, one military engagement to the next, that he had no time to make proper use of his elephants. Horses and men had to be trained not to fear them and to fight alongside them as a cohesive force. Alexander had no time for such lessons. So for the moment, he simply used his elephants to transport the army's supplies and equipment and to stand ceremonially and majestically at the entrance to his throne room.

After more than five years of ceaseless campaigns, during which Alexander conquered Asia Minor, Egypt, Palestine, and Mesopotamia, his elephants were still not integrated into his army. This proved a problem for him when he came to confront Porus, the seven-foot-tall king of the eastern Punjab. Alexander arrived in India in the spring of 326 BC. Omphis, king of Taxila, a Punjab principality, welcomed him at once, figuring that resistance was futile. But Porus refused to send to the invader envoys bearing tokens of submission. Alexander did not take kindly to this insubordination. He would have to put Porus in his place.

Yet as he stood on the north bank of the Hydaspes, the great river in northern India, preparing to engage Porus in battle, Alexander's task looked daunting. Porus's troops lined the south bank of the river, which was swelled to a huge, impassable torrent by monsoon rains. The Greeks had to cross this violent, muddy surge under a hammering downpour and still be in shape for battle on the other side. The segment of the riverbank where Porus had encamped, moreover, was guarded not only by a vast enemy force but also by a chain of some one hundred elephants. Attired in dazzling decorated blankets, their bodies looming above horses and men, their tusks covered in metal tips that transformed them into battering rams, the elephants were an overwhelming impediment. Spurred to fury by fermented wine given to them to make them more wild and by the urgent commands of their drivers, the beasts, trumpeting blood-chillingly, terrified the Greeks.

How could Alexander tackle such an enemy? Reconnoitering the area for possible solutions, he discovered an island in a bend of the river some seventeen miles from his camp. He would use this as a stepping-stone for his crossing. Surrounded by his generals — Ptolemy, Seleukos, Perdikkas, and Lysimachos — and accompanied by a cavalry of 5,000 and an infantry of 10,000, Alexander pushed his contingent across the river under the cover of night during a tremendous thunderstorm. The thunderclaps and rain concealed their advance, the clatter of arms and shouted commands. As soon as Porus learned of Alexander's maneuver, he sent his son with 120 chariots and 2,000 cavalry to rout the advancing Greeks. Although Alexander lost his beloved horse Bucephalus in the battle, he soon defeated this division. Now he was ready to take on Porus himself.

At close range, however, Porus's elephant formation appeared even more forbidding. To the Greeks, the line of giant beasts looked like massive defense works — the huge animals jutting out like towers from the curtain wall of infantry stationed between them. Alexander devised a battle strategy. He ordered his men to encircle the elephants and to hurl javelins at their mahouts (drivers). At first "the beasts charged into the line of [Alexander's] infantry," writes ancient historian Arrian, "and whichever way they turned, began to devastate the Greek phalanx, dense though it was." The elephants crushed the Greek soldiers underfoot, speared them with their tusks, and seized them with their trunks, dashing them with full force against the ground or passing them up to their riders to be dispatched.

After sustaining massive losses, Alexander's forces rallied and ultimately proved superior to the Indians both in strength and experience. They drove Porus's cavalry back into the elephants and surrounded them and the horsemen within one choking ring. Since many of the elephant drivers had been shot, the beasts became weary, and many of them were wounded. Distressed, "they no longer kept their separate formation in the battle, but, as if maddened by suffering, attacked friends and foes alike and in all sorts of ways kept pushing, trampling, and destroying." The Indians lost nearly 20,000 infantrymen and 3,000 horsemen. Their chariots were smashed to pieces, and two of Porus's sons were killed. Porus, though wounded, survived. Alexander was so impressed with his courage that he set him free and restored him to his kingdom. He did, however, keep Porus's remaining elephants.

The Greek casualties were fewer than the Indian, but the horror of fighting against the elephants was engraved on the memories of even the most battle-hardened veterans. Alexander, of course, was undaunted. Buoyant and eager to reach "the end of India," he urged his troops onward, driving them through forests thick with poisonous snakes, punishing heat, and bone-soaking rain. But when rumors began to circulate throughout the army that twelve days beyond the Beas River, in the direction of Alexander's advance, lay a still greater river, and beyond it a tribe that fought with four thousand elephants, the soldiers would have no more. Worn down by years of merciless fighting, dreadful weather, harsh terrain, and myriad diseases, they had no stamina left for another encounter with elephants. Alexander's ambitions were brought to a halt.

The great conqueror fumed and harangued his veterans with stirring speeches. He sulked alone in his tent. He stalled, trying to save face. But his men would not be cajoled. Alexander had no choice but to turn around and embark on the long, miserable trek homeward. The dread instilled in his soldiers by war elephants proved decisive in ending Alexander's invincible march of conquest.

After he returned to Babylon, Alexander died suddenly following a two-day drinking party in June 323 BC. It was probably not the alcohol alone but the cumulative effects of hard campaigning, wounds, and tropical diseases that did him in, although some said it was poison. Alexander never got around to transforming his herd of two hundred elephants into a tool of war. As his former companions and generals divided up his sprawling empire, they also split the elephants between them. They trained their troops to fight alongside the giant animals and proceeded to use them against one another as they vied for Alexander's legacy and for supremacy. They assessed each other's strength by the number of elephants each possessed. It became a kind of ancient arms race.

In reality, the elephants did not always guarantee victory. Superior strategy and command proved more decisive, as Alexander had demonstrated at Gaugamela and Hydaspes. Still, the appearance of strength mattered, and so the successors continued to deploy the massive beasts — when they could. All elephants in those days were procured in India, to which most of Alexander's successors had no access. How could they fight one another over their newly gained territories without comparable animal corps? This question especially worried Ptolemy Philadelphos.

THE MAN WITH the most elephants was Seleukos, who, in the division of Alexander's territories, took northern Syria, much of Asia Minor, Persia, and Mesopotamia. He also hoped to extend his domain to northern India, so he set off to challenge the rajah Chandragupta, who, after Porus's death, came to rule this area. Seleukos soon realized that it was foolhardy to take on a man with the wealth of India behind him. He struck a bargain with

Chandragupta instead. He would cede to the rajah the Seleukid territories west of the Indus. In return, he would take something infinitely more useful to him: a force of elephants some five hundred strong. This number was probably somewhat exaggerated by ancient writers, but clearly Seleukos obtained a huge and intimidating number of these beasts. His rivals soon called him "the Master of the Elephants," and he began to stamp his coins with his portrait on one side and an elephant on the reverse. What is more, Seleukos controlled the route to India, so he could procure more elephants when he needed them, while keeping his enemies from getting any at all.

Ptolemy, meanwhile, had relatively few elephants and no way to increase their number. Some beasts remained from Alexander's herd; others he captured in various battles against his fellow successors. For example, he had seized forty-three animals from Antigonos the One-Eyed, inheritor of Macedonia, whom he defeated at Gaza in 312 BC. But as the years went by, Ptolemy's herd dwindled. Some of the elephants died of old age, others of war wounds or disease. Whatever calves may have been born in captivity were insufficient to replenish his supply. Meanwhile, the path to India remained cut off by Seleukos. To preserve and consolidate his kingdom in the face of constant threats from other successors, Ptolemy was desperate to augment his elephant numbers. For him, and even more so for his son Ptolemy Philadelphos, elephants were not a luxury but a necessity in demonstrating the strength of their kingdom and securing it in its formative stage.

THE PTOLEMIES, BEING Greeks, faced a double challenge in ruling Egypt. They had to ensure the subjugation of their Egyptian subjects and keep Alexander's other successors from encroaching on their newly acquired domains. Ptolemy, whom the historian Quintus Curtius described as a fine soldier — modest, steadfast in his duty, and levelheaded — turned out to be a savvy king. The very choice of Egypt revealed his judicious instincts. Egypt was the richest of Alexander's provinces and the most self-contained. Cut off from the rest of the world by its geography, it could flourish in isolation and splendor. As the ancient historian Diodorus wrote:

> Egypt seems far to surpass in natural strength and scenic beauty the places bordering on the kingdom. On the west it is protected by the desert and the beast-infested wilderness of Libya, so vast in extent, whose aridity and total lack of food make a passage not only difficult but extremely dangerous. And the southern parts are defended by the cataracts [rapids] of the Nile and the mountains surrounding them. Indeed, beyond the land of the Trogodytes and the highest uplands of Ethiopia, for almost a thousand and five hundred stades, it is not easy to sail via the river nor to travel overland, unless one has the wherewithal of a king or an absolutely enormous fortune.

These natural barriers gave Ptolemy a great advantage, but his northern frontiers remained vulnerable. He moved swiftly to bring Cyprus, Cyrenaica (the north coast of Libya), and part of Syria under his sphere of influence and built a mighty navy to safeguard his Mediterranean flank.

At the same time, he adapted the ruling customs of the pharaohs to keep his Egyptian subjects under control. He continued local religious practices, including building temples to Egyptian deities, and assumed ownership of most of the land in Egypt and its fruits. He strictly regulated all commercial activity in his kingdom, worked hard to augment the country's wealth, and strove to guarantee its territorial integrity and autonomy. When given the possibility to become the de facto head of Alexander's empire, Ptolemy declined. He preferred the solidity and security of ruling over Egypt to a glamorous but ever-tottering position as leader of a sprawling and unstable realm. In fact, he devised a shrewd ploy by which to consolidate his authority both at home and in the larger Hellenistic world.

Symbolism was an important component of successful rule, and each of Alexander's generals sought to show that he was the great conqueror's true successor. When Alexander died in Babylon, his body was mummified and set aside in a golden sarcophagus until a magnificent hearse would be ready to take it to its final resting place. Some successors wanted it to go back to Macedonia, to be buried in the dynastic tomb complex at Vergina. Others argued that on his deathbed Alexander had requested that he be taken to Memphis, to the temple of Ammon, who had recognized and saluted him as son of Zeus. After two years, in the fall of 321 BC, the funeral cortege was ready for its final journey. While Perdikkas, another of Alexander's generals and the custodian of his body in Babylon, was away in Anatolia dealing with his enemies there, Alexander's hearse left Babylon under heavy escort. Perdikkas had planned to take it to Macedonia, where he had been offered the hand of Alexander's sister, with all that implied. Ptolemy mobilized an army, marched out to meet the funerary procession, and diverted it to Memphis.

Perdikkas flew into a rage when he heard of this brazen body snatch. Livid, he invaded Egypt in the spring of 320 BC intending "to deprive [Ptolemy] of his office, to install a lieutenant of his own in Egypt, and to get back the body." But Ptolemy stood prepared. When Perdikkas failed to breach Ptolemy's defenses on the Nile, Perdikkas's army mutinied, and his staff murdered him in his tent. Ptolemy retained control of Alexander's body, and after letting it rest for some time at Memphis, to commune with Ammon, he took it to Alexandria. There he encased it in a gold and crystal sarcophagus and placed it in a specially constructed mausoleum, called the Sema, at the heart of the city that Alexander had founded. Thus Ptolemy laid a solid foundation for his son's rule, but he also established a legacy of astute planning and bold military action that his son would have to uphold.

Ptolemy Philadelphos had been groomed for kingship from his boyhood by the best teachers. The natural historian Straton of Lampsakos, his chief tutor, ignited in his pupil a love of zoology and geography. Philetas of Kos, an influential poet and philologist, and his student Zenodotos of Ephesos, a Homeric scholar and the first director of the Library of Alexandria, taught the boy to appreciate and foster literature. His own father, having witnessed and assisted in Alexander's triumphs, offered valuable historical lessons and set his son's political course.

But Philadelphos was quite different from his father. Unlike the rugged and fearless general who had fought for years alongside Alexander, Philadelphos was sickly and sensual. "He had a more than ordinary leaning to affairs of love," his son wrote in his memoirs. He was smitten by Didyme, a native Egyptian girl of extraordinary beauty, then by Bilistiche, then by Agathokleia. In honor of his mistress Stratonike, he erected a monument on the seashore near Eleusis. He celebrated Kleino, his cupbearer, with sculptures set up throughout Alexandria showing the tantalizing girl in a body-hugging tunic, offering up a drinking horn. Philadelphos's houses bore the names of Myrtion, one of the most notorious variety actresses of the day, and of the flute girls Mnesis and Potheine.

The king acquired his epithet, Philadelphos, meaning "sister-loving," when he married his sister Arsinoë. Some historians say that she was the driving force behind the throne. She was certainly smart and canny (the Ptolemaic dynasty produced several impressive women, the last being the famous Cleopatra), but Philadelphos was no fool, either in conducting affairs of state or in selecting a useful partner. Sibling marriages were, in any case, a pharaonic tradition. The Egyptians took Philadelphos's marriage in stride and grew quite fond of Arsinoë. When she died in 270 BC, at age forty-six, they mourned her with genuine grief. But the more prudish Greeks, who formed the administrative and intellectual elite of the Ptolemaic kingdom, were scandalized. The poet Sotades, thinking himself very clever, published a lampoon with the biting line, "You are pushing the prod into an unholy hole." Philadelphos was not amused. He threw the impudent poet into prison. When several years later Sotades managed to flee Alexandria and hide on the tiny island of Kaudos, off the south coast of Crete, the king sent his admiral Patroklos to hunt him down, take him out to sea, and sink him in a lead coffin. Philadelphos may have been soft in body and habits, but his mind was tough.

Philadelphos would also turn out to be an astute and imaginative ruler who would turn Alexandria into the cultural capital of the Mediterranean. According to the geographer Strabo, Philadelphos was "of an inquiring disposition, and on account of the infirmity of his body was always searching for novel pastimes and enjoyments" — by which Strabo seems to have meant more than delights of the flesh. Aelian, another ancient author, notes that Philadelphos was "highly cultured." Although his father founded the Museum and Library in Alexandria, it was Philadelphos who made this complex into the preeminent think tank of the ancient world.

Modeled on Aristotle's Lyceum in Athens — a similar, though much smaller, center of intellectual pursuits — the Museum (literally the shrine of the muses) and its adjacent Library were erected in the royal quarter. Strabo recounts, "The city has extremely beautiful public precincts and also the royal palaces, which cover a fourth or even a third of the whole city area. . . . The Museum is also part of the palace complex; it has a covered walkway, a hall with seats and a large house, in which there is a common dining hall for the learned men who share the Museum. This group of men have communal possessions and a priest in charge of the Museum, who [is] appointed by the king." The king paid and fed the Museum scholars out of his treasury. In return, he expected them to advance knowledge through their research, to give public lectures on their findings, and to groom the kingdom's ruling elite. Timon of Phlius, a skeptic philosopher, quipped that "in the populous land of Egypt there is a crowd of bookish scribblers who get fed as they argue away interminably in the bird-coop of the Muses."

Ironically, the man who made Alexandria a repository of all knowledge has nearly vanished from history himself. The destruction of the Library in a succession of disasters — first in 47 BC, when Julius Caesar accidentally burned down part of the city as he set fire to his ships in the harbor during his war against Pompey, then during the religious strife that swept Alexandria in the 390s AD, and finally when the Muslim caliph Omar took the capital in AD 642 — robbed us of much documentation about Philadelphos. Now we can only tease out his qualities, ambitions, and achievements from traces of his actions in a few literary texts, administrative records, archaeological remains, and the larger history of this period. Such meager details only spur one's curiosity about the king, whom one ancient writer, Athenaeus, praised in no uncertain terms: "King Philadelphos surpassed most kings in riches; and he pursued every kind of manufacturing and trading art so zealously, that he also surpassed everyone in the number of his ships. . . . And concerning the number of his books, and the way in which he furnished his libraries, and the way he collected treasures for his Museum, why need I speak? For everyone remembers all these things."

Being a sensualist and an intellectual, how did Philadelphos turn into a man of action like his father and face Antiochos, who, with his army of elephants, not only challenged him for control over Coele-Syria but also threatened the integrity of his kingdom as a whole? Philadelphos's pursuit of elephants provides the greatest insight into his personality and accomplishments. It was this quest that ultimately cemented his shaky inheritance into a dynastic power that would last for nearly three centuries, until it was conquered by Rome.

WE KNOW PHILADELPHOS had a curious nature and was well schooled. He certainly had read Herodotos and Aristotle, the two authors who had reported that elephants lived in the African hinterland, areas now encompassed by eastern Sudan, Somalia, Eritrea, and Ethiopia. So he sent his explorers south to investigate. They were to travel along the Nile River and the west coast of the Red Sea, describe the regions they traversed, survey the natural resources, and bring back interesting specimens. Of course Philadelphos wanted live elephants that could be trained for battle — a formidable challenge for men not experienced in capturing and transporting these great beasts. But the young king was also eager to best Alexander the Great, who had gathered much scientific information during his eastern campaign. Together with the literary and historical holdings of the Library, any unusual animals, vegetation, or minerals his men found would form an encyclopedia of knowledge unique in the Mediterranean world.

Unfortunately, all that survives of the accounts of Philadelphos's explorers are scattered fragments in the writings of later Greek and Roman authors. One of Philadelphos's admirals, Philon, visited the kingdom of Meroë (Sudan) and Isle of Topaz in the Red Sea (now St. John's Island off the southeastern tip of Egypt). He recorded his journey in a book called *Aethiopika*, the name ancient Greeks gave to the region that covered most of what is today Sudan and northern Ethiopia. This book does not survive, but echoes of Philon's investigations resonate through Strabo's *Geography*, written more than two centuries later: "The

Aethiopians lead for the most part a nomadic and resourceless life, on account of the barrenness of the country and of the unseasonableness of its climate and of its remoteness from us, whereas with the Egyptians the contrary is the case in all these respects."

Another Ptolemaic explorer, Dalion, investigated and described the Nile Valley south of Meroë. Ariston, meanwhile, studied the Arabian coast. How sad that all we know of their intrepid efforts are snippets that barely hint at months-long expeditions through desolate landscapes of hot sand and baked mountains. How many men were there in each expedition? What did they think and feel about their mission, besides being hot and thirsty, apprehensive about encountering hostile natives and wild beasts, and unsure of how soon they would return home? The only certain thing is that the king expected them to persevere. He needed his animal army to consolidate his reign.

The Trogodyte coast offered the first promising lead in Philadelphos's quest. This region along the Red Sea stretched from Suez to Bab el Mandeb, the strait opposite Aden at the southern tip of the Arabian Peninsula. It was inhabited by people whom the Greeks called Trogodytes, which means cave dwellers ("troglodyte" is a misspelling of the original word). The Trogodytes adapted the openings in the mountains along the Red Sea as their shelters and eked out a living from the meager resources of the sun-scorched land and treacherous sea. Herodotos, writing in the fifth century BC, described the Trogodytes as the swiftest of men, who ate snakes and lizards and spoke "like bats squeaking."

Agatharchides of Knidos, an Alexandrian geographer of the mid-second century BC, described various groups of Trogodytes who "live a nomadic life off their flocks, each group with its own tyrant." Although he did not observe them himself, he based his treatise *On the Red Sea* on accounts of explorers sent out by Philadelphos and later Ptolemies, whose reports were deposited in the royal archives in Alexandria. There were diverse tribes of Trogodytes.

The Fish-Eaters went about completely naked, possessed their women and children in common, inhabited primitive dwellings by the coast, and caught a variety of fish in tidal pools, which they constructed out of large boulders. The Turtle-Eaters lived near Bab el Mandeb and made countless uses of the great sea animals after which they were named. Agatharchides admiringly remarked that "nature seems to have granted them with one gift the satisfaction of many needs, for one and the same gift is their food, container, house, and boat."

The Fiber-Eaters, in their turn, foraged for tender twigs in the upper branches of trees, leaping from one tree to another like birds. They were so adept at climbing to the topmost branches that they seldom fell, and if they did, the explorers reported, they were so slender and light that they did not get hurt. Agatharchides does admit that their life was not one of carefree flight: "Most of them die as a result of being worn down by hunger."

And then there were the Elephant-Hunters, who dwelled in the bushy and forested area inland from the Red Sea. Philadelphos dispatched an explorer named Satyros to enlist their help in procuring the beasts he so urgently sought. Not only did these people know where to find the elephants, but they also were skilled in the complicated and dangerous business of capturing them.

Living in the vicinity of the great animals and dependent on them for many staples, the Elephant-Hunters had developed various ways of pursuing the beasts. According to one method, they began a hunt with one man climbing up into the tallest tree in a thick forest to spy on a herd of animals. He waited patiently as the column of elephants streamed by and watched for the last or the weakest one. As the unsuspecting creature walked past, the hunter leapt down from the tree and landed on the elephant's haunches. He planted his feet on the beast's left flank, grasped its tail firmly with his left hand, and hung on in this suspended acrobatic position as the animal began to run to escape. As the elephant ran, the hunter gripped in his right hand a light, sharp ax, and with fast and furious blows he hacked at the beast's hamstrings. The animal charged forward in pain and fury, but, sinews severed, it soon collapsed.

Sometimes, if the hunter did not leap off in time, the falling beast would crush him under its massive flank. Or, infuriated by its wounds, it might try to squeeze its assailant against a rock or tree. But more often, the panicked and suffering creature would try to flee across the plain, until the hunter, still hanging on, managed to sever its tendons and paralyze it. As soon as the elephant fell, the rest of the hunting party quickly surrounded it and began to chop it into bite-size pieces, staging a feast on the spot.

In the 1770s the Scottish explorer James Bruce described a similar scene that he observed near the source of the Blue Nile. Except there, naked hunters, "dark-skinned with European features," worked in pairs and on horseback. The front rider directed the horse, the back one wielded a broadsword. When they selected their prey, the hunters rode up to the animal, and while the front man assaulted it with a barrage of words to get it riled up and distracted, the second man slipped off the horse, snuck up behind the elephant, and hacked at its hamstrings. The horseman then swiftly picked up his companion, and they galloped off at full speed to a safe distance. When the elephant finally collapsed, the hunters returned and finished it off with a javelin or lance.

Trogodyte Elephant-Hunters who were of a more cautious nature, or not inclined to engage in a wild ride, resorted to another method. Teams of men wielding large bows and arrows coated with snake venom lay in wait in the bush alongside the elephant trail. Once they selected the most likely prey, they shot the arrows, aiming at the animal's head or flank in the hope of striking its brain or heart. The wounded elephant would try to escape, but the poison would soon take its toll and bring it down. A trail of blood directed the hunters to their catch. This method, involving seven-foot-tall bows, was also described by Bruce and by early twentieth-century travelers to Africa.

Yet another hunting method stemmed from the ancients' belief that elephants could not lie down and had to sleep resting against a tree. Some Elephant-Hunters would saw nearly through a tree trunk favored by a particular animal. When the elephant arrived for a nap, it would topple the tree and fall beneath it. The ancients also thought that elephants had jointless legs and could not get up once prostrate on the ground. Thus the hunters would swiftly attack fallen animals and cut them up for food, tusks, and other vital parts. Although elephants can, actually, lie down, they also like to rub against trees and to rest and sleep against them. Their legs do have joints, and they can get up from the ground, if rather clumsily, rocking their massive bodies to get momentum. But if hunters move quickly, they can gravely wound or kill an elephant while it is down.

Whatever their method, the Elephant-Hunters were clearly quite proficient, but their expertise was only partly helpful to Philadelphos's men. Since the Trogodytes relied on elephants for meat and used their ivory for trade, their goal was to kill the animals. Dead elephants, however, were of little use to Philadelphos. Agatharchides reports that the king's envoy Satyros tried to plead with the hunters, urging them not to slaughter every beast so that the king might take some live ones for his wars. "Although he promised them many wondrous things, he not only did not persuade them, but he heard that their reply was that they would not exchange his whole kingdom for their present way of life."

We don't know whether Philadelphos was furious, disheartened, or undaunted at this response. Whatever the case, the shadowy traces of his men's movements and bits of the archaeological record indicate that the king's opportunism prevailed over setbacks and that, in search of both elephants and hunters willing to capture them alive, his teams proceeded farther south. They did not promptly find the beasts, but they made what was perhaps an equally valuable discovery — gold mines.

Elephants alone could not secure Philadelphos's kingdom. He also needed gold to finance his elephant-hunting expeditions, pay his troops, build his ships, and present to the world a facade of great splendor. Even if, in the short run, it somewhat delayed his quest for elephants, the discovery of gold mines was an opportunity the king could not help seizing.

The hills and mountains along the coast of the Red Sea are one vast geological museum. The mountains of Wadi Allaqi (the southern part of the Eastern Desert of Egypt) and Wadi Gabgaba (northern Sudan), rising between the Nile and the Red Sea (south of Aswan and east of Abu Simbel), were particularly rich in gold. By the third century BC, the former gold-bearing regions, such as Macedonia and Lydia in Asia Minor, had become fairly depleted. The mines of Lower Nubia, used by the pharaohs for centuries, remained productive, but because of the sparse population and inhospitable climate, they were prospected only sporadically. As soon as his explorers came upon these mines, Philadelphos sent down troops to secure their possession. Then he set up a mining town to exploit this resource systematically. He named it after his mother, Berenike Panchrysos ("All-Gold").

The new settlement of modest dwellings for the miners and their overseers occupied an area of less than a square mile and was protected by two forbidding stone strongholds. All around stretched a desolate landscape of mountains and sand. Berenike Panchrysos was like an anthill in the middle of the desert. Its population is estimated to have been at least ten thousand, for, as Agatharchides reports, Philadelphos sent down a number of mining specialists and a huge labor force of criminals and prisoners of war, as well as men who had been unjustly accused of some crime and had been imprisoned because they had reacted angrily to the royal police. When they were dispatched to the mines, their families were sent along as well.

So sprang up a prison colony that does little credit to Philadelphos, though of course he did not see it that way. Men, women, and children, all bound in chains, toiled ceaselessly, day and night, under appalling conditions, in one of the hottest places in the world. Foreign guards, probably Nubian mercenaries in the royal service, stood watch over the laborers. Because they spoke a language different from that of the prisoners, they were impervious to conversation or human appeal. Duties in the mine were divided by age and sex. The younger men tunneled into the mountains by hand, crawling with burning oil lamps attached to their foreheads, following the gold veins. Children dragged out the hewn pieces of quartz to the surface. Old men hammered them into pebbles. Women, naked, ground the fragments to dust in spar mills, turning the spars three abreast in place of the oxen that would normally perform such an arduous task. Agatharchides, who described this miserable scene, was sympathetic to their terrible lot:

> Since there is general neglect of their bodies and they have no garment to cover their shame, it is impossible for an observer to not pity the wretches because of the extremity of their suffering. For they meet with no respite at all, not the sick, the injured, the aged, not a woman by reason of her weakness, but all are compelled by blows to strive at their tasks until, exhausted by the abuse they have suffered, they die in their miseries. For this reason they think that the future always will be more fearful than the present and they consider death more desirable than life.

Philadelphos apparently lost no sleep over the fate of his mine laborers. He seemingly valued the lives of animals more than those of the people who worked to procure them or the means to pay for them. Of course he also never saw their hardships first-hand. Like many rulers, he closed his eyes to the human cost of his ventures. Meanwhile, glorious Alexandria was built not only through Philadelphos's vision and ambition but also through the toil of untold thousands of men and women who executed his grand projects. The king, for his part, urged his explorers onward. He still needed his elephants. With the new gold to pay for this coveted resource, he pushed his men to continue their quest in the kingdom of Meroë.

This kingdom, which the Egyptians called "the land of Kush," lay south of Aswan, in the territory of modern Sudan. In Strabo's words, it had "both numerous mountains and large thickets; it [was] inhabited partly by nomads, partly by hunters, and partly by farmers; and it [had] mines of copper, iron, gold, and different kinds of precious stones. It is bounded on the Libyan side by large sand-dunes, on the Arabian side by continuous precipices, on the south by the confluences of the three rivers, and on the north by the next course of the Nile."

The Meroites had borrowed from their Egyptian neighbors the use of hieroglyphic script and the practice of building pyramidal royal tombs, but otherwise they had their own distinct culture. From about 900 BC to the early third century BC, their capital was at Napata, which lay close to the fourth cataract of the Nile (near Kuraymah, in northern Sudan). In the early third century BC, the capital was moved to Meroë, farther south along the Nile (some fifty miles northeast of Shandi).

After the harsh and primitive conditions of the Trogodyte coast, Philadelphos's explorers must have found the city of Meroë a pleasant change of scenery. Spread on the eastern bank of the Nile, it had temples and shrines, a royal palace surrounded by a garden fragrant with fruit trees, and a sprawl of houses built from mud brick and interwoven pieces of split palm wood. Trade routes passing by the capital brought in goods from central Africa, the Red Sea, and Arabia, for Meroë was the transfer point for shipments of salt, copper and iron, gold and precious stones, valuable woods and ivory, and lion and leopard skins.

Lying within the rain belt, Meroë was relatively green, with seasonally productive surrounding land and a scrub forest where rhinoceroses and elephants dwelled. The savanna country, which began roughly on the level of Meroë, was much richer in water and vegetation in antiquity. Locals hunted here for leopards, cheetahs, giraffes, monkeys, and other animals, which they sent to Egypt as tribute. Meroites were skilled and versatile hunters, and unlike the Trogodytes, they did not kill every beast that came their way. They did slaughter some elephants for ivory, but they also tamed and trained them for practical and ceremonial purposes. (It is a myth that African elephants cannot be trained.) Sculptural reliefs that once adorned Meroite temples and palaces depict kings and gods riding elephants. Their major god, Apedemak, a lion-headed man dressed in armor, was often shown standing or sitting on an elephant or holding elephants and lions on leashes.

Altogether, Meroites seemed very promising partners who might be amenable to helping Philadelphos capture live elephants. Their trade links with Arabia were also of interest to him. And their ruler was more willing to conduct negotiations than the Trogodytes had been.

Ergamenes, the king of Kush, was Philadelphos's match in ambition and vision. It had been a custom in his land for high priests, when they saw fit, to send a message to the king, from the great god Ammon, declaring that the time of the king's rule on earth was finished and that he must be tired and in need of sleep. Traditionally, the king dutifully obeyed the divine order and took his own life. When Ergamenes received this message, however, he begged to differ. He was feeling quite awake, thank you, and with plenty of energy to spare. So he dared to flout Ammon's command. "With the determination worthy of a king," writes Diodorus, "he came with an armed force to the forbidden place where the golden temple of the Ethiopians was situated and slaughtered all the priests, abolished this tradition, and instituted practices at his own discretion." To make the break more radical, Ergamenes decided that from then on, Meroite kings would be buried not in Napata, but in Meroë, where he built his own tomb. It seems likely that he was the driving force behind the move of the capital from Napata to Meroë. In addition, the king fostered novel styles in architecture and art. He also replaced the Egyptian language and writing with the native Nubian language, expressed in a newly devised alphabet of twenty-three hieroglyphic and cursive letters.

But Ergamenes was not satisfied with local reforms. He was as eager for a link with Mediterranean commerce as Philadelphos was for one with the Arabian market. The kingdom of Kush relied on the barter system. Was Ergamenes ready to offer the king of Egypt some help with the elephants in exchange for access to Mediterranean trade? The two rulers would eventually collaborate in renovating the temples of Lower Nubia, sacred to both Kush and Egypt. It seemed likely that they would be partners in elephant capture as well, if Ergamenes could persuade his people to teach Philadelphos's men the Meroites' hunting skills.

To get live elephants, Meroite hunters relied on corrals and teams of trained animals, a method also used by the Indians in capturing Asian elephants. We have no contemporary description of this practice in Meroë, but Megasthenes, an Ionian Greek who served as Seleukos's ambassador to King Chandragupta, describes in detail how this was done in India. The hunters selected a level place open to the sun's heat and dug a circular ditch wide enough to contain a camping army. The earth removed from the ditch was piled up to form a wall around it. They made a single dirt bridge over the ditch. When the corral was ready, the hunters led in a few tame female elephants and left them there. During the night, foraging wild elephant bulls, attracted by the scent and sounds of the enclosed females, searched out the opening in the wall around the ditch and rushed along the bridge to meet the ladies. Once they got in, the Indians quickly removed the bridge. Because of their bulk, elephants cannot scale steep slopes, so the newcomers were trapped.

In the morning the hunters came to inspect the captives and sent messages to the surrounding villages that the hunt was ready to begin. The villagers mounted their most disciplined and spirited elephants and hurried toward the corral. All this took several hours, during which the wild animals remained enclosed under the scorching sun and grew increasingly frightened, as well as tormented by hunger and thirst. When the wild elephants looked sufficiently dispirited, the hunters reerected the bridge and entered the enclosure atop their domesticated beasts. The tame elephants and their wild counterparts briefly engaged in a battle, but the trapped ones, already worn-out by anxiety and deprivation, soon gave way. At that point the riders dismounted, tied ropes around the hind feet of the wild elephants, and ordered the tame ones to strike the captives repeatedly until the beasts fell to the ground in distress.

Finally, the hunters approached their quarry, threw nooses around their necks, and climbed on their backs. To ensure complete submission, and to guarantee that the elephants did not throw them off, the hunters cut an incision on the neck of each animal and placed the noose around the wound. If the elephant made any sharp movement, the rough rope would immediately grind into the fresh cut. The poor beasts quickly learned to keep their heads and necks perfectly still to avoid the pain. Sensing that they had been conquered, they allowed themselves to be led out of the enclosure on the heels of the tame elephants.

The natural historian Pliny the Elder, writing in the first century AD, says that Africans used corrals in similar ways: "In previous times, for the sake of capturing beasts for training, the kings used to drive them with cavalry into a man-made gorge." This method was still employed in Africa, particularly in the southern Sudan, into the twentieth century. Hunters selected a gorge leading to an enclosed valley, often along the path that elephants traveled to their watering place. Once horsemen and spearmen had driven the herd into it, men atop trained elephants rode into the corral to pick young animals and calves for domestication, bound their feet to restrict their movement, and led them away.

To learn the skills necessary to carry out this involved process, Philadelphos's men needed to recruit experienced Meroite hunters. But would they cooperate? Ergamenes may have been willing to order his subjects to assist Philadelphos, but the Meroite population was rather spread out, and the king of Kush did not exert as much control over his people as did the king of Egypt. Judging by the fact that Philadelphos's elephant-hunting parties included soldiers, the Meroites were not necessarily welcoming hosts. Did they feel that Philadelphos was pillaging their natural resources by taking elephants? Did they fear his conquest of their land? Whatever the cause for mutual distrust, it seems that Philadelphos decided to put into place his own infrastructure: well-paid hunters, soldiers to protect them, and stations from which they could work. We do not know for sure whether Philadelphos granted Ergamenes access to Mediterranean trade, but given that the king of Egypt also stood to gain from extending his commercial network, it is likely that he did.

Philadelphos drew commanders for his hunting parties from his own army officers. The rank-and-file hunters were his Egyptian subjects and recruits from farther afield. Some of them carved their names into the giant statues of the pharaoh Ramses at Abu Simbel: "Krateros the son of Leukaros came elephant-hunting"; "Ariston son of Timodoros the Kourian [from Cyprus] came elephant-hunting with Ariston." As the operations became established, the hunting parties grew quite large — up to two hundred men, presumably including soldiers.*

How to tempt so many men to enlist for long, exhausting expeditions in unwelcoming territories, under intolerable heat, and with unreliable water and food supplies? The most efficient way, of course, was with financial incentives. In 223 BC, under Philadelphos's son, royal hunters were paid 20 drachmas per month, compared to 13.5 drachmas per month received by a very highly paid clerk in the capital. Philadelphos handsomely remunerated private entrepreneurs who supplied him with other rare beasts. Presumably he was as generous with the hunters on whom he had staked the success of his elephant venture and his kingdom's military might.

Because the cataracts of the Nile made it difficult to transport any goods along the river, especially massive animals, the Red Sea was the preferred shipping route for both delivering supplies to the hunters and sending captured animals to the capital. To make the operations more efficient, Philadelphos established stations up and down the coast and at several points inland where elephants were commonly found. These stations had housing for hunters, handlers, soldiers, and other personnel. There also had to be sheds for the newly captured elephants and for the enormous amount of food they consumed every day. Food for men was sometimes procured locally, but much of it had to be brought from up north. If the ship bearing provisions was wrecked along the way, explorers, hunters, and soldiers were stranded with little sustenance.

Ptolemais of the Hunts (near the modern-day Sudanese port of Suakin) is the best documented of these hunting stations. Accord-

---

*We do not know how long it took for the new system to begin running on this scale, but in 275 BC Philadelphos would display nearly one hundred elephants in a grand parade on the eve of the Syrian war.

ing to *Periplus of the Erythraean Sea,* the ancient merchant guide-book to the area, it was "a little market town on the shore. The place has no harbor and is reached only by small boats." At first the locals were not thrilled by the appearance of Philadelphos's men in their midst, perhaps fearful that they would take over the region. Strabo reports that Eumedes, whom Philadelphos dispatched to found the settlement, "secretly enclosed a sort of peninsula with a ditch and wall; and then, by courteous treatment of those who sought to hinder the work, actually won them over to be friends instead of foes." The wall was probably intended to protect Philadelphos's men from the hostile natives, but it seems that Eumedes managed to avoid hostilities and cultivated good relations with the natives while advancing the king's business. He recorded his accomplishments in an inscription at the site: "He built a great city to the king with the illustrious name of the king. . . . He made there fields and cultivated them with ploughs and cattle [so as to feed the settlers]. . . . He caught elephants in great numbers for the king, and he brought them as marvels to the king, in his transports on the sea."

Whatever the skills of Philadelphos's soldiers and hunters, before the newly captured elephants could be transported to Alexandria, they had to be sufficiently tamed to get on the boats and to be manageable along the way. Philadelphos needed the services of skilled mahouts. These trainers had a special bond with the animals in their care, which is why when elephants were taken prisoner in battle, they were ideally captured together with their mahouts. Without their personal trainers, the giant beasts were a liability rather than an asset. When Alexander fought Porus at Hydaspes, he ordered his archers to shoot not at the elephants, but at their drivers. Deprived of their mahouts, the elephants panicked and trampled their own troops.

The best mahouts were Indians, as Indians had been using war elephants since at least 1100 BC. (The word "mahout" derives from the Sanskrit *mahamatra,* meaning "one having great measure.") Elephant training in India was a hereditary profession, and it was so firmly associated with the Indians that the Greeks called all elephant drivers *Indos,* even if they were Greeks who had learned the craft. Philadelphos was once presented with a young elephant that had been brought up in the Greek language, which was deemed a marvel, as everyone believed that elephants understood only the language of the Indians.

Philadelphos probably had a small staff of Indian mahouts inherited from his father along with the elephants. Some of these men must have been very old by the time Philadelphos sent out his expeditions; others may have been the sons of these men or their Greek pupils. In any case, the king needed many more trainers for his newly captured animals, so he dispatched his emissary Dionysios to India, to the court of King Asoka, the grandson of Chandragupta. (This is the same Chandragupta who had established the first Indian empire and supplied Seleukos, Antiochos's father, with five hundred elephants.)

Asoka was keen to foster relations with the successors of Alexander. Having converted to Buddhism after a youth spent in many ruthless military campaigns, he had sent out missionaries to spread the faith not only to Kashmir, Persia, and Sri Lanka, but also to the kingdoms of Antiochos I, Ptolemy Philadelphos, Antigonos of Macedonia, Alexander of Epiros (in northern Greece), and Magas of Cyrene (in Libya). One suspects that he had broader aims than merely preaching peace, morality, and good works. For one thing, India shipped many of its natural and man-made products to Egypt and the Mediterranean and needed the goodwill of the rulers in those regions. It is likely, then, that Asoka welcomed Philadelphos's emissaries and that Philadelphos got his mahouts, because by 275 BC the elephants were well enough trained to be shipped to Alexandria in sizable numbers.

Shipping elephants to the capital, however, was not a trivial task. It took ten to twelve days to walk the animals from Meroë to the Red Sea coast. Then the difficulties began. The waters of the Red Sea were shallow and greenish from the jungles of weeds below the surface. Rowboats might manage to clear this tangle, but ships carrying elephants needed a deep enough draft to bear the enormous weight of the animals, yet they had to be shallow enough not to run aground. No such boats existed, so Philadelphos had his naval engineers develop a special design. The new elephant carriers, called *elephantagoi* (from the Greek *elephas,* "elephant," and *agos,* "driver"), were propelled by sails and had a wide hold that accommodated elephants on the way north and food and supplies for the hunting stations on the way south. Between October and May winds on the Red Sea blow prevalently from the south, ensuring a rapid voyage north; from June to September they come from the north, speeding supply boats.

The *elephantagoi* tended to travel by night, as strong winds at sea often prevented them from putting into harbor or anchoring overnight. In addition, the Trogodyte coast was inhospitable for navigation. It had some breaks in the coral reef hugging the shore (created by watercourses entering the sea, since coral does not grow in fresh water), but few harbors were large enough for the *elephantagoi.* Night travel also spared people and animals the relentless heat of the sun. But navigating in the dark was treacherous, as it was all too easy to strike the reef or run aground.

"The disasters that befall the elephant transports arouse great pity for their victims from spectators," Agatharchides writes. "Sudden waves impale the ships on rocks or drive them onto sandbars and make rescue impossible for the sailors who man them." The stranded men might hope for a while that a tide would lift them off and release them from their unintended mooring, but the tide rarely came. Nor could they manage to dislodge the ship by pushing it away from the rocks with punt poles, because the water around the sandbars was too deep. "Those who experience such a misfortune, at first, bewail their fate moderately to a mute land as they have not completely abandoned hope of ultimate salvation," Agatharchides continues. But as food began to dwindle, the sailors jettisoned everything except for provisions. Then the stronger men would throw the weaker ones overboard to make the supplies last several days longer.

Agatharchides does not say whether elephants were thrown overboard or eaten by the desperate sailors, but they certainly met an untimely end, as did the men. When no rescue came, the remaining sailors fell into "great despair because there is neither island nor headland nor another ship to be seen in the vicinity. For these places are completely inhospitable, and rarely do people sail through them in ships. Besides these evils the tide quickly throws so great an amount of sand around the hull of the ship and heaps it up in so remarkable a way that a circular mound is built up, and the ship becomes bonded to the land as though it were done intentionally." And so the men gradually died of starvation, "dividing the process of dying into many wretched moments." The ships themselves "remain like cenotaphs for a long time buried on all sides in sand. With their sails and masts set, they impel to pity and sympathy for the dead sailors people who see them from afar. For there is a royal decree that they be left as markers to signal to mariners the places that produce destruction."

Yet royal decree also commanded the transport of elephants to continue. The ships that made the sea passage without disaster landed at Berenike, a port that Philadelphos founded (and again named after his mother) on the west coast of the Red Sea to facilitate the flow of elephants, gold, and other goods toward Alexandria. The dangers of shipping by sea, including treacherous reefs and pirates operating from the Arabian Peninsula, made a safe landing place as far south as possible indispensable. The pirates probably had little use for elephants, but since *elephantagoi* also carried other precious goods, they were potential targets.

Berenike fell just within the domain of Egypt, in its southernmost part, where the Nile approached the sea and where a large peninsula protected a natural harbor from the prevailing winds.

During the trading season, between February and August, ships loaded with elephants and other prized commodities made their perilous way to Berenike. The distance from Ptolemais of the Hunts, some 470 miles, could be sailed in eight days if the weather was good and the sea cooperated. From the most distant port, near Cape Guardafui (Somalia), the trip took about a month. There were also a number of hunting stations in between. Besides wild animals, Berenike received and sent to the capital ivory, tortoiseshell, and rhinoceros horn from Ethiopia and Meroë; spices, frankincense, and myrrh from Arabia; and "slaves of the better sort" from the Horn of Africa. From India and its trading partners came diamonds, sapphires, pearls, turquoise, lapis lazuli, agate, and carnelian; cotton and silk; and sugar and pepper. Ships loaded with companies of archers patrolled the shore and protected these treasures from pirates.

From Berenike, elephants still had to travel a long overland route toward Alexandria. Along with other goods, they were unloaded and walked in caravans through the Eastern Desert to Apollonopolis (now Edfu) or Coptos, in the Nile Valley. To ease the journey by land, Philadelphos sent soldiers to clear tracks, sink wells in the desert, dig and plaster cisterns, and establish watering stations at twenty-mile intervals on the arid route from the port to the Nile. In addition to setting up these caravan routes, Philadelphos introduced the one-humped Arabian camel, or dromedary, into Egypt. The animal was used extensively by Arabian traders, since no other animal could make the long trek through the desert carrying heavy loads of spices, resins, and other prized commodities. The camel's padded feet could walk on shifting, scorching sand. Its digestive system could subsist on the toughest thornbushes. It could ingest up to forty gallons of liquid at a time, drinking water too salty for humans, and proceed without further liquid for about ten days. Besides, the beast yielded a variety of useful products. Female camels could furnish milk for humans to consume along the way. Camel hair was spun into cloth and rope. Its skin served for saddlebags, sandals, and water buckets, and its dried dung made good cooking fuel in the treeless desert. The animal was the most versatile moving system one could desire in that climate and geography. Recognizing its importance to the commerce of his kingdom, Philadelphos began to import camels through his Arabian trading contacts.

The journey of camel and elephant caravans from Berenike to Coptos, a stretch of some 265 miles, took twelve days. Men and beasts traveled during the night to avoid the extreme heat. In the daytime they rested at protected watering stations, called *hydreumata*, and were happy for water, shelter, and some sleep. The hunters were also pleased to be returning home. At El-Kanayis, the penultimate *hydreuma* on the road from Berenike to Edfu, a man named Dorion recorded his return with a picture of an elephant carved on a rock. Once at the Nile, men and beasts boarded riverboats and sailed north to Memphis. Since the chief purpose of the elephants was to serve in the Syrian war, it was best to keep most of them at the royal depot there. From Memphis they could reach Egypt's eastern border and Syria much faster than if they were to march from Alexandria across the full width of the delta and its network of waterways.

A MAN WITH a less agile mind might have stopped at procuring gold and war elephants and expanding his trade networks. But Philadelphos, as ancient writers note, was driven by grander ambitions and by curiosity. As a highly educated Greek nobleman, he valued learning, both as a political tool and as a goal in itself. Even as his elephant hunts were going on, he began building on the achievements of his father and making the Museum of

Alexandria into a preeminent research institution, usurping cultural leadership from Athens.

Philadelphos wanted the Museum scholars to carry out studies in all areas of knowledge. Thus Euclid, whose *Elements* would remain the standard textbook of elementary mathematics for two thousand years, worked and taught in Alexandria. The renowned engineer Ktesibios (a local barber's son), also thrived under Philadelphos's patronage. He was the first to make devices operated by pneumatics, constructing the first accurate water clock and a water organ, marvelous automata (self-propelled mechanical devices) for the king's festivals, and war catapults for his military campaigns. Meanwhile, the physician Herophilos performed dissections on cadavers to unlock the secrets of the brain, which he saw as the organ of the soul (while his contemporaries believed the soul was in the heart or liver), and studied the eye, liver, and sexual organs. He also discovered the nerves and the rhythm of the pulse, and in his medical practice he devoted careful attention to diagnostics and the use of drugs, diet, and exercise. Straton, Philadelphos's chief tutor, wrote books on ethics and logic, cosmology and psychology, and physics and zoology. He argued that the processes of nature must be explained by natural causes rather than by the actions of the gods. And Philadelphos himself composed a treatise on trees.

At the same time, a contingent of literary scholars at the Museum studied, analyzed, and preserved for posterity the body of Greek literature and that of other cultures. Philadelphos invited foreign philologists to his court, including a group of religious scholars from Jerusalem, who came to Alexandria to translate the Torah into Greek for the Library. The king and his successors were so intent on gathering all of the world's extant books that they not only scouted the major book markets at Athens and Rhodes, but they also engaged in book piracy. They would seize scrolls found on board ships docked in Alexandria's harbor, have them copied, return the copies to the owners, and keep the originals in the Library with the words "from the ships" on the shelf mark.

Philadelphos approached his quest for elephants the same way he approached the Museum and the Library. He encouraged his explorers to procure not only these beasts but all exotic animals, including creatures unknown even to Aristotle, who had written the massive *History of Animals*. Philadelphos's animals, gathered at the palace zoo, were at once a by-product of his elephant quest and a complement to the studies at the Museum. They formed a living library of the natural world. The collection became one of the earliest and most celebrated menageries in antiquity and an archetype for later zoos, just as the Library was for subsequent repositories of books.

According to Diodorus, "Philadelphos, who was passionately fond of the hunting of elephants and gave great rewards to those who succeeded in capturing against odds the most valiant of these beasts, expending on this undertaking great sums of money, not only collected great herds of war-elephants, but also brought to the knowledge of the Greeks other kinds of animals which had never before been seen and which were objects of amazement."

Diodorus tells the story of a forty-five-foot snake captured in Ethiopia, famous in antiquity for its huge reptiles. Of course he embellishes both his tale and the snake's size, but the African rock python, *Python sebae,* can indeed be very large and has big fangs, a vicious bite, and a bad temper. It likes to wait near pools or watering holes, its coiled body perfectly motionless. "But at the appearance of an animal which came down to the spot to quench its thirst," writes Diodorus, "it would suddenly uncoil itself, seize the animal in its jaws, and so entwine in its coils the body of the creature which had come into view that it could in no wise escape its doom." Then the snake stretches its mouth over the animal — whether an impala or an unlucky man — swallows it whole, and curls up for a contented while to digest.

Diodorus reports that a group of hunters, tempted by the prospect of a royal reward, decided to capture a giant python for Philadelphos. They first thought to ensnare it with ropes and nooses, which they threw around the snake's tail. But the python whirled around with a dreadful hiss, rose swiftly above the first hunter, and seized him in its jaws. The rest of the hunters, in cold terror, threw down their ropes and ran for their lives. But one more man was out of luck. As he tried to flee, the snake caught him from a distance with a coil, wound itself about him, and crushed him in its muscled embrace.

The remaining men returned to their huts. Some thought it wise to give up the hunt, but others, greedy for Philadelphos's recompense, devised a long, circular basket shaped like a great fish trap. When the python slithered away from its den, they hastily blocked the entrance with a mixture of earth and stones, dug a new hole nearby, and put in the basket. They also assembled a small army of bowmen, slingers, horsemen, fighting dogs, and trumpeters. When all was ready, they hid in the surrounding bushes to await the snake's return.

At dusk the python slithered back to its home and was baffled to find it sealed off. Suddenly, the hunters and their crew leapt out of the bushes and, from a safe distance, assaulted it with stones and arrows, trumpet blares, and their dogs' barks. Disoriented and frightened, the snake darted into the hole dug by the hunters, whereupon the men swiftly pulled the ropes at the mouth of the basket to tie it shut. Straining against the snake's thrashing weight, they dragged it out of the hole and heaved it onto a timber platform. To tame the beast along the way to Alexandria, they starved it, sapping its strength and ferocity. By the time the python arrived in the capital, it was gentle and compliant, and ready to be Philadelphos's pet.

The king was delighted with this addition to his menagerie and paid the resourceful hunters a hefty fee. He kept his marvelous reptile well fed and proudly exhibited the rare creature to his visitors and foreign guests.

IT HAD BEEN only seven years since Philadelphos assumed the throne, but elephants and their by-products — other exotic beasts, newly mined gold, and myriad valuable trade commodities — now streamed into Alexandria. These acquisitions, no less than Philadelphos's armies and weapons, would demonstrate to his enemies and allies the extent of his power and organization as he stood poised for a war over Coele-Syria. Philadelphos thought of a way to show off all these gains to their greatest effect. He would parade his new treasures during the Ptolemaia, a festival simultaneously honoring his deified father, Ptolemy, Alexander the Great, and the Olympian gods. Philadelphos had instituted the Ptolemaia in 280/79 BC, to be celebrated every four years, like the Olympic games, which he hoped to rival in renown. The festivities lasted for several weeks, from late December until mid-February, and spectators and participants were treated to an array of magnificent processions dedicated to various gods and to the Ptolemaic dynasty. They were also entertained by athletic games, musical and dramatic competitions, military parades, and sumptuous feasts.

The second Ptolemaia was coming up, and the timing was auspicious. Antiochos was not the only rival whom Philadelphos hoped to overawe. Not long before, his own half brother Magas, the viceroy of Cyrene, had married Antiochos's daughter and, with his father-in-law's backing, decided to march on Egypt to oust Philadelphos from the throne. Alas, as soon as Magas left Cyrene, Libyan nomads staged a revolt against him, and he was forced to rush back to deal with the insurgents. He quelled the uprising but felt too vulnerable to resume his Egyptian campaign.

Philadelphos was prepared to pursue Magas to punish his impudence, but as he got ready to leave for Cyrene, his own Celtic mercenaries rebelled against him. The king moved swiftly to punish them, luring them to a deserted island on the Nile and having them slaughtered. At this point he, too, decided not to scatter his military resources and to give up his confrontation with Magas. Instead, he would put on a spectacle that would send all his enemies a clear message that he was not to be trifled with. The Ptolemaia would give him an occasion to showcase his own African war elephants and to astonish and intimidate the Mediterranean world with the new riches he had acquired while searching for them.

IN THE WINTER of 275–274 BC, Alexandria buzzed with excitement. Thousands of spectators assembled to observe and take part in the Ptolemaia. The streets undulated with cosmopolitan crowds — Thracians and Macedonians; Greeks from the mainland, Sicily, and Ionia; visitors and immigrants from Asia Minor, Persia, Syria, and Judaea; and native Egyptians. The foreigners marveled at the imposing buildings, the grand colonnaded streets of extraordinary width, the gleaming marble everywhere, and the lush gardens flowering in the middle of winter. Kallixenos, author of *On Alexandria,* waxed lyrical about the flowers, "which, in any other city could have been found only with difficulty to make up a single wreath, [but here] were lavished in a wealth of wreaths upon the multitude of guests [especially the dignitaries invited to special banquets], and, moreover, lay scattered profusely on the floor of the banqueting pavilion, truly presenting the picture of an extraordinarily beautiful meadow."

The best way to view the city — which Philadelphos had transformed into a splendid metropolis thanks to his imported riches — was from the sea, which is how many visitors arrived for the festival. From the long and flat coastline, the city rose like a magical apparition. To enter the Great Harbor, one sailed to the east of Pharos (a long, narrow island lying parallel to the coast) and could thus admire up close the splendid lighthouse on its eastern tip. The lighthouse, which took its name from the island, rose as a stepped tower, with a light beam at its summit that could be seen from miles away. (The light was probably created by fires burning inside it and reflected by mirrors.) It had only recently been completed by Philadelphos and at once became one of the seven wonders of the world. To the left of the Pharos lay the hilly promontory called Lochias, which marked the eastern limit of the Great Harbor. Beyond Lochias stood the barracks and the armories, while on its summit spread the royal palace complex, shaded by lush vegetation. The waterfront was lined on the left by the brightly painted lodges and cool groves of the royal precinct and on the right by public buildings — the theater, the agora (marketplace), customs offices, warehouses, and temples, all linked by pavements, porticoes, and colonnades. The buildings were clad in bright limestone, marble, and granite and adorned inside with stucco decorations and mosaics.

Disembarking and stepping into the town proper, visitors found much more to admire. Alexandria was shaped like an outspread chlamys — a military cloak that Alexander the Great allegedly threw on the ground to provide the blueprint for his new settlement. It was roughly a rectangle, washed on its long sides by the Mediterranean and Lake Mareotis, its streets laid out in a grid. Two great avenues intersected at the heart of the city. The Canopic Way ran for about three and a half miles east–west, starting at the Canopic Gate, also known as the Gate of the Sun, and ending at the Gate of the Moon, which led to the Necropolis, a residential and cemetery district with many gardens and groves, as well as embalming establishments. The Canopic Way was some thirty-two yards wide and paved with large, regular-shaped stones. It was lined with columns and illuminated at night by oil lamps, a costly and luxurious amenity. This street was always busy. Not only visitors but also locals had to take care not to be crushed by the heavy traffic. "I barely got here alive through all the crowds and chariots," complained one lady in the poet Theokritos's *Fifteenth Idyll.* "Big boots and men in soldiers' cloaks all over the place, and the road going forever." At the center of the city, the Canopic Way was crossed by the tree-lined Street of the Sema (tomb), equally wide but only about a mile long. This street got its name from the mausoleum of Alexander, which rose where the two main avenues met.

The Sema, being the symbol of Ptolemy's legitimacy as the heir of Alexander, stood within the palace precinct, which stretched over the north-central area of Alexandria. Here, too, were located the Museum and the Library, the royal buildings, and extensive pleasure grounds with opulent gardens and Philadelphos's magnificent zoo. The civic portion of Alexandria lay to the south, where visitors could admire various shrines, public monuments, and the Gymnasium, surrounded by a tall colonnade.* In the center of town stood the court of justice and an artificial hill, shaped like a fir cone and reached by a spiral road. The hill was devoted to the woodland god Pan, and from its summit one could take in the whole of Alexandria. It had been a remarkable feat of planning, engineering, and management of Egypt's material and labor resources to erect this splendid city, and it testified to Philadelphos's sophistication. The same vision and ambition that he had put into obtaining his elephants had driven his transformation of Alexandria into a cultural metropolis whose fame would endure for millennia.

The attractions of the city were not limited to its center. Visitors could also explore the residential neighborhoods and craft

---

Gymnos means "nude" in ancient Greek, and the Gymnasium was where men exercised in the nude.

districts. East, beyond the royal palaces, lay the Jewish quarter, with its great synagogue along the Canopic Way. The southwest district, called Rhakotis, was the original settlement that had stood before Alexander's arrival. It still housed the native Egyptian population, the poorest in the city. Some of the spectacles of the Ptolemaia, including the animal parade, were staged in this neighborhood's stadium. In numerous craft shops scattered throughout the city, visitors were tempted by local specialties: exquisite jewelry hammered by Alexandrian goldsmiths, cosmetics and perfumes made from the resins and spices Philadelphos obtained via southern trade routes, elegant vessels created by glassmakers, thin yet durable papyrus, and fine linen fabrics — all highly prized Alexandrian exports.

But how much time would one spend sightseeing when the Ptolemaia was in full swing? The Canopic Way heaved with spectators jostling on either side of the passage, kept clear with difficulty by soldiers for the upcoming processions. Elbowed and squeezed from every side, the motley crowd envied the exalted guests — Alexandrian dignitaries and foreign ambassadors — who were privileged to observe the proceedings from the comfort of the stadium seats.

And now the pipes and cymbals, the rising hum of the excited crowd, and the wafts of incense heralded the approach of the most fabulous part of the festival — the procession devoted to Dionysos, god of wine. The Ptolemies claimed descent from this god, and Philadelphos in particular fostered his cult in Alexandria. Dionysos was believed to have captured Egypt before proceeding to India, as did Alexander. So Philadelphos celebrated his own rule over Egypt and his expansion south and east by likening himself directly to Dionysos and implicitly to Alexander.

Preceding Dionysos in the parade were satyrs, who pushed back the onlookers surging into the path of the procession. Then an altar, nine feet long, came into view. Covered with gilded foliage, it was surmounted by a great crown made of vines entwined with striped ribbons. The rising scent of frankincense, myrrh, and saffron — borne by boys dressed in purple chitons (long tunics) — announced the advent of the god himself.

Dionysos, a fifteen-foot-tall statue pouring a libation from a golden vessel, rode on a massive four-wheeled cart pulled by 180 men. The god wore a purple chiton draped all the way down to his feet and a transparent outer robe of saffron cloth that enveloped him in an aura of light. Above him was a lush canopy of ivy vines and fruits and before him a golden table groaning with massive gold plates. Priests, priestesses, maenads, and devotees followed the cart in an exuberant display of joy.

Then came a thirty-foot-long cart pulled by three hundred men. On it stood a huge press full of grapes. Sixty satyrs, singing to the music of flutes, trampled the grapes with their bare feet. The grape juice trickled from an opening in the press floor and flowed through the street like a red mantle trailing the cart.

The most astounding spectacle, however, was the enactment of Dionysos's triumphal return from India with a retinue of exotic animals, a wealth of luxurious goods, and a train of ecstatic followers. Dionysos appeared at the head of this tableau as an eighteen-foot-tall statue dressed in a purple cloak and a golden ivy crown, riding on an enormous artificial elephant directed by a seven-foot satyr perched on its neck. He was followed by twenty-four quadrigae (chariots) drawn by four live elephants each — ninety-six in all. Some of these beasts — those with smaller ears and humped backs — were the remaining Indian elephants that Philadelphos had inherited from his father. Others, with larger ears and concave backs, were the fruits of Philadelphos's recent hunting campaigns. The dignitaries of foreign kingdoms, specially invited to witness this display, must have shaken their heads as they recalculated the balance of Mediterranean power, now that Philadelphos possessed his own source of these animal tanks.

After the elephants came *bigae* (two-horse chariots) drawn by goats, saiga antelopes (hump-nosed ruminants from the Urals), oryx with their bright white bodies and horns rising like tall spears, swift hartebeests (hump-shouldered fawns with long, narrow faces), and ostriches. Behind them still more African, Ethiopian, Arabian, Syrian, and Persian beasts drew chariots — all of them driven by boys dressed as charioteers and girls armed with lances and shields.

No animal array of such diversity had ever been seen in Alexandria or in any other Greek city. Some spectators gawked in wonder. Others recalled Aristotle's learned descriptions of strange beasts dwelling in distant lands and marveled at how far Philadelphos's power had spread. But they could not ponder any species for long, as more and more animals and other prized goods streamed past, trumpeting yet another conquest of land, commerce, and diplomacy. There were *bigae* drawn by camels, as well as carts carrying Indian women, other exotic foreigners, and prisoners huddled under colorful tents. There were further carts loaded with hundreds of pounds of frankincense and myrrh, saffron and cassia, cinnamon and orris, and many other spices from Arabia and India — brought to Alexandria to be turned into the finest ointments, perfumes, and cosmetics and then shipped to clients across the sea. Next marched Ethiopian tribute bearers, walking slowly, bent low under the weight of six hundred elephant tusks, two thousand ebony logs, and dozens of large vessels full of gold — testaments to Philadelphos's expansion down the Trogodyte coast and into Meroë.

As a coda, trainers led one large white bear — either a Thracian variety or an albino from Syria — fourteen leopards, nine cheetahs, four caracals, and two marvels: a giraffe (an animal unknown even to Aristotle), and a two-horned white Ethiopian rhinoceros.

Both of these strange beasts had been shipped from Meroë, and they made an indelible impression on the onlookers. The Jewish scholars translating the Torah at the Museum included the giraffe in Deuteronomy 14 among the beasts that can be safely eaten by Jews. The animal does not appear in the non-Greek version of this text.

In the days after the Dionysian procession, statues of the deified Ptolemy I and Alexander the Great, borne by quadrigae of elephants, were paraded through the city, honoring the men who had made Philadelphos's kingdom possible. There were also celebrations of Zeus and other Olympian gods. And it took an entire day for Philadelphos's army — some 57,000 infantry, 23,000 cavalry, and massive quantities of military hardware bought with the new gold — to pass before the spectators, leaving them in no doubt of the king's readiness for war.

It seems incredible that Philadelphos could have amassed so much, especially so many elephants, in so short a time — from the moment he took the throne in 282 BC to the celebration of the Ptolemaia in 275 BC. Yet here they were, nearly one hundred beasts marching before the astonished spectators, plus everything that followed in their wake. Determined to defend and extend his kingdom in the face of various enemies, Philadelphos had moved with efficiency and determination, opportunism and vision. In the process of building a corps of his animal warriors, he had made his kingdom far richer and stronger than it had been when he had received it from his father. And now he was informing Antiochos that he also had his own potentially vast supply of African elephants. The former imbalance of power had been redressed.

LATER THAT YEAR Philadelphos marched east, to wrestle Coele-Syria from his rival. Yet despite all his resources, he was turned back. Was it because, while he had been busy consolidating his kingdom, Antiochos had been honing his fighting skills in a succession of military engagements across his sprawling territories? Were Philadelphos's elephants still inexperienced in battle compared to those of the Seleukid king? Or were the elephants themselves less crucial than good generalship and battle strategy? The ancient historians do not say, or their opinions have perished together with Alexandria's Library. All we know is that only in 271 BC, when Antiochos simply abandoned the Syrian campaign, did Philadelphos win by default.

In the long run, however, Philadelphos won a far greater victory. Antiochos became merely one of many Hellenistic rulers struggling to hold on to Alexander's legacy, his resources scattered too widely for him to fashion a lasting heritage. But Philadelphos built a mighty kingdom that would remain in the dynasty's control for generations and ushered in the golden age of Alexandria, whose renown endures to this day. He may have been self-indulgent and unconcerned with the lot of those toiling on his behalf, but he was certainly a gifted and creative ruler. In the process of hunting for his war elephants, he developed new trade centers and caravan routes, diplomatic links and territories, and wealth and learning that made his capital the queen of the Mediterranean world.

Philo, a Jewish philosopher who lived in Alexandria two and a half centuries later, left the following assessment of Philadelphos:

> In all the qualities which make a good ruler, he excelled not only over his contemporaries, but all who have arisen in the past; and even till today, after so many generations, his praises are sung for the many evidences and monuments of his greatness of mind which he left behind him in different cities and countries, so that even now, acts of more than ordinary munificence or buildings on a specially grand scale are proverbially called Philadelphian after him. To put it shortly, as the house of the

Ptolemies was highly distinguished compared to other dynasties, so was Philadelphos among the Ptolemies. The creditable achievements of this one man almost outnumbered those of all the others put together, and, as the head takes the highest place in the living body, so he may be said to head the kings.

TWO

CONTROLLING NATURE
IN THE ROMAN ARENA

I happened to go to one of the lunchtime interludes,
expecting there to be some light and witty entertainment . . . far from it. In the morning men are thrown
to the lions and the bears; but it is to the spectators
that they are thrown in the lunch hour.

SENECA,
Epistles 7.3–4

In 55 BC Gnaeus Pompeius Magnus was desperate to recapture his fading popularity. Only recently he had been a national hero. He had conquered three continents and served as
consul (chief magistrate) of Rome without having held any of the
preliminary posts required for that lofty office. He had risen from
modest provincial roots to become the first citizen of the state.
Yet the astonishing victories on land and sea that made his reputation and his meteoric rise to the pinnacle of power now seemed
for naught. Upon returning from laying the foundations of
Roman rule in the East in 61 BC, Pompey failed to master Rome.
Instead, he began to lose esteem and authority by the day. How
could he win back the people and overawe his adversaries? He
decided to put on exotic animal games.

Wild beast displays and contests were beloved spectacles in

ancient Rome. They had their roots in gladiatorial shows, which in their turn originated in funeral celebrations. Fed by Rome's subjugation of foreign lands and their resources, exotic animal combats grew in size and splendor with each territorial conquest. They began as a way to entertain and control the populace and to give it a symbolic share in the glory of the state. But as the people got more and more addicted to these exhibitions, politicians had to sponsor them to ensure popular support. Their reputations came to depend on the games they put on.

Pompey's wild beast spectacles proved unforgettable. They were talked about for centuries afterward. Their fame endured in part because of their unprecedented scale and magnificence, but far more because they, like Pompey's career, went contrary to expectations.

FROM HIS YOUTH Pompey seemed favored by fortune. Born on September 29, 106 BC, into a family of provincial knights in Picenum (a region in The Marches, in east-central Italy), he began to distinguish himself as a teenage boy. His father, Gnaeus Pompeius Strabo (not the same as the geographer), had schooled him in the military arts, and by age seventeen Pompey was already fighting in his father's army in the Social War.* Pompey and his father fought mercilessly on the side of Rome and were instrumental in its victory.

---

*This was a conflict in which Rome's former Italian allies rebelled against Rome's refusal to grant them full rights. The word "Italy" in Pompey's day referred to most of the Italian peninsula south of Liguria and the Po Valley. As the ancient historian Velleius Paterculus describes this conflict, "All Italy took up arms against the Romans. . . . The fortune of the Italians was as cruel as their cause was just; for they were seeking citizenship in the state whose power they were defending by their arms . . . , and yet were not admitted to the rights of citizens in a state which, through their efforts, had reached so high a position that it could look down upon men of the same race and blood as foreigners and aliens."

Two years later, while Strabo was lending Rome his help in fighting against Cinna, a Roman consul who was waging a civil war against his co-consul and the Roman Senate, Pompey saved his father's life. One night, during dinner at camp, Pompey overheard that his tentmate had been bribed by Cinna to kill Strabo and set his tent on fire. Pompey stayed calm through the rest of the meal, drinking heartily and not letting on about his discovery. When everyone retired for the night and his tentmate went to sleep, Pompey stole out of his tent, warned his father, and set a guard around him. As soon as Strabo's soldiers heard of the foiled plot, they attempted to stage a revolt against their general, whom they hated for his greed and perfidy. Strabo hid in fear, but Pompey went up and down among the soldiers, beseeching them to desist, then threw himself on the ground in front of the gates to the camp, inviting those who were still determined to march against Strabo to trample him first. The soldiers, shamed, drew back, and most of them gave up the revolt.

According to Pompey's biographer Plutarch,

> There were many reasons for the love bestowed on Pompey; his modest and temperate way of living, his training in the arts of war, his persuasive speech, his trustworthy character, and his tact in meeting people, so that no man asked a favor with less offence, or bestowed one with a better mien. . . . He had a countenance which helped him in no small degree to win the favor of the people, and which pleaded for him before he spoke. . . . His hair was inclined to lift itself slightly from his forehead, and this, with a graceful contour of face about the eyes, produced a resemblance, more talked about than actually apparent, to portrait statues of King Alexander [the Great]."

Young Pompey was as charismatic as his father was odious. Strabo was loathed for his avarice and treachery and for rendering military aid to the Roman state only when it suited him, rather than helping whenever he was needed. When Strabo died from plague in 87 BC, a mob pulled his body from its bier and dragged it through the mud on a hook. Taking to heart his father's negative example, Pompey would forever be sensitive to popular opinion and keen to win supporters and friends.

Soon after his father's funeral, Pompey was put on trial for the theft of public property. He quickly discovered that most of the theft had been committed by one of his father's former slaves. He proceeded to argue his innocence so eloquently, says Plutarch, that with "acumen and poise beyond his years, he won great reputation and favor, insomuch that Antistius, the praetor and judge in the case, took a great liking to him and offered him his own daughter in marriage." Pompey accepted and was promptly acquitted.

Since Rome was a militaristic and imperialistic society, the way for a man to build his career was through military exploits abroad: fighting the enemies of the state and expanding its frontiers. Pompey's first success came when, at age twenty-three, he led a private army of three legions, assembled from his father's old soldiers in Picenum, into battle on behalf of Sulla, the dictator of Rome.

Although Rome was usually ruled by two consuls, in times of political unrest a "dictator" was appointed to restore order. The post was normally granted for six months, but Sulla retained it for three years, until he resigned from politics in 79 BC. The scion of an old patrician family, Sulla had gained fame and power by conquering foreign kings. His unrivaled luck in battle led people to call him Felix, "the Fortunate." He was also a brilliant and ruthless politician, all the more dangerous for being quite unpredictable: he could be both deeply greedy and most generous, able to order a man beaten to death for no good reason or to pardon a recalcitrant political foe.

Upon gaining power in 82 BC, Sulla proceeded to butcher his political opponents, instituting a reign of terror. Pompey was lucky to be on his good side. So when Sulla, impressed with Pompey's military skills and administrative abilities, decided that he wanted to bind the young man closer to himself through marriage, Pompey quickly consented. This was far from convenient, as it meant that he had to divorce his wife of five years, Antistia, while his new bride, Sulla's stepdaughter Aemilia, had to leave her husband, whose child she was carrying. But Roman political elites often arranged and broke marriages for political advancement, and so the previous unions were dissolved and the new match was made.

Soon afterward Sulla gave his protégé a great opportunity to distinguish himself by dispatching him to pursue and defeat Sulla's enemies in Sicily, Spain, and Africa. Eager to prove himself, Pompey fought so fiercely in Sicily and Spain that his opponents nicknamed him "boy-butcher." In Africa, he "conquered all who came his way," writes Plutarch,

and made potent and terrible again the Barbarians' fear of the Romans, which had reached a low ebb. Nay, he declared that even the wild beasts in African lairs must not be left without experience of the courage and strength of the Romans, and therefore spent a few days in hunting lions and elephants. It took him only forty days all told, they say, to bring his enemies to naught, get Africa into his power, and adjust the relations of its kings, though he was but twenty-four years of age.

Although Sulla had given Pompey this opportunity to advance his career, he was unnerved by the efficiency and growing power of his son-in-law. When Pompey's mission in Africa was completed, Sulla ordered him to disband his army and await the arrival of the general who would succeed him. But when Pompey informed his soldiers of this order, they refused to leave their commander. Following the tactics of Alexander the Great when faced with mutinous troops in India, Pompey first addressed his soldiers with rousing speeches, proclaiming his abhorrence of rebellion against his superior. Then he retired to his tent in tears at the troops' reluctance to heed his high-minded words. Next he threatened to commit suicide if they pushed him into wrongdoing.

When word of Pompey's conscientious conduct and of his army's loyalty reached Sulla, the dictator realized that it was better to embrace rather than suppress the increasingly popular young general. As Pompey approached Rome with his army, Sulla went out to meet him in great state and saluted him in a loud voice as Magnus, "the Great," a deliberate reference to Alexander.

Encouraged, Pompey boldly demanded a "triumph" — a formal celebration of his African victories. He wished to appear in this procession riding a chariot through the streets of Rome toward the temple of Jupiter on the Capitoline, accompanied by his troops, the spoils of his campaign, and his prisoners of war. The senators and all the magistrates of Rome would escort him.

Pompey's request was brash in the extreme. To receive the honor of a triumph, a victorious general had to have held one of two top magistracies in Rome, that of either consul or praetor.* Pompey had never held even a junior office. Yet he was intent not only on wearing the laurel crown of a *triumphator* but also on riding through Rome in a chariot drawn by war elephants walking four abreast, in the manner of Alexander the Great. In fact, Pompey had captured a number of the giant beasts from the Numidian king Iarbas and brought them back from Africa just for this purpose.

Understandably, Sulla refused to do the bidding of a young man "who had scarcely grown a beard." But Pompey, self-confident and determined, would not be cowed. As Plutarch reports, he

---

*Rome was governed by two consuls who ruled jointly for a one-year term. Consuls convened and presided over the Senate and popular assemblies, initiated and administered legislation, served as generals in military campaigns, and represented Rome in foreign affairs. Praetors were primarily responsible for administering law. Eight praetors served per one-year term under Sulla.

"bade Sulla reflect that more [people] worshipped the rising than the setting sun, intimating that his own power was on the increase, while that of Sulla was on the wane." Sulla either did not hear the words clearly or would not acknowledge their impudence, for he was speechless for some time as those around him stood agape. Finally Sulla replied, "Let him triumph!" And so Pompey marched through the city to great fanfare, although his chariot was drawn by horses, as the city gates proved too narrow for a quadriga of elephants to pass. Through his triumph Pompey clearly established himself as one for whom the state would make allowances and bend the rules. He also became a popular hero, beloved for his good looks and charm, his courage in battle, and his political success.

Pompey's next big coup came almost a decade later, when Rome struggled to suppress the slave revolt headed by the valiant and charismatic Thracian gladiator Spartacus. Breaking out of a gladiatorial school at Capua in 73 BC, Spartacus fled to Mount Vesuvius, where he raised a rebel army said to have comprised seventy thousand escaped slaves. When Rome sent troops to squelch the uprising, Spartacus defeated them in a succession of battles in southern Italy and proceeded north. He apparently wanted to march his army out of Italy and into Gaul, so that his men could return to their homes in the various countries from which they had been captured by the Romans. But either on his own or under pressure from his followers, who were eager to plunder Roman towns, Spartacus turned back and successfully fought the Roman legions sent against him, making Rome more nervous with each battle he won.

In 72 BC the rebels returned to southern Italy, where they continued to humiliate the Romans by defeating the legions commanded by Marcus Licinius Crassus. Early in 71 BC Crassus isolated Spartacus's army on the Calabrian peninsula by building a wall across the isthmus and cut off the slaves' supplies. But taking advantage of a snowy night, Spartacus filled in a construction ditch Crassus's men had dug, led his army over it, and escaped to Brundisium (modern-day Brindisi). Frustrated in his attempts to destroy the rebels, Crassus wrote to the Senate asking for reinforcements. The Senate told Pompey, just returning from his campaigns in Spain, to hurry to southern Italy to help put an end to this ludicrous war. Rather than rejoicing at Pompey's approach, Crassus redoubled his efforts to defeat Spartacus. He wanted the glory of winning to himself.

Crassus came from a well-established plebeian family and became the wealthiest man in Rome thanks to Sulla's tyranny. When Sulla took control of Rome in 82 BC, he issued proscriptions — lists of his real and purported enemies — and paid handsome bounties to informers for denouncing traitors, whose lives and properties were then forfeited. Crassus grew rich by buying up the property of the condemned at ridiculously low prices and thus building up vast real estate holdings. According to contemporary accounts of his greed and mean-spiritedness, he would also show up at the site of a burning building and begin to bargain for the property. If the owner accepted his low price, Crassus's henchmen would promptly put out the blaze. If the owner refused to sell, Crassus would stand by and relish the sight of the house burning to the ground. While Crassus thus increased his fortune at the cost of being widely despised, Pompey built a reputation as a military superstar and a darling of the Roman people. It was no wonder that Crassus deeply resented the young upstart.

Now that Pompey was on his way to lend his hand in eliminating Spartacus, Crassus moved into high gear. He fought a great battle with Spartacus's army at Lucania (south of Salerno), and this time met with success, or so he thought. The Romans killed more than twelve thousand of the enemy, including the indomitable Spartacus, whose body was never found amid the mounds of the dead on the battlefield. Some six thousand of the captured slaves were crucified along the Via Appia from Capua to

Rome and left to rot, as a deterrent to other potential rebels. Five thousand slaves, however, escaped and fled north toward Rome. They were intercepted by Pompey, just arriving from Spain. He cut the fugitives to shreds and promptly wrote to the Senate that although Crassus had overthrown the slaves in battle, he, Pompey, "had plucked up the whole war by the roots."

The Romans, embarrassed by the indignity of having to wage a full-out war against slaves who had terrorized the entire peninsula and had required eight legions to put them down, seemed to prefer the notion that the rebellion was simply brushed aside by a brilliant young general on his way back from a victorious Spanish campaign. The popularity Pompey had built up in foreign wars also helped, and so he again became the hero of the day. This time he requested not only a triumph — for his Spanish accomplishments — but also the consulship for the following year, 70 BC, skipping the requisite lesser posts.

Pompey may have been a hero of foreign wars, but he was a novice in Roman politics, which were mercurial in the extreme. Shifting alliances, bribery, and political assassinations were rampant, as were conflicts between the aristocratic and populist parties. Pompey came from a respectable but somewhat provincial background, and from a family without a long history in the city of Rome. So he could not draw on the nexus of ties and friendships inside and outside the Senate, often reaching back many generations, on which power in the capital was habitually built.

To stand a better chance of being elected consul, Pompey decided to team up with Crassus. There was, of course, no love lost between the two men, but both wanted the consulship and felt that they could help themselves by helping each other. There were three main classes of free Roman citizens — senators, knights, and plebeians. Pompey could bank on his popularity as the darling of the plebeians and knights. Crassus relied on his immense wealth to buy the necessary votes among the senators — which is how Roman politics functioned, quite openly, in those days.

Plutarch writes that people considered the partnership a proof of Pompey's splendid distinction, as Crassus, "the richest states-man of the time, the ablest speaker, and the greatest man, who looked down on Pompey himself and everybody else, had not the courage to sue for the consulship until he had asked the support of Pompey." The alliance paid off. Together they won the election, and Pompey became a head of state at the age of thirty-five, having skipped the slow climb up the political ladder by which Romans usually ascended to this summit. He attained the supreme office when he was seven years younger than the minimum legal age.

Because Pompey rocketed straight to the top, he had no politi-cal experience. When he entered the Senate for the first time in his new role, he had to rely on a handbook composed by his friend Varro so as not to embarrass himself before his new peers. His lack of connections would also make it difficult for him to in-fluence senatorial debates and manipulate popular assemblies. (Though technically an advisory body, in reality the Senate was the chief organ of government in Rome, controlling public finances and foreign affairs, assigning military commands and provinces, and debating and passing decrees.) As a result, Pompey's first consulship was not particularly distinguished. He and Crassus differed on all points and were constantly in collision, although they did succeed in passing some laws that restored to the knightly and plebeian classes powers that Sulla had severely cur-tailed. These acts served to strengthen Pompey's popular support.

After his term ended, Pompey still had plenty of energy and ambition. But according to Roman law, he would not be eligi-ble for another consulship for ten years. What to do in the in-terim? Fortune smiled on him again. For some time now the Mediterranean had been infested by pirates who ceaselessly ha-rassed and impoverished coastal towns and disrupted trade. They were not only formidable but also obnoxiously ostentatious, sailing ships with gilded masts, purple sails, and oars plated with silver. Several Roman generals had been sent to tackle the problem, but with minimal results, and the situation was becoming dire. As the pirates continued to prey on maritime traffic, merchants feared taking their wares to sea, and Rome, which imported its grain from Sardinia, Sicily, and Egypt, was beginning to experience shortages. If these were allowed to worsen, public riots were not far off.

In 67 BC Pompey's supporter, the tribune Aulus Gabinius, proposed to the Senate that Pompey be assigned to lead the anti-pirate campaign. The senators balked at the idea, as they feared entrusting the enormous powers required to combat the vast piratical network to the extremely ambitious young general. Seeking to force the Senate, Gabinius put Pompey's candidacy before the popular assembly — composed of all males who were full Roman citizens. They immediately demanded that he be given charge. Pompey himself made a show of being forced to accept the command against his will. According to the historian Dio Cassius, "it was always Pompey's way to pretend as far as possible not to desire the things he wanted most, and on this occasion he did so more than ever because of the jealousy that would follow if of his own accord he had laid claim to the leadership, and because of the increased honor which he would enjoy if he should be appointed against his will as the man most worthy of command."

After some wrangling and grand speeches by Pompey, Gabinius, and the senators, the Senate finally voted to grant Pompey supreme command over the Mediterranean sea, its islands, and all the mainland to a distance of fifty miles inland. He was given three years and an unprecedented amount of resources to accomplish this task: 24 legates (military deputies) from the Senate to assist him, 500 ships, 120,000 troops, 5,000 horsemen, and as much money from public treasuries and tax collectors as he needed. Pompey's reputation and the popular expectation of his success caused the price of grain to drop sharply before he even began his campaign. People said that "the very name of Pompey had put an end to the war."

Pompey embarked on his new task with the same resolve and efficiency that he had brought to his previous foreign wars and domestic career building. He divided the Mediterranean basin, from Spain to the Levant and from the Black Sea to North Africa, into thirteen districts, assigning to each sector an officer in charge of a flotilla of ships, some infantry, and some cavalry. In this manner, rather than chasing after the pirates across the sea, he covered every segment of the Mediterranean, every harbor, and every coastal town, cutting off supply and escape routes. The sea was clear of pirates within three months.

Pompey then treated the captured pirates with great acumen. He reflected, writes Plutarch, "that by nature man neither is nor becomes a wild or an unsocial creature, but is transformed by the unnatural practice of vice, whereas he may be softened by new customs and a change of place and life; also that even wild beasts put off their fierce and savage ways when they partake of a gentler mode of life." (Ironically, this is not how the Romans approached wild animals themselves, as we shall see.) Rather than capturing and executing thousands of pirates and their families or selling them into slavery, Pompey resettled them into agricultural communities, giving them a chance to earn an honest living while increasing the productivity of Roman-controlled lands. Another historian, Florus, elaborates, "With remarkable wisdom he removed those maritime people far from the sight of the sea, and by tying them down to the cultivation of fertile areas of the interior he at once restored the land to its proper inhabitants and recovered the use of the sea for trade."

Pompey's reward for this achievement was what he had dreamt of most: supreme command of the war against Rome's most formidable foe. Mithradates VI of Pontus aspired to build a new Eastern empire of Asians and Greeks. After murdering his mother and brother, he had conquered the Crimea and gained control of most of the coasts of the Black Sea, which gave him an almost inexhaustible supply of men and materials for further military conquests. He then swept through much of Asia Minor and annexed Bithynia and Cappadocia (northwestern and central Turkey). Proclaiming the evils of Rome, he ordered his armies to massacre Roman and Italian residents in his lands and won over most of Greece, receiving a welcome in Athens. In 87 BC Sulla had sailed to Greece with five legions, defeated the Pontic armies, besieged and sacked Athens, and pushed Mithradates back to Asia Minor. The king surrendered and was allowed to retire to Pontus, but he continued to despise and threaten Rome and to assist the pirates.

Now Pompey had a chance to vanquish Rome's most dangerous enemy for good. Of course he made the usual pretense of being reluctant to be loaded with further burdens. "Alas for my endless tasks!" he lamented. "How much better it were to be an unknown man, if I am never to cease from military service, and cannot lay aside this load of envy and spend my time in the country with my wife!" But as he said this, Plutarch writes, "even his intimate friends could not abide his dissimulations."

Pompey's Eastern campaign proved his greatest achievement. Mithradates, weakened by years of war, was defeated almost immediately. Although he managed to flee and Pompey's attempts to pursue him over the Caucasus failed, the king was no longer a player. When he committed suicide in the Crimea four years later, it was welcome, but not earth-shattering, news. (Inured to poison by years of taking it in preventative doses, Mithradates had to ask his bodyguard to run him through with a sword.) Meanwhile, between 65 and 62 BC, Pompey proceeded to conquer Tigranes the Great, king of Armenia and Mithradates' son-in-law, and Antiochos XIII of Syria, whose territory he annexed for Rome. He subdued the Jews and captured Jerusalem. He founded numerous new colonies and laid the foundation for subsequent Roman rule in the East. As Dio Cassius summarizes in his *Roman History*, Pompey "had opened up many lands and sources of revenue to the Romans, and had established and organized most of the nations in the continent of Asia then belonging to them with their own laws and constitutions, so that even to this day [in the early third century AD] they use the laws that he laid down." Pompey himself boasted that he had found Asia the remotest of the provinces and made it a central dominion of Rome.

The Eastern campaign brought Pompey even more fame, a vast personal fortune, and a clientele of foreign kings and provincial governors from whom he could request favors, from military aid to exotic beasts with which to impress his rivals and wow the populace at home. He would call on these clients in a few years when his authority was at risk.

Returning home from the East, Pompey began his further career-building in Rome with a bang. His third triumph, staged on September 28, 61 BC, on the eve of his forty-fifth birthday, was, in Plutarch's words, of "such a magnitude that, although it was distributed over two days, still the time would not suffice, but much of what had been prepared could not find a place in the spectacle, enough to dignify and adorn another triumphal procession." Before Pompey other Roman generals may have earned the honor of three triumphs, but he was the first to triumph over three continents — Africa, Europe (Spain), and now Asia. As Pompey rode through the city in a gem-studded chariot wearing the cloak of Alexander the Great (or so he claimed), which he had taken from Mithradates' wardrobe, placards carried at the head of the procession named the countries he had conquered: Pontus, Armenia, Cappadocia, Paphlagonia, Media, Colchis, Iberia, Albania, Syria, Cilicia, Mesopotamia, Phoenicia, Palestine, Judaea, and Arabia. Every nation was represented by distinguished captives, none of them bound and all marching in colorful national costumes. (After the triumph, instead of executing them, Pompey magnanimously sent them home at the state's expense.)

At the center of the Pontic exhibition was a golden statue of Mithradates, twelve feet high and made of solid gold. Endless carts bore objects made of gold and studded with precious stones captured in Mithradates' palaces, as well as works of art from Greece and Asia Minor, trees and plants new to Rome, and an array of exotic beasts that could be shown to great political profit in the animal combats in the arena. Additional banners proclaimed that Pompey had captured no fewer than 1,000 fortresses, just short of 900 cities, and 800 pirate ships and that he had founded 39 cities. He would later boast that whereas in the past the revenues of the state from taxation had been 200 million sesterces, his extension of the empire now brought in 350 million more.

Pompey was impatient to translate these spectacular accomplishments into his lasting supremacy in Rome — to put his booty and the vast wealth that now far overshadowed even that of Crassus to use in becoming the "prince of citizens." But this would prove harder to achieve than subjugating Spain, Africa, Asia, and the pirates. As Plutarch grimly writes, "How happy would it have been for him if he had ended his life at this point, up to which he enjoyed the good fortune of Alexander! For succeeding time brought him only success that made him odious, and failure that was irreparable."

POMPEY HAD GROWN accustomed to military command and victories on his own terms while abroad. But attaining preeminence and control in Rome — building a power base for his next run for consulship, triumphing over competitors, dictating his will to the Senate through political clout rather than high office — was quite another matter. Here he found himself in a snake pit of equally ambitious and often more ruthless contenders for power. In fact, Dio Cassius praises the general's restraint — his unwillingness to use violence or disregard the laws. Given his great achievements in the East, his control over sea and land, his wealth and foreign clientele, Pompey could have easily tried to make himself sole master of Rome, says Dio. But he chose not to usurp power because he did not want to repeat the tyrannical and hated practices of Sulla, who had been wont to gain obedience through fear. Pompey strove instead to win friends and to avoid open clashes with his rivals that might damage his image and pride.

But it was tricky to garner popularity and authority in the quicksand of Roman politics. Power in the capital was often gained and lost in violent clashes between contenders and their supporters. The dubious credit for this state of affairs goes to two brothers, Tiberius and Gaius Gracchus, who profoundly contaminated Roman politics in the 130s and 120s BC. In their day Rome was on the verge of a crisis in which small landowners and the lower classes felt disenfranchised, while people in other Italian cities and regions were frustrated at being denied full participation in Roman affairs. Tiberius Gracchus, the son of one of Rome's leading families, entered politics on a reform platform, seeking to improve this situation. When faced with opposition to his bills, however, he resorted to removing his major opponent from office by force, an extraordinary assault on a public official. This and his other high-handed actions came to haunt him when he sought an unprecedented second term as tribune. During the reelection campaign, he was assassinated on the steps of the Capitoline hill by a mob of senators.

Tiberius's brother Gaius followed him into politics and pursued the reform cause even more forcefully — and more successfully. But when, in 122 BC, Gaius proposed giving Roman citizenship to Latins and other Italian allies to protect them from Roman excesses, he met with the violent opposition of both the Senate and the people. The next year, his legislation still under attack, Gaius resorted to armed insurrection but in the process was murdered, along with three thousand of his supporters, in a riot in the Forum led by followers of the senatorial party. The assassination of the Gracchus brothers made violence and partisan unrest part of Roman politics for the next hundred years.

Although Pompey's efforts to solidify his position in Rome were more peaceful, they were not entirely aboveboard. As soon as he returned from the East, he divorced his wife, Mucia (another relative of Sulla's whom he had married after Aemilia died in childbirth), to form a new, more advantageous alliance. He implied that Mucia's adultery spurred his decision, but it seems that he wanted more useful in-laws. Full of vanity, and counting on his illustrious reputation, he sought the hand of a niece of Cato, a powerful and outspoken politician. He knew that Cato was likely to prove a thorn in his side, so a marriage alliance was an efficient way to neutralize him, if not actually to gain his support. But Cato refused to compromise his political freedom and resolutely turned down Pompey's request. The incident was a huge blow to Pompey. At the time when he was trying to build a power base for himself for his next move, he lost the goodwill of his former in-laws and earned the scorn of Cato, making a fool of himself just when he needed to appear strongest.

Pompey's skills on the battlefield were proving incompatible with the crafty behind-the-scenes manipulations necessary to stay afloat in Rome. Once his third triumph had come and gone, he found himself unable to capitalize on his foreign glory. Senators, envious of his past victories and fearful of his future ambitions, blocked his requests to confirm his settlements in the East and to make land available to his veterans. Cato in particular opposed Pompey and set other politicians against him. As each of his requests was refused, Pompey's dignity, heroic reputation, and credit with his veterans and with the common people were undermined, and his prospects of returning to high office grew dimmer. The great orator Cicero was saddened to see Pompey, the man who used to have so much confidence and esteem, cast down, discontented with himself, and distasteful to others within only a few months of returning home. Cicero reports that "popular sentiment has been most apparent at the theater and the shows. . . .

At the Games of Apollo the actor Diphilus attacked our friend Pompey quite frankly: 'By our misfortune art thou Great' — there were a dozen encores."

In an attempt to strengthen his standing, Pompey decided to team up with Crassus again, as well as with Julius Caesar, six years Pompey's junior and the new star on the Roman scene. Like Pompey, Crassus was hungry for another consulship but could not attain it on his own. Together they stood a better chance. But the two men did not trust each other to share power equally, so they formed an alliance with Caesar to neutralize their mutual enmity. They also thought that by fostering Caesar's career, they could manipulate him while riding on the coattails of his military victories and growing authority in Rome. Little did they know how badly they miscalculated their protégé.

Pompey solidified the new alliance by marrying Caesar's daughter, Julia, in 59 BC. (He was forty-seven; she was fourteen.) The marriage, born of political expedience, actually proved very happy. For a time, Plutarch reports disapprovingly, Pompey "gave way weakly to his passion for his young wife, devoted himself for the most part to her, spent his time with her in villas and gardens, and neglected what was going on in the forum." It is likely he was also happy to get away from more political embarrassments in the capital.

The link with Caesar seemed to pay off at first. As Caesar was serving his first term as a consul in 59 BC, an office he gained with Pompey's and Crassus's help, he finally satisfied Pompey's demands for ratification of his Eastern settlements and for land to be granted to his veterans. But the coalition of the three men was resented by the people, who saw them as grabbing power for their own gains. A triumvirate was an unprecedented and unconstitutional move, clearly intended to give the three generals greater authority and benefits than was their due. And Pompey was criticized the most because, being extremely concerned with public opinion, he appeared most easily swayed by various factions to further bend the rules. As Plutarch says, "That political power which he had won by his own legitimate efforts, this he used in the interests of others [especially Caesar] illegally, thus weakening his own reputation in proportion as he strengthened them."

Despite his tarnished image, and thanks to Cicero's brilliant oratory — an act of gratitude for Pompey's securing his return from exile that year — in 57 BC Pompey was granted control of Rome's grain supply for five years. This "once more made Pompey master of all the land and sea in Roman possession," writes Plutarch. "For under his direction were placed harbors, trading-places, distributions of crops — in a word, navigation and agriculture." It was another chance to make a show of his dedication to the welfare of the people and to recapture their esteem. Plutarch continues,

> Having thus been set over the administration and management of the grain trade, Pompey . . . sailed to Sicily, Sardinia and Africa, and collected grain. When he was about to set sail with it, there was a violent storm at sea, and the ship-captains hesitated to put out; but he led the way on board and ordered them to weigh anchor, crying with a loud voice: "To sail is necessary; to live is not." By this exercise of zeal and courage attended by good fortune, he filled the sea with ships and the markets with grain.

Pompey was back in his element, commanding and organizing. Yet his efforts and achievements were being eclipsed by Caesar's triumphs in Gaul, a rich new province for Rome and a great power base for Caesar.* Pompey's grain commission was prestigious, to

---

*Gaul comprised the Po Valley in northern Italy and its mountain fringes from the Apennines to the Alps, as well as areas from the Pyrenees and the Mediterranean coast of modern France to the English Channel, and from the Atlantic to the Rhine and the western Alps.

be sure, but as he had learned early in his career, military glory led much more directly to popularity and power in Rome.

In April 56 BC Pompey, Caesar, and Crassus agreed on a mutually acceptable distribution of their control over Roman politics and territories for the next six years. Pompey would get a consulship for the next year and after that would command Spain for five years. Crassus would hold the consulship with Pompey and then govern Syria for five years. And Caesar would assist their candidacy by sending large numbers of his soldiers to vote for them and then would receive command of Gaul for another five years. Pompey seemed to be getting the best deal: because of his office as grain commissioner, he would govern his Spanish provinces from Rome and thus remain at the heart of political control and intrigue.

This high-handed partitioning of power by the three partners "gave displeasure to the chief men of the state." To prevent it, Cato urged and persuaded Lucius Domitius to stand up against the tyrants "for liberty" by running against them in the upcoming elections. Plutarch reports that,

> Pompey and his partisans, seeing the firmness of Cato, and fearing lest, having all the senate with him, he should draw away and pervert the sound-minded among the people, would not suffer Domitius to go down into the forum, but sent armed men and slew the link-bearer [torchbearer] who was leading his company, and put the rest to flight; Cato was the last to retire, after being wounded in the right arm while he was fighting to defend Domitius.
>
> By such a path they [Pompey and Crassus] made their way into the office they sought, nor even then did they behave more decently.

When, at the end of Election Day, Pompey came home with blood on his toga, the sight so alarmed his pregnant wife that she suffered a miscarriage. Pompey, it seems, was learning the ways of Roman politics — not only the machinations and the bending of constitutional rules but also the use of violence to attain victory. Given so much hostility and opposition surrounding him, Pompey yearned more than ever to gain back the love and respect of the Roman people. He decided to use a method that had worked for other politicians: bread and circuses. As grain commissioner, he was already feeding the Romans. Now he would offer them a magnificent spectacle featuring exotic animals.

WILD BEAST SHOWS, along with gladiatorial fights, were a favorite entertainment of the Romans. Staged only a few times a year, they were always special events, anticipated with great eagerness and much talked about afterward. Exotic animal displays showed off the Romans' command of foreign lands, but unlike the creatures paraded by Ptolemy Philadelphos, which went back to the royal zoo after the Great Procession, beasts presented in the Roman games were mostly killed in the course of the spectacle as a public exhibition of the sponsor's largesse.

Rome was a violent place, even for humans. In the city itself, it was dangerous to walk down the street because of roving bands of thugs, and not only during the elections. Outside its walls war veterans often turned into bandits and prowled the countryside, which is why giving land to them, as Pompey sought to do, was so important. Beyond the frontiers of the empire, the Roman army conquered foreign peoples with highly organized and merciless onslaughts. Caesar boasted that during his campaigns, he killed more than a million people. Violence in the arena was an extension of the violence of the state.

Roman society was also highly stratified. Those who appeared in the arena were perceived as lesser beings than the spectators and were thought to deserve their fate. Gladiators, who fought against men, as well as *bestiarii* and *venatores*, who sparred with exotic animals, were either slaves sold to gladiatorial schools or free men who voluntarily gave up the rights and privileges of citizens to escape debt or to obtain a guaranteed subsistence.* This was certainly a desperate measure, since when they took the oath of subjugation to the owner of the gladiatorial troupe, they swore to submit themselves "to be branded, fettered, flogged, and killed with an iron weapon."

But there was also fame to be won in this profession. A certain Celadius of Pompeii, a contemporary graffito declares, was a "heartthrob of the girls." A *bestiarius* named Carpophorus inspired the poet Martial to write a series of epigrams about him and to compare him to Hercules. Martial describes how Carpophorus speared a boar, a bear, and a lion of unprecedented size and killed a leopard with a lance. On another occasion he dispatched twenty beasts in a single bout. Such was the macho charisma of gladiators that men of the knightly and senatorial class had to be legally prohibited from pursuing this profession as utterly unsuitable to their rank.

The gladiator's position in Roman society was clearly paradoxical. He was both despised for his lowly occupation and vaunted for his bravery, skill, and sex appeal. He was trained for mortal combat yet was too precious to be summarily killed in the arena; he was more profitable if he survived the fight. If the gladiator was killed, his owner lost his investment, and the sponsor of the games paid one hundred times the sum he would have been charged if the fighter had lived. But the decision to kill or to spare the fallen gladiator could not be merely economic. On the one hand, if the fighter was spared when the spectators wanted his blood, they might think the organizer a cheapskate, trying to save himself the expense. On the other hand, if the sponsor chose to dispatch a gladiator to show his largesse, while the viewers really

*There were many types of gladiators, each trained to fight with different weapons and tactics.

desired clemency, he would incur their disapproval. So the crowd's mood had to be gauged carefully. Still, since gladiators were lesser beings, when they died, it was par for the course.

Wild beasts were also seen as justly deserving their treatment. They were inferior creatures, violent and aggressive by nature, so it was appropriate for humans to vent their own aggression on animals and to exploit them for a spectacle. Aristotle argued that animals lacked rationality, which opened the possibility of treating them without concern for the justice that was due to men. Of course, he warned, wanton cruelty toward animals was inadvisable, as it might accustom humans to brutal conduct toward one another. But for the Romans, the sight of fighting and dying beasts was, by and large, not wanton. It demonstrated their state's triumph over exotic lands and control over nature — a very Roman notion that also found expression in architecture. (While the Greeks carved their theaters into hills to save themselves the labor of erecting a complex sloping structure on even ground, the Romans, including Pompey, built theaters where it suited them and invented cement to make their buildings defy gravity and terrain.)

The Romans thronged by the thousands to watch gladiators and beasts engage in bloody contests in the arena. Some may even have tried to bring youngsters to these spectacles, judging by the regulations advising nurses not to take children along. And the poet Ovid recommended gladiatorial games in the Forum and chariot races in the Circus Maximus as excellent occasions for young men to meet and seduce women.

Contests between unequal opponents excited Romans the most: a lightly armed but mobile fighter pitted against a better-equipped but relatively static foe; a man facing down a wild beast; an elephant sparring with a bull; a lion versus a rhinoceros. Which beast would prevail? Would human intelligence win out over brute strength? The more wild and terrifying the beasts, the greater the chance for a show of bravery by humans or tamer animals. Cicero and other writers extol the chance the games gave combatants to display the supreme Roman virtues of physical and moral courage. Viewers paid careful attention to how men, as well as animals, comported themselves and how they fought: fiercely or cautiously, with intelligence or sheer force. Gladiatorial graffiti from Pompeii immortalizes the most successful fighters. One graffito, showing two contestants, reads: "Severus, of free status, victorious 13 times, earned a reprieve. Albanus, left-hander, of free status, victorious 19 times, won."

The uncertainty of the outcome in the arena, the spectacle of life hanging in the balance, was addictive. Saint Augustine described how his friend Alypius, who had for a long time been reluctant to attend the games, finally went to the Colosseum. At first he sat there with his eyes shut. But as the sound of the crowd's excitement grew more and more compelling, he opened his eyes and was lost in the show. "At the sight of that blood he drank a deep draught of it in all its monstrous horror, and did not turn away; instead he lost his reason at the sight of it and took great gulps of madness. He had no idea what he was doing, but he was enchanted by the evil contest and became drunk on bloodstained pleasure."

Obviously Saint Augustine was not an enthusiast of the games. Cicero and a number of other highbrow Romans feigned boredom at witnessing yet another slaughter of exotic animals, yet they could hardly stay away. Libanios, a Greek rhetorician living in Antioch in the fourth century AD, conveys the addiction of regular people to the animal games: "People like racing, as you know, and they enjoy stage shows, but nothing attracts them as much as men fighting animals; escape from the beasts seems beyond the bounds of possibility, yet through sheer intelligence the men succeed in mastering them. The crowds go off to the other games early in the morning, but for the wild beast shows they queue up all night."

Romans also thrilled at unequal contests of another kind: the execution of criminals and prisoners of war by exotic animals. Public executions were widespread in the Roman world. They aimed both to deter and reassure. Crucifixions lined the high-ways; gallows stood at important crossroads. Rebels and slaves received particularly brutal treatment — crucifixion or condemnation to the beasts. (As you may recall, when Crassus defeated Spartacus's army, he crucified all the survivors he captured.) In Roman thinking, wrongdoers deserved to suffer for their crimes and to do so publicly, and persons without the protection of Roman citizenship should suffer extremely. Unlike the *bestiarii*, who went out to match their skills against the animals with spears or swords in hand, prisoners of war and criminals were led into the arena with their hands tied behind them. Wearing only loincloths and with tablets bearing their verdicts dangling from their necks, they were pulled out by ropes or wheeled forth on carts on which they stood bound to posts. Then starved leopards, lions, bears, or other wild animals were let loose on them as the excited crowd cheered and jeered.

At times condemnation to the beasts took quite imaginative forms. The Roman geographer Strabo records that in the second half of the first century BC, probably under Augustus, who was then cracking down on slaves and brigands,

> a certain Selurus, called "son of Etna," was sent up to Rome because he had put himself at the head of an army and for a long time had overrun the environs of Etna with frequent raids; I saw him torn to pieces by wild beasts at an organized gladiatorial fight in the forum: he was put onto a tall contraption, as though on Etna, and the contraption suddenly broke up and collapsed, and he went down with it into fragile cages of wild beasts that had been set up beneath the contraption for that purpose.

When the emperor Titus was dedicating the Colosseum in AD 80, among his inaugurating spectacles was a reenactment of the story of Orpheus, but with a twist. In the myth, the bard, lamenting the death of his wife, Eurydice, moved animals, trees, and rocks with his song. The poet Martial records that during the performance in the Colosseum, "cliffs crept and a marvelous wood ran forwards such as was believed to be the grove of the Hesperides. Every kind of wild beast was there, mixed with the flock, and above the minstrel hovered many birds." The enactment probably unfolded gradually, with harmless beasts let out into the arena first through multiple trapdoors. "But," Martial continues, "the minstrel fell, torn apart by an ungrateful bear. Only this one thing happened contrary to the story." Orpheus was probably restrained by netting, as condemned criminals often were, and thus unable to escape a goaded bear. The irony of the bard failing to charm *all* the animals was meant as a delightful joke.

Accounts differ on whether Pompey's animal games featured criminals or professional beast fighters. But his show was certainly meant to be the greatest spectacle staged to date, to enthrall the masses, overawe his political rivals, and solidify his position.

BRINGING THE GAMES together on such a stupendous scale would have been a daunting feat. The prerequisite for its success was contact with and influence in regions where desirable beasts lived. Cicero's letters offer a vivid picture of such hunting and gathering. In 51 BC Cicero was serving as the governor of Cilicia (in southern Turkey). His friend Marcus Caelius Rufus was back in Rome preparing to run for the office of aedile (an official charged with supervising public places, public games, and the grain supply). As soon as he got elected, Caelius would need to put on an animal show to garner popular support for the next stage of his career. Since Cilicia was rich in exotic game, Caelius kept pestering Cicero to get him some panthers.

In one letter Caelius writes, "[for] my games, . . . since give them I must, I should be glad if you would take the trouble — I have been perpetually asking you this favor — to let me have something in the way of beasts from where you are." In another letter he persists, "If you only remember to . . . send for some hunters from Cibyra. . . . In this matter you will have no trouble except to say a few words — that is, to give orders and instructions. For as soon as the animals are caught, you have the men I sent . . . available to feed them and see to their being shipped to Rome." When no panthers seemed forthcoming, Caelius nudges again, "It will be a disgrace to you if I have to go without any panthers."

To get Caelius off his back, Cicero sent a noncommittal reply:

> About the panthers, the business is being carefully attended to according to my orders with the aid of those who hunt them regularly. But it is surprising how few panthers there are. And they tell me that those there are bitterly complain that in my province no snares are set for any living creature but themselves; and so they have decided, it is said, to emigrate from this province into Caria. Still my people are busy in the matter. . . . All the animals caught will be at your service; but how many there are, I have no idea.

Sponsors of the games also may have called on Roman troops stationed in the conquered provinces. In the imperial period (after Augustus came to power in 31 BC) soldiers certainly captured and transported exotic animals for the games in the capital; they likely did so earlier as well. A letter on papyrus, written by a Roman soldier stationed at Wadi Fawakhir in Egypt in the late first or early second century AD, reports on the regiment's hunt for local animals: "From the month of Agrippina until now we have been hunting all species of wild animals and birds for a year under the orders of the prefects. We have given what we caught to Cecealis and he sent them and all the equipment to you." Native hunters probably helped the Romans, but soldiers themselves specialized in different aspects of hunting, earning exemptions from certain routine duties thanks to their skills. Army documents mention trackers who located the animals, hunters who captured bears and lions, and veterinarians who cared for the army's horses and baggage animals, as well as for captive exotic beasts.

Transporting wild creatures from distant provinces to Rome was another complicated business. Here the Roman fleet came into play. Merchant galleys, which served as both cargo vessels and men-of-war, depending on circumstances, were one means of conveyance. Transport ships for ferrying army horses, called *hippagogoi* — with a large hull in the back and a flat bottom — were another. Ferocious beasts were brought on board and kept in cages for the duration of the journey. Larger or calmer animals were secured on deck by ropes or chains attached to their feet. Pliny the Elder reports a charming anecdote about disembarking the elephants at the southern Italian port of Puteoli (modern Pozzuoli). The animals got frightened by the length of the gangway stretching from the boat to the shore, so of their own accord, they turned around and crossed it backward to cheat themselves in their estimation of the distance.

Animals destined for Rome were disembarked at Ostia, the closest port to the capital. Here the cages and loose animals were transferred to flat-bottomed boats that went up the Tiber River. On reaching Rome the cages were stacked at the docks until the appropriate officials came to collect them. Pliny mentions that the sculptor Pasiteles was once so absorbed in studying an African lion at the docks, peering at it so as to depict the creature most accurately, that he nearly lost his life when a leopard burst out of a nearby cage.

Even if they arrived in good time and decent shape, unhindered and undamaged by storms at sea, exotic beasts required proper care and feeding to perform in the games. Symmachus, a consul who staged opulent animal hunts in AD 391, had imported a number of crocodiles for his show, but they refused to eat for fifty days. Were they given the wrong food? Did they pine for freedom? When the appointed day arrived, the crocodiles had. tle pluck left in them. Emaciated, they had to be dispatched in a hurry, before they expired on their own from the stress of being dragged into the arena and attacked by armed men. The spectators could hardly have been pleased with the show.

Despite such challenges, Pompey managed the logistics of organizing his games with the same military discipline and administrative savvy he had employed in conquering and resettling the pirates and subjugating the East. And he outdid his predecessors by a wide margin. Sulla had created a sensation in 93 BC when he had displayed 100 lions. Pompey imported 600. In 58 BC the extravagant aedile Marcus Scaurus had exhibited 150 female leopards for the first time in Rome. Pompey ordered 400 for his show, as well as 20 elephants. He also took care to procure animals the Romans had never before seen in the arena. There were Ethiopian baboons, which Pliny described as having "hind feet resembling the feet of a man and legs and forefeet like hands" and as being extremely ferocious. The Gallic lynx, "with the shape of a wolf and leopard's spots," according to Pliny, was also a novel creature. So was the rhinoceros, which would become a favorite in Rome, bred to fight elephants by slicing their stomachs with its sharp horn.

That he was able to assemble such a spectacular array of exotic animals reflected Pompey's far-flung influence and command. Despite his political problems at home, he was able to call in favors and obligations from his numerous clients across the ancient world. In Africa he could rely on the Numidian king Hiempsal, whom he had put on the throne. In Egypt king Ptolemy Auletes was in Pompey's debt for his restoration to power. Having conquered Pontus, Armenia, the Caucasus, and Syria, Pompey could request rare beasts from rulers in these lands. He probably obtained his 600 lions from Africa, Arabia, Syria, and Mesopotamia; his 400 leopards from Asia and Africa; and his 20 elephants probably also from Africa. There were other animals as well, more

ıus not enumerated by eyewitnesses and histori-
ıt, this was undeniably the largest wild beast hunt
ɔme. Would the magnificent games restore Pom-
er glory?

IN LATE SEPTEMBER and early October 55 BC, Rome was more crowded, noisier, and smellier than ever. The city was packed with people who had come from all over Italy and the provinces to attend Pompey's festivities. There were many entertainments on offer, some in the Circus Maximus, others in Pompey's newly built theater.

Shortly after his return from the East, Pompey had begun to build the first permanent theater in Rome.* The new edifice, made of stone with red granite columns, was three arcaded stories high on the outside and profusely adorned with statues throughout. Some sculptures represented marvels of history, such as Eutychis, a woman of Tralles who bore thirty children, and Alcippe, who gave birth to an elephant. Others were allegorical depictions of the nations Pompey had subdued. The vast auditorium, some 164 yards in diameter, seated 11,000 spectators. The stage was the size of half of the Colosseum's arena (built a century later), and the stage building — a permanent architectural backdrop for plays — measured 104 yards wide.

Behind the stage building stretched a great portico: two cov-

---

*Up to that time theatrical productions in the city were presented in temporary wooden structures. Each play was dedicated to a particular god and thus most suitably offered in his or her sanctuary. More to the point, theater was a venue for popular gatherings, and thus was potentially a threat to the ruling elite, so a permanent theater had, for many years, been effectively blocked by conservative senators. Pompey circumvented the senatorial opposition in part thanks to his stature as the conqueror of Europe, Africa, and Asia, and in part by a clever bit of architecture. He erected a temple of Venus the Victorious — the goddess to whom he credited all his conquests — at the summit of his new structure. This way the theater was, ostensibly, just a monumental stairway to the temple.

ered colonnades a hundred columns long displaying Pompey's collection of paintings by famous masters (brought from Greece) and shimmering gold tapestries from Pergamon. Between the colonnades was laid out Rome's first public garden, planted with trees and shrubs Pompey had imported from Asia Minor. As the Roman natural historian Pliny the Elder notes, "It is a remarkable fact that ever since the time of Pompey the Great even trees have figured among the captives in our triumphal processions."

At the far end of the portico, Pompey erected a meeting hall for the Senate. It was there that Caesar, the man who would cause Pompey's downfall, would be assassinated. On the Ides of March, 44 BC, the Senate met in Pompey's edifice. When Caesar was attacked and repeatedly stabbed by conspirators, "either by chance or because he was pushed there by his murderers," writes Plutarch, "he fell down against the pedestal on which the statue of Pompey stood, and the pedestal was drenched in his blood, so that one might have thought that Pompey himself was presiding over this act of vengeance against his enemy, who lay at his feet, quivering from so many wounds." But this vengeance was, in 55 BC, still unearned. For now Pompey was content to assert his supremacy over Caesar by peaceful, if ostentatious, means.

The inauguration of Pompey's theater was supposed to be the main event. Here, beneath the temple of Venus, Pompey put on dramatic and choral performances carefully selected and staged to recall his military successes. Cicero, consoling his friend Marcus Marius, who had been too ill to attend, cattily remarked that it had been painful to sit through so many farces and to endure the actors who returned to the stage out of respect for Pompey, having left it out of respect for themselves. The sheer spectacle of such magnificence had taken all the fun out of the thing, for what possible pleasure could one derive from the sight of six hundred mules onstage in the *Clytaemnestra*, or three thousand vases in the *Trojan Horse*, or all the varieties of arms and armor worn by whole regiments of foot soldiers and horsemen who appeared in every battle scene? For those who were bored with the plays, Pompey prepared another entertainment — his splendid animal combats. In fact, of all the events, the games proved the most popular spectacle.

THE CIRCUS MAXIMUS, the elongated valley between the Palatine and Aventine, was the oldest games venue in Rome. Here 150,000 people gathered for each of Pompey's animal shows, and as there were two shows a day for five days, the crowds hardly subsided. Vendors, astrologers, fortune-tellers, prostitutes, and pickpockets did a marvelous business under the Circus's exterior arcades. Inside, the 600-yard-long, 87-yard-wide racetrack seemed to pulsate with the energy of three tiers of spectators, the nobler ones occupying the cushioned stone seats closer to the arena, the others taking wooden seats higher up.

Pompey, handsome in his embroidered purple toga and gold laurel crown, gazed at the assembled masses from the box at the northwest end of the Circus, above the twelve starting gates closed off by ornamental grillwork. His pride and vanity were richly rewarded by the sight of thousands of delighted Romans flocking to partake of his magnanimity. He must have been very pleased with himself for having prepared for them the most amazing games Rome had ever seen.

The arena, set up with an artificial landscape of mountains, forests, shrubs, and flowing streams, was ready to receive its actors. Behind the scenes the hunters and beast fighters checked their equipment for the last time. The wild animals roared in their cages. The animals to be used for "padding" — the sheep and cows whom the wild cats would hunt between battles with humans — stood in fearful clumps, sensing predators in the air. Around the arena, the noise of thousands of eager viewers grew deafening. It was six in the morning, the hour to commence the show before the sun rose too high and baked spectators and animals alike.

For four days majestic lions and leopards appeared in contests with less exotic animals and with beast fighters. Smoked out of their cages and driven with bundles of burning straw along the vaulted passages into the arena, the wild cats fought fiercely. A number of men had to be carried from the arena on stretchers, bleeding profusely from gashes inflicted by claws and fangs. But the animals suffered the most casualties. Transfixed with spears, lions and leopards rolled on their backs in agony, tried to extract weapons stuck in their throbbing flesh with their teeth, howled in anguish, and died torturous deaths. The baboons, lynx, and rhinoceroses also provided great entertainment with their fighting abilities and noble demise.

And then came the grand finale. Wild elephants would match their massive strength against lithe and swift Gaetulian hunters, whom Pompey had imported from Africa along with the beasts. To the sounds of the chanting crowd and the fanfare of organ, trumpets, and horns, some twenty elephants entered the arena, moving ponderously to the center. Assaulted by the noise and smell of thousands of humans, the elephants flapped their ears, raised their trunks in the air, rumbled, and warily watched the men with javelins on the far side of the ring. At last Pompey gave a sign, and the contest began.

Early on in the program one hunter managed to kill an elephant with a single blow. His javelin pierced the animal just under the eye, instantly reaching the brain. The crowd roared with delight. The music soared. Then another elephant put on a magnificent performance. Its feet wounded, it crawled on its knees against its enemies, snatching up their shields and tossing them high in the air. The spectators, Pliny reports, were thrilled by the curving flight of the falling shields, as if they were thrown by a skilled juggler and not an infuriated wild animal.

But then things began to go wrong. A group of elephants, finding themselves cornered, panicked. They stampeded toward the iron railing that enclosed the arena and tried to burst through.

The closely packed spectators, terrified, ran for their lives, tumbling over and trampling one another. The lofty occupants of the front seats lost all dignity as they scrambled for the exits.

And then the doomed beasts, pursued at spear point and seeing that there was no escape, did something that no one had anticipated. They turned the sympathy of the usually bloodthirsty spectators toward themselves. Dio Cassius recounts:

> Contrary to Pompey's wish, [the elephants] were pitied by the people when, after being wounded and ceasing to fight, they walked about with their trunks raised toward heaven, lamenting so bitterly as to give rise to the report that they did so not by mere chance, but were crying out against the oaths in which they had trusted when they crossed over from Africa, and were calling upon Heaven to avenge them. For it is said that they would not set foot upon the ships before they received a pledge under oath from their drivers that they should suffer no harm.

The Romans believed that the elephants could understand human language. Pliny, who particularly admired these noble beasts (along with dolphins, nightingales, and bees), thought them "the nearest to man in intelligence: [the elephant] understands the language of its country and obeys orders, remembers duties that it has been taught, is pleased by affection and by marks of honor, nay more it possesses virtues rare even in man, honesty, wisdom, justice, also respect for the stars and reverence for the sun and moon." He tells a lovely story of one literate elephant who could trace in Greek letters in the sand, "I, the elephant, wrote this," and another about a slow learner who was so embarrassed by his failure to master his lessons, and tired of being beaten for it, that he would practice alone in the night.

According to Pliny, "Pompey's elephants, when they had lost all hope of escape, tried to gain the compassion of the crowd by indescribable gestures of entreaty, deploring their fate with a sort of wailing, so much to the distress of the public that they forgot the general and his munificence carefully devised for their honor, and bursting into tears rose in a body and invoked curses on the head of Pompey for which he soon afterwards paid the penalty."

The audience begged Pompey to spare the animals who had supplicated for his clemency. Supplication was, after all, a legitimate part of a fight. Gladiators who fought well could ask for a *missio,* an honorable dismissal from the arena. Why not the elephants, who appeared to be partly human already? They had fought bravely and skillfully, and it was the courage, rather than the pathos, of a fighter that won him a reprieve.

But Pompey seems not to have understood popular sentiment, or he simply chose to ignore it. He apparently decided that he could show his power and wealth better if he readily disposed of the exotic creatures he had obtained and brought to Rome at enormous expense. Acting as the warrior he was, rather than as the savvy politician he aspired to be, Pompey ordered the elephants hunted down and slaughtered. The cost of his decision proved greater than he had calculated. The games went down in history as a flop.

POMPEY'S BOTCHED GAMES did not in themselves spell the end of his career. In the years that followed, Rome plunged into increasing chaos. When, in late February 52 BC, no consuls were elected because of prevailing disorder and corruption, Pompey was made sole consul, another bending of the rules for him. But the death of his wife, Julia, Caesar's daughter, in childbirth, weakened the bond between the former colleagues. And Crassus's death in battle, in Syria in 53 BC, further upset the fragile balance of power. As the poet Lucan comments, Caesar could allow no man to be his superior, and Pompey no man his equal. The only way out was civil war.

After a few years of fighting each other across the Italian

peninsula and the Mediterranean, Caesar and Pompey met at the Battle of Pharsalus (in northern Greece). Caesar won a decisive victory. Hoping to regroup, on the eve of his fifty-eighth birthday, Pompey made his way to Egypt to seek the support of King Ptolemy XIII, brother of Cleopatra VII and son of Ptolemy Auletes, whom Pompey had restored to the throne. He went to the king of Egypt as an ally, relying on the bond of obligation. But either the fifteen-year-old ruler or his counselors decided that Pompey was a poor bet and it was wiser to side with Caesar.

Just as he came ashore, Pompey was stabbed to death by Ptolemy's henchmen. His head was cut off, to be embalmed and presented as a gift to Caesar. His body was tossed into the waves. Pompey's faithful freed slave, Philip, dragged it out onto the sand, wrapped it in his own tunic, and cremated it on a pyre of broken fishing boats. The historian Velleius Paterculus summed up the pathos of Pompey's end: "Such was the inconsistency of fortune in his case, that he who but a short time before had found no more lands to conquer now found none for his burial." But some Romans said that it was the curse of the elephants that brought him down.

After his death Pompey continued to be overshadowed by Caesar, in part because Caesar emerged victorious over him and became a dictator of Rome, but also because Caesar had true genius as both a general and a statesman. Yet Lucan, in his epic poem *Pharsalia,* which describes the civil war, painted a more positive picture of Pompey than of Caesar. Altough Pompey dangerously misgauged both the public sentiments and his opponent's abilities, he demonstrated overall respect for the laws of Rome, whereas Caesar flouted all rules in his quest for power. Lucan writes of Pompey's demise:

A fellow-citizen has passed from among us who fell below the standards set by our ancestors in recognizing the bounds set by law; however . . . he was powerful without destroying liberty, . . . and though he directed the Senate, it was the Senate that still remained a true governing body. He made no demands based on the rights which armed force bestows, and although there were things which he desired, he was prepared to see them denied him. . . . He took up the sword, but he knew also how to lay it down. . . . He has been a great and reputable name among the nations of the world, and one which in no small degree advantaged our own country.

DESPITE THE FAILURE of Pompey's games, animal hunts remained popular in Rome. Caesar would incur public displeasure because he took paperwork with him to the games, carrying on with his business rather than paying undivided attention to the fighting in the arena. Augustus, the savviest of Roman politicians, would boast that among the great achievements of his reign, "in my own name, or that of my sons or grandsons, on twenty-six occasions I gave to the people, in the circus, in the forum, or in the amphitheater, hunts of African wild beasts, in which about three thousand five hundred beasts were slain." This number would grow higher and higher with each emperor. Trajan would have eleven thousand animals killed in the games celebrating his Dacian triumph in AD 106.

What had incensed the spectators of Pompey's games was not necessarily his inhumane treatment of the elephants, but a breach of expectations and decorum. They had come to see a theatrical subjugation of inferior creatures, but once the elephants appeared human, full of dignity and pathos, their fate seemed unjustly brutal, evoking in the onlookers shame and guilt. It was fine to stage a violent spectacle, so long as it exploited non-persons, so long as it was "they" who suffered and not "us."

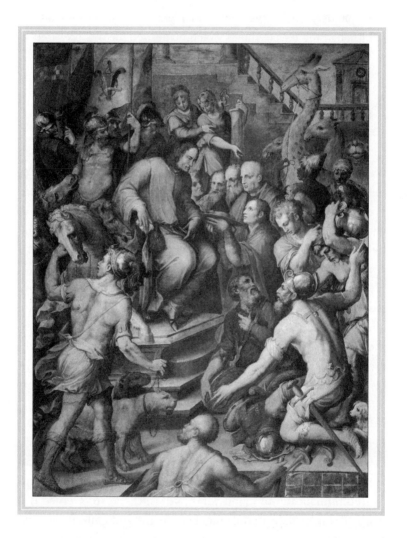

THREE

HOW A GIRAFFE TURNED A
MERCHANT INTO A PRINCE

It is unnecessary for a prince to have all the good qualities I have enumerated, but it is very necessary to appear
to have them. . . . Every one sees what you appear to
be, few really know what you are, and those few dare
not oppose themselves to the opinion of the many.

NICCOLÒ MACHIAVELLI,
The Prince

Palazzo Vecchio, the town hall of Florence, dominates the
Piazza della Signoria. Lavishly adorned with frescoes, its
halls honor the achievements of various members of the Medici
clan. Lorenzo the Magnificent's room is crowned by a painting
showing him receiving homage from foreign ambassadors. Lorenzo,
seated on an elevated platform, is thronged by jostling visitors
bearing valuable gifts. From the right a mustachioed man bends
low under the weight of a vase made of precious metal. Below
Lorenzo another man leads in two horses and two lions. The most
prominent and striking offering appears opposite Lorenzo and
commands almost equal attention: it is a giraffe. To us, accustomed to extolling Lorenzo for ushering in the golden age of art
and culture in Renaissance Florence, it may come as a shock that
the fresco celebrates instead an exotic animal sent to him by the

Egyptian sultan Qaitbay. But to Lorenzo, his contemporaries, and his heirs, it was a perfect symbol of what he had attained.

LORENZO CAME TO power on December 3, 1469. As he would later write in his memoirs,

> The second day after my father's death, although I, Lorenzo, was very young, that is to say, only in my twenty-first year, the principal men of the city and of the state came to our house to condole with us on our loss, and to encourage me to take on myself the care of the city and of the State, as my father and grandfather had done. This proposal being against the instincts of my youthful age, and considering that the burden and danger were great, I consented to it unwillingly. But I did so in order to protect our friends and property; for it fares ill in Florence with any one who possesses wealth without any control in the government.

Lorenzo knew well how the Florentine system worked. Florence was a republic with a constitution carefully designed to spread political power among a large group of citizens. It was safeguarded by various legal devices intended to prevent the formation of political parties or the domination of the city by one family or one man. Government officials served for two to six months, depending on the post, which kept power from being gathered in too few hands. Most officers, moreover, were selected not by popular elections, but by lot — their names being literally drawn out of a bag.

The Medici were bankers and merchants. They had bank branches throughout Europe and traded in numerous lucrative wares: cloth, olive oil, spices, precious metals, artwork, and even choirboys. Initially they entered politics to protect their fortunes. By arranging marriages with prestigious Florentine families and creating a circle of "friends" — clients who linked themselves to the Medici in return for their support — the family formed an unofficial party, a web of men who voted along Medici lines when serving in the government and fostered a pro-Medici atmosphere in the city's trade guilds.

Lorenzo's grandfather Cosimo de' Medici, who began the Medici political dynasty in this backhanded way, was a master of operating the city's political system from behind the scenes. By manipulating his supporters, he achieved his goals without breaking Florence's constitutional laws. As his biographer Vespasiano da Bisticci wrote, "He acted privately with the greatest discretion in order to safeguard himself, and whenever he sought to obtain an object he contrived to let it appear that the matter had been set in motion by someone other than himself."

A rational and calculating entrepreneur and a cautious politician, Cosimo was careful to appear only as an old-fashioned merchant with simple tastes (although his residence was rather splendid) and as merely a citizen of the republic. Thanks to his international banking activities, and especially his position as the pope's banker, Cosimo was often entrusted with conducting Florence's foreign policy, which gave him significant power and prestige. But despite his authority abroad, Cosimo did his best to maintain an unassuming conduct at home.

Unlike his grandfather, Lorenzo was not satisfied with the status of a mercantile magnate. He wanted to rise to the rank of an unequivocal prince. In addition to the great wealth and clout he inherited from his family, he was blessed with natural political gifts. He would go on later in life to consolidate his power in Florence and in Italy at large without holding any political office. His path to securing this authority, however, would be treacherous and trying. The giraffe immortalized on the ceiling in the Palazzo Vecchio symbolized Lorenzo's creative and showy approach to building his rule.

Lorenzo was, as his contemporaries noted, two men in one, his personality as contradictory as his appearance. According to his biographer Niccolò Valori, he "stood above the average height, was broad shouldered, robustly built, muscular, remarkably agile, and olive complexioned," but so "short-sighted that he saw very little from a distance," and he had a "flat nose and a harsh voice." Contemporary portraits show a broad face with high cheekbones, a nose that is caved in and askew (he had no sense of smell), a jaw protruding slightly forward, and small hooded eyes. He looks very much like a thug. Standing before his death mask in the Pitti Palace, one struggles to discern in these features Lorenzo's fabled refinement and humor, subtle intelligence and great sensitivity to art.

He was a clearheaded and astute politician, as well as a poet who loved classical literature and bawdy songs. He was deeply pious yet skeptical; he mixed easily with simple folk yet strove to be taken for an aristocrat. As a boy he received a superb education and early training in diplomacy. He was sent around to Italian courts to learn political protocol and familiarize himself with his future allies and foes. As a young man he was unruly and chased women. When it came time to groom him for political leadership, the elders of the Medici party took him in hand and admonished him to follow in the wise, measured footsteps of Cosimo. Lorenzo was dispatched to study moral philosophy with the celebrated humanist Marsilio Ficino, under whose tutelage he wrote a complex philosophical poem on the Supreme Good. But he did not abandon his youthful pleasures and took great delight in composing rude carnival ditties and staging lavish chivalric tournaments, in which, naturally, he was the star. Arrogant, cruel, and vindictive toward his enemies, Lorenzo was charming, kind, and attentive to his friends and political superiors. His critics decried his pride; his supporters praised his humility and humanity. But his major preoccupation was his honor.

Living in a hierarchical society, Lorenzo was keenly aware of the difference between tradesmen and aristocrats. He had been born into a family of merchants and into a city that had no tolerance for monarchy. But he grew up like a prince in a luxurious home and spent significant time at foreign courts. He also observed how during the visits of important dignitaries to Florence, his grandfather, striving to enhance the Medici prestige, entertained them in ways more characteristic of a de facto ruler than of a mere rich citizen.

In April 1459, for example, when Lorenzo was ten years old, he witnessed Cosimo's reception of Pope Pius II and Galeazzo Maria Sforza, son of the powerful Duke of Milan. In preparation for the visitors, Cosimo dressed the family palace in the utmost splendor. A member of the Sforza entourage, dazzled, described

> the studies, chapels, salons, chambers, and garden, all of which are constructed and decorated with admirable mastery, adorned on every side with gold and fine marbles, with carvings and sculptures in relief, with pictures and inlays done in perspective by the most accomplished and perfect of masters even to the very benches and floors of the house; tapestries and household ornaments of gold and silk; silverware and bookcases that are endless and without number.

All this finery, though notable, was not in itself unusual. Every prince was expected to have a splendid home stuffed with artwork that reflected his cultured mind. Although the Medici were not princes in Florence, they wanted to give the impression of being such to foreign dignitaries. So Cosimo decided to awe his guests with something more, something outstanding that would dazzle even Pope Pius II, a man of vast erudition who had traveled widely. To make the greatest impression, Cosimo would organize an animal combat such as was staged by the great statesmen of ancient Rome. He would borrow the stars of his show — the noble lions — from the city but finance the other expenses of the spectacle himself.

Lorenzo actively helped his grandfather receive the honored guests. When Galeazzo Maria Sforza arrived at the Medici Palace, Lorenzo welcomed him with a verse recited with perfect poise. In honor of the pope, he led a cavalcade of Florentine youths from the best families on a nighttime tourney, outshining all the other boys. An eyewitness recorded,

> Now that genuine youth moves
> Upon a horse marvelously ornate,
> Everyone watches what he does . . .
> His dress surpasses easily that of
> All those of whom we've spoken,
> And well shows that he is *signore*.

On the day of the eagerly anticipated animal combat, Lorenzo sat near Cosimo, the pope, and the young Duke of Milan, and struggled to rein in his excitement and look like a grown-up nobleman. The Piazza della Signoria had been transformed into an arena by blocking off the streets leading into it, lining its perimeter with grandstands, and erecting protective barriers between the seats and the stage. Thousands of spectators — Florentines as well as foreigners who had heard of the upcoming spectacle — crowded the wooden stands, the windows of surrounding buildings, and their rooftops.

At last the show began. A wild boar, two horses, four bulls, two young buffalo, some goats, a cow, and a calf were led into the arena. Given a few minutes to adjust to the noise of the animated crowd, they wandered around timidly, nervously sniffing the air. Then twenty-six lions were brought in. Terror ran through their intended prey, and the poor beasts cowered against the walls of the enclosure. The spectators held their breath as the majestic predators ambled around nonchalantly, letting out an occasional roar. Suddenly one lion, in a great effortless leap, pounced on a horse, "showing himself the emperor of the beasts," one observer recorded. The viewers braced themselves for the bloody combat. But the lion lost interest in the horse and showed none for the other animals. Having surveyed the motley assembly of trembling beasts with indifferent glances, the lions yawned, lay down, stretched out, and fell asleep.

Cosimo was horrified. He had staked his reputation on the performance of the lions. What a miscalculation! The beasts turned out not to be in a hunting mood. They had been fed too regularly and too well and were not the least bit hungry.

Lions — fierce, proud, and exotic creatures — were among the oldest symbols of Florence. Live lions had resided in the city since the thirteenth century and were generously cared for at the government's expense. The animals' custodian — required to wear a beard and long side-whiskers, either to look more leonine or to be readily recognized and treated with due deference — was carefully selected. He had to be "most honorable, capable, and noble" and was privileged to sit with the aristocrats during the Councils of the Republic.

The Florentine lions lived at the very heart of the city. Their first home was on the site of the future Loggia dei Lanzi, right in front of the town hall. They were clearly happy there, because they reproduced well, increasing in number from a couple in the thirteenth century to twenty-four in the fourteenth. (Some animals also were presented to Florence as gifts from foreign states.) Well-fed lions can live a long time in captivity and become quite domesticated. Given about nine pounds of good meat a day, they grow healthy and nicely plump — and not very motivated to hunt. By 1350 the Florentine lions had become too numerous for their quarters in the Piazza della Signoria and had to be moved to a new home, behind the town hall, in the street that still bears the name Via dei Leoni. There they remained for two centuries, until another Cosimo de' Medici decided to transform the town hall into his private residence.* As he enlarged the building to suit his needs, the lions got in his way, so he relocated them to a new dwelling, in the Piazza San Marco, opposite the Hospital of San Matteo. The patients in the hospital complained bitterly about the continual roaring, but the grand duke remained unmoved.

The lions were so important to Florence's image that visiting dignitaries were always taken to see them during tours of the city. (Lesser folk could view the beasts for a fee.) In the rare snowy winters, "snow-lions" popped up in the streets. The fifteenth-century diarist Luca Landucci records that during one four-day snowstorm, "a number of most beautiful snow-lions were made in Florence by good masters; amongst others there was a very large and fine one next to the campanile of Santa Maria del Fiore [the Cathedral], and one in front of Santa Trinità."†

The Florentines read all sorts of signs into the lions' actions. When a lioness gave birth to cubs, it was considered a good omen. If a lion died, it boded ill for the city. Even the usually skeptical historian Francesco Guicciardini would write that the death of Lorenzo de' Medici in 1492 "was indicated to be of the greatest significance by many portents. . . . Some lions fought among themselves and a very beautiful one was killed by the others."

At once exotic and deeply Florentine, the lions had seemed to Cosimo a perfect showpiece with which to regale Pope Pius II and Galeazzo Maria Sforza. What an embarrassment they turned

---

*Cosimo I, as he would be called, was a member of a different branch of the family. He would rule the city from 1537 to 1574 and become the grand duke of Tuscany.

†In addition to the lions, Landucci records, the snow prompted other expressions of creativity: "Many nude figures were made also by good masters at the Canto de' Pazzi; and in Borgo San Lorenzo [the Medici neighborhood] a city with fortresses was made, and many galleys; and so on, all over Florence."

out to be! To rouse the indolent beasts, and to save face, Cosimo dispatched into the arena a kind of "Trojan giraffe" — a wooden animal set on wheels that contained a team of armed warriors who tried to tease and prod the lions into action, but to no effect. The show proved a failure. The pope grumbled that more wine was spilled in his honor than blood.

We tend to think of Renaissance Italy as a more familiar and less bloodthirsty place than ancient Rome. At the mere mention of Florence, we readily beam our imaginations to the Duomo crowned by Brunelleschi's majestic dome, take a mental stroll around the Piazza della Signoria, pause in awe before Michelangelo's *David* at the Accademia, and bask in the sensual lines of Botticelli's *Birth of Venus* in the Uffizi (conveniently airbrushing away all those throngs of tourists like ourselves). Yet fifteenth-century Florence was a violent place, too. Luca Landucci recounts frequent public executions: "10 April 1465. A young woman, who was the daughter of Zanobi Gherucci, was tried, for having killed, and then thrown into a well, the little girl of Bernardo della Zecca, a goldsmith, for the sake of stealing a pearl necklace and certain silver ornaments that the child wore round her neck. She was taken away in the executioner's cart, and was beheaded." At moments of political crisis, mob brutality easily got out of hand. So a bloody animal spectacle would not have shocked the Florentines with its violence, only with its failure to please the illustrious guests.

Watching Cosimo's disastrous animal show, little Lorenzo was learning valuable political lessons. He saw that a splendid residence filled with artwork was crucial to impressing foreign delegations and that an animal display created a memorable spectacle. But, as he had read in the books by ancient authors that his tutors urged him to master, the most successful animal shows featured far more exotic beasts than a bunch of overfed lions. Moreover, these animals had not been Cosimo's own possessions, obtained by skill or force from faraway lands, but the property of the commune. When he grew up, Lorenzo dreamt, he would acquire more remarkable animals that would make him a real prince respected by all.

Unlike his grandfather, who was content to act as an ordinary man and to rule Florence surreptitiously, Lorenzo aspired to a higher status and more obvious authority. He yearned to rise above his mercantile roots, take greater control over the Florentine government, and acquire the stature of heads of other Italian states, such as the Duke of Milan, the king of Naples, and the pope. He wanted to command respect not through money, but through real political power at home and abroad.

LORENZO'S FIRST DECADE as the unofficial head of the Florentine republic would test his determination and his mettle almost to the breaking point. In June 1472 Volterra, a town subject to Florence, revolted and refused to submit to a decision of the Florentine government regarding local disputes. Eager to show his toughness, Lorenzo insisted that the city must be cruelly punished to forestall any further insubordination. The mercenary captain Federigo da Montefeltro, Duke of Urbino, was hired for the job. He besieged Volterra for a month, and when the city surrendered and opened its gates, his army brutally sacked it, burning, pillaging, and raping for days. Lorenzo would not live down the opprobrium for this savagery for a long time.

In the next few years Lorenzo found himself on deteriorating terms with the notoriously nepotistic Pope Sixtus IV (the builder of the Sistine Chapel).* Having ordained six of his nephews as cardinals, Sixtus wanted to secure for them lucrative properties in northern Italy, but Lorenzo stood in his way. In the fall of 1473

---

*This conflict and the ensuing Pazzi conspiracy are vividly described and analyzed by Lauro Martines in *April Blood,* to which I owe the quotes from the pope and many other details of these dramatic events.

Lorenzo refused to lend Sixtus the sum of forty thousand ducats for the purchase of the town of Imola for his nephews Cardinal Pietro Riario and Count Girolamo Riario. The Pazzi family — Medici rivals both in Florence and in international banking, on which both families' fortunes depended — promptly obliged the pontiff by lending him the money, but Lorenzo still would not sell the towns. Sixtus made the Pazzi the principal papal bankers, taking the accounts away from the Medici, who had held them for decades. The pope calculated that without these finances, Lorenzo would not have sufficient resources to hold on to Florence and the towns Sixtus wanted for his family. Still Lorenzo would not cave in. The aggressively proud Florentines, who also prized the ample tax paid by subject towns, supported Lorenzo's refusal to yield to the pope. All this left Sixtus increasingly angry and scheming how to get rid of Lorenzo. Irritated, he threatened darkly, "We may have to use our irons, so as to help [Lorenzo] see that he is a citizen and we are the pope, because thus has it pleased God."

Meanwhile, within Florence itself, Lorenzo's strong-arm tactics toward his political rivals were creating seething resentment. As we have seen, since Cosimo's days, the Medici had wielded power by manipulating an extensive network of friends and clients. Although government officers were theoretically selected by having their names drawn from a purse, in reality Lorenzo, through his supporters, controlled whose names were put into the purse and pulled from it. If one were rich or prominent in Florence, not serving in the government was a dishonor. The Pazzi were among those whom Lorenzo pushed out of Florentine politics, taxed punitively, and even thwarted in their matrimonial plans. (Since the marriages of leading families were political alliances, Lorenzo also interfered in them through his "friends.") The Pazzis' patience was running out.

In 1478 Lorenzo's conflict with the pope and the Pazzi finally exploded. Sixtus IV formed an audacious plot together with Francesco de' Pazzi, Francesco Salviati (whom the pope had recently made archbishop of Pisa in the face of Lorenzo's fierce opposition), and Count Girolamo Riario, who was still vying with Lorenzo over Imola. The conspirators also enlisted the services of the mercenary commander Giovan Battista da Montesecco to ensure the takeover of Florence once Lorenzo was removed. The pope told his coconspirators, "I greatly desire a political change in Florence. I want that government taken from Lorenzo's hands, because he is a villain and a wicked man and has no respect for us. Once he is out of Florence, we'll be able to do as we wish in that republic and this would be very much in keeping with our plans." Although the pope claimed that he was firmly against shedding blood, the plot hinged on the assassination of Lorenzo and his younger, more handsome, and more popular brother Giuliano. To ensure the demise of the Medici's power, both brothers would have to die.

At first the conspirators intended to murder Lorenzo and Giuliano during a luncheon banquet that Lorenzo was hosting at his villa near Fiesole for another of the pope's nephews, the seventeen-year-old Cardinal Raffaele Sansoni Riario. But Giuliano felt indisposed (the Medici were a sickly family) and did not attend the event, so the plotters had to devise another plan in haste. The Riarios sent word to Lorenzo that the cardinal longed to see the famous art collection in the Medici Palace. Lorenzo, eager to show off his splendid treasures, invited the cardinal and his retinue, which included Francesco de' Pazzi and Archbishop Salviati, to lunch in Florence the following Sunday immediately after High Mass.

On Sunday morning, April 26, Lorenzo and his guests gathered at the Medici Palace to proceed together to Mass in the Duomo. To their frustration, the conspirators learned that Giuliano would again not be attending the lunch. They decided to strike while they had the chance — in the Duomo during the service. Once the assassination plot shifted to the church, however, the mercenary commander Montesecco balked, refusing to commit murder on sacred ground, so the task was divided between the remaining men: Francesco de' Pazzi and his supporter Bernardo Baroncelli would kill Giuliano; two renegade priests, Maffei and Bagnone, would slay Lorenzo. Meanwhile, Archbishop Salviati would direct Montesecco's troops into the Piazza della Signoria so they could take over the town hall.

The High Mass began. The conspirators discreetly exchanged glances and nodded their resolve. Suddenly Francesco de' Pazzi and Bernardo Baroncelli realized that Giuliano was nowhere to be seen. Had he not been with them on the short walk from the Medici Palace to the church? Had he slipped away and returned home? They rushed back to the Medici residence. Giuliano was there, not feeling well. Francesco and Bernardo cajoled, joked, and nudged him to join them just for the service. They did not want to risk attacking him in the Medici Palace, where servants would come to his aid and cut off the killers' escape. Finally Giuliano agreed, and they all walked back to the Duomo. Along the way, jesting and hugging him playfully, Francesco and Bernardo ascertained that Giuliano was not wearing any armor under his jacket. Violence was so widespread in Renaissance Florence that prominent men often walked around prepared for a chance encounter with a blade.

At last everyone was assembled in the Duomo. After a prearranged signal (and while Mass was in progress) the assassins struck. Francesco de' Pazzi and Bernardo Baroncelli attacked Giuliano with ferocity, stabbing him nineteen times. Collapsing in a pool of blood, he died on the spot. Francesco de' Pazzi had jabbed so frantically that he gravely wounded himself in the leg. Lorenzo, meanwhile, was assailed by the two priests and wounded in the neck, just under his right ear. Whirling around in a flash, he parried the next few thrusts with his short sword. Then he jumped over a low wooden railing into the octagonal choir, ran in front of the high altar and into the north sacristy, and barricaded himself behind its heavy bronze doors. Confused and frightened,

Lorenzo and a few trusted friends huddled in the sacristy for some time, unsure whether the assassins were gone or still lying in wait. Lorenzo was in pain from his neck wound and on the verge of hysteria, and he kept asking about Giuliano — he had not seen his stabbing. No one would answer his anguished questions. When eventually the coast was clear and they left the Duomo, Lorenzo's supporters made sure to lead him around the south side of the choir so that he would not see Giuliano's lifeless body sprawled in profuse gore.

Just before the attack on the Medici brothers, Archbishop Salviati had slipped away from the church under the pretext of visiting his ailing mother and hurried to the town hall with thirty armed men. The Florentine magistrates, suspecting foul play at the sight of the archbishop and his armed entourage, took Salviati and his soldiers captive, even though they had not yet heard of the events in the Duomo.

For a few hours tension and uncertainty hovered over the city. It was rumored that both Medici brothers had been killed, and "everyone held back, not quite knowing what to do." Bewildered and on edge, the citizens wondered whether they should throw in their lot with the conspirators. But then word got out that the coup had failed. In the late afternoon Lorenzo sent an urgent letter to his ally, the Duke of Milan, imploring military assistance. In growing outrage over the sacrilegious assault in the Duomo, the Florentines began to rally behind their unofficial lord. Lorenzo was clearly still alive and wielding authority, and apparently gearing up to unleash his fury on the conspirators, so it seemed unwise to side with them after all. Over the next few hours support for Lorenzo swelled, and the hammering of the alarm bell stirred the Florentines to action.

The roundup of culprits began. Florence was, for its time, a fairly large city, with a population of around fifty thousand. But it was also a rather intimate town, with closely knit neighborhoods and high visibility for prominent citizens as they made their way around the city. Therefore, the culprits' faces and those of their friends and allies would be easily recognizable to most citizens.

In the heat of the moment, Lorenzo's supporters zealously hunted down the Pazzi, their associates, and probably others with whom they wished to settle old scores. Most were captured the same day as Giuliano's murder, or the next day, and executed on the spot. These first two days yielded a gruesome harvest of some eighty to one hundred mangled bodies, a large number even given Florence's propensity for civic unrest. Machiavelli wrote that there were "so many deaths that streets were filled with the parts of men." The scattering of bloody limbs, the stench of decaying flesh, the screams of victims being slaughtered, and the jeers of rampaging crowds turned the refined Renaissance city into a hellhole — Dante's *Inferno* come to life.

Many men, including Archbishop Salviati, were hung from the windows of the town hall and the Bargello (police headquarters), and the city's major artists were ordered to depict them in this way as a record of their infamy and as an admonition to other conspirators. Leonardo da Vinci's sketch of Bernardo Baroncelli shows his dangling body, his arms tied behind his back and his face bruised.

Once the plotters and those associated with them were dead, their corpses were dropped to the ground, to be torn apart by the crowds assembled below. Soon a mass of shredded bodies littered the Piazza della Signoria, and throughout Florence bands of citizens trooped around dragging the limbs of dismembered men and carrying them speared on swords and lances. One jubilant group came knocking on the door of the Medici Palace with a pair of legs and a head impaled on the point of a lance, "and another part with an arm, borne aloft on a spit." These were the remains of an aide to Archbishop Salviati.

The upheaval diminished after the first couple of days, but the violence and rage lasted for weeks. Even the dead were not safe. The broken body of the head of the Pazzi family, old Jacopo, was disinterred by a gang of youths, who proceeded to kick it around town, throw it into the river, and fish it out again to shred it some more, despite the nauseating stink of decomposed flesh. Lorenzo, meanwhile, systematically annihilated the Pazzi name and fortune. He seized all their liquid assets, merchandise, houses, and landed estates and unleashed a campaign to erase from the city any sign of the clan. Their coats of arms and dedicatory plaques were removed and destroyed, and the surviving family members, including distant cousins, were ordered to change their surnames and coats of arms within six months.

The Pazzi conspiracy and Giuliano's murder would influence Lorenzo's actions for years. Tension and suspicion lingered in the city as Lorenzo pounced on any real or supposed potential assailant. Luca Landucci records in his diary that on September 27, 1481, more than three years later,

> a certain hermit came to the house of Lorenzo de' Medici at the Poggio a Caiano [one of his suburban villas]; and the servants declared that he intended to murder Lorenzo, so they took him and sent him to the Bargello, and he was put on the rack. 15th October. This hermit died at Santa Maria Novella [the city's hospital], having been tortured in various ways. It was said that they skinned the soles of his feet, and then burnt them by holding them in the fire till the fat dripped off them; after which they set him upright and made him walk across the great hall; and these things caused his death. Opinions were divided as to whether he was guilty or innocent.

Although the conspiracy had failed, Lorenzo's and Florence's troubles only grew worse. The pope was furious at the failure to remove Lorenzo from power, at the execution of Archbishop Salviati and other clerics involved in the coup, and at the imprisonment of his nephew, the young cardinal (Lorenzo did not dare to kill a relative of the pope). Sixtus demanded Lorenzo's surrender. Lorenzo refused. The pope imposed an interdict (an exclusion from participating in worship and certain holy rites) on the entire Tuscan state and excommunicated the Medici, calling Lorenzo "the child of iniquity and the nursling of perdition." Excommunication was a grave sentence, similar to but more severe than an interdict, as it cut the punished off from Christian society and barred them from Communion and other blessings of the Church.

Other princes rushed in to take advantage of Florence's perceived weakness. King Ferrante of Naples, already keen on invading the Florentine territories, sided with the pope and threatened the city with total destruction unless it expelled Lorenzo. Luca Landucci writes, "The King of Naples sent a herald to Florence, with the proclamation displayed, stamped with the arms of the king, and he went to the *Signoria* [Florentine government] to declare war, being deputed to tell us that the king and the Holy Father would oblige us in any way, if we sent away Lorenzo de' Medici: to which the citizens would not agree; and so war began." Soon thereafter "the Sienese invaded our territory and took booty and prisoners." They also "captured [the town of] Rincine and destroyed it, and took away men and women of all classes; and our soldiers were worse than they, pillaging and working great havoc all through Valdelsa. . . . Each day there was some incursion or other, and the enemy overran Panzano, pillaging and burning." By the end of 1478 things were still dismal. "And at this Christmas-time," Landucci lamented, "what with terror of the war, the plague, and the papal excommunication, the citizens were in sorry plight. They lived in dread, and no one had any heart to work . . . , so that all classes suffered."

For two more years Florence lived in turmoil, losing its subject cities, suffering skyrocketing prices, and enduring assaults on Florentine merchants abroad. As anxiety in the city mounted and its resources and spirit declined, Lorenzo desperately pondered how he could survive all these disasters without losing his power and his life.

In 1480 he took a bold step. He would go to Naples, put himself at the mercy of his enemy, King Ferrante, and try to persuade him to cease hostilities and side with Florence against the pope. In a letter to the Signoria, Lorenzo humbly declared:

> I have chosen to expose myself to some degree of danger rather than to allow the city to suffer longer under its present trials. . . . Since I am the one whom our enemies are pursuing primarily, by putting myself into their hands, I might be the means of bringing peace back to our city. . . . Perhaps God desires that since this war began with my brother's blood and mine, so too that it should end by my hands. What I most desire is that my life and death, and what is good and bad for me, be ever for the benefit of our city.

The letter, read aloud in public, moved people to tears. By linking the survival of Florence with his selfless action, Lorenzo regained a measure of popular support.

In reality, a master of turning problems and challenges into political gold, Lorenzo had prepared the trip with great care, and his personal risk was small. He set off for Naples laden with gifts for the king and members of his court. The king's son, the Duke of Calabria, dispatched his galleys up from Naples to escort Lorenzo with all the honors due an important state visitor. Ferrante gave him a gracious welcome and decorated his quarters with royal furnishings. Lorenzo remained in Naples for nearly two and a half months, wooing the king with his charm, a large fortune in cash, and a promise to deliver a Florence loyal to Ferrante as long as Lorenzo stayed in power. Besides, Lorenzo had strong ties with the king of France, another useful resource for Naples. And without Ferrante's support, Lorenzo intimated, Florence might have to turn to an alliance with Venice, the enemy of Naples, which the king surely did not want. Lorenzo sweetened his diplomatic efforts with luncheons and dinners for Ferrante at the Neapolitan palazzo of the Medici Bank, where he resided. And so, through a combination of rhetoric, hospitality, charm, and cash, he won the king over.

The cost of all this diplomacy was vast both financially and emotionally. One of Lorenzo's aides noted that he was "like two men: full of grace and confidence during the day, presenting himself as light-hearted and self-assured, but at night he would complain wretchedly about his and Florence's *fortuna*." But then Lorenzo was always anxious about appearing more powerful and confident than he really was. How could he not be when he tried to rule like a prince a city that was a republic, and one that stood at the heart of Italy yet was weaker than other major states? Lorenzo knew he was always vulnerable to a coup by his rivals and to further assassination attempts, yet day after day he put on a show of strength that masked his vulnerability. The trip to Naples confirmed for him a vital political truth: what you appeared to be mattered more than what you were.

Having successfully negotiated peace with Ferrante, Lorenzo returned to Florence a hero. More than one hundred of the most eminent citizens and all the foreign ambassadors rode out of the city to meet him, a ceremonial practice previously reserved for noble rulers, not upstart merchants. Lorenzo would boast afterward that "there was no man in Florence, whatever his condition, who did not come to touch my hand and kiss me." Characteristically, he used this triumph to make his control over his city more autocratic than before.

Lorenzo now realized that the strength of his position in Florence depended on the respect he was accorded by the potentates of Italy and other countries. Good personal relations with other rulers had also been the key to his grandfather's and father's influence. The ambassador from Ferrara confirmed that "without their esteem, he would not be so highly regarded at home." To shore up his standing in the next few years, Lorenzo formed a league with his new ally, the king of Naples, and with the Duke of Milan, both much more powerful rulers than he. Unfortunately, Lorenzo did not have enough clout to compel his allies to uphold their end of the pact for mutual support. He could only fume in frustration when Milan would not help Florence regain Sarzana, a strategic fortified town that Florence had lost to Genoa in the war after the Pazzi conspiracy. "I don't have the means of His Excellency [the Duke of Milan] to defend myself," he complained to his ambassador in Milan. And while Lorenzo had helped King Ferrante suppress a rebellion of Neapolitan barons, the king also declined to support Florence in the Sarzana affair, with the excuse of being too financially drained. Lorenzo had to find a way to shore up his position at home and to gain authority in larger Italian politics. He came up with two stratagems.

For years he had been dreaming of enhancing his family's prestige by procuring a cardinal's hat for his son Giovanni. Genuine princely families routinely obtained such distinctions for their boys. Of course, given his bitter feuds with Pope Sixtus IV, Lorenzo had made little progress in this matter. With the ascension of Pope Innocent VIII in 1484, Lorenzo saw an opportunity. Innocent was, on the whole, well disposed toward Lorenzo, and Lorenzo made sure to be most helpful in mediating the pope's troubled relations with the king of Naples. By the end of 1486 the pope and Lorenzo had reached an accord. Lorenzo's thirteen-year-old daughter, Maddalena, her mother's favorite, would marry the pope's illegitimate son Franceschetto — twenty-four years her senior, small, fat, boring, perpetually drunk, and a compulsive gambler. Lorenzo would provide a dowry of 4,000 florins for his daughter and a loan of 30,000 florins for the pope. Whatever qualms he might have felt about sacrificing his daughter to political expediency (it was, actually, common for teenage girls to marry much older men, and Lorenzo would later plead with Innocent "to be a pope" and provide the couple with the means to live in comfort), the gains of this rapprochement were enormous. For just 95,000 florins more, paid into the coffers of the Apostolic Chamber, the pope would make Giovanni de' Medici a cardinal.

But Lorenzo wanted something more to solidify his standing, and he found an original and showy way to demonstrate that he was no longer just a wealthy merchant and banker, but a ruler of international rank.

AS HIS GRANDFATHER Cosimo had, Lorenzo took a page from the Romans' playbook — in particular, from that of the brilliant statesman with whom Lorenzo already had an affinity. In 48 BC, after defeating Pompey, Julius Caesar led a successful campaign in Asia Minor and Egypt (where he fell under the spell of Cleopatra and left her with a son, Ptolemy Caesar). To celebrate his accomplishments and to assert his power back in Rome, Caesar staged a series of spectacular triumphs. Among the spoils he paraded through the city were hundreds of lions, leopards, black panthers, baboons, green monkeys, Egyptian saluki dogs, parrots, flamingos, and ostriches. Forty elephants carrying lighted torches in their trunks marched alongside Caesar up the steps of the Capitoline. But the most astonishing animal, a marvel he obtained in Cleopatra's Egypt, was a giraffe.

The appearance of this extraordinary beast caused a sensation in Rome. Today we are used to seeing giraffes in zoos, books, and on television programs, and still these animals never fail to amaze us. Edmund Blair Bolles, in his book *A Second Way of Knowing: The Riddle of Human Perception,* writes that many people who first see giraffes on a prairie in Africa register only one animal where there are actually several nibbling on acacia branches. "Giraffes are so unusual they seem to overwhelm the senses. The brain does not know what to do with its input." For the Romans, who had never even known that such a beast existed, seeing a giraffe for the first time must have been even more amazing.

Ptolemy Philadelphos had exhibited a giraffe to memorable effect in his Great Procession in Alexandria in 275 BC, but that had been more than three centuries earlier and on a different continent. Caesar's giraffe was the first to be brought to Europe. Unsure what this alien-looking creature was, the Romans called it by a name that seemed to describe it most closely: camelopard, a mixture of a camel and a leopard. (Our scientific name for this animal is still *Giraffa camelopardalis*.) Strabo, trying to grapple with the nature of this bizarre animal, disagreed with this comparison:

> They are in no respect like leopards; for the dappled marking of their skin is more like that of a fawn, which is flecked with spots. Their hinder quarters are so much lower than their fore quarters, that it seems as if the animal were sitting upon its rump. It has the height of an ox, although its forelegs are as long as those of the camel. The neck rises high and straight up, but the head reaches much higher up than that of camels. . . . It is, however, not a wild animal, but rather like a domesticated beast, for it shows no signs of a savage disposition.

The natural historian Pliny added that since the giraffe displayed no ferocity, it earned for itself the nickname "wild sheep."

Caesar's ability to procure this fantastic animal was a great coup. Pliny emphasized that "it was first seen at Rome in the circus games held by Caesar, the Dictator." As if to imply that he could easily replenish such a treasure, Caesar had the giraffe torn to shreds by lions in the games following his triumph. The Roman poet Horace reproached his fellow citizens for enjoying the spectacle of the death of so wondrous a beast: "Demokritos, if he were still on earth, would deride a throng gazing with open mouth at a beast half camel, half panther." But Caesar's animal spectacle helped him solidify his power by demonstrating his military might and political reach. Shortly afterward he usurped complete power over Rome.

So why shouldn't Lorenzo emulate Caesar? His opponents already likened him to the ancient dictator because of his style of rule, a comparison that flattered Lorenzo more than it bothered him. As he saw it, they had much in common. Both men had attained success despite many internal and external enemies; both had won respect even though they were accused of violating republican principles and becoming tyrants; both were objects of assassination conspiracies. However, the parallels between Lorenzo and Caesar did trouble other Florentines such as the humanist Alamanno Rinuccini, who wrote the secret *Dialogue on Liberty* a year after the Pazzi conspiracy. He intended to publish it if Lorenzo was overthrown, but in the end the *Dialogue* was printed only after World War II.

Rinuccini praised the conspirators for championing the cause of liberty by opposing a tyrant; he compared them with Brutus and Cassius, the slayers of Caesar. "I see people . . . bullied by the whims of one young man," Rinuccini inveighed. "Many noble minds and men of eminent seniority and wisdom wear today the yoke of servitude and hardly recognize their own condition. Nor, when they do see it, do they dare avenge themselves." Rinuccini recognized that Lorenzo's brilliance was what made him so dangerous.

Lorenzo was a man endowed by nature, training, and practice with such enormous ingenuity, that he was in no way inferior to his grandfather Cosimo. . . . He had so able and versatile a mind that whatever he turned to in his pursuits as a boy, he learned and possessed perfectly, and better than others. So it happened that he learned to dance, fire arrows, sing, ride, join in games, play diverse musical instruments, and do many other things, all going to grace and delight his youthful years. And I believe that being inspired by the magnitude of his ability, when he found our citizens timid and of a servile spirit, having been rendered so by his father, he resolved to transfer to himself all public dignity, power, and authority, and in the end, like Julius Caesar, to make himself lord of the republic.

Lorenzo had read with great interest about Caesar's triumph and his giraffe, although it is not clear when he first had the idea to get one of his own. (He had in his library Dio Cassius's *Roman History* and Pliny the Elder's *Natural History*, both of which describe Caesar's momentous animal display.) Given that he did not set out to assemble a whole menagerie, he clearly saw this beast as a tool for political advancement, a great coup that on its own would be more potent than if it formed part of a larger collection. The giraffe was not, of course, Lorenzo's single key to political sovereignty. It was only one component of his multilayered strategy of social ascent. His art collecting was similarly focused and deliberate. He bought few paintings and sculptures by contemporary artists, whose work was accessible to any well-to-do merchant, and instead went after truly noble artifacts — rare vases carved from semiprecious stones, ancient gems and cameos, antique statues in stone and bronze — that bespoke a more princely taste. Appearing magnificent through ostentatious and luxurious possessions was part of the art of looking more powerful than others. And so a live giraffe, not seen in Europe since antiquity, would lift Lorenzo's prestige above that of all his contemporaries, who may have had other exotic mammals, but certainly none as extraordinary.

Of course Lorenzo knew that giraffes lived in Africa. The wooden giraffe that his grandfather had used in 1459 to stir into action the self-satisfied lions was likely modeled on a drawing brought to Florence by the merchant and humanist Ciriaco d'Ancona, one of Cosimo's protégés. Ciriaco had traveled throughout the Mediterranean and the East and returned home with fascinating pictures of all sorts of remarkable sights, including a giraffe he had seen in Cairo. But to bring to Florence a drawing of a giraffe is one thing, to import a live animal quite another — especially since, unlike the Romans, the Florentines did not command an extensive empire from which to exact countless and varied beasts. Procuring even a single giraffe was a major challenge that no European ruler had surmounted since the days of ancient Rome. But Lorenzo, as Rinuccini said, "was endowed with enormous ingenuity," and when he noticed a window of opportunity, he took advantage of it.

ANTIQUITY PROVIDED THE model for Renaissance men, but the East supplied the means. Exotic beasts, as well as spices and dyes coveted by Europeans, came from lands controlled by their religious enemies, the Ottoman and Mamluk dynasties. The Venetians had been getting rich from trade with them for centuries. The Florentines had concluded a commercial treaty with the sultan of Egypt and Syria in 1422 and had established a state shipping line to transport goods to and from the East, but these efforts never bore significant fruit.

In the mid-1480s, hurting financially from the post–Pazzi conspiracy wars, the Florentine government and merchants decided to try again. They were keen to buoy up the city's economy by trading with Egypt directly rather than going through middlemen such as the Venetians. Alexandria exported pepper and ginger in vast quantities, as well as cloves and cinnamon, spikenard, galangal, camphor, and incense. The Florentines were eager to obtain these valuable spices, at good prices, along with tanning products for their domestic textile industry. Fine Alexandrian linen, as well as cotton and sugar from Cyprus, was also of interest. In return, they wanted to sell their own products directly to the Egyptians: high-quality woolen and silk cloth (the eastern Mediterranean was the principal market for the Florentine cloth industry); olive oil, nuts, and other agricultural products. And so in 1485 a Florentine ambassador, Paolo da Colle, went to Cairo to the court of the sultan of Egypt, Qaitbay, to negotiate new trade links between the two states.

The sultan welcomed the Florentine ambassador in the great ceremonial Throne Hall of his Citadel — a vast space surrounded by gigantic red granite columns from which sprang pointed arches and then a huge dome. Qaitbay — whom one European traveler described as well into his seventies, with a long white beard, and showing signs of having been in his youth a graceful, well-built, and powerful man — received the visitors dressed in a white robe and a high turban with multiple horned projections. He sat cross-legged on a small gold- and silver-plated chair, surrounded by exquisite hangings and fine carpets. On the sultan's left, on an ornate cushion, lay his gilded sword and a shield decorated with intricate colored-metal inlays. To his right stood a half tent under which sat his attentive counselors, secretaries, and clerks.

The Florentine ambassador was instructed to kneel and kiss the floor three times upon arriving before the sultan, and to continue kissing it as he approached his host. At twelve steps from Qaitbay he was permitted to stand upright and present his message to the sultan's interpreter. The interpreter passed on the message to a high official, who repeated it to a man of higher rank, who then repeated it to Qaitbay. The sultan was meant to be "inaccessible like a high wild mountain that hides animals of prey," according to the Mamluk manual for princes. "The Sultan's visitors should feel like visiting a wild lion; but once having been admitted the encounter with the Sultan should bestow glory upon the visitor."

Part of the visit with the sultan included a tour of the public quarters of the Citadel — adorned with fine marbles, opulent carpets, and elegant paintings and metalwork — as well as a stop at the stables where the sultan kept his splendid horses, hunting falcons, and other valued beasts. The stables stood at the heart of the Citadel's ceremonial life. The sultan's residence overlooked them, so he could admire his animals at all times. He held judicial audiences in the stables' loggia, from which he also watched fireworks on festive days. It is here that the Florentine ambassador must have spotted what Lorenzo wanted as much as trade privileges for his city: a strange animal that the locals called Zerafa.

Many European visitors to Cairo were astonished by this remarkable creature. The Castilian merchant-adventurer Pero Tafur went to see a giraffe in Cairo the way he went to see other notable sights in the city and its environs: the preserve of the elephants, the sultan's balsam groves, the pyramids. Tafur was mesmerized by the giraffe. "It is very tame," he noted in his diary. "If they give it bread to eat with the hand it lowers its head and makes a great arc with its neck. They say that these creatures live to a great age, and that this one has been here more than 200 years." Actually, a giraffe's life span is only twenty to thirty years, but the animal seemed ever present at the court in Cairo because the sultans made sure always to keep one in their menagerie. When the Mamluks annexed Sudan to Egypt in 1275, they required that the country send its new lords an annual tribute of oxen, dromedaries, panthers, elephants, and giraffes.

We do not know whether Lorenzo instructed Paolo da Colle to get him a giraffe before he left Florence, or urged him to obtain the animal as soon as he received a report of the splendid beast in Qaitbay's stables. Lorenzo certainly kept close tabs on all correspondence from foreign ambassadors and requested that they write to him personally more detailed accounts of what they did, saw, and heard abroad. (However, he reminded one diplomat, "when you write to the Eight [the Signoria], never mention writing to me about anything important.") Besides, Florentine ambassadors tended to be chosen from Lorenzo's close friends.

Whatever way Lorenzo came to hear about the giraffe, Paolo da Colle would have been in an ideal position to put in a request to the sultan.

Sultan Qaitbay was quite willing to listen. He was keen to foster commercial relations with the Florentines, and he, too, had a major favor to ask of Lorenzo. Qaitbay's reign was, like Lorenzo's, a golden age of art and culture against a background of political tensions and economic hardships. Both men combined in their personalities hard-nosed politicking with refined artistic sensibilities. A contemporary historian, Ibn Iyas, described the Sultan as "serene and dignified. . . . Highly intelligent, sound of judgment, skilled in state affairs, talented in administration . . . he always reflected carefully before implementing a decision [yet was also] renowned for his bravery. . . . He was proficient in all military arts, and yet obsessed with a lust for money."

Qaitbay's sense of justice, even temper, and noble deportment were not qualities fostered by his milieu. The sultans of Egypt were elected from among non-Muslim slaves who began as palace guards and soldiers and rose through the military hierarchy. This caste was called Mamluk. (The word "Mamluk" is derived from the Arabic root meaning "to own.") Contemporary Europeans were astonished by this political system. Pero Tafur, who visited Egypt in the 1430s, wrote in fascination that the Mamluks,

> whom we call renegade barbarians, . . . the Sultan buys . . . for cash in the Black Sea, and in all places where the Christians sell them. When they arrive here they become Moors (Muslims), and they teach them the law, and instruct them in horsemanship and to shoot with the bow. Then they are examined by the chief Doctor, and are given wages and rations and sent to the city. No man can become Sultan, nor admiral, nor have any honor or office except he be one of those renegades, nor can any Moor by birth ride on horseback under the penalty of death.

It is the Mamluks who have all the honors of knighthood. Their sons have somewhat less honor, and the grandchildren still less again, and after that they are counted Moors by birth.

The German Felix Fabri explained in his travel account that by using the inexhaustible reservoir of soldiers from outside, the rulers of Egypt did not have to depend on the availability and loyalty of native Muslims. "The governors, legal officials, princes, army commanders, and emissaries are all Mamluks. The [prospect of] emancipation and freedom and the hopes of attaining the highest offices attract numerous Christians [and other slaves]. There are also the payments and daily stipends, the security, but also the weakness of the flesh and the prospect of possessing several women." The lure of such rewards kept the Mamluks loyal to the system and ambitious for advancement. But the qualities for which adolescent boys were selected for this path were physical agility, aggressiveness, and intelligence, not the calm temper and abiding sense of justice for which Qaitbay was praised.

Qaitbay had been born in the Circassian district of the Caucasus between 1416 and 1418. Mamluk merchants made regular trips to Circassia and to the Black Sea steppes to find promising youths. Like most Circassians, Qaitbay had a light complexion, fair hair, and gray-blue eyes. The German knight Arnold von Harff heard during his stay in Cairo that Qaitbay came from a family of shepherds and was bought for five ducats.* Qaitbay was purchased by the merchant Mahmud ibn Rastam, who was looking for adept horsemen, archers, and lance throwers. The boy displayed talent in all these activities and impressed his contemporaries by effortlessly directing the most boisterous mount. He was comely, tall, and agile, and he possessed remarkable stamina. Later in life,

---

*The Florentines also acquired Circassian slaves. Cosimo de' Medici fathered a son, Carlo, by a Circassian slave in his household. He brought him up along with his legitimate sons and set him on the path to a successful career in the Church.

even into his sixties and seventies, he loved rigorous outings and often outpaced men decades younger.

The Circassian youth arrived in Egypt in 1435 and rose meteorically through the Mamluk military hierarchy, moving from being a palace guard to amir (commander) of a thousand Mamluks, to commander of the royal guard, and finally to marshal. Qaitbay was clearly not just a gifted officer but also a shrewd politician. In a system plagued by factionalism and turmoil surrounding the succession of each sultan (it being a nonhereditary post), he managed to stay clear of conspiracies and destructive intrigues. Over the span of thirty-three years Qaitbay served nine sultans, yet, Ibn Iyas notes, not once was he arrested, imprisoned, or exiled — an extraordinary record given the gnawing fear of revolt the sultans lived with and the severe measures they took to purge real and perceived enemies. Qaitbay exuded loyalty and steadfastness, and thus, patiently and persistently, he rose to the top.

Qaitbay became sultan in the winter of 1468, a year before Lorenzo came to power in Florence. He was already in his fifties, but he would go on to govern for almost three decades — again, a remarkable achievement given the typically high turnover of sultans. Like Lorenzo, Qaitbay made a show of accepting the reins of power reluctantly. According to Ibn Iyas, just as he was about to be invested as sultan, Qaitbay broke down in tears and refused the position. The august assembly of caliphs, *qadis* (judges), and amirs had to force him to assume the throne. Once in power, however, Qaitbay had absolutely no doubt that he was the only man capable of leadership in the treacherous Mamluk system. In 1478–1479, just as Lorenzo was going through the ordeal of the Pazzi conspiracy and subsequent wars, Qaitbay's reign was imperiled by opposing factions. The sultan restored order by threatening to resign. It is a testament to his political savvy and authority that his ploy worked.

Qaitbay's rule came after half a century of political, economic, and artistic decline, and his contemporaries hailed him as a savior from chaos. He was also greatly admired as a defender of Islam and a patron of scholars, all the more so because he was self-taught. Given their humble origins and military careers, many Mamluks were not well schooled, but Qaitbay was better educated than most. He significantly increased book production during his reign. And despite ongoing fiscal crises, he built a vast number of mosques, colleges, hospices, orphanages, libraries, fountains, and caravansaries in Mecca, Medina, and Jerusalem (where he lavished great care on the city in order to impress European pilgrims and enhance his reputation in the West), as well as in Cairo and Alexandria. Linking himself with the glorious past of Alexandria, he also erected a splendid fortress on the site of Ptolemy's great lighthouse, the Pharos.

Although Qaitbay's rule was more peaceful and prosperous than those of his predecessors, concern over money loomed large during his reign, in part because he spent so much of it on building projects, in part because military operations against the Ottomans on his northern borders continually drained his treasury, and in part because of the decline of the Egyptian economy that he inherited when he came to power. Major plague epidemics had been decimating the population every few years for much of the fifteenth century, bringing down productivity and precipitating a trade deficit. Qaitbay worked assiduously to boost the commerce of his kingdom by spurring local manufacture, especially of the fine metalwork and carpets much prized in Europe and eagerly collected by the Medici, among others. By granting new privileges to foreign merchants, he would eventually bring about a golden age of European trade in Egypt and Syria. But in the mid-1480s his courtship of Europeans was still new, and a commercial accord with Florence held out promise of alleviating some of Qaitbay's financial worries.

There was also a political favor Qaitbay wanted from Lorenzo. The Mamluk territories were threatened by the Ottoman sultan Bayezid II. For the time being, Bayezid's own political problems kept him from waging an all-out war on Egypt. Qaitbay wanted Lorenzo's help in keeping it that way. At issue was the dynastic struggle between Bayezid and his brother, Djem.

Bayezid was the older son of Sultan Mehmet the Conqueror, who had sacked Constantinople in 1453. When Mehmet died suddenly in May 1481, Bayezid expected to succeed his father, but he was challenged by his younger brother. Djem tried to defeat Bayezid in battle but failed, and fled to the protection of Qaitbay. The Mamluk sultan extended a courteous but cautious welcome to Djem, who spent a few months in Egypt and then made another attempt to unseat Bayezid. Failing again, he fled in 1482 to the protection of the Knights of St. John on Rhodes, who eventually took him to France as something of a hostage.

Qaitbay wanted Djem returned to Egypt, so that he could serve as a deterrent against Bayezid's aggression. In response to a hostile move from Bayezid, Qaitbay could put Djem at the head of an army and send him to dethrone his brother. Meanwhile, Pope Innocent VIII also stood to benefit from taking custody of Djem, for Bayezid had threatened to invade Europe as well. Such an arrangement was an acceptable second choice to Qaitbay, as the threat of Djem's leading Christian armies against Bayezid would also keep the Ottoman sultan from attacking Egypt. If only Qaitbay could persuade the French to give Djem up. As it happened, the Medici had a long-standing friendship with the French, and Lorenzo was just then forging a familial relationship with Pope Innocent, so he was in a perfect position to help Qaitbay with his dilemma.

The timing of the Florentine embassy to Cairo corresponded with Qaitbay's especially acute need for Djem. In 1485 Bayezid concluded peace with Hungary, Venice, Ragusa, and the Danube provinces, and he was ready to commit larger forces against Egypt. He was provoked into an offensive by Qaitbay's insult of stealing presents that an ambassador from India was bringing to Bayezid. It is not clear why Qaitbay decided to risk this theft, given the already tense situation, but he appropriated the exotic luxury goods intended for his Ottoman rival — opulent textiles, gemstones, and pearls. He left alone the elephants, giraffes, gold, and spices, which he could readily obtain at home. Now that Bayezid was on the warpath against him, Qaitbay wrote to France, where Djem was being held, offering 100,000 ducats for his transfer to Egypt. He also appealed to Lorenzo for help. Lorenzo was prepared to entertain Qaitbay's request for diplomatic assistance. It seems that in return, he requested a giraffe. This was Lorenzo's chance to obtain the scarcely known exotic beast that could seal his status as a statesman.

Historical records are, unfortunately, largely silent on this bargain. But given Lorenzo's need to cement his power, Qaitbay's documented appeal for his aid, and the arrival of the animal in Florence in 1487, it seems that an agreement was struck: a giraffe for an Ottoman prince.

Qaitbay, a shrewd reconciler, would have been happy to give Lorenzo the beast in return for securing Djem. For him a giraffe was not a high price to pay for the safety of his kingdom. In addition, Qaitbay held out to Lorenzo the commercial treaty craved by the Florentine merchants (and equally useful to the Mamluks), an economic accord that stood to benefit Lorenzo by enhancing his image as a ruler working for the good of his people. Lorenzo seemed satisfied with the arrangement, because he wrote to Anne, the queen of France, offering to forward the giraffe to her in exchange for her aid. If he could obtain a giraffe and then use it as diplomatic currency with France, Lorenzo's stature as a prince wielding international authority would only be amplified. His willingness to surrender the rare and precious creature to the queen rather than keep it for himself suggests that he wanted it less for curiosity and enjoyment than for political profit.

But before giving up the giraffe, Lorenzo would use it to full advantage at home. The fantastic animal was his bargaining chip not only with Anne but also with his fickle Italian allies, the king of Naples and the Duke of Milan, who were still reluctant to uphold their end of the agreement for mutual assistance. It could also be persuasive in Lorenzo's delicate negotiations with the pope for a cardinal's hat for his son. As one scholar of the period writes, Lorenzo's diplomatic style was one of "shrewd compensation for weakness."

Lorenzo was very close to realizing his giraffe scheme when his plans nearly got derailed by a series of disasters that beset the sultan. In the early months of 1486, several of Qaitbay's trusted civil officials died, and the Egyptian economy took a turn for the worse, owing to poor harvests and hoarding, which caused food prices to soar. Military hostilities with the Ottomans intensified over control of the province of Cilicia. Then, in March, while the sultan was exercising a spirited new horse in the palace courtyard, he violently reined in the animal. The horse reared and bucked, the rider was thrown to the ground, and the mount fell on top of him.

Qaitbay suffered bad bruises and lacerations, and his femur was shattered, with the bone jutting out of his thigh. He lost consciousness from the pain and blood loss, and his aides were terrified that he had died. They carried him into his quarters and summoned his physician, who ascertained that Qaitbay was still alive and set the fracture, but could not guarantee that the sultan would recover. Alarm spread through the capital at the prospect of a power struggle should Qaitbay expire from his injuries. Luckily, no one broke allegiance to the sultan while his life hung by a thread.

After a few days of tense uncertainty, Qaitbay began to recover. By the next month he could again sign decrees and receive delegations, and by the end of June he rode unassisted to preside over Friday prayer in the Citadel mosque. Clenching his teeth to fight the pain and struggling to appear effortless as ever on his mount, he passed upright before the saluting harem eunuchs perfumed with saffron, the princesses distributing sashes of gold silk to the spectators, and the assembled subjects cheering the sultan's fortitude.

Despite Qaitbay's show of a full return to his powers, unrest smoldered among his subordinates, the economy kept sinking, and escalating campaigns against the Ottomans drained the country's treasury and spirits. The sultan needed Lorenzo's assistance more than ever to improve the fiscal health of his state and to keep Djem, and therefore Bayezid, in hand. He was all the more motivated to dispatch the giraffe to Florence. Ironically, Lorenzo had found his most reliable ally not among his fellow Christian rulers, but in a Muslim sultan.

On Sunday, November 11, 1487, the Florentines woke up to an astonishing sight. A procession of blue-eyed foreigners in flowing white robes and high turbans was moving through the city, followed by swarthy attendants carrying exquisitely tooled metal boxes and bundles of costly Eastern textiles. They looked like the Magi arriving to greet the birth of Christ. After them moved a train of strange animals. The lion and bay horse were familiar to the Florentines, but peculiar goats with extremely long ears that dangled like a rabbit's made them giggle, and a flock of sheep whose fat tails hung to the ground and were more than a foot wide caused men and women to point and exclaim.

But what took the spectators' breath away was a sixteen-foot-tall creature that looked at once bizarre and beautiful, muscular and dainty, moving both its slender right legs in one stride and its left ones in the next. Its spotted coat stood out brightly in the gloomy autumn air. This fantastic apparition glided past the somber stone palazzi, sniffing at the grocers' and artisans' stalls, and towered over the crowd of gawking Florentines assembled in the streets and piazzas. Its eyes in particular were magical: dark brown, large, and lustrous, gazing softly at the onlookers from under long, thick lashes. The Florentines were dumbfounded and beguiled.

The Mamluk visitors were escorted to their lodgings and the animals taken to the city menagerie, where the lions had to be hastily moved around to make room for the Egyptian guests. The next day, as the keepers marveled at their new charges, a grave accident marred their delight. Luca Landucci recounts in his diary that

> there was an attendant who looked after the lions, and with whom they were quite tame, so that he could go into their cages and touch them, especially one of them; and just lately, a boy of about fourteen . . . wished to enter the lions' cage with this tamer. But after he had been inside a little while, this lion threw himself upon him [the boy], seizing him by the back of the head; and it was only with difficulty, by shouting at the beast, that the tamer got him away. But the lion had so torn and mauled the boy, that he died in a few days.

The lion was probably agitated by the arrival of the new animals and the commotion around them. The mishap must have made the keepers jittery and anxious about the new beasts. They seemed tame, but in truth the Florentines had no idea of their temperaments, how to handle them, and what to expect. They did not have time to ponder these mysteries idly, though, for they had to acclimate the Egyptian animals to their new surroundings and to ready them for the official reception, in less than a week, of the Mamluk delegation.

On Sunday afternoon, November 18, the Egyptian ambassador, Muhammad ibn Mahfuz al-Maghibi (known as Malfota), a preeminent expert in the world of commerce who had negotiated for Sultan Qaitbay in Europe for almost two decades, arrived in the Piazza della Signoria. As he stepped ceremonially across the square, he was followed by his entourage, the animals that had arrived the week before, and porters carrying other offerings sent by Qaitbay.

Malfota took a seat in the midst of the Signoria officials on the *ringhiera,* a raised platform at the foot of the town hall decorated for the occasion with painted cloth backdrops and carpets strewn on the floor. Every Florentine merchant trading in the Levant in the first part of the century had been required to bring a carpet to the Signoria upon his return. The Florentine government had accumulated a sizable collection and was now showing it off before the Mamluk ambassador as a gesture of welcome and an invitation to continue their trade relationship.

After everyone was settled, Malfota and the Florentine magistrates exchanged greetings. Then the ambassador spread before the Signoria and Lorenzo the gifts sent by Qaitbay. There was a profusion of ceramics, including precious Chinese porcelain, whose secret the Florentines were eager to discover and which an eyewitness deemed to be "finer than anything seen before." There were also rich textiles: cottons, muslins, and a magnificent striped ceremonial tent, an emblem of royalty among the Mamluks that Qaitbay bestowed on Lorenzo as a special gift. An assortment of Eastern sweetmeats, myrobalans (astringent fruits used for dyeing and tanning), ginger, musk, benzoin (used for cosmetics and healing), aloe wood, and balsam from the sultan's own groves filled the air with marvelous scents. And then, of course, there were the animals, nervously eyeing the crowd of strange-looking and -smelling Florentines.

Following the show of presents, Malfota pulled out a long scroll filled with elegant Arabic script: the terms of the commercial treaty the sultan was prepared to offer to Florentine merchants. These would be translated while he stayed in the city and discussed in more detail later on. While these grave diplomatic matters occupied the ambassador, the Signoria, and Lorenzo, a great mass of citizens gathered in the piazza before the town hall. Everyone came to gape at the peculiarly dressed Egyptians and their wondrous offerings, especially the strange beasts, which evoked distant lands. It was the first time such gifts were displayed in Lorenzo's rule. The onlookers felt that his power must indeed be immense to command such amazing offerings from a faraway heathen king.

A week later, on November 25, the Mamluk ambassador had a personal audience with Lorenzo, whom Qaitbay addressed in his letters as "king of Florence" and "valiant and fierce lion," while titling himself "Alexander of the Age." Malfota communicated to Lorenzo the sultan's greetings and the favors he was asking regarding Djem. Lorenzo conveyed to the Egyptian diplomat what he was prepared to do for the sultan. Mutually pleased, they parted. Malfota went to his lodgings to write a report home. He was gratified with his reception in Florence. In his expert opinion, it promised to be a very productive relationship.

Malfota remained in Florence for a year. In that time the Florentine merchants translated the draft treaty sent by Qaitbay, scrutinized it, debated additions and corrections, and presented them to the Signoria, to be passed on to the sultan. Malfota was soon forgotten by most inhabitants of the city, but the giraffe kept Florence abuzz. She (alas, her name has not been preserved) was painted by various artists throughout the city. Numerous Florentines sang her praises. A coppersmith named Bartolomeo Masi recorded in his diary that the beasts sent by the sultan were the most marvelous ever seen in the city and that the giraffe was as sweet as a lamb. Another Florentine, Antonio Costanzi, wrote an epigram recounting how when the giraffe was led through the streets, she gracefully accepted tasty nibbles from her admirers. Tame and gentle, she delicately ate from the hands of children who offered her bread, hay, and fruit.

A giraffe's tongue is some seventeen inches long, thin, and purple, and it torques as it pulls in food. The animal uses it with great subtlety and can take bits of fruit or leaves in the daintiest way from human fingers — or from ladies' hats, as has happened in modern zoos. Lorenzo's exotic belle developed a particularly affectionate rapport with the second stories of the noble houses of the city, where she went every day to receive sumptuous morsels from the hands of the ladies who adopted her. Docile and clever, she mesmerized the Florentines with her sweet disposition, large moist eyes, and attentive ears, as well as the elegant way in which she turned her long neck to gaze at her surroundings.

News of the giraffe traveled across Italy and even to other countries. On December 20 the Signoria dispatched a letter to the Florentine consul in Pera (Constantinople) informing him of the visit of the Mamluk ambassador with the giraffe and asking that the Ottoman sultan Bayezid be notified of this event (of course, not only because of the giraffe itself but also because of its role in the Djem affair). Anne of France was also apprised of the giraffe's arrival and waited with great impatience for the animal Lorenzo had promised her.

Lorenzo took the greatest care of his beguiling pet. He installed her in special stables on the Via della Scala and made sure her lodgings were kept heated through the winter months so she would not get sick in the damp cold of Florence. He probably regretted having to part with her, but she had already brought him new respect across Italy and Europe, and all the way to Constantinople. Now it was time for him to fulfill his side of the bargain with Qaitbay.

In June 1488 Lorenzo wrote to the sultan, recommending to his favor a Florentine ambassador, Luigi della Stufa, who was to accompany Malfota on his journey back to Cairo to discuss the emended commercial treaty. En route the two would stop in Rome to obtain the pope's permission to buy Qaitbay the weapons he needed for his war against Bayezid. The pope forbade arms sales to the infidels, but the Venetians, for whom business superseded religious scruples, had long been ignoring the ban and selling arms to the Ottomans, while carefully erasing any evidence of such sales from their books. Qaitbay — who hoped that if Djem were not sent to Egypt, he would at least be brought into the custody of the pope — did not want to antagonize the Holy Father with an illicit arms deal. So he asked Lorenzo to facilitate negotiations with Innocent VIII. The talks went well, and on January 17, 1489, the Florentine ambassador reported to Lorenzo that the weapons had been purchased with papal authorization. After some delays and hassles, the delegation finally sailed from Naples to Alexandria with its cargo of arms.

Lorenzo continued his efforts on behalf of Qaitbay. In March 1489 Djem was brought from France to Rome to be placed in the custody of the pope. On November 18 of that year, Qaitbay, obviously pleased with Lorenzo's help, wrote to him that he had granted the petition of the Florentine ambassador and had ordered the writing of the final copy of commercial privileges for Florentine merchants. A thirty-two-article document stipulated that "when one of the Florentine merchants or one of their community arrives at the God-guarded port of Alexandria or another of the Islamic ports and discharges his goods, such as cloth or silk or soap or olive oil or hazelnuts or antimony or sulphur or coral or other . . . such commodities, that the importer of those be secured in respect of his person and of his goods, and that he may sell for cash or by barter to whom he chooses, and no one shall trouble him nor extort from him even a single dirham."

Meanwhile, back home Lorenzo was also reaping the results of his diplomacy. In January 1488 his daughter Maddalena was married to the decadent Franceschetto Cibo. And on March 19, 1489, Lorenzo received the news he had dreamt about for years: his thirteen-year-old son, Giovanni, was made a cardinal by Innocent VIII (and though he had never studied legal texts, the boy was also awarded a doctorate in canon law). The pope stipulated that because the new cardinal was so scandalously young, his appointment must be kept secret for three years, but of course Lorenzo could not wait to tell the world, and the pope let him get away with immediate disclosure. The news echoed across Italy.

Florence erupted in celebrations. Lorenzo, beside himself with joy, declared that this was "the greatest honor ever conferred upon our house." In fact, this was only the beginning. In 1513, after Lorenzo's death, Giovanni de' Medici would become Pope Leo X. Ten years later, his first cousin, the illegitimate son of the murdered Giuliano, would ascend the papal throne as Clement VII. The two Medici popes would ensure that members of the Medici family would rule Florence as grand duke of Tuscany for the next three centuries. And they would also intermarry with the French royal house (Clement VII arranged the marriage of Catherine de' Medici to the future Henry II of France in 1533, and Maria de' Medici wed King Henry IV in 1600). All this was set in motion when Lorenzo procured the cardinal's hat for his son.

From that moment on, Lorenzo enjoyed complete influence with the pope, and those seeking Innocent's favor would beseech him for help. As the ambassador from d'Este court reported, "The pope sleeps with the eyes of Lorenzo." The peninsula's great power broker had risen at last to the position to which he had aspired through all his perils and hardships. As he had hoped it would, Lorenzo's authority abroad translated into greater control over Florence. In his final years he ruled the city more or less as a dictator. He strolled around surrounded by an armed escort and a caravan of aides, friends, and sycophants, while other prominent citizens, pushed out of decision making, were reduced to watching from the sidelines.

The deal between Lorenzo and Qaitbay that hinged on the exchange of Djem for the giraffe worked out better for the two rulers than for their pawns. Djem, still a political hostage, died in February 1495 in Naples, where he had been taken by King Charles VIII of France, Anne's brother. Charles had come to conquer Italy in 1494 and compelled the pope to hand over the Ottoman prince for use in his own planned crusade.

As for the giraffe, she did not live even that long. Her new home proved her undoing. Giraffes are nervous beasts, which makes them dangerous to transport, as they are liable to break their necks by suddenly twisting about in their traveling boxes. This is what seems to have happened to Lorenzo's Egyptian beauty. One day her head got stuck in the beams of the barn in which she was kept with so much care. Panicked, she must have jerked her head too hard, breaking her neck and collapsing dead on the floor, to the grief of Lorenzo and the entire city. One chronicler says that the sad event occurred as early as January 1488; another claims that the giraffe lived a while longer. In April 1489 Anne of France nudged Lorenzo to forward the promised animal:

> You know that formerly you advised me in writing that you would send me the giraffe, and although I am sure that you will keep your promise, I beg you, nevertheless, to deliver the animal to me and send it this way, so that you may understand the affection I have for it; for this is the beast of the world that I have the greatest desire to see. And if there is anything on this side I can do for you, I shall apply myself to it with all my heart.

But by then there was nothing to send; the poor creature was dead. Lorenzo's agent in France suggested placating the queen with some exotic Egyptian perfume.

Lorenzo himself died in April 1492, at age forty-three, from gout, the illness that had also killed his grandfather and father. In his last years he also suffered from arthritis, stomach and kidney problems, and asthma. It is astonishing that he achieved so much given his dismal health. Yet even after his death, the giraffe continued to define Lorenzo's political triumph. In the mid-sixteenth century, when Medici control over Florence became absolute, Grand Duke Cosimo I de' Medici decided to turn the former republican town hall into his private home. He had each room of the remodeled palazzo decorated with paintings that extolled his ancestors' most notable deeds. In the room devoted to Lorenzo, he ordered his court painter Giorgio Vasari to create a center-piece for the ceiling: a tableau of Lorenzo's greatest feats. The three brightest spots in the painting are Lorenzo in a light blue gown, his young son in the crimson cardinal's robe kneeling before him, and the tawny-colored giraffe.

Although it may seem strange to us, it was not the arts and letters that Cosimo I celebrated as Lorenzo's crowning glories, but the exotic animal sent by Sultan Qaitbay to the "king of Florence." The splendid beast was one of many political instruments Lorenzo employed to build his power and enhance the position of the Medici. But it was clearly seen by his successors — and mythologizers — as the finest symbol of his ascent.

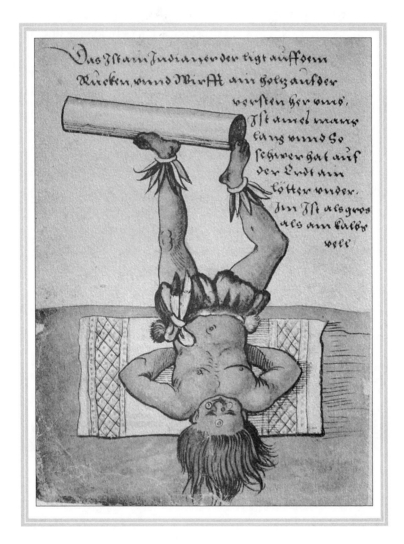

Das Ist ain Indianer der ligt auff dem
Rucken, vnnd Wirfft ain holz aus der
versten her vmb,
Ist auch manns
lang vnnd so
schwer hat auff
der Erdt ain
klötter vnder,
Im Ist als gros
als ain kalbs
vell

FOUR

HUMAN ANIMALS IN THE NEW
WORLD AND THE OLD

O, the strange bestiality of these people, in many things
they have good discipline, government, understanding,
capacity and polish but, in others, strange bestiality
and blindness.

DIEGO DURÁN,
The History of the Indies of New Spain

In the spring of 1528, seven years after conquering the Aztec
Empire, Hernán Cortés returned to Spain to reclaim his
authority and reputation. He had sacked and taken over the
Mexican capital, Tenochtitlán, in the summer of 1521 and a year
later was nominated governor and captain-general of New Spain.
Not yet forty years old, he was at the peak of his power. Bursting
with ambition for further glory, he set off in 1524 to subjugate the
land that would later be called Honduras, departing with a cavalcade of several thousand, including native kings and jugglers,
dancers and harpists, jesters and Franciscan friars.

Two years later he staggered back to Mexico with a bedraggled
group of fewer than one hundred survivors, only to find a judge
from Spain come to set in motion a commission of inquiry against
him. The judge soon died, having eaten bad bacon at Cortés's
table. Another Spanish magistrate promptly followed the first.
Suspicions of poisoning swarmed around the conqueror, and his

friends in Spain warned him that enemies were circulating serious political charges. Cortés decided it was time to sail home, to argue his merits personally before the ruler of Spain, the Holy Roman Emperor Charles V.

To show what he had added to Spain's overseas possessions, Cortés filled two vessels with the riches and wonders of the Aztec realm. Into the holds went 20,000 gold pesos, 10,000 pesos' worth of unminted gold, 1,500 marks of silver, many jewels, splendid feather-decorated mantles and fans, intricately sculpted scepters and obsidian mirrors, and other exquisite Aztec artifacts. Locked in stout wooden cages were jaguars, ocelots, and other wild cats native to the New World; pelicans and brightly plumed parrots; and two animals entirely new to Europe: an armadillo, which the Spanish named after its armored appearance, and an opossum, which, according to Cortés's secretary Francisco López de Gómara, taught its offspring to eat while in the mother's pouch. But most remarkable were the human specimens: male and female dwarfs and hunchbacks, a band of men and women "whiter than Germans" (albinos), Aztec jugglers and ballplayers, and Mexican noblemen — including three of the vanquished emperor Montezuma's sons, who wore opulent feather mantles and sported jewels set into their foreheads, cheeks, noses, and lips. Arriving in Spain with this astonishing retinue, Cortés, one contemporary marveled, "came as a great lord."

Cortés was not the first European explorer and conqueror to bring home barbaric strangers — Columbus had transported a number of natives from his voyages to the New World — but Cortés's troupe made the greatest impact. The Aztecs were representatives of a highly developed civilization that tantalized the European imagination, thanks to the wide circulation of Cortés's letters to his sovereign. Yet these people were also seen as aliens with murderous habits of human sacrifice and ritual cannibalism. By including these impressive savages in his suite, along with the unusual white-haired and pale-skinned humans who had previously served as treasured pets in Montezuma's menagerie, Cortés signaled that he had tamed the mighty barbarians. And whatever his enemies said about him, he would show that he deserved to rule the Aztec realm on behalf of the crown.

How did the fierce and proud Aztecs end up as trained monkeys on a Spanish chain? What did the Spaniards make of them? What did "human" and "animal" mean to the Spaniards — and to the Aztecs? The slippery boundary between men and beasts bedeviled the encounter between Old Europe and the New World.

NINE YEARS EARLIER, on November 8, 1519, the sons of Montezuma and their fellow citizens watched with unease and awe as a small Spanish army streamed into their capital, Tenochtitlán. White men with fair hair and beards, covered in suits of steel, rode in on strange, massive animals that forcefully pawed the ground, glistened with sweat, and emitted terrifying neighs. Preceding the riders ran huge dogs (unknown to the natives), sniffing furiously at unfamiliar smells, panting, and barking. Troops of foot soldiers shimmered menacingly with their armor, lances, and swords.

Who were these strangers, and who was their leader — a fair, youthful man with a plume of feathers waving atop his helmet and a gold medallion shining on his chest? Was he a god or a divine ancestor returning home with his companions, as the emperor Montezuma believed? Or was he the leader of pillaging invaders who came from across the sea "to rob and to conquer," as the emperor's brother Cuitláhuac had warned? Should the strangers be welcomed and revered as deities, or captured as enemy warriors and sacrificed to the gods?

Cortés and his band of three or four hundred Spaniards in turn looked apprehensively at the inquisitive faces of the Aztecs.

The causeway into the city, recalled Bernal Díaz del Castillo, a Spanish adventurer who took part in the expedition and later wrote a vivid chronicle of it, "broad as it is, was so crowded with people that there was hardly room for . . . all . . . who had come out to see us, so that we were hardly able to pass by the crowds of them that came; and the towers and quays were full of people as well as the canoes from all parts of the lake. It was not to be wondered at, for they had never before seen horses or men such as we are." The Spaniards' eyes darted between the teeming masses of tense inhabitants and the beautiful views of the city opening up ahead.

Tenochtitlán was a stunning place. The Spaniards had heard that the city was rich, but they had anticipated a settlement of savages. Yet here, miraculously, rose a metropolis wealthier and more stately than any they had encountered in Europe: a Venice of the New World. In a report to Charles V, Cortés himself gushed:

> Most Powerful Lord, in order to give an account to Your Royal Excellency of the magnificence, the strange and marvelous things of this great city of Temixtitan [sic] and of the dominion and wealth of this Mutezuma [sic], its ruler, and of the rites and customs of the people, and of the order there is in the government of the capital as well as in the other cities of Mutezuma's dominions, I would need much time and many expert narrators. I cannot describe the hundredth part of all the things which could be mentioned, but, as best I can, I will describe some of those I have seen which . . . will, I well know, be so remarkable as not to be believed, for we who saw them with our own eyes could not grasp them with our understanding.

Tenochtitlán was built to impress. Its very setting was spectacular: a city perched on an oval island measuring some five square miles, set in the middle of Lake Texcoco, in the vast

Valley of Mexico, situated 7,250 feet above the sea and ringed by forested mountains. Two snowcapped volcanoes, Iztaccihautl and Popocatepetl, loomed majestically in the distance. "At the top of this mountain [Popocatepetl], which is a quarter of a league around," wrote an anonymous conquistador, "there is a crater from which a great column of smoke issues furiously twice a day and sometimes at night. No matter how strong the wind is, the smoke rises as high as the first bank of the clouds without dispersing, and mixes with the clouds forming a solid mass."

The Valley of Mexico, Cortés estimated, was over two hundred miles in circumference: "In this plain there are two lakes which cover almost all of it. . . . One of these lakes is of fresh water and the other, which is larger, is of salt water. A small chain of very high hills which cuts across the middle of the plain separates these two lakes." Tenochtitlán was situated in the salty lake, the more turbulent of the two and subject to strong winds and currents, but also a great source of food. Its fish and turtles, insect larvae and green slime scooped off the surface — a great delicacy, said to taste like cheese — nourished its inhabitants and those of surrounding towns. Some fifty towns speckled the shores of the lakes, but only Tenochtitlán emerged directly out of the water — a disadvantage turned to great profit by the Mexica (as the Aztecs called themselves) and proof of their indomitable spirit. When the Mexica had arrived in this valley two centuries earlier, the low-lying island in the salt lake was the only remaining place to settle. The other tribes that had come here earlier had found it too undesirable to colonize. But the Mexica, resolute and fearless, set to work and turned it into a thriving and invincible capital. From it they conquered a vast empire.

Tenochtitlán was linked to the mainland by three artificial causeways, "each as wide as two cavalry lances" (about twenty feet), the Spaniards reckoned. The causeways converged at the center of the city and served as its main avenues. The rest of the streets were meticulously laid out on a grid, and many of them were canals, as in Venice. The city, wrote an anonymous conquistador, ". . . has many beautiful and wide streets, although except for two or three main streets all the avenues are water on one side and earth on the other. The people walk on the dirt side or ride canoes on the water. The canoes are of concave wood, and large enough sometimes to carry five people comfortably."

Francisco de Aguilar, one of Cortés's companions in arms, found the profusion of boats at the approach to Tenochtitlán threatening. "The water was so full of canoes loaded with people who were watching us that it was frightening to see such multitudes," he wrote. Aguilar and his fellows had good reason to worry. They were vastly outnumbered by the inhabitants of the city — some quarter of a million of them to three or four hundred Spaniards and a few hundred of their recently co-opted native allies. And the Spaniards had already witnessed the gruesome human sacrifices practiced by the Aztecs.

As Cortés marched toward Tenochtitlán, Montezuma did his utmost to honor the stranger and his company while keeping them at bay. The Aztec emperor was filled with dread at the news of Cortés's approach: "His soul was sickened, his heart anguished." Was the fair newcomer the bloodthirsty god of the sun and war, Huitzilopochtli? The more benign Quetzalcoatl? The mercurial Tezcatlipoca, god of "affliction and anguish," who enjoyed cheating people out of their property and "brought all things down"? Or some other divinity? Whoever he was, his advance spelled trouble.

To conciliate the mysterious foreigner, Montezuma plied him with lavish gifts. Among other offerings, an Aztec chronicler recounted, Montezuma

> sent captives to be sacrificed, because the strangers might
> wish to drink their blood [as Aztec gods liked to do]. The envoys sacrificed these captives in the presence of the strangers,
> but when the white men saw this done, they were filled with

disgust and loathing. They spat on the ground, or wiped away their tears, or closed their eyes and shook their heads in abhorrence. They refused to eat the food that was sprinkled with blood, because it reeked of it; it sickened them, as if the blood had rotted.

Fear and apprehension gripped both sides. While the Spaniards were en route to Tenochtitlán, Montezuma's messengers anxiously reported to their lord that "the strangers' bodies are completely covered, so that only their faces can be seen. Their skin is white as if they were made of lime. They have yellow hair, though some of them have black. Their beards are long and yellow, and their moustaches are also yellow. Their hair is curly, with very fine strands." Montezuma was amazed. The Mexica did not grow beards, or only very thin ones, and they cut their hair short and wore loose, open clothes. White skin was so rare among them that those who possessed it were collected in the emperor's zoo.

The newcomers' animals were equally strange and terrifying, as horses were unknown in Mexico. "Their deer," which is how the messengers interpreted the horses brought by the conquistadors, "carry them on their backs wherever they wish to go. These deer, our lord, are as tall as the roof of a house." "Their dogs," the messengers continued, referring to the fighting hounds and mastiffs brought along by the Spaniards as live weapons of war, "are enormous, with flat ears and long, dangling tongues. The color of their eyes is a burning yellow; their eyes flash fire and shoot off sparks. Their bellies are hollow, their flanks long and narrow. They are tireless and very powerful. They bound here and there, panting, with their tongues hanging out. And they are spotted like an ocelot." Another Aztec echoed, these "wild animals on leashes" were "so ferocious that they ate people." This may well have been an exaggeration, but the Spaniards' dogs were trained for attack and were fearsome to the Aztecs, who only had small, plump, silent dogs, which they raised for food.

The appearance and behavior of the Mexica were equally bizarre to the Spaniards. As they entered Tenochtitlán, they gaped at the men who, shockingly, wore nothing but loincloths and blankets knotted at the right shoulder and hung under the left arm. The commoners' blankets were coarse, made of maguey fibers or rough cotton, while those of rich merchants and noblemen were visibly softer and more elegant, woven of fine cotton and decorated with colorful designs. Elite warriors looked fierce in tall feather headdresses and costumes made to resemble eagles and jaguars.

The women's dress seemed more familiar: brightly embroidered white cotton wraparound skirts and loose tunics tied with narrow belts. But why did some women think it attractive to paint their faces yellow with ocher and to draw red patterns on their cheeks? It was fine that they dyed their hair with indigo to make it glisten. But staining their teeth scarlet with cochineal? Some men, too, looked menacing in their makeup of bars, stripes, and dots of red, green, blue, or black pigment. The Spaniards greedily eyed the profusion of gold, silver, and obsidian jewelry worn by Aztec nobles. But while the women glittered in fairly normal earrings, the men deformed their ears with large plugs and passed bulky ornaments through the septa of their noses and through holes in their lower lips. More attractive, though still peculiar, was the Aztec custom allowing only the upper classes to carry and smell bouquets of fragrant flowers.

The most striking sight was the emperor Montezuma himself. He came out to welcome the foreigners, since all his attempts to thwart their arrival had failed. He had certainly tried every trick. He had claimed his own ill health and a shortage of food. He had sent magicians to make the intruders turn back and had had his ambassador tell Cortés that his zoo was full of fierce animals and reptiles that would tear the Spaniards to shreds if they were let loose. All this made Cortés only more intent on reaching the capital. Clearly Montezuma had great riches that he was trying to keep from the Spaniards. Now good manners obliged the emperor to greet the unstoppable strangers with pomp. Looking majestic in his richly embroidered cloak, tall headdress of green quetzal feathers, and gold sandals studded with precious stones, Montezuma rode out in a litter carried by noblemen and profusely adorned with fragrant flowers and cacao blossoms, wreaths, garlands, and gold bands. The litter's canopy of green feathers was embellished with gold and silver embroidery and jade fittings. A group of noblemen preceded the emperor, sweeping the ground before him.

Montezuma welcomed Cortés with words that mixed customary hospitality with submissiveness, in case the stranger really was a god. "Our lord," he said through interpreters, "you must be tired, you have experienced fatigue, but you have arrived at your city." He then told Cortés of "the lord who brought us, the Mexica, to Tenochtitlán," and explained the Aztec belief that "those who descended from him would one day come back . . . and take us as vassals." Linking Cortés with that sacred progenitor, Montezuma went on, "So be assured that we will obey you and hold you as our lord, in the stead of that great lord. . . . And in all the lands which I hold in my power you can command as you will, for you will be obeyed."

Cortés interpreted Montezuma's welcome as a concession of power and assessed the imperial capital with an eye to reigning over it. "The city itself is as big as Seville or Córdoba," he wrote in his report to Charles V.

[It] has many squares where trading is done and markets are held continuously. There is also one square twice as big as that of Salamanca, with arcades all around, where more than sixty thousand people come each day to buy and sell, and where every kind of merchandise produced in these lands is found; provisions as well as ornaments of gold and silver, lead, brass, copper, tin, stones, shells, bones, and feathers. . . . There is a street where they sell game and birds of every species found in this land: chickens [actually turkeys; there were no chickens in Mexico], partridges and quails, wild ducks, fly-catchers, widgeons, turtledoves, pigeons, cane birds, parrots, eagles and eagle owls, falcons, sparrow hawks and kestrels, and they sell the skins of some of these birds of prey with their feathers, heads, and claws. They sell rabbits and hares, and stags, and small gelded dogs which they breed for eating.

Small hairless dogs called *itzcuintlis* (they looked something like Chihuahuas) were a staple of the local diet. The Aztecs had no pigs, goats, cows, or sheep, but they raised several varieties of edible canines. Diego Durán, a Dominican friar from Seville who came to New Spain as a child, learned Nahuatl (the language of the Aztecs), and wrote *The History of the Indies of New Spain* based on interviews with natives and a close study of their history and culture, recorded that

it was established that dogs were to be sold in the periodic market at Acolman and that all those desirous of selling or buying were to go there. Most of the produce . . . consisted of small- and medium-sized dogs of all types, and everyone in the land went to buy dogs there. . . . One day I went to observe the market day there, just to be an eyewitness and discover the truth. I found more than 400 large and small dogs tied up in crates, some already sold, others still for sale. When a Spaniard who was totally familiar with that region saw my amazement, he asked, "Why are you so astonished? I have never seen such a meager sale of dogs as today!"

It seems, however, that dog meat was considered inferior to turkey. Another Spanish chronicler, Bernardino de Sahagún, commented that "in dishes the turkey-meat was put on top, and the dog underneath, to make it seem more." But perhaps he misunderstood, and it was the other way around: could the tastiest morsels have been saved for last?

The Spaniards were bedazzled by Tenochtitlán's thriving commerce: "Among us were soldiers who had been in many parts of the world, at Constantinople, all over Italy and at Rome; and they said they had never seen a market so well ordered, so large and so crowded with people."

Of the merchandise sold in Tenochtitlán, some was brought in as trade, but vast quantities were delivered as tribute. The Mexica waged constant wars to enlarge their empire, gather its riches, and obtain captives to be sacrificed to the gods, who required regular doses of human blood. Their weapons may at first have seemed primitive to the Spaniards, but the Mexica were skillful in wielding their slings, arrows, and obsidian-tipped spears. In their battles with the conquistadors, their *macana* — paddle-shaped wooden clubs edged with obsidian blades — beheaded Spanish horses with a single stroke. At times the bold Aztec kings went to war over a specific luxury resource: one sent out a military expedition to Tlaxiaco, in Oaxaca, to obtain *tlapalizqquixíchitl,* a tree bearing beautiful perfumed flowers.

In only two centuries the Mexica had extended their domain from an island in the middle of the lake to a realm stretching from the Pacific to the Gulf coasts and from central Mexico to present-day Guatemala. By 1519 Montezuma ruled over a mosaic of 38 provinces and some 450 cities. As long as they paid tribute, the conquered cities and provinces retained their political and administrative autonomy. But if they rebelled, the Aztec army marched in and meted out cruel punishment.

The range of tribute delivered to Tenochtitlán by the Mexica's far-flung vassals was vividly conveyed by Diego Durán:

Great quantities of gold, in dust and worked as jewels.
Large amounts of green stones [jade], of crystal, of carnelian, bloodstones, amber, besides many other types of stone which

these people loved greatly. The basis of their idolatry was the adoration of these stones together with the feathers which they called, "Shadow of the gods." These feathers were multi-colored or green, blue, red, yellow, purple, white and striped.

Vast amounts of cacao.

Cotton in large bundles, both white and yellow. . . .

Exceedingly rich mantles for the lords, differently woven and worked, some of them had rich fringes done in colors and feather work; others had insignia on them, others serpent heads, others ocelot heads, others the image of the Sun, and yet others had skulls, or blowguns, figures of the gods — all of them embroidered in many colored threads and enriched with the down of ducks, all beautifully and curiously worked. . . .

Live birds, too, sent by the Chichimecs — green, red, blue; parrots large and small; other splendid and handsomely colored birds such as eagles, buzzards, hawks, sparrow hawks, ravens, herons and wild geese.

Wild animals such as ocelots, jaguars, wildcats. All of these fierce animals were brought in cages.

Great and small snakes, some poisonous, others not, some fierce, others harmless.

It was marvelous to see the great variety of snakes and other small beasts that were brought in large pots. Vassals even paid tribute in centipedes, scorpions and spiders! The Aztecs were Lords of All Creation; everything belonged to them, everything was theirs!

From the coast came everything that could be found in the sea; scallop shells, large and small snails, curious fish bones, large turtle shells, great and small turtles, stones from the sea, pearls baroque and smooth, amber stones.

From other places were brought deer and rabbits and quail, some uncooked and others in barbecue. As tribute also came gophers, weasels, and large rodents, which thrive in the woods.

Toasted locusts, winged ants, large cicadas and little ones, in addition to other small animals. Those who lived near lagoons sent everything that thrives in the water, such as algae, a certain type of insect that walks on the water, and small worms.

There was also tribute of food and flowers, clothing for men and women, armor and weapons for warriors. "Provinces that lacked foodstuffs and clothes paid in maidens, girls and boys, who were divided among the lords — all slaves. . . . There were such vast quantities of all these things that came to the city of Mexico," Durán summed up, "that not a day passed without the arrival of people from other regions who brought large amounts of everything, from foodstuffs to luxury items, for the king and for the lords."

The flow of all these goods and creatures into the Valley of Mexico was all the more astonishing because the Aztecs did not have draft animals or wheeled transport. Most commodities were borne by human porters carrying loads of some fifty pounds on their backs. Securing the goods in woven cane containers strapped to carrying frames and covered with hides to protect the contents, they marched in relay fashion, traveling about fifteen miles a day. Larger and bulkier items, such as caged animals, were carried by teams.

The amount and range of tribute sent to Tenochtitlán, Durán concluded, showed "the magnificence and strength of the Aztec nation and how they came to be called and held to be lords of all created things, upon the waters as well as upon the earth."

Seeking to further impress the foreigners, Montezuma proudly showed them one of the highlights of his capital: the Great Temple at its heart, "so large that within the precincts, which are surrounded by a very high wall, a town of some five hundred inhabitants could easily be built," opined Cortés. From the summit of the Great Temple opened a stunning panorama of the city.

Montezuma pointed out to his guests the causeways and the orderly grid of streets and canals, the sprawl of adobe houses with picturesque gardens on their flat roofs, the vast marketplace, and the sumptuous royal residences that included lush botanical gardens and, of course, the emperor's famous zoo. To the Aztecs and to their allies and foes, all these sights were evidence of the undisputed and far-flung authority of the emperor. To Cortés they were an appetite-whetting preview of the realm he intended to make his own.

AT THAT TIME Cortés was thirty-four years old. Of medium height, about five feet four inches, he was thin and bowlegged, with broad shoulders, a barrel chest, pale skin, long fair hair, and a thin fair beard. Hailing from a modest but cocky hidalgo (lowest nobility) family from Medellín, in Castile, he was keen to attain riches and glory in the New World. As a youth he had studied law briefly at the University of Salamanca but gave it up in favor of a military career. Sailing west in 1504, at age nineteen, he quickly distinguished himself in the suppression of a native revolt in Hispaniola and in the conquest of Cuba. "Always a leader in war as well as in peace," according to Francisco López de Gómara, Cortés was courageous and charismatic, imaginative and ruthless, and fond of pleasure and pomp.

He was much given to consorting with women, and always gave himself to them. The same was true with his gaming, and he played at dice marvelously well and merrily. He loved eating, but was temperate in drink, although he did not stint himself. . . . He was a very stubborn man, as a result of which he had more lawsuits than was proper to his station. He spent liberally on war, women, friends, and fancies, although in other things he was close, which got him the name of new-rich. In his dress he was elegant rather than sumptuous, and was extremely neat. He took delight in a large household and family, in silver service and dignity. He bore himself nobly, with such gravity and prudence that he never gave offence or seemed unapproachable.

Another Spaniard, Bartolomé de Las Casas, said that Cortés behaved as if he were a lofty lord, "as if he had been born in brocade." No wonder the conquistador was impressed with Montezuma's court and covetous of his empire.

Motecuhzoma Xocoyotzin (the proper name of the anglicized Montezuma) was, at the time of the Spaniards' arrival, "about forty years old," Bernal Díaz del Castillo guessed,

of good height and well-proportioned, slender and spare of flesh, not very swarthy, but of the natural color and shade of an Indian. He did not wear his hair long, but so as just to cover his ears; his scanty black beard was well shaped and thin. His face was somewhat long, but cheerful, and he had good eyes and showed in his appearance and manner both tenderness and, when necessary, gravity. He was very neat and clean and bathed once every day in the afternoon.

— a marked contrast with the inattentive grooming habits of most Spaniards.

According to Gómara, Montezuma was

of an amiable though severe disposition, affable, well-spoken, and gracious, which made him respected and feared. Moctezuma [*sic*] means a furious and solemn man. . . . His people endowed him with such majesty that they would not sit in his presence, or wear shoes, or look him in the face, with the exception of only a few great lords. . . . He changed his [clothes] four times a day and never wore the same garment twice. His used garments were saved and given as rewards and presents to servants and messengers, or, as a token of favor and privilege, to soldiers who had fought and captured an enemy. The many and beautiful mantles that he sent to Cortés were of such.

Francisco de Aguilar added that "he was very astute, discerning and prudent, learned and capable, but also harsh and irascible, and very firm in his speech." The emperor himself told Cortés that the way to rule was to inspire people with fear, not affection. The Spaniards perceived Montezuma as more amiable than fierce, but they still took him prisoner, putting him under house arrest shortly after arriving in Tenochtitlán in order to gain greater control over the city. Through a combination of flattery and threats, Cortés succeeded in turning the ferocious warrior into a meek lamb, as Montezuma was too afraid of the Spaniards' terrifying fire weapons, huge and aggressive animals, and potentially divine nature to resist his captors.

Cortés intended to rule Tenochtitlán through Montezuma as his puppet king, so while keeping the Aztec emperor under close Spanish guard, Cortés allowed him to continue his royal lifestyle. Montezuma's regal conduct and elaborate court etiquette were awe inspiring and comparable to those of the loftiest European and Muslim rulers. At dinner "his dishes were brought in by four hundred pages, gentlemen's sons," Gómara marveled.

Moctezuma would enter and look over [the prepared dishes], pointing to those he liked, whereupon they would be set on braziers of live coals, to keep them warm and preserve their flavor. . . . Before he sat down to eat, as many as twenty of his wives would enter, the most beautiful or shapely, or those serving their weekly turn, who very humbly brought him his food, after which he sat down. . . . During his meals he would listen to the music of pipes, flutes, conches, bone fifes, drums, and other instruments of the kind, for they have no better ones, nor can they sing, I say, because they do not know how, and their voices are bad besides. Always present at his meals were dwarfs, hunchbacks, cripples, and so on, all for his entertainment and amusement, and these, along with the jesters and mountebanks, were given the leavings to eat at one end of the hall.

If the Spaniards were impressed by the lavish and varied entertainments at Montezuma's court, they would be even more astonished by his encyclopedic menagerie. In fact, nothing captured their imagination more, or came to symbolize more clearly both the civilization and the savagery of the Aztecs, than the emperor's zoo.

This collection — which, along with his great hunting parks, Montezuma continued to visit — was the most extensive and well-managed animal assemblage anywhere in the world. Even Cortés, whose chief preoccupation was gold — as much of it to be squeezed from the emperor as possible — devoted more space and time to his account of the zoo than to any other aspect of Tenochtitlán. He wrote to Charles V only briefly about Montezuma's palace, built of alabaster, jasper, and black stone with veins of red and white, and adorned with images of eagles and jaguars.* But he described the zoo at great length.

There was one section, set in a lovely garden devoted to birds, that the emperor came to admire from specially constructed

---

*"He had," Cortés reported, "both inside the city and outside, many private residences, each one for a particular pastime. . . . The palace inside the city in which he lived was so marvelous that it seemed to me impossible to describe its excellence and grandeur. Therefore, I shall not attempt to describe it at all, save to say that in Spain there is nothing to compare with it." This was quite a daring declaration to the Spanish ruler.

observation balconies. Cortés and Gómara noted here "lanners, hawks, kites, vultures, goshawks, nine or ten varieties of falcons, and many kinds of eagles, among which were some fifty a great deal larger than our red-tails. . . . All these birds were given chickens [turkeys] to eat each day and no other food." Gómara marveled that at one feeding each of the birds of prey would eat "a turkey of the country, which is larger than our peacock. . . . They consumed some 500 turkeys every day." A separate staff of three hundred servants waited on these birds, "not counting the hunters, who were numberless."

In addition to the birds of prey, Montezuma also assembled a profusion of waterfowl in ten different pools. The seabirds were kept in a saltwater pool, the river fowl in fresh water, both kinds of basins being regularly drained, cleaned, and refilled. A staff of three hundred men cared for these birds, making sure that each species received the same kind of food it ate in the wild, be it fish, worms, or grain, and taking care of any sick creatures. Gómara added that "some [caretakers] cleaned the ponds; others caught fish for [the birds]; others fed them; others deloused them; others guarded the eggs; others threw out the brooders; and still others had the most important duty of plucking them. Of the feathers, rich mantles, tapestries, shields, plumes, flyflaps, and many other things were made, adorned with gold and silver, of exquisite workmanship."

Feather mosaic was a spectacular New World art form. Bartolomé de Las Casas, a great advocate of the Aztecs, wrote admiringly that

> the activity in which they seem to excel over all other human intellects and which makes them appear unique among the nations of the earth is the craft they have perfected of representing with real feathers, in all their natural colors, all the things that . . . other excellent painters can paint with brushes. They used to make many different things of feathers, including animals, birds,

men, cloaks or mantles, apparel for the priests . . . , shields
and flyswatters, and a thousand other things. The feathers they
used were green, red, golden, purple, crimson, yellow, blue or
pale green, black and white, and all other colors, mixed and
pure. None was tinted by human industry, but all were natural,
taken from different birds. For this reason these people greatly
valued all sorts of birds and made use of every variety.

Feathers of parrots, macaws, quetzals, and other colorful birds
were sent as tribute to the capital from lowland provinces and
cloud forests. Sorted by professionals, the dazzling plumes were
carefully fastened onto net backings of cotton or vegetable fibers
and made into splendid garments, accessories, and works of art.
Objects adorned with feathers counted among the most valuable
in Aztec culture. Feather fans were signs of rank and symbols of
ambassadors. Tunics made of quetzal feathers — plucked from a
sacred bird with iridescent emerald plumage — were bestowed
only on the loftiest men for supreme achievement.[*]

The most unusual feature of the aviary, however, was "a room
in which were kept men, women, and children who had, from
birth, white faces and bodies and white hair, eyebrows and eye-
lashes." They were considered so unusual as to be "almost miraculous, so seldom did they occur."

According to Aztec legend, the Mexica hailed from a land
called Aztlán, which means "Whiteness" or "Place of the Herons."
As native lore had it, upon arriving on the island in the middle
of Lake Texcoco, the Mexica wandered among the reeds and

---

[*]Cortés sent as a present to Charles V a spectacular Aztec royal headdress
made of 450 long quetzal tail feathers (plucked from 225 birds) arranged in the
form of a fan. Originally this fan was mounted on a pure gold helmet, but the
Spaniards melted it down into bars. Still, the feathered crown, 45¼ inches tall
and 69 inches wide, amazed the emperor and was passed down through the
Habsburg family as a treasured heirloom. Today the headdress, its radiant beauty
undiminished by time, resides in Vienna's Museum of Ethnology.

rushes, looking for a permanent home. In Durán's transcription of the story,

> They came upon a beautiful spring and saw wondrous things in the waters . . . a juniper tree, all white and very beautiful, and the spring came forth from the foot of this tree . . . a group of willows around the spring, all white, without a single green leaf. The reeds there were white also, and so were the rushes surrounding the water. White frogs and fish came out of the water. There were water snakes, too, shiny and white. . . . The priests and elders, remembering what their god had told them, wept with joy and became exuberant, crying out: "We have now found the promised land."

Given this symbolism, the Mexica valued albinos and people with very white skin as special creatures — part human, part divine. Gathered into the house where Montezuma kept his most important and sacred birds, as well as his personal treasury of gold, silver, jewels, and feather work, these precious captives were attended by keepers and regularly admired by their owner, who seems to have been untroubled by enclosing humans in a zoo.

Montezuma's menagerie was not limited to majestic birds and miraculous humans. In the house next to the aviary, Cortés continued, "there were several large low rooms filled with big cages, made from heavy timbers and very well joined. In all, or in most of them, were large numbers of lions, tigers, wolves, foxes and cats of various kinds." Actually, the wild cats were probably jaguars, pumas, and ocelots native to Mexico, rather than lions and tigers, which live in Africa, but Cortés and other Spaniards did not know Mexican animals and were interpreting them through European eyes.

The variety of fauna assembled by Montezuma prompted Gómara to declare:

There was no kind of four-footed beast that was not represented, and all for the purpose of Moctezuma's being able to boast that, however fierce they might be, he dared to keep them in his house. They were fed turkeys, deer, dogs, and game. In other rooms, in great earthenware jars, pots, and vessels filled with water or earth, reptiles were kept, such as boa constrictors, vipers, crocodiles [revered by the Aztecs and imported from the lowland jungle] . . . , lizards of other kinds, and suchlike vermin, as well as land and water snakes, fierce and poisonous, and ugly enough to frighten the beholder.*

Gómara noted with awe an amazing number of keepers taking care of birds, beasts, and serpents in this house. But while "the diversity of the birds, the ferocity of the beasts, and the serpents swelling with poisonous fury" delighted the Spaniards, the animals also terrified them by "their frightful hissing, the hideous roaring of the lions, the howling of the wolves, the screams of the tigers and lynxes, and the yelps of the other animals, owing to hunger or perhaps to the thought that they were caged and could nor give vent to their fury. And truly, at night the place was a picture of hell and an abode of the devil."

What made the zoo still more unsettling to the Spaniards was its human denizens. As Cortés wrote in amazement, Montezuma kept "many deformed men and women . . . dwarfs and hunchbacks . . . and each manner of monstrosity had a room to itself; and likewise there were people to look after them." A number of Spaniards alleged to have heard that some of these cripples were broken and made crooked in babyhood for the glory of the king. Whether this is true or not, life for these unfortunates may well

---

*Díaz furnished further details about the "many vipers and poisonous snakes which carry on their tails things that sound like bells. These are the worst vipers of all, and they keep them in jars and great pottery vessels with many feathers, and they lay their eggs and rear their young."

have been easier in the royal menagerie, where they had their own quarters and keepers to tend and feed them, than in the wider world, where their survival would have been far less certain and their life an endless hardship. European rulers also retained as their pages one or two dwarfs, but nothing on the scale of Montezuma.

The Spaniards apparently found it barbaric to keep humans in cages. Yet anomalous humans at Montezuma's zoo received better treatment than noble warriors the Mexica captured in war and offered up to their bloodthirsty gods. Of course the Spaniards themselves at that very time were heading the Inquisition in Europe and feeling few qualms about burning heretics and torturing suspected religious subversives.

For Montezuma unusual humans were valuable natural specimens to be collected, cataloged, and enjoyed on a par with curious and mesmerizing birds and animals. The Aztecs revered nature and prized its study. Aztec children were educated in natural history, and "almost all," wrote a Spanish observer, "know the names of all the birds, animals, trees, and herbs, . . . and what they are good for." Montezuma's anthology of rare fauna enhanced his image as a lord over land and sea and as a sovereign of intellectual distinction.

Although other Aztec rulers had gathered flora and fauna, Montezuma's collection was the biggest, and the array of his exotic species conveyed his political control over a vast empire, as well as his affinity with the gods who ruled all creation. When he could not obtain or keep alive certain animals, he had court goldsmiths fashion exemplars in precious metals. Gómara wrote with delight that "they can cast a parrot that moves its tongue, head, and wings; a monkey that moves its feet and head, and holds a distaff in its hands, so naturally that it seems to be spinning, or an apple that it appears to be eating. All this was much admired by our men, for our silversmiths have not such skill."

A microcosm of Montezuma's empire, the zoo also served as an encyclopedia of its natural history. Mexico is one of the most biodiverse countries in the world, with 10 percent of the earth's flora and fauna. The abundance of wildlife stems from the region's wide variety of topographic and climatic zones, with hundreds of species thriving in each. Montezuma's animals came from all corners of his realm. And the quality of care given to the royal pets reflected a sophisticated knowledge of various species and their diets and health requirements.

For the Spaniards, however, the emperor's zoo was a source of puzzlement and unease. The Mexica were clearly an advanced people, yet their highly developed understanding of natural history, astronomy (they had an accurate 365-day calendar, divided into 18 months), town planning, and hygiene — "on all roads," noticed Díaz, "they have shelters made of reeds or straw or grass, so that the people can retire when they wish to do so, and purge their bowels unseen" — coexisted with technical backwardness. They lacked wheeled vehicles and beasts of burden, steel and nails, candles and pulleys, guns and warships. Yet Cortés wrote admiringly that "these people live almost like those in Spain, and in as much harmony and order as there, and considering that they are barbarous and so far from the knowledge of God and cut off from all civilized nations, it is truly remarkable to see what they have achieved in all things." No less bewildering was the contrast between the deluxe treatment of animals and deformed humans in Montezuma's menagerie and the readiness with which healthy and handsome people were sacrificed to the Aztec gods.

The Spaniards' anxiety about the nature of the emperor's zoo, of the Aztecs themselves, and of the tenuous boundary between men and beasts in this alien culture coalesced in their repeated claim that Montezuma's animals were fed the flesh of sacrificed humans. "The snakes and their mates were given the blood of men killed in sacrifice, to suck and lick, and some even say they were fed on the flesh, which the lizards devoured with great gusto." The picture of jaguars and crocodiles chomping on human carcasses was certainly hair-raising, if fed more by fevered imagination than fact. Sacrificial victims were deemed substitute gods by the Aztecs, so it would seem sacrilegious to turn them into animal feed. (It was a different matter when people ate sacrificed warriors to draw bravery and strength from their flesh.)

The Spaniards admitted that they did not personally witness animals feasting on humans, but they did assert that the ground of the animal and reptile pavilion was "all crusted with blood, as in the slaughterhouse, which stank horribly and quaked if a stick was thrust into it." The blood was probably that of the dogs, turkeys, and deer normally fed to the animals. Yet to the Spaniards it seemed all too likely that should they fall into the hands of the Aztecs, they would be sacrificed and eaten, whether by Aztec gods, animals, or men.

HUMAN SACRIFICE — ABHORRED by the Spaniards and constantly invoked by them as evidence of the Mexica's beastliness — stood at the heart of the Aztec religion. According to the Mexica foundation myth, the gods had sacrificed themselves for the good of humankind — the deities Nanauatzin and Tecuciztecatl threw themselves into a raging bonfire to create the sun and the moon, and Quetzalcoatl spilled his own blood to give birth to people — so humans were in divine debt. Sacrifice was a prerequisite for bringing forth new life.

There were hundreds of gods and goddesses in the Aztec pantheon, each representing a different aspect of existence. Not all of them called for the ultimate offering, but some required regular doses of human blood, in accordance with the agricultural calendar, to ensure good crops and the well-being of the community. And the supreme Aztec divinity Huitzilopochtli, god of war and the sun, had to receive a daily offering of the most sacred of all foods to guarantee that the sun would blaze forth at dawn. Otherwise a universal disaster would erupt.

Gods accepted human blood in various ways. On regular days, to appease the divinities, certain individuals drew their own blood, usually with sharp maguey thorns. Rulers regularly performed autosacrifice by piercing their earlobes or upper ears. Sometimes other body parts were deemed more appropriate — the tongue, thigh, upper arm, chest, or genitals. Common people performed their own bloodletting at some point in their lives to ask for special favor from the gods, and priests engaged in autosacrifice every night. Their shredded flesh, long, filthy, blood-matted hair, blackened faces, and black robes terrified and disgusted Cortés and his men.

The offering of a human heart, however, was the supreme ritual performed during holidays associated with the eighteen monthly ceremonies of the Aztec calendar. The majority of sacrificial victims were enemy warriors captured in battle. In fact, the purpose of many wars was to seize captives for future offerings to the gods. But victims were also drawn from slaves, commoners, and children — the latter especially required by certain deities, such as Tlaloc, god of rain and agriculture.

It was a great honor to be a sacrificial offering, because in this way a human temporarily became a god. Beforehand, he was treated with appropriate pomp and ceremony, dressed in the clothing and insignia of divinities, worshipped and given various luxuries, from delicacies to eat to women for sexual gratification. The emphasis on war and sacrifice in Aztec society may have prepared its members for such a fate, to an extent. The fact that, before sacrifice, victims were often given the intoxicating drink *pulque,* a liquor distilled from agave, suggests that they might not all have been keen to embrace this destiny.

On the appointed day the victim was led up the 114 steep steps of the Great Temple, the hundred-foot-high pyramid towering over the center of Tenochtitlán. Two shrines shared its summit. The sanctuary facing north, painted white and blue, was dedicated to Tlaloc. The other one, facing south, was devoted to

Huitzilopochtli, "Hummingbird on the Left." It was ornamented with carved skulls painted white on a red background.

Having ascended the pyramid, the victim took in for the last time the panorama of the great city below: the tall stepped temples and flat-roofed adobe houses bright with flowers, the crowded marketplace murmuring and humming with trade, the three causeways leading to the mainland, the aqueduct bringing in fresh water from Chapultepec, the lake teeming with canoes loaded with produce and merchandise, and, beyond, the forested mountains and snowcapped volcanoes.

The victim was laid on a convex sacrificial stone, and four priests held down his arms and legs. The fifth priest, with a swift gesture, sliced his chest open with a sharp obsidian blade (probably making two long cuts parallel to the sternum on either side of the chest to reach the heart). Seizing the still-beating heart, he severed the vessels at its top, ripped it out, and offered it to the gods. He then cut off the victim's head so that it could be strung on a massive skull rack next to the pyramid and sent the lifeless corpse tumbling down the steps of the temple, splattering them with blood. And so the sacrificed human repeated the original selfless act of the gods and helped save the world.

Some sacrifices also involved flaying the bodies, after which the priests donned the victims' skins. On certain ritual occasions portions of the bodies were eaten. Bernardino de Sahagún, a Franciscan friar who assiduously studied native culture through local informants, reported that the emperor received the thighs of sacrificed victims. The warriors who had captured them in battle took the rest. Cooking the flesh in a special stew with dried maize and beans, they served it at a family feast, thereby ingesting courage and strength.

Thousands of people met this fate every year. The Spaniards were revolted and appalled. Díaz, having gone up the Great Temple with Cortés, choked on the sight and smell of layers of human blood. "There were some braziers with incense which they call copal, and in them they were burning the hearts of the three Indians whom they sacrificed that day. . . . All the walls of the oratory [the shrine of Huitzilopochtli] were so splashed and encrusted with blood that they were black, the floor was the same and the whole place stank vilely. . . . The walls were so clotted with blood and the soil so bathed with it that in the slaughter houses of Spain there is not such another stench."

The Aztecs justified so much blood with the same rationale that fueled their constant warfare: it was a sacred cosmic duty required by the gods, especially Huitzilopochtli, whose chosen people they were. "War is your desert, your task," a midwife would tell a newborn boy; "perhaps you will receive the gift of the flowered death by the obsidian knife [sacrifice to the gods]." Aztec boys were brought up to be soldiers, and warriors were treated with great honor. Those who captured a certain number of prisoners earned the right to wear the costumes of animals — jaguars and eagles — the most prestigious attire of their class.

Other noble warriors wore splendid tunics covered with the feathers of parrots, cotingas, herons, and other brightly plumed birds. The colors and decoration signaled their military rank and accomplishments. Even the Spaniards were impressed with this dress. An anonymous conquistador described how Aztec warriors wore quilted cotton armor one or two fingers thick and sturdy enough to repel arrows. Over this armor they donned bodysuits

. . . covered with feathers of different colors and they look very jaunty. One company of soldiers will wear them in red and white, another in blue and yellow, and others in various ways. The lords wear certain smock-like coats which among us are of mail but theirs are of gold or silver gilt, and the strength of their feathered garments is proportionate to their weapons, so that they resist spears and arrows, and even the sword. To defend their head they wear things like heads of serpents, or tigers, or lions or wolves, and the man's head lies inside the animal's jaws as though it were devouring him. These heads are of wood covered on the outside with feathers or incrustations of gold and precious stones, and are something wonderful to see.

With such exaltation of war and human sacrifice, were the Aztecs just bloodthirsty savages? Perhaps they were ruthless opportunists who used religion as an excuse to wage highly profitable wars and to discourage foreign and domestic subjects from resistance. Or were they deeply faithful people with complex and fatalistic religious beliefs? Cortés and his men, fired by crusading zeal as well as their own ambitions, tended toward one of the first two interpretations and saw it as their duty to obliterate the devilish Aztec rituals while converting the natives to Christianity. Cortés boasted to Charles V that after gaining control of the city, he went up to the summit of the Great Temple and entered the shrines where the sacred images of the Aztec gods were kept.

The most important of these idols, and the ones in whom they have most faith, I had taken from their places and thrown down the steps; and I had those chapels where they were cleaned, for they were full of the blood of sacrifices; and I had images of Our Lady and of other saints put there, which caused Mutezuma and the other natives some sorrow. First they asked me not to do it, for when the communities learnt of it they would rise against me, for they believe that those idols gave them all their worldly goods, and that if they were allowed to be ill treated, they would become angry and give them nothing and take the fruit from the earth leaving the people to die of hunger. I made them understand through the interpreters how deceived they were in placing their trust in those idols which they had made with their hands from unclean things. They must know that there was only one God, Lord of all things, who had created heaven and earth and all else and who made all of us . . . and they must adore and worship only Him.

The conquistadors felt little doubt about the barbarism of native beliefs and the superiority of Christianity, which the historian Stephen Greenblatt, in his book *Marvelous Possessions,* describes as

a religious ideology centered on the endlessly proliferated representation of a tortured and murdered god of love. The cult of this male god . . . centered on a ritual in which the god's flesh and blood were symbolically eaten. Such was the confidence of this [European] culture that it expected perfect strangers . . . to abandon their own beliefs, preferably immediately, and embrace those of Europe as luminously and self-evidently true. A failure to do so provoked impatience, contempt, and even murderous rage.

In the wake of the conquest of Granada in 1492, the Spanish conquistadors were driven by the romance and the possibility of vanquishing the infidel. Besides, most of them came from Castile, the land of the Inquisition, which sanctified violence against those who did not conform to Christian norms. Was Cortés himself a religious man? The Franciscan priest Motolinía, his confessor later in life, thought that "even though he was a sinner, he had faith and did the work of a good Christian." But Diego de Ordaz, who formed part of Cortés's expedition, wrote in 1529 that his leader had "no more conscience than a dog." Both views had truth in them. Cortés, like most Europeans at that time, was brought up as a devout Catholic, and yet his conduct toward the Mexica was ruthless.

It did not matter to Cortés and his compatriots that their "Christian" ways provided a rather uninspiring model to the Aztecs. When Cortés arrived in Tenochtitlán, he had permission only to explore and trade, so he hoped to win the city without a battle. Taking Montezuma prisoner to ensure compliance, and alternating threats with promises, he proceeded to dictate what the inhabitants of the city could and could not do. In the spring of 1520 the Mexica asked permission to hold the feast of Toxcatl, a celebration as important as Easter and occurring at roughly the same time. Cortés happened to be away, having gone to the coast. His deputy, Pedro de Alvarado, first granted permission for the celebration, but then, fearing that the festival would serve as a pretext for an uprising, changed his mind. Several Aztec chronicles record the wretched outcome:

> At this moment in the fiesta, when the dance was loveliest and when song was linked with song, the Spaniards were seized with an urge to kill the celebrants. They all ran forward, armed as if for battle. They closed the entrances and passageways. . . . They posted guards so that no one could escape, and then rushed into the Sacred Patio to slaughter the celebrants. . . .
>
> They ran in among the dancers, forcing their way to the place where the drums were played. They attacked the man who was drumming and cut off his arms. Then they cut off his head, and it rolled across the floor.
>
> They attacked all the celebrants, stabbing them, spearing them, sticking them with their swords. They attacked some of them from behind, and these fell instantly to the ground with their entrails hanging out. Others they beheaded, . . . or split their heads to pieces.
>
> They struck others in the shoulders, and their arms were torn from their bodies. They wounded some in the thigh and some in the calf. They slashed others in the abdomen, and their entrails all spilled to the ground. Some attempted to run away, but their intestines dragged as they ran; they seemed to tangle their feet in their own entrails. No matter how they tried to save themselves, they could find no escape.
>
> Some attempted to force their way out, but the Spaniards murdered them at the gates.

The massacre accomplished precisely what Alvarado had sought to forestall. The outraged Mexica rose in revolt. Trying to subdue them, on June 26 Cortés took Montezuma to the rooftop of his palace so that he would appeal to his subjects to stop hostilities. But the Mexica captains replied that they had elected a new lord to replace the emperor who had capitulated to the Spaniards: Montezuma's brother Cuitláhuac, who from the start had argued that the newcomers were criminals who had come to steal the kingdom. Under their new king the Mexica swore to fight until all the invaders were dead. As for Montezuma, the enraged people released a volley of missiles at their deposed leader, "as if the sky was raining stones, arrows, darts, and sticks." Montezuma was hit three times, gravely wounded, and hastily taken below. He died on June 30, whether from the wounds inflicted by his former subjects or from fresh ones expediently added by the Spaniards, it is not clear.

On July 1, 1520, under cover of night and drizzling rain, the Spaniards — short of food, water, and gunpowder, and with the Aztecs closing in on them — decided to flee Tenochtitlán. Discovering their retreat, the Mexica attacked the conquistadors escaping along the causeway with such fury that scores were killed and drowned, and vast quantities of the gold they had extorted from Montezuma were lost in the lake. More than three hundred Spaniards (their ranks augmented since their arrival the previous fall) were captured and sacrificed. Of course, this only confirmed the Spaniards' view of the Aztecs as devil-worshipping savages who deserved to be killed or enslaved.

Cortés and his beaten army retreated to Tlaxcala, a city just over the mountains to the east of the Aztec capital and hostile to the Mexica. It took the Spaniards a year to recover and to reinforce their ranks with the native enemies of the Aztecs. Finally, on May 30, 1521, Cortés came back to Tenochtitlán and laid siege to the city for seventy-five days. When he finally entered the starved and decimated capital, he not only slaughtered countless inhabitants and razed the temples, palaces, and dwellings that he had once sought to possess and preserve, but also deliberately burned down Montezuma's zoo.

Gleefully, he reported the destruction of Montezuma's palace building, including the house where the emperor had kept "every species of bird found in these parts. Although it distressed me, I determined to burn them, for it distressed the enemy very much more." Cortés's secretary Juan de Rivera, however, felt pity for the hapless victims, recalling "the howls of the lions, tigers, bears, and the wolves while they were burning in the houses, and the deplorable catastrophe which overtook the natives." The conquistadors then proceeded to treat the surviving Aztecs as animals, though, with few exceptions, not nearly as well as Montezuma had treated his pets in the zoo.

THE QUESTION OF whether the Aztecs and other inhabitants of the New World deserved to be handled as humans or as beasts preoccupied Europeans both at home and abroad. Layers of prejudice, ideology, and realpolitik infused this debate.

The discussion was prompted most of all by the institution of *encomienda*. This system, set up in the West Indies in 1493 by the crown of Castile, assigned to deserving Spanish colonists groups of Indians, living at particular geographic locations, to serve them with labor and tribute. The system gave the conquistadors a cheap workforce and control over the native population. In return, the Spaniards assumed the feudal obligation to defend their Indian subjects and the land they inhabited, and to instruct them in Christianity.

The word *encomienda* derives from the Spanish *encomendar*, to entrust. In truth, there was no trust from either side, and for the natives the experience proved horrendous. Regarding the laborers as brute beasts rather than people, the colonists in Cuba, where the system was first introduced, subjected them to such dreadful hardships — treating them inhumanely and often working them to death — that they decimated the population even before Cortés arrived in Tenochtitlán. Still, the institution persisted, and soon after defeating the Aztecs, Cortés began to amass *encomienda* himself and to grant them to his followers for their services in the conquest. He admitted that the system was abusive and had produced disastrous results. And he felt compelled to notify Charles V of his decision to begin this practice in the newly subjugated Aztec territories because he had no legal authority to do so. But when the emperor forbade Cortés to make *encomienda* grants and ordered him to revoke the ones he had already distributed, Cortés refused to obey and instead tried to convince Charles V of the necessity of this practice in administering New Spain.

European views of Native Americans as inferior beings — and thus worthy of inhumane treatment — were not uniform. They were based on a variety of sources, which only made the debate about the natives' nature and proper handling more heated. Some expected them to be bizarre monsters, as described in the medieval best seller *The Travels of Sir John Mandeville* (written in the mid-fourteenth century). According to Mandeville, who seems to have compiled his book largely from travel accounts by other writers and from fanciful lore, races dwelling in distant regions of the East — the presumed destination of Renaissance explorers — were composite beasts. There were cannibals who ate their own families; dwarfs who had no mouths and communicated by hissing; Cyclopes who consumed nothing but raw flesh; headless people with eyes on their shoulders; people with horse hooves on their feet; others with such large upper lips that when they slept in the sun, they used them to shield their faces; and so on. In illustrated Renaissance editions of Mandeville's *Travels*, these exotic creatures look like extraterrestrials from modern science fiction: their humanoid bodies sprout grotesque heads or appendages that reveal their alien, untamed, or dangerous natures.

Christopher Columbus fully expected to meet such hybrids, and upon encountering the natives on his first voyage, he wrote in surprise, "They are well-built people of handsome stature. In these islands I have so far found no human monstrosities, as many expected; on the contrary, among all these people good looks are esteemed." When Cortés set off toward Mexico, among his orders was to discover the whereabouts of the Amazons and to ascertain whether it was true that there were people on those distant frontiers who had the faces of dogs and huge ears that hung down to their knees.

Another tale informing the European perception of Native Americans was the medieval myth of Wild Men, savage creatures said to be living in European forests, whose ancestry went back to pagan fauns, centaurs, and satyrs. Something between men and animals, Wild Men went about unclothed, their bodies covered with shaggy hair, and wielded clubs hewn from tree trunks. In fits of rage they uprooted trees and attacked animals and men who trespassed on their territory. Lustful and at times cannibalistic, they possessed no human speech and were thus devoid of reason. Needless to say, they were ungodly creatures. In the European view, Native Americans shared a number of these characteristics. Amerigo Vespucci, whose letters were printed in numerous translations and widely read, wrote animatedly about their cannibalism, "for they eat one another, the victor the vanquished, and among other kinds of meat human flesh is a common article of their diet. . . . I knew a man whom I also spoke to, who was reputed to have eaten more than three hundred human bodies. . . . I say further, they themselves wonder why we do not eat our enemies and do not use as food their flesh, which they say is most savory."

Not all European explorers were prejudiced against the inhabitants of the New World. A variant myth described Wild Men as noble savages leading a simple, harmonious life free from the burdens and injustices of civilization.* And Columbus's second letter reporting his discoveries praised the innocence of the American Indians: "They are of simple manners and trustworthy, and very liberal with everything they have, refusing no one who asks for anything they may possess, and even themselves inviting to ask for things. They show greater love for all other than for themselves."

Similarly, not all Spaniards felt that the Aztecs deserved inhumane treatment. Díaz wrote with sympathy about Montezuma and declared that once the king was taken prisoner by the Spaniards, "it was not necessary to give orders to many of us who stood guard over him about the civility that we ought to show to this great cacique [chief]. . . . Whenever I was on guard, or passed in front of him, I doffed my headpiece with the greatest respect." And when the king died, "Cortés wept for him, and all of us Captains and soldiers, and there was no man among us who knew him and was intimate with him, who did not bemoan him as though he were our father." Yet at the end of his memoirs, even Díaz virulently condemned the Aztecs as a whole for their human sacrifices and cannibalism and accused them of sodomy and incest, "a common practice among them."

It was the *encomienda* system, however, that incited the greatest debate as to how the natives ought to be viewed and treated. The inhabitants of the West Indies were so hideously abused — starved,

---

*Philippus Aureolus Paracelsus, the Swiss alchemist and physician active in the first half of the sixteenth century, postulated a new theory. It was hard to believe, he suggested, that people who had been found "in out-of-the-way islands" were "of the posterity of Adam and Eve, for the sons of Adam by no means departed into out-of-the-way islands. It is most probable that they are descended from another Adam. For no one will easily prove that they are allied to us by flesh and blood." Perhaps, he reasoned, they had been born "after the deluge, and perhaps they have no souls. In speech they are like parrots." This theory of multiple genesis was heretical and did not catch on, but it did reflect how the Europeans struggled with the strangeness and strangers of the New World.

tortured, and massacred — by their new lords that Charles V ordered Cortés to stop *encomiendas* in New Spain, "because God created the Indians free and not subject." Cortés, however, had a valuable ally in changing the emperor's mind: his friend Juan Ginés de Sepúlveda, a distinguished classical scholar, historian, and theologian with close links to conquistador circles. Citing Aristotle's theory of natural slavery — according to which some people, due to their superior abilities, are naturally fit to rule, while others, because of their brutishness and limited reasoning, are meant to be slaves — Sepúlveda postulated in learned disquisitions that the Aztecs deserved the status of "natural slaves" because of the gravity of the acts that they committed, "especially their idolatries and their sins against nature."

A number of missionary friars who came to the New World to convert the conquered natives disagreed with Sepúlveda and Cortés and spoke in defense of the Aztecs. Of course they, too, had a vested interest: they wanted to win souls, and if the conquistadors continued to abuse their charges, no conversions would take place. As the bishop of the province of Santa Marta (Colombia) reported to Charles V:

> It is my considered opinion that the greatest obstacle that stands in the way of the pacification of the New World, and with it the conversion of the people to Christ, is the harshness and cruelty of the treatment meted out by "Christians" to those who surrender. This has been so harsh and so brutal that nothing is more odious nor more terrifying to the people than the name "Christian," a word for which they use in their language the term *yares*, which means "demons." And such a usage is amply justified, for what has been done to them by the Spanish commanders and by their men has been neither Christian nor indeed the work of devils; and so, when the locals find themselves on the receiving end of such merciless butchery, they assume that such actions are standard among Christians and

that they derive ultimately from a Christian God and a Christian King. Any attempt to persuade them otherwise is doomed to failure and quite understandably occasions snorts of derision, jibes about Christ and jeers at him and His laws.

The Dominican Bartolomé de Las Casas was the most outspoken advocate of the Aztecs (it is he who quoted the bishop of Santa Marta's appeal in his *Short Account of the Destruction of the Indies*). Opposing Sepúlveda's thesis of the natural inferiority and depravity of the natives, Las Casas argued that the Aztecs were "fully rational beings with a culture which, though certainly 'primitive' in its technology and in a large number of its practices, was equal to anything which the Old World had produced." They were eminently qualified to live the good Christian life, and he wanted to lead them to it.

Las Casas was all the more vehement in his defense of the natives because he had undergone a moral conversion. He had initially sailed for Hispaniola in 1502 and, upon acquiring land and slaves there, began to prosper. But seeing the horrors brought about by *encomiendas*, he experienced a change of heart and took Holy Orders. He argued before Charles V that the dreadful cruelties inflicted on the Indians in the West in the name of Spain and Christianity must be stopped. The natives, he lamented, were being treated "just as if . . . [they] were pieces of wood that could be cut off trees and transported for building purposes, or like flocks of sheep or any other kind of animals that could be moved around indiscriminately, and if some of them should die on the road little would be lost." He likened the Spanish conquest to the descent of famished wolves, tigers, and lions on a flock of sheep. And he described the suffering of the Indians in *encomiendas* in piteous detail:

> When they have been brought to the very edge of collapse by the labors to which they are put and begin to drop from hunger

and toil as they stumble through the mountains with enormous loads on their backs, the Spanish kick them and beat them with sticks to make them get up and resume their wearisome trudge. They do not allow them to stop and gasp for breath, and even knock their teeth out with the pommel of their swords. Their only response to such treatment is: "I give up, You are evil and wicked. I cannot go on any longer. Kill me now. I do not want to live another moment." This they say as they lie groaning and clutching their chests in what is clearly great agony. Oh, would that I could describe even one hundredth part of the afflictions and calamities wrought among these innocent people by the benighted Spanish!

Anxious to protect the natives from the conquistadors' murderous greed, in 1517 Las Casas urged a group of important Spanish theologians and doctors of the University of Salamanca to hold a debate on the nature of the natives and their rights. Upon extensive deliberation, these wise men drew up a series of conclusions. They decreed that whoever denied the humanity and potential for faith of the natives must be burned at the stake as a heretic.

Las Casas was fired by a grander vision. He was the first proponent of the doctrine of self-determination. The *encomienda* system should be suppressed altogether, the natives liberated from all servitude except a small tribute to the Spanish crown, and their states and rulers restored. The Spanish monarch should preside over the Indian states as "Emperor over many Kings" only to fulfill his sacred mission of bringing the natives to the Catholic faith and the Christian way of life. But Las Casas's voice was unusual. The majority of the clergy opted for a compromise: let *encomiendas* remain to ensure the prosperity and security of the New World, but have them regulated to guarantee the welfare of the natives.

In the end the Aztecs, like other inhabitants of the New World, fared poorly. They were wiped out in appalling numbers by Cortés's soldiers and by slave labor in *encomiendas*. And those who did not die by the hands of the Spaniards perished from European diseases. A smallpox epidemic that had begun in Hispaniola in 1518 spread to Cuba the following year and reached the Valley of Mexico in September 1520, just as Cortés was arriving. It ravaged Tenochtitlán, making the grand city more susceptible to Cortés's siege the following summer. As an Aztec chronicler recounted:

> A great plague broke out here in Tenochtitlán. It began to spread during the thirteenth month and lasted for seventy days, striking everyone in the city and killing a vast number of our people. Sores erupted on our faces, our breasts, our bellies; we were covered with agonizing sores from head to foot.
>
> The illness was so dreadful that no one could walk or move. The sick were so utterly helpless that they could only lie on their beds like corpses, unable to move their limbs or even their heads. They could not lie down or roll from one side to the other. If they did move their bodies, they screamed with pain.
>
> A great many died from this plague, and many others died of hunger. They could not get up to search for food, and everyone else was too sick to care for them, so they starved to death in their beds.

Perhaps the luckiest were those Aztecs whom Cortés ferried across the Atlantic along with other curious animals and colorful birds. Made into human pets, they received kinder treatment, more like that accorded animals and human monsters in Montezuma's menagerie. Although he had destroyed that unsurpassed collection, Cortés now assembled his own miniature version from the vestiges of Montezuma's kingdom and took it to Spain to shore up his own power. Just like the wild animals in the emperor's zoo, the Aztecs were tamed and paraded as exotic novelties for European diversion.

AFTER HIS CONQUEST of Tenochtitlán, Cortés went on to extend Spanish control over areas within and beyond the boundaries of the Aztec Empire, and by 1524 he occupied a nearly all-powerful position in New Spain (the territory of all of Mexico). As the governor and captain-general of the new colony, he had virtually unlimited authority over its political, social, and economic affairs, and he had secured a vast personal fortune by acquiring properties in the richest districts. But then his luck began to turn.

In the spring of 1524, prompted by reports of Cortés's abuses, the emperor sent a delegation of treasury officials to New Spain to investigate his conduct and to revoke his grants of *encomiendas*. Cortés and his lieutenants ignored the imperial directive, but his position was threatened. The following autumn Cortés set off with several thousand men to subjugate Honduras. Two years later, fewer than a hundred Spaniards returned to Tenochtitlán in a pitiable state. They were the only ones to have survived the dreadful hardships of trudging through the jungle in unknown territories, crossing innumerable rivers, suffering from disease, hunger, and thirst, and to have remained loyal to their commander in a mutiny. Soon after his return in May 1426, Cortés was forced to relinquish his governorship to an appointed successor, and at the same time the crown opened a formal inquiry into his misdeeds in New Spain. In 1527 Cortés dispatched two agents to Charles V to try to improve his position at court, but they failed to convince the monarch that Cortés was willing to subordinate his own interests to those of the crown. And so, early in 1528, Cortés decided to sail home to defend himself personally before his emperor and to restore his status, possessions, and reputation.

Cortés set sail in March 1528. After a forty-two-day crossing, he landed on his home coast and made his way toward the court of Charles V. He orchestrated his arrival with great care. He came accompanied not only by his proud and cocky fellow explorers but also by the glimmering riches of the New World: vast quantities of gold and silver — some of it in coins and some wrought into beautiful works of art — plus shimmering mantles, fans, and shields adorned with exquisite feather work. When the famous German artist Albrecht Dürer saw a sampling of Aztec artifacts, he was deeply impressed:*

> I saw the things which have been brought to the King from the new land of gold, a sun all of gold a whole fathom broad, and a moon all of silver of the same size, also two rooms full of armor of the people there, and all manner of wondrous weapons of theirs, harness and darts, very strange clothing, beds, and all kinds of wonderful objects of human use. . . . These things were all so precious that they are valued at 100,000 florins. All the days of my life I have seen nothing that rejoiced my heart so much as these things, for I saw among them wonderful works of art, and I marveled at the subtle Ingenia of men in foreign lands. Indeed I cannot express all that I thought there.

But more amazing still were Cortés's human treasures: three of Montezuma's sons and several other Aztec nobles attired in radiant feather mantles and with jewels in their faces; eight jugglers and twelve ballplayers; male and female dwarfs, hunchbacks, and albinos. The Europeans gaped at these exotic specimens as if at trained monkeys. The humanist Peter Martyr was both enthralled and repulsed:

> These natives are brownish color. Both sexes pierce their ears and wear golden pendants in them and the men pierce the ex-

---

*He saw the Aztec treasures on display in Brussels, at the court of Charles V's aunt Margaret of Austria.

tremity of the underlip, down to the roots of the lower teeth. Just as we wear precious stones mounted in gold upon our fingers, so do they insert pieces of gold the size of a ring into their lips. . . . I cannot remember ever to have seen anything more hideous; but they think that nothing more elegant exists under the human circle.

One wonders how astonished and disoriented the Aztecs were by their journey from Tenochtitlán to Spain, what they felt at crossing the vast ocean, traveling as far as only the gods went, and arriving in an alien land of fair-skinned strangers who wore odd close-fitting costumes and ate bizarre foods. The hardships of such human specimens (who would be brought to Europe as exotic diversions well into the nineteenth century, when various animal dealers and showmen did a thriving business in exhibitions of "native behavior") is sadly exemplified by the better-recorded story of the Eskimos whom Martin Frobisher imported to England from Baffin Island in 1576 and 1577.

Frobisher had sailed north in search of new commercial opportunities for the English crown and a supposed Northwest Passage leading to the riches of China. His captives were meant as publicity for English colonial expansion and as intriguing specimens. Unfortunately, as the English struggled to capture the Eskimos, they killed several of them, and a few others threw themselves into the sea, preferring to die rather than be caught, so the harvest proved meager. The only man brought to England in 1576 died fifteen days after arriving from an unspecified European disease to which he had no immunity.

During the second attempt the following year, Frobisher's men seized one man and a woman with her twelve-month-old baby. In the course of capture the little boy was shot in the arm by an English arrow. The salves applied by Frobisher's surgeon did little good, but the mother cured the wound "by continual licking with her own tongue." Upon their arrival in England the Eskimos aroused great curiosity, prompting several artists to record their strange faces and costumes. The man, called Kalicho, was put on display within a few days of his landing in Bristol. In October 1577 he was made to paddle up and down the Avon River at high tide in his kayak as a sort of show for the mayor and a number of other spectators. He also killed two ducks with his "dart."

Demonstrating their savage nature, the Eskimos were said to eat nothing but raw meat. A contemporary French account claimed, wrongly, that Kalicho was presented to the queen, who allowed him to kill her swans on the Thames. (In fact, the queen neither saw Kalicho nor gave him permission to hunt her birds.) It added that the Eskimos "once killed a fowl and ate all the entrails including the dung." The woman, called Arnaq, meanwhile, enchanted the onlookers by the way she carried her baby, Nutaaq, on her back inside her parka and "gave suck casting her breast over her shoulder."

All three Eskimos died a little over a month after their arrival. The doctor who examined Kalicho as his health deteriorated detected "an 'Anglophobia,' which he had from when he first arrived." When Kalicho died a few days later, the doctor performing the autopsy "was bitterly grieved and saddened, not so much by the death of the man himself, as because the great hope of seeing him which our most gracious Queen had entertained had now slipped through her fingers, as it were, for the second time."

Cortés's Aztecs faired somewhat better. Most of them survived their stay in Europe, and they were treated more kindly there than were their countrymen back in New Spain. But like the Eskimos, they were used rather like circus animals and made to show their native tricks. The Europeans were particularly enchanted by the Aztec ballplayers and jugglers. The chronicler Gonzalo Fernández de Oviedo y Valdés thrilled at the sight of these jugglers, naked but for little britches and feathered ankle bracelets, performing "in a manner never seen or heard in Spain." Each juggler in turn would lie on his back and balance, toss, and retrieve a heavy log with his feet to the accompaniment of songs and chants by his companions. Sometimes, while the log was up in the air, another juggler would quickly replace the one who tossed it and catch it on its descent. Gómara reported that Montezuma had loved to watch

> jugglers who use their feet as ours do their hands. They hold between their feet a log as big as a girder, round, even, and smooth, which they toss into the air and catch, spinning it a couple of thousand times, so cleverly and quickly that the eye can hardly follow it. Besides this, they perform other tricks and comical acts with astonishing skill and art. They also perform grotesque dances, in which three men mount one above the other, resting upon the shoulders of the bottom man, while the top man does extraordinary things.

Now Montezuma's jugglers were diverting their new lord, Charles V.

The ballplayers, meanwhile, played a game they called "batey" with a large, solid ball "made from the milk of certain trees" (rubber, still unknown to the Europeans), which they propelled with their buttocks. In teams of two against two or three against three, the players aimed to bounce the ball through a stone ring affixed vertically to a wall (like a basketball hoop), which won the game, or to score points by hitting it over the wall or against an opponent's body (except his buttocks). Gómara says that Montezuma had enjoyed watching this game as well.

> The ball itself is called *ullamalixtli,* which is made of the gum of the *ulli,* a tree of the hot country. . . . The game is not played for points, but only for the final victory, which goes to the side that knocks the ball against the opponents' wall, or over it. The players may hit the ball with any part of the body they please,

although certain strokes [e.g., with the hands] are penalized by loss of the ball. Hitting it with the hips or thighs is the most approved play, for which reason they protect those parts with leather shields. The game lasts as long as the ball is kept bouncing, and it bounces for a long time. They play for stakes, wagering, say, a load of cotton mantles, more or less, according to the means of the players [cotton mantles and cacao beans were Aztec currency]. They also wager articles of gold and featherwork, and at times even put up their own bodies.

Another Spanish chronicler asserted that Indian lords often wagered a town or a province, and poorer folk bet themselves as possible slaves. So popular was this sport that Aztec nobles maintained their own teams of players. Those brought by Cortés had likely originally belonged to Montezuma.

The remarkable performances of these players and jugglers was captured in a series of drawings by Christoph Weiditz, a draftsman and medal maker from Augsburg. He depicted various members of the Aztec party: the nobles in their feathered mantles, with jewels glimmering in their faces, an Indian holding a brightly plumed parrot. To convey the curious antics of the performers, he used a cartoon-strip technique. On three sheets of paper he showed jugglers tossing up a log, spinning it in the air, and catching it again, while on a double sheet two ballplayers kick a ball with their buttocks from one page to the next. Weiditz also depicted Cortés standing proudly next to a shield emblazoned with his coat of arms and cast his portrait medal, usually the privilege of rulers in those days. These are, in fact, our earliest contemporary images of the conquistador.

Cortés's entourage of exotic humans and animals proved a great success. "The whole kingdom was agog with his fame and the news of his coming," boasted Gómara, "and everyone wanted to see him." Prominent court figures received him with adulation.

The emperor was both startled and impressed by the conqueror's spectacular appearance. The bad bacon that had felled imperial officials sent to investigate his conduct in New Spain seems to have been forgotten, along with the conquistador's willful disregard of his superior's orders to cease establishing *encomiendas.*

Impressed by the marvels Cortés had captured in the Aztec kingdom, Charles V showered him with honors and privileges. In a ceremony on July 6, 1529, the emperor conferred on Cortés the title of Marquis of the Valley of Oaxaca, with a right to twenty-two pueblos. He also confirmed him as captain-general of New Spain and "Governor of the islands and territories he might discover in the South Sea," and gave him the right to retain the twelfth part of what he should conquer in perpetuity for himself and his descendants. These titles and concessions ensured Cortés first rank among the conquistadors and colonists of New Spain.

Cortés was pleased with the emperor's renewed goodwill, but he also wanted to gain recognition and favors from the pope. So he dispatched his agents to Rome and, to make his case more convincing, sent along his Aztec performers. Pope Clement VII (the nephew of Lorenzo de' Medici) was so delighted by the Indians "who juggled the stick with their feet," reported Díaz, that "His Holiness greatly appreciated them, and said that he thanked God that such great countries had been discovered in his days." Clement VII legitimized three of Cortés's natural children, issued a bull granting him patronage powers, including the right to collect ecclesiastical tithes and first fruits on his estates in New Spain, and pronounced that Cortés and his soldiers, in Díaz's words, "had rendered great service, first of all to God, and then to our Lord the Emperor Charles V and to all Christendom, and that we were worthy of great reward. Then he sent us a Bull to absolve us from the blame and punishment of all our sins."

The overall experience was less enjoyable and advantageous for the Aztecs. After parading them before the emperor and the pope and obtaining from Charles V and the Holy Father the favors he sought, Cortés no longer needed his exotic retinue. He sent the majority of the Aztecs to Seville, to await transport back to New Spain. Charles V undertook their expenses and ordered that they be given gifts and clothes, as well as church images and devotional objects, "so that they would return content" and, presumably, spread the word back home about their kind new master, the European emperor. Seven principal Aztecs, Charles decreed, were to be dressed in blue velvet sleeveless coats, doublets of yellow damask, and capes and breeches of fine scarlet cloth. (Judging by Weiditz's drawings, they had been wearing their traditional Aztec garments during their exhibitions throughout Europe.) In addition, each was to receive two shirts, shoes with ribbons, leather gaiters, and a cap of blue velvet. These foreign clothes must have felt confining and hot to the Aztecs, used as they were to loose and flowing garments. And the closed Spanish shoes probably pinched their toes, which were habituated to sandals. Twenty-nine other Indians were issued sleeveless coats of yellow cloth, doublets of white cotton fustian, and mulberry-colored capes. They, too, received two shirts apiece, shoes with ribbons, regular breeches and gaiters, and caps of scarlet cloth. Not included in the group sent to Seville were thirty or so jugglers, ballplayers, dwarfs, and albinos, who likely remained with Cortés as part of the great lord's entourage.

While the Aztecs lingered in Seville, the emperor also ordered that they be lodged and fed at the crown's expense. Thirteen men were put up by Hernando de la Torre, the Franciscan canon; a certain Alonso Sánchez de Hortega took in the rest. But royal bureaucracy had its glitches. The Aztecs' overseer, Fray Antonio de Ciudad Rodrigo, reported to Charles V that the names of three Indians had somehow been omitted from the document ordering their clothing. The unaccounted men were going about naked. A few of them fell ill, and one died on May 17, 1529. Unfortunately, the friar failed to mention, or notice, that the omission was perpetuated in the royal order regarding food for the Aztecs, so while the crown issued additional garments to the overlooked men, it did not feed them. Since the canon was being paid to house and feed only ten Aztecs, whereas thirteen were living under his care, the unlucky three went hungry (or, if their companions shared their rations, everyone was underfed). Four more Aztecs died. The remaining ones apparently sailed home in two groups, one in late August 1529 and the other the following year when Cortés himself returned to New Spain.

THE POPULARITY OF Cortés's Aztecs in Europe did not change the fate of their countrymen at home. While Europeans debated the character and treatment of people in the New World, Spanish domination and savage handling of native populations continued. The emperor granted Cortés twenty-three thousand Indian vassals, and this grant was perpetual, to be passed on to his heirs. Thus thousands of natives were subjected to forced labor and harsh taxation for generations on end.

It is ironic that on the site of Montezuma's destroyed "bird house" in Tenochtitlán, the Spaniards erected the principal monastery of the Franciscan order in New Spain. In the Christian tradition, Saint Francis was the lover of all creation and so compassionate that he could communicate with wild birds and animals, which stopped to listen to him preach the Word of God. Saint Francis's most famous exploit was taming a wolf that terrorized the Italian town of Gubbio, regularly devouring not only animals but people as well. According to legend, the vicious beast killed all who attempted to hunt it down, but Francis bravely ventured outside the city gates to meet it. Upon seeing him, the wolf charged with jaws agape, but when Francis made the sign of the cross, the animal stopped and closed its mouth. Then, in the name of Christ, Francis admonished the beast, "Brother Wolf, I want you to make peace between you and the people of Gubbio. They will harm you no more and you must no longer harm them. All past crimes are to be forgiven." They sealed their agreement with a pledge and a hand-to-paw shake, and from then on the wolf and the people of Gubbio lived in peace and mutual respect. Alas, there was no Saint Francis in Mexico, and precious little regard for the natives. Francis had treated even animals with kindness. The Spaniards would go on for centuries treating humans as beasts.

FIVE

RUDOLF II'S
EMPIRE OF KNOWLEDGE

[There is] . . . a certain Chinese encyclopedia called the
Heavenly Emporium of Benevolent Knowledge. In its
distant pages it is written that animals are divided into:
(a) those that belong to the emperor; (b) embalmed ones;
(c) those that are trained; (d) suckling pigs; (e) mermaids;
(f) fabulous ones; (g) stray dogs; (h) those that are included in this classification; (i) those that tremble as if
they were mad; (j) innumerable ones; (k) those drawn
with a very fine camel's-hair brush; (l) etcetera; (m) those
that have just broken the flower vase; (n) those that at
a distance resemble flies.

JORGE LUIS BORGES,
"John Wilkins' Analytical Language"

Nothing is more beautiful than to know everything.

PLATO

With little warning, on a cold winter day in early January
1612, the favorite lion of Rudolf II, the Holy Roman
Emperor and king of Hungary and Bohemia, died. Rudolf was
devastated when the servant brought the news. Not only was the
lion his dearest pet, allowed to roam the palace at will, terrifying

the servants, it was also the heraldic beast of Bohemia. Its death could only be an evil omen. Surely it presaged the imminent end of Rudolf himself.

And the omen proved true. On January 20 the emperor expired in his great echoing castle perched on a hill above Prague. Refusing last rites, he died a bitter, disillusioned man, stripped of his crowns and his imperial dignity by his hateful brother Matthias. How did it come to pass that he began his reign as the loftiest monarch of Europe only to end it as a humiliated prisoner in his own home?

Rudolf's detractors said that his preoccupation with nature and alchemy caused him to lose his mind and his reign. Certainly these had been his abiding passions and his therapy for his political and mental ills. With Rudolf's death, his beloved Royal Garden full of exotic plants and his ponds stocked with rare fish were left bereft of their admirer. The foreign beasts in his menagerie and the tropical birds in his aviaries had lost their devoted master and scholar. Rudolf's *Kunstkammer* — a cabinet of wonders composed of four large halls filled to the brim with natural history specimens from around the globe, the most advanced scientific instruments, and works of art by the greatest craftsmen — lay abandoned. This unsurpassed collection, the wonder of its age, had been the soul of this complex and troubled man. He had failed miserably as the ruler of the Holy Roman Empire, but the empire of knowledge he created in his castle ensured his lasting fame.

RUDOLF II CAME into the world on July 18, 1552, the firstborn son of a discordant union between the charismatic and open-minded Holy Roman Emperor Maximilian II Habsburg and his stern and bigoted cousin Maria of Spain, daughter of the former emperor Charles V. Maximilian was a popular ruler who presided over a lively and intellectually vibrant court. He conversed with his subjects and guests in German, Spanish, Italian, French, Czech, and Latin. A lover of music, he attracted splendid performers into his employ; Orlando di Lasso, one of the greatest composers of polyphony in the late Renaissance, deemed Maximilian's chamber music so wonderful that "neither tongue could describe it nor ears take enough of it."

Fascinated by ancient history and literature and by natural sciences, Maximilian lured to his court the leading practitioners in these fields and encouraged them to conduct further research. When Maximilian's favorite diplomat, Ogier Ghislain de Busbecq, returned from an imperial mission to Constantinople, he brought back for his lord's garden the first tulip to reach Europe. Busbecq also taught young Rudolf about botany and imparted to him an admiration for natural philosophy. Meanwhile, Rudolf fell in love with animals at the two menageries his father had founded near Vienna, at Neugebau and Ebersdorf. The year Rudolf was born, Maximilian was thrilled to acquire an elephant, an exceedingly rare and precious beast. Alas, it died only four months after reaching Vienna, a victim of improper diet and severe climate change. But Rudolf avidly observed and fell under the spell of many other beasts in his father's collection. He would retain his fascination for them all his life and take it to new heights when he grew up.

From his father Rudolf also learned religious tolerance and openness to talent regardless of creed. This was an era of bitter struggles between Catholics and Protestants, battles that would plague Rudolf's reign. The fault line ran right through his own home. Maximilian sympathized with the Protestants, granted them freedom of worship in his territories, and worked for reform in the Catholic Church, including letting priests marry. But his progressive efforts were thwarted by the opposition of the militantly Catholic Spanish royal house to which his wife, Maria, belonged. Maria was a staunch Roman Catholic who despised her husband's Protestant leanings. Fearful for her children's souls at the liberal Viennese court, and more strong willed than her husband, she insisted that Rudolf and his younger brother Ernest be dispatched to Spain, to be educated in the true faith and in the dignities of their exalted rank by her brother Philip II.

And so, in 1563, eleven-year-old Rudolf and ten-year-old Ernest, his favorite brother, were sent away from Vienna to spend the next eight years at the Spanish court. The boys felt miserable at leaving their father's warm and sparkling home. The prospect of living with their uncle — a distant, suspicious, pedantic, and remorseless man — chilled their young hearts. It was common knowledge that Philip was universally disliked by his subjects. A Venetian ambassador described the atmosphere at the Spanish court as being as "cold as ice." Philip, always attired in a somber black habit, was conspicuously pious. He attended endless religious services and even arranged his apartment at the Escorial monastery, which he adopted as his residence, in such a way as to be able to see the high altar from his bed. He disapproved of such hedonistic pleasures as hunting and feasting, and banned polyphonic music from his liturgy in favor of organ and plainsong.

Under Philip's stern watch, the boys' joyful and carefree childhood came to an end. Rudolf and Ernest had to focus on their humanistic studies, write letters in Latin, and help their uncle serve Sunday Mass. Philip allowed them certain joys due young princes: they could hunt, dance, and participate in chivalric tournaments. But he kept a vigilant eye on their religious education and instructed them in what he considered to be regal conduct. Whereas Maximilian's relationship with his courtiers was warm and hearty, Philip's was formal, aloof, and majestic, and he demanded tremendous reverence during his audiences. When the boys returned home from Spain, people commented that they had become distant and haughty. Maximilian even ordered his sons to "change their bearing," but their uncle's behavior had become ingrained in them. Rudolf would maintain Spanish fashion — dark clothes and hats with feathers — and a stiff manner for the rest of his life. Yet he would never embrace his uncle's strident and bloodthirsty Catholicism. His father's moderate views and intellectual interests, which Rudolf had absorbed as a boy, would remain at the core of his personality.

As the eldest son, Rudolf began to step into his father's political shoes at age twenty, when he was crowned king of Hungary in 1572. Maximilian's health was in decline — he suffered heart attacks, the excruciating pain of gout, and bouts of "kidney colic" — so Rudolf was groomed for succession. In 1575 he was crowned king of Bohemia, and in 1576, when Maximilian died, Rudolf became Holy Roman Emperor.

The emperor presided over a complex of territories in western and central Europe — a successor state to the one Charlemagne had founded in 800 in an attempt to revive the Roman Empire. While the pope was the vicar of God on earth in spiritual matters, the emperor claimed to be God's temporal vicar, and thus the supreme ruler of Christendom. In reality, the power of the Holy Roman Emperor was illusory. Rudolf was accorded diplomatic precedence over other rulers, and his domain included what is now Germany, Austria, the Czech Republic, Switzerland, eastern France, the Low Countries, and parts of northern and central Italy. The German lands were his primary area of sovereignty, however, and his control over international affairs was limited.

In person Rudolf was a likable but hardly an imposing presence. The Venetian envoy to Prague, Girolamo Soranzo, described him as

> a rather small figure, of quite pleasing stature and relatively quick movements. His pale face, nobly formed forehead, fine wavy hair and beard, and large eyes looking around with a certain forbearance, made a deep impression on all who met him. The Habsburg family likeness was evident in the largish lips which curled towards the right. There was nothing haughty in

his comportment; he behaved rather shyly, avoided all noisy society and took no part in the usual amusements; jokes pleased him not, and only rarely was he seen to laugh.

Rudolf had received a princely education and spoke German, Latin, French, Spanish, and some Czech — all the languages necessary for political and intellectual discourse in his realm. But from the start, his reign was beset by difficulties. He hoped to preside over a united Christendom, but the Holy Roman Empire was an unruly domain. A loose confederation of more than three hundred political entities of varying sizes and importance — each with its own sovereign, army, and laws — it was characterized by particularism and disunity. How could it not be when it included Germans, Swiss, Czechs, Flemings, Dutch, and Danes, as well as warring Catholic and Protestant groups within them?

Europe in the second half of the sixteenth century was consumed by religious wars, as Catholics and Protestants clashed violently, especially in the northern countries. The crisis had begun earlier in the century when various reformers had openly attacked the Catholic Church for its corruptions: priests keeping mistresses, popes selling religious offices and indulgences to finance their own luxurious lifestyles and political agendas. Then Martin Luther postulated that one could attain salvation through a personal relationship with God, rather than one mediated by the clergy. This idea fell on many ready ears, especially in light of widespread disapproval of the priesthood, and the Protestant movement spread like wildfire. Naturally, the Church lashed out against its critics, and for the next few decades conflicts between Catholics and Protestants divided not only countries but also individual cities and communities, and involved all members of society, from laborers to rulers.

An agent of the Fugger banking firm, which had many international branches, vividly conveyed the feeling of such religious clashes in his report from Antwerp in May 1581: "Eight days ago the soldiery and the Calvinists mutilated all the pictures and altars in the churches and cloisters of Belgium. The clergy and about five hundred Catholic citizens were driven out and several among them cast into prison." Two months later he wrote again:

> In the past days the Calvinists here have wrought much havoc. . . . They ravaged the Church of Our Lady, the Churches of St. Jacques, and the Palace Chapel, as well as the Convent of St. Michael, where up to now the Catholics held their religious exercises and ceremonies, in such fashion that they have wrecked everything therein, with the exception of the organ and a few pictures. . . . Not one person did protest against this, since the rule of the clergy is completely destroyed and at an end here.

In response to these disorders, and to the larger rebellion of the Low Countries against its Spanish overlords, Philip II sent his nephew the Duke of Parma at the head of a powerful army to crush the Netherlandish Protestants.* Parma captured and subdued the rebel towns in the southern provinces, taking Antwerp in August 1585. The Dutch rebels fled to their northern strongholds, which eluded Spanish control.

But religious clashes continued to flare up elsewhere in Rudolf's empire. Another Fugger agent wrote from Steyr in October 1599 that the ruler of that territory, Ferdinand of Austria, removed two Protestant pastors from a parish in the mining town of Eisenerz and replaced them with two Catholic priests. As soon as he left town, however, the people drove out the Catholic clerics. Ferdinand, annoyed, sent his officers and six hundred soldiers to reinstate his priests and keep order. As soon as Ferdinand's men entered town, they arrested the heads of the municipality, the aldermen,

---

*Although this region technically fell under the jurisdiction of the Holy Roman Emperor, it was governed by the king of Spain, whose methods deeply troubled Rudolf.

the burghers, and other real and potential rebels and ordered all citizens to surrender their arms. Then they erected seven gibbets in the marketplace and prepared to begin the

> hangings, beheadings, impalings and other torments, tortures and agonies, to find out by means of suffering whether there was an understanding between them and other places and districts. Altogether it is a grievous state of affairs. Everyone who can, flies from the parish. Women with their children are driven from their houses and are obliged to watch in terror and pain the miserable existence of their husbands. Although it was intended to execute the ringleaders and the heads of the town at once, it is said that Imperial Commissaries have arrived these last days, who have sternly forbidden, in the name of His Majesty [Rudolf II], any harm to be done unto any man or to put any one to the rack or torture. It is greatly hoped that His Majesty will show mercy.

Rudolf had to adjudicate such incessant religious confrontations, as well as contend with conflicting political factions in his domains. His sovereignty was continually challenged by independent-minded princes, particularly in his German lands, who were keen to pursue their own religious and political agendas. His own brothers, jealous of his power, further undermined his reign. At the same time, the Ottomans were trying to invade Europe across his empire's eastern frontiers.

After capturing Constantinople in 1453, the Ottomans continued their expansion, and in the next half century they conquered the Black Sea, the Balkan Peninsula, and Greece. In 1529 Suleiman the Magnificent laid siege to Vienna. He did not succeed in taking this city but proceeded to subjugate a large portion of Hungary — a Habsburg territory — and from there to threaten the rest of Europe.

All these problems required a strong ruler to resolve them. Rudolf, however, was more given to contemplative study than to decisive political action. "Rudolf of few words," as he was called, not only spoke little in person but also left few written statements. A complex and elusive man, he baffled his contemporaries. One moment he presented himself as a wise and charismatic sovereign; the next he appeared to be an absentminded prince who, though courteous, was eager to withdraw into his study, which seemed to matter more to him than his throne. Yet it is hardly surprising that Rudolf should have been conflicted. He strove for stability and peace, while his family and foes constantly undercut his aspirations. He was tolerant and open-minded yet surrounded by religious strife and bigotry. He detested his uncle's dogmatic Catholicism, having spent his childhood under its shadow for eight years in Spain. Now, in adulthood, he watched its brutal implementation in the Netherlands. Although he remained within the Catholic faith, Rudolf welcomed refugees from the Netherlands at his court and engaged Protestant artists and scientists — something many of his peers refused to do. And though he preferred to devote as much of his time as possible to scholarship, the demands of his office distracted him from these cherished pursuits.

An intellectual and a dreamer, Rudolf was prone to "melancholy," a form of severe depression that ran in the family and probably resulted from too much Habsburg inbreeding. (Rudolf's parents shared the same grandmother, Joanna the Mad of Castile, who was quite mad indeed: she refused to bury the body of her deceased husband for almost a year, believing in the prophecy of his resurrection.) Within a year of becoming emperor, Rudolf cracked under the pressure. The first severe bout of illness seized him in 1577. Only twenty-five years old, he developed acute gastric problems and suffered a mental breakdown. He remained sick on and off for four years, lost weight, and became reclusive.

Such physical and emotional afflictions would continue to torment Rudolf for the rest of his life.

ALTHOUGH RUDOLF WAS the absolute ruler of the empire and paid his siblings ample annual allowances, his three brothers (aside from Ernest) caused him incessant embarrassment and grief through their smoldering ambitions. Their political machinations, combined with constant harping about Rudolf's failings as a ruler, frustrated him to no end. His mother, too, refused him moral support, suspecting him of sympathy toward Protestants and of neglecting the duties of a Roman Catholic monarch. Hoping for greater independence and peace, as well as relief from his melancholy, Rudolf decided in 1583 to leave Vienna and settle in Prague.

Prague was a venerable city with a glorious past. In the late fourteenth century, under King Charles IV, it had thrived as a cosmopolitan cultural center and a lively university town. Since then its glory had dimmed, and it had become somewhat provincial. But it offered Rudolf significant advantages. The kingdom of Bohemia, with its four million souls, was the most densely populated, richest, and best developed region in central Europe. Bohemia was also more religiously diverse and tolerant than Austria, and farther away from the Vatican and the pope, whom Rudolf profoundly disliked. Bohemia's mountains provided greater protection against the Ottoman armies than did the open Hungarian plains leading to Vienna. And being removed from his family was a major boon.

When Rudolf first came to Prague, the city was both enchanting and rough around the edges. Lying in a broad basin formed by a bend of the Vltava River, it is fringed by gently sloping hills. The densely settled right bank of the river, with its skyline of numerous church spires, was home to three districts. The Old Town was inhabited by rich patricians residing in narrow, multistory stone houses. The adjacent New Town was a more modest municipality with market squares, booths, storehouses, and counting-houses. On the other side of the Old Town stood the crowded Jewish ghetto, with its closely packed homes. Thanks to Bohemia's religious tolerance and the financial usefulness of the Jewish community, Prague developed into the most significant central European center of Hebrew scholarship and publishing.

On the left bank, the Lesser Town nestled between the castle and the Charles Bridge. A residential and service area of the castle, the Lesser Town was the neighborhood of courtiers and court craftsmen, including the large community of northern Italian stonemasons, bricklayers, stucco workers, and painters whom Rudolf had summoned to Prague to renovate the castle. A major fire had destroyed much of the Lesser Town in 1541, so it was abuzz with building activity as members of the aristocracy snapped up the vacant lots and erected imposing new palaces on this prime real estate.

Prague was not large, its population totaling only about fifty thousand. The relocation of the imperial seat there brought new vigor and growth to the city, along with noise, dirt, and crowds of beggars, criminals, and prostitutes. The streets were often muddy, the squares piled with manure, and channels of filthy water ran from the courtyards of aristocratic residences. With time Rudolf's presence and his patronage of the arts and sciences would turn Prague once again into a cultural mecca and usher in its second golden age.

While the city bustled with activity, Rudolf kept to himself in his castle on the hill, removed from all this commotion. Hradcany, as this district was called, was a town unto itself. In addition to the royal palace, there stood the Cathedral of St. Vitus, the residence of the archbishop of Prague, and the imposing homes of leading Bohemian nobles. The mighty ramparts and the deep Stag Moat (a dry ravine encircling the palace) made the castle appear inaccessible and majestic, and the surrounding gardens cloaked it in a mantle of peace. It was just what Rudolf wanted.

ALAS, PRAGUE DID not remove the emperor from the political and religious turmoil he had hoped to escape. On Christmas Eve 1590 a Fugger agent reported to the home office on the growing tensions in the city. Apparently a rumor had spread around town that Catholic priests were planning to forcibly occupy several Hussite Protestant churches.* Rudolf, notified of this imminent confrontation, ordered an inquiry and then issued a proclamation, posted in all public places, calling for calm. But people were still in an ugly mood, and

> in all parts of Prague there broke out disturbances. It has been ordered that a number of burghers hold night-watch in all the suburbs of Prague. Likewise, house-to-house visitation was carried out in order to ascertain how many strange guests there be with each citizen, how named, from whence, and of what nature their business. This had to be reported to His Majesty. Moreover, it was ordered that whosoever should know or hear of any danger should give tidings thereof to His Majesty or the Council. This scheme may lead to great bloodshed, theft and pillaging, if by chance a daring murderer or robber make use of this rumor [of the Catholic takeover] to start an outcry and raise disorder in the town of Prague.

---

*Hussites were followers of Jan Hus, a religious leader burned for his heretical teachings in 1415. A powerful force of religious dissent in Bohemia and Moravia, they demanded freedom to preach, Communion of wine and bread for the laity as well as priests, the limitation on property holding by the Church, and civil punishment of mortal sins, including simony (the buying and selling of Church offices). The Hussite movement was the first substantial attack on the Roman Catholic Church, and it helped pave the way for both the Protestant Reformation and the rise of modern nationalism.

In addition to these internal conflicts, Rudolf's territories, particularly his Hungarian frontiers, were threatened by a renewed Ottoman offensive. As we have seen, the conflict between the Europeans and the Ottomans was long-standing, with both sides seeking to crush the "infidel" and gain vital economic territories and shipping routes. The Ottomans enjoyed a period of remarkable westward expansion after their conquest of Constantinople and suffered a major blow from the Europeans only in 1571, when their navy was demolished at the Battle of Lepanto by the Holy League (composed of papal, Spanish, Italian, and other European forces). Despite the massive Turkish defeat, the tensions and rivalries among the Europeans prevented them from pressing their victory and attaining a lasting supremacy over the Ottomans. By the early 1590s the Turks had regrouped and began a new action against the Europeans, their line of attack starting at the doorstep to Rudolf's lands.

Rudolf was keen to fight them, but he could not do it alone. Other rulers within the Holy Roman Empire, as well as the pope and Philip II, refused to cooperate with him on his terms or to give their support without some guarantee of control over the war. At the same time, poor generalship and squabbles between commanders on the battlefield further hampered Rudolf's military efforts. These setbacks aggrieved him intensely. Although he was a religious moderate when it came to Christianity, he was imbued with the traditional Habsburg zeal for crushing the enemies of Christendom and impetuously wished for either a complete victory over the Ottomans or none at all. Instead, he became mired in a protracted conflict that lasted for a decade and a half.

Rudolf was also distressed by his failed plans to marry, even though it was largely his own fault. His family — his mother and brothers — were alarmed at the absence of an heir and pushed him into what seemed to be the most advantageous match, with his Spanish cousin Isabella, daughter of Philip II. But Rudolf could not abide falling under his uncle's immediate influence.

The negotiations dragged on for fifteen years. Finally, Isabella was betrothed to Rudolf's younger brother Albrecht. Although Rudolf had let the union slip through his hands, he flew into a rage at the news, feeling utterly betrayed. He then tried to negotiate a marriage with Maria de' Medici, daughter of the grand duke of Tuscany, but this match also came to nothing, again because of his procrastination. Once more he was desolate when Maria married Henry IV of France instead.

Rudolf's inability to marry had nothing to do with his physical capacities. He was well known for his illicit liaisons and had a long-term mistress in Katharina Strada, the daughter of his favorite court antiquary, Jacopo Strada. Katharina even bore him several children who were brought up at court. The problem was a reluctance to trust anyone, which perhaps stemmed from Rudolf's childhood, when he was sent away from home by his mother. His mistrust was exacerbated by the political intrigues around him and by his propensity for depression and paranoia. As a result of all these political and personal difficulties, Rudolf grew more morose and removed from the world. He turned for solace to his intellectual pursuits.

THROUGHOUT HIS LIFE Rudolf actively patronized the fine arts and natural sciences. He collected paintings and sculptures by the best artists, bought scientific instruments, and amassed an impressive collection of flora and fauna, both alive and dead. As a powerful ruler he was expected to set up an art gallery and a cabinet of wonders in his palace, so his collecting was in part consonant with his position. But it was spurred far more strongly by his insatiable curiosity and his quest for knowledge.

Thanks to new developments in natural history, the sixteenth century was a great age of collecting and studying a variety of man-made and natural creations. With the discovery and exploration of the New World by Cortés and other adventurers, novel birds, animals, and plants streamed into Europe, arousing wonder and in-spiring changes in scientific thought. Until then scholars had relied on the works of Aristotle and Pliny when interpreting nature, but the influx of unfamiliar species made natural scientists rethink the old system of knowledge. Stimulated by encounters with exotic creatures, they began to study afresh the familiar ones as well.

The Swiss naturalist Konrad Gesner revolutionized the in-vestigation of the animal world in particular with his *Historia Animalium* (History of Animals), a five-volume encyclopedia pub-lished between 1551 and 1558. In this massive publication — 4,500 pages long, with nearly 1,000 woodcut illustrations — Gesner compiled all that had been written on animals by ancient and me-dieval authors, as well as all he himself could learn from the di-rect study of live beasts, their skins and bones, and drawings and descriptions sent to him by correspondents from around the world. Reveling in the idea that seeing led to knowledge, Gesner and his contemporaries placed new emphasis on empirical evidence.

Gesner divided the animals into five Aristotelian categories — mammals, four-legged animals that lay eggs, birds, animals that live in water, and serpents, including dragons. (He planned a sixth volume, on insects, as well as a vast *History of Plants* but died prematurely of plague in 1565.) Gesner arranged the animals alphabetically — not an ideal system, but a sensible one. He be-gan his discussion of each animal with its name in many lan-guages, then offered a precise description and information on its morphology, diet, reproduction, ecology, and enemies. After that he addressed the particular uses of a given creature in medicine, agriculture, and other spheres of human activity. In the final sec-tion he considered the symbolic, allegorical, and moral meanings of the animal in different civilizations, thus providing its cultural history.

Ulisse Aldrovandi, another great naturalist of the age and the author of *Ornithologiae* (Ornithology) (1599) and *De animalibus insectis libri septum* (Seven Books About Insects) (1602), described to his patron, Cardinal Barberini (the future Pope Urban VIII), his study of insects in the field.

What my labors have been, and to what lengths I went, I could wish you to judge; and when I reflect on the many days I have given to this study, and what expenses I have incurred, I cannot but wonder how I have been able to obtain possession of, and to examine, and to describe such a number of minute creatures. For the attainment of my object, I was in the habit of going into the country for months during the summer and autumn, not for relaxation, like others; for at these times I employed all my influence, as well as money, to induce the country-people to bring me such insects, whether winged or creeping, as they could procure, in the fields or under ground, and in the rivers and ponds. When any were brought me, I made inquiries about its name, habit, locality, &c. I often, too, wandered over the marshes and mountains, accompanied by my draughtsman and amanuenses, he carrying his pencil, and they their notebooks. The former took a drawing if expedient, the latter noted down to my dictation what occurred to me, and in this way we collected a vast variety of specimens.

Collecting an extensive assortment of live and preserved fauna and flora became essential to the new approach to natural history. By assembling his own array of specimens, a scholar had knowledge at his fingertips. As natural history turned into the passion of the age, rulers eager to be at the forefront of scientific inquiry began to amass their own collections of animals, minerals, plants, and other natural marvels. Rudolf eagerly embraced this trend.

Of course sixteenth-century natural history was not yet "pure science." Nature was still viewed above all as a manifestation of divine creativity. And man's purpose in studying it was to marvel at God's ingenuity. As the humanist Giovanni Pico della Mirandola wrote in his *Oration on the Dignity of Man* (1486), after creating the world and populating it with animal life, the Divine Architect "longed for a creature which might comprehend the meaning of so vast an achievement, which might be moved with love at its beauty and smitten with awe at its grandeur." The French naturalist Pierre Belon, in his *Natural History of Birds* (1555), contended that it was one of the chief duties of a well-bred man to improve his understanding of the universe by studying and admiring God's creations. And the English clergyman cum naturalist Edward Topsell promoted the study of nature as a guide to salvation. In his *Historie of Foure-Footed Beastes and Serpents* (1607), he argued that God saved the animals from the Flood in order to allow humans access to divine genius. "Surely, it was for that a man might gaine out of them much knowledge, such as is imprinted in them by nature, as a spark of that great wisdome whereby they were created."

Indeed, the story of Noah's ark served as a major inspiration for collecting animals, both live and preserved, and for classifying them as a step toward attaining this true knowledge. Sixteenth- and seventeenth-century natural philosophers were engrossed by the ark. They wrote treatises and made elaborate calculations trying to figure out its size and design, composition and organization. But to re-create it fully, one also had to gain a complete understanding of the species of animals, their sizes, habits, diets, and life cycles. Aldrovandi, who assembled one of the most famous natural history collections of his day, was called a "second Noah."

Rudolf, spurred in part by his desire to grasp the wonderful variety, beauty, and purpose of divine creation and in part by his wish to escape his political and personal problems, avidly hunted for specimens from every possible source. He enlisted merchants, with their far-flung contacts, to seek out diverse creatures, urged his diplomats to acquire animals for him from distant countries, kept an eye on rare beasts procured by other rulers, and tried to cajole them to cede the creatures to him. His hunger for exotic fauna had no bounds, and he spared no effort or expense to assemble a complete compendium of it in Prague.

THE INCREASED MARITIME traffic to the New World, Africa, and Asia channeled a steady stream of new birds and beasts to Europe. They aroused astonishment and delight in some, greed and competition for ownership in others. When the Portuguese, having set out in search of gold, returned to Lisbon with strikingly colored parrots and adorable monkeys from South America, these instantly became prized commodities. In 1522 Magellan brought home stuffed birds of paradise, native to New Guinea and the Moluccas. These ethereal creatures fascinated the Europeans and made them eager for more. When Rudolf's uncle Philip II added the throne of Portugal to his possessions in 1580, he inherited its trading posts in Brazil, the East Indies, and India. He enchanted his daughters back in Madrid with news of the arrival in Lisbon of ships from India loaded with precious spices and fabulous animals, including an elephant, still a great rarity in the West.

The Fugger banking house added exotic animals to its portfolio. At Antwerp — Europe's major port, which received shipments from around the world — it set up next to its business offices a large garden full of cages where foreign beasts could be temporarily kept before being sold to collectors across Europe. The business was so brisk that the Antwerp branch managers complained to the head office in Augsburg of the large amount of work involved in handling "monkeys" from India, Africa, and South America. In Amsterdam the Dutch East India Company, founded in 1602, built special warehouses and stables on the quayside to hold exotic creatures before selling them off to an enthusiastic international clientele. (The company also had an intermediary animal depot at its colony on the Cape of Good Hope.)

Meanwhile, Dutch sea captains returning from distant voyages displayed the animals they brought back for a lucrative fee. It was thanks to Dutch traders that Rudolf obtained the first live cassowary ever to come to Europe.

The cassowary is a large, flightless bird that dwells in the tropical forests of Australia and New Guinea. It has glossy black plumage that looks like thick hair, a bright blue neck with a patch of brilliant red skin on the nape, and two long red wattles dangling in front. A domed horny helmet rises atop its head, over the eyes and beak, giving it its name, which derives from the Papuan word meaning "horned head." The bird uses this helmet to push aside vegetation as it runs through the rain forest with its head bent down. The cassowary's stout, powerful legs end in long, three-toed feet. The inner toe has a deadly 4½-inch-long spiky claw, which the bird uses for defense.

Rudolf's cassowary had had quite an adventurous life. It made its first recorded appearance on December 4, 1596, as a gift from the king of Java to a Dutch ship captain sailing in search of spices. The bird, however, was "as much a stranger to the inhabitants of Java as it is new for us," remarked the French scientist Carolus Clusius. The king of Java had probably received the cassowary as a diplomatic gift, although from whom it is not recorded. Given the rarity and the spectacular appearance of the creature, the king must have figured that it would make an excellent goodwill offering to the Dutch traders, known for their fierce conduct in the East Indies. The Dutch gladly accepted the bird and managed to preserve it alive and in good health on the long journey home. The cassowary disembarked in Amsterdam in July 1597. For several months it was put on display, and locals and foreigners passing through the bustling port gawked at it — for a fee. After its novelty had worn off a bit, it was sold to Count Georg Eberhard von Solms, who collected animals in his park at La Haye.

When news of the remarkable bird reached Rudolf, he at once undertook to secure the fascinating stranger for his menagerie.

Did it offer him some consolation from the rage he felt upon hearing that his bride-to-be Isabella had just been betrothed to his brother Albrecht? Rudolf threw great effort into obtaining the cassowary, calling on a local duke to help persuade the count to give the bird to him. Rudolf may well have expected a truly fantastic creature, for rumors said that the strange "Indian" bird ate embers and red fire. Four months later, the cassowary arrived in Prague. It did not peck at coals, but it was a spectacular specimen, with its long cobalt blue and raspberry red neck, which was visible from afar in the Royal Garden, and its rounded helmet, giving it regal hauteur. Rudolf was thrilled with his acquisition, generously rewarding the courtiers who delivered it to him.

Rudolf was now the only man in Europe to possess such an extraordinary pet. To honor and safeguard his distinguished animal, he erected in the Royal Garden an imposing aviary especially for the Indian bird and engaged the painter Bartholomäus Beranek to decorate the cassowary's home with pretty pictures — perhaps evocations of its natural habitat. While the emperor was clearly elated, it is harder to know how happy the cassowary was in its new abode or how long the tropical creature lasted in the wintry Prague climate. By 1607 it was listed as a stuffed specimen in Rudolf's *Kunstkammer*. Not quite as splendid in death as in life, it was still a valuable sample that could be studied for its body structure, plumage, and distinctive features.

Rudolf was also delighted to secure a dodo — very likely the first live one to reach Europe. This gawky and defenseless bird was discovered by Dutch sailors on the island of Mauritius on September 18, 1598. Five Dutch ships had come upon this uninhabited island in the Indian Ocean while heading for the East Indies. After landing, the sailors spotted a strange bird waddling around the island and showing no signs of fear at their approach. The undaunted creature had a heavy, ungainly body, stubby wings too small to lift it off the ground, and a large beak shaped like a lobster claw. Originally the dodos, or rather their ancestors, probably did fly, but when they landed on Mauritius and found plenty of food and no predators, they evolved into ground dwellers. Accustomed to their comfortable life on the island, dodos had no idea that the newly arrived Europeans were a dangerous species that would pounce on them and turn them into an easy and tasty meal.

One could well understand the excitement of the Dutchmen — tired of rancid meat and stale, maggot-eaten biscuits — joyfully plucking the bizarre birds from underfoot and savoring their fresh meat, even as they tried to puzzle out what these creatures were. A mixture of scientific perplexity and gastronomic fixation pervades all Dutch accounts of the dodo. First commissar Jacob van Heemskerck described it to the best of his ability: "There is also there a kind of bird the size of a goose, which has legs as those of an ostrich and feet of an eagle, and a very large beak. . . . It has a few feathers in its legs, its wings are like those of jackdaw; they are very fat and their legs, once de-feathered, are very good, but their skin a bit tough." Helmsman Heyndrick Dirrecksen Jolinck jotted down in his diary: "Moreover we found large birds whose wings are the size of those of pigeons, of the kind that cannot fly and that the Portuguese call pingouins. These birds have a stomach [breast] so large that two men can make a royal meal out of it, and it is also their tastiest part." Another helmsman, Philip Grimmaert, echoed the culinary theme: "There were also here big birds, the size of lamb, and we ate them equally; we called them Doederssen [*dodoor* being a Dutch word for a sluggish person]." This may have been the origin of the name dodo.

When the Dutch returned to Amsterdam in late July 1599, they apparently brought aboard a live dodo. It says much about the scientific passion of the age (and the profit to be derived from selling foreign fauna) that the sailors did not eat the bird along the way. Such a fate certainly befell many exotic animals on homeward journeys as food supplies dwindled and fascination with their strangeness dulled. Once the dodo reached Europe,

Rudolf jumped at the chance to add it to his collection, probably buying it from a Dutch merchant who sold him other animals, including birds of paradise.

Did the dodo provide an uplifting distraction from the anxieties and fears Rudolf felt at the approach of the millennium — feelings that would soon push him over the edge? Again he asked one of his court artists to paint the uncanny creature for his compendium of fauna illustrations. (Illustrations of animals became in this era a crucial component of natural history studies because they supplied valuable visual data. As Konrad Gesner wrote, the reader of his *Historia Animalium* could look at the woodcut images of the animals he discussed wherever he pleased, whereas the ancient Romans could see exotic beasts only for the duration of the games.) Likely using this painting as his model, Carolus Clusius made a printed image of the dodo, thus bringing it for the first time to the eyes of Europeans. He included it in his *Exoticorum libri decem* (Ten Books of Exotica), an up-to-date and extremely influential presentation of new animals and plants published in 1605 and based in part on Rudolf's menagerie.

It is unclear how the dodo adjusted to its new life in Prague. By 1609 its embalmed body also resided in Rudolf's *Kunstkammer.* The mortality rate of exotic animals and birds was tragically high once they had been transported to unfamiliar climates and fed inappropriate food. Rudolf probably mourned the demise of his dodo as of his other singular pets, but it seems he was more motivated by a collector's zeal and scientific curiosity than a deep love for the animals. He clearly found them as fascinating and useful when they were in his menagerie or his aviaries in the Royal Garden as when they passed into his anthology of preserved specimens inside the Prague Castle. Not that Rudolf did not care whether his animals were dead or alive; he looked for living beasts first and was mesmerized by them. But his intellectual interests led him to prize stuffed creatures, too, because he could gather more of them than of the live ones, enabling scholars to draw wider conclusions about the properties and peculiarities of each species. The stuffed dodo would acquire even greater value once the bird became extinct only a hundred years after its discovery, having fallen pathetically easy victim to the appetites of the Europeans who landed on Mauritius and the cats, rats, and pigs they brought along.

Rudolf could more readily obtain exotic birds than mammals for his menagerie because birds were easier to bring to Europe. Ships returning from the New World, as well as from the East Indies, often sailed with long rows of birdcages aboard, hoping that their inmates would survive the journey and realize a good profit. Thus the emperor was able to augment his aviary with New World parrots, such as blue macaws with yellow breasts and scarlet macaws with blue and yellow wings, which enlivened the Royal Garden with their tropical colors and loud chatter. He also acquired lovebirds — small parrots with green-blue bodies and red faces and beaks — that live in pairs in tropical Africa and Madagascar. And from Amboine, in the Moluccas, Dutch East India Company merchants brought him a purple-naped lory, a parrot with a red body, green wings, blue feet, and a purple "hat" and wing tips. Rudolf had one of his court artists paint a portrait of the lory cheerfully pecking at a pear, which it holds in place with its claw. Sweet and affectionate creatures, lories make lovely pets. If the portrait does not lie, it would seem that the lory got on quite contentedly in Rudolf's care. The emperor's salmon-crested cockatoo — with its striking white plumage, orange crest, and beak whose curved upper and lower portions overlap like round scissors — lasted through seven Prague winters thanks to the devoted care of the old valet de chambre Christoph Ranft. When it died in August 1608, Ranft received a handsome severance pay of one hundred florins "for seven years of caring for the white parrot and feeding it with the food of its native island [southern Moluccas]."

Rudolf's two ostriches had a rougher time. They were brought from Africa aboard a Venetian galley in 1603. Purchased in Venice by the emperor's agents, the large birds were loaded on carts and transported by an overland route via Innsbruck (Austria), then transferred onto a boat and taken by water to Linz, unloaded onto a cart again, driven to the Vltava, and put on another boat to Prague. The distance between Venice and Prague is 335 miles, but the journey lasted twenty-eight days and taxed the spirits of the birds and their four attendants. Not only was it exhausting to heft crates with heavy and stressed birds on and off carts and ships, and to bump for days along uneven roads and through mountain passes, but the travelers also had to contend with crowds of locals assembled to gawk at the bizarre creatures at every stop along the route. Nor did the ostriches enjoy a long life once they reached the Royal Garden. By 1607 they appeared in the inventory of Rudolf's *Kunstkammer* as mere skins and bones.

Rudolf bought at least some of his birds of paradise — crow-like birds with gorgeous plumage and trailing tail feathers — only as preserved specimens. His supplier in this case was the merchant Hans van Weely, who regularly sold him exotic fauna. The emperor would eventually accumulate sixteen such birds, of different varieties, including the king bird of paradise, with a bright red body, white stomach, blue legs, and two long antenna-like tail feathers ending in a green spiral curl; and the lesser bird of paradise, with a brown body and long, bright yellow and white tail plumes. (Both came from New Guinea.)

Over the course of his reign Rudolf's passion for fauna had become common knowledge, and the fame of his menagerie spread throughout the realm. Though not open to the wider public, it was accessible to Rudolf's visitors and to some well-placed foreigners, who penned accounts of their visits to his zoo. The collection grew thanks to direct purchases and gifts, as those wishing to please or court the emperor would send him exotic beasts. In this way, for example, despite the European war with the Ottomans, Rudolf acquired several dromedaries — very rare in central

Europe at this time. Rudolf's subjects in Hungary, which lay closest to the Ottoman Empire, procured these animals via Turkish intermediaries and presented them to Rudolf. When the English traveler Fynes Moryson visited Prague in 1591, he counted a dozen dromedaries in the Royal Garden. They must have looked incongruous and marvelous, chewing contemplatively as they strolled about the manicured castle grounds.

It was lucky that some animals came to Rudolf for free, for he spent huge sums not only on obtaining so many beasts but also on housing them at his castle. Most of the live animals and birds lived in the Royal Garden, where Rudolf liked to promenade on horseback. His ancestors had previously built a small zoo, but he greatly expanded the premises and their inhabitants. The Royal Garden lay on the north side of the castle and was separated from it by the Stag Moat, where game that Rudolf hunted for diversion was allowed to graze. (Though fascinated by exotic creatures, the emperor had no difficulty killing more common species for sport, and stuffed deer heads abundantly decorated the interior of the castle.) A covered wooden bridge led from the castle to the garden, allowing Rudolf to come and go without being seen, which suited his introverted nature. He preferred to spend time alone here. In addition to the deer ambling around the grounds, buffalo, aurochs, and central Asian sheep with white fleece and black faces and ears munched contentedly on specially allocated meadows.

Rudolf's predecessors had also built a series of pleasure amenities in the garden. His uncle Ferdinand of Tyrol had erected the Belvedere pavilion at the eastern end of the park, with a large ballroom for summertime dance parties. Rudolf was not interested in such pastimes, so he converted the Belvedere into an observatory for Tycho Brahe when the famous astronomer came to his court at the turn of the century. Later he made it into a museum of scientific instruments.

Rudolf's desire to surround himself with the creatures of his passion continued inside the palace. In the castle courtyard, he set up a large perch for his eagle, a symbol of the Holy Roman Emperor. Depictions of this raptor were ubiquitous on the imperial insignia, but Rudolf went to the trouble of keeping a live one. The bird made international news when a Fugger agent reported to the home office that "a short while ago, His Imperial Majesty wished to betake himself to his apartments. . . . Thereupon the eagle, who has his stand in the courtyard by the cistern of the fountain, flew towards His Majesty through the corridor and into his own chamber. There, upon a table, a snow-white dove was to be seen, whereat His Majesty was greatly surprised, for it was unknown to him that white doves were bred in that part of the country." The Fugger agent marveled at the prominence of animals in Rudolf's castle and wondered if the birds' behavior was some kind of an omen.

Rudolf's lions also lived in close proximity to the emperor. He was exceedingly fond of these beasts, having inherited his love for them from his father. Like Maximilian, Rudolf kept a lion in the castle, as if it were a domestic cat, and let it prowl the corridors and curl up by his side, to the astonishment and fear of onlookers. His other wild cats resided in the Lion's Court in the northern part of the Royal Garden. When Rudolf first came to Prague, there had been a wooden animal pavilion there. He replaced it with a stone building with seven large enclosures (10½ by 15 feet each), all facing east, which gave a more comfortable exposure to his animals by letting in the morning light and not overheating the cages during the day. A corridor led from this building to a small adjacent yard through which animal keepers came to clean cages, bring food, and make appropriate heating arrangements in the winter. A spiral staircase in one corner of the courtyard led up to the visitors' gallery overlooking the cages. Rudolf would stand there for long periods, admiring his majestic cats.

Between his affection for big felines and their high mortality rate, the emperor regularly bought lions, tigers, and leopards. The cost of feeding a whole menagerie of hungry animals, on top of paying for their purchase and transport, was a heavy burden on the imperial treasury and on Rudolf's subjects, who were expected to subsidize it. Upkeep was expensive, as the lions required some thirteen pounds of meat per animal per day.

There was, in fact, not always enough money to feed the voracious beasts, and they were often hungry. (Rudolf's wars and other expenditures drained his finances, and he was in desperate need of new sources of wealth.) This might explain why on several occasions the emperor had to recompense servants and subjects mauled by his felines. On September 15, 1581, the imperial treasury was ordered to pay the court barber Matthäus Schrag, the halberdier Hans Rider, and an unnamed woman a compensation for having been attacked and wounded by the emperor's lion inside the Prague Castle. The barber survived the encounter, but the halberdier and the woman died of their wounds. (Presumably their families received the payment.)

Rudolf's tigers caused similar problems. The largest of wild cats, adult male tigers can reach up to 9 feet in length and 660 pounds. Yet Rudolf apparently let them run around half-hungry. In 1580 Peter Zitardus — the guardian of the felines at the Ebersdorf palace, where Rudolf continued to maintain the zoo founded by his father — had to pay an indemnity to a blacksmith whose young child had been wounded by a tiger. The beast must have escaped his cage and begun prowling the palace grounds in search of food. In 1596 the surgeon Georg Schaller received twenty florins to care for another poor boy wounded by His Majesty's tiger. It seems that Rudolf's menagerie eluded his control, just as did the larger political realm he struggled to rule. In the aftermath of each animal attack, it must have been nerve-wracking for Rudolf's servants and courtiers to walk down the castle corridors and grounds, wondering when they might be pounced on by a colossal cat.

Tigers were rarer than lions, which resided in royal and municipal menageries throughout Europe, and thus were considered more valuable and prestigious beasts. The same was true of leopards. Unfortunately, Rudolf's leopards — brought to Europe from Africa, Asia, and India — seem to have been of greater danger to themselves than to humans. In 1579 an Austrian baron bought two leopards for Rudolf for a princely sum of 568 florins. (A sixteenth-century foot soldier was paid 4 florins per month and a veteran soldier 8 florins.) As the animals were being shipped from Venice to Vienna, one of them turned unruly and began to tear violently at its collar. It ripped at it so ferociously that it punctured its own neck. Then, before its guardians could come to the rescue, the poor beast strangled itself, probably by pulling too fiercely on its leash. It was a sad loss, though not a complete one. Rudolf received one live leopard for his menagerie and one hide for his *Kunstkammer*. In 1587 his master of the hunts, Wolf Sigmund, Baron of Auersberg, presented Rudolf with two more leopards plus one English dog.

While lions, tigers, and leopards commanded attention at the Prague Castle, Rudolf's cheetahs added luster to the Star Villa, his hunting lodge outside Prague. Renaissance princes who could afford it kept cheetahs as prized hunting accessories. Keen to take advantage of these cats' hunting qualities and instincts, men over the centuries had perfected the art of catching adult chee-tahs in the wild, taming them within a few months, and training them to work with humans. On the day of the hunt, a cheetah, much like a falcon, had its head covered to keep it from seeing its prey too early and taking off after it. It was led to the hunting area on a leash, in a cart, or on the back of a horse, where it sat behind the rider. Once near its quarry, the animal's head was uncovered, and the cheetah sprinted away. Then, after it had captured the desired game, the trainer would reward it with a piece of meat, which reinforced the contract between man and beast.

Rudolf enjoyed the thrill of the chase and the elegance and skill with which his working animals — horses, dogs, and fal-cons — played their part in the hunt. His cheetahs' grace and

speed made the sport all the more splendid. Because they reproduced poorly in captivity, cheetahs had to be continuously imported from Africa and Asia, so they remained costly and exotic.
Fynes Moryson was very impressed with these magnificent
beasts at Rudolf's hunting lodge:

> The Emperour hath two inclosures walled about, which they
> call Gardaines, one of which is called Stella, because the trees
> are planted in the figure of starres, and a little faire house
> therein is likewise built, with six corners in forme of a starre.
> And in this place he kept 12 Cammels, and Indian Oxe, yellow,
> all over rugged, and hairy upon the throate, like a Lyon; and an
> Indian Calfe, and two Leopards [actually cheetahs*], which
> were said to be tame, if such wild beasts may be tamed. They
> were of a yellow colour spotted with blacke, the head partly
> like a Lyon, partly like a Cat, the tayle like a Cat, the body like
> a Greyhound, and when the hunts-man went abroad, at call
> they leaped up behind him, sitting upon the horse like a dog on
> the hinder parts; being so swift in running, as they would eas-
> ily kill a Hart.

Prized and exotic in a different way were Rudolf's albinos. In
1603 Pierre Bergeron, upon visiting Prague, noted, "Then there
was a menagerie with lions, leopards and civets, as well as a crow
as white as snow." Like Montezuma, Rudolf saw albino animals
as miraculous beings (though, happily, he kept only animal pets,
not humans). He had a live albino raven, magpie, and stag, which
aroused wonder in visitors. Other *Kunstkammer* specimens that
reflected nature's variety included the foot of a sparrow hawk
with twelve claws, the skin of a fawn with two heads, a quail with

---

*People often confused cheetahs and leopards because of their similar appear-
ance. They are two distinct species, and cheetahs were the ones trained to hunt
with men.

three legs, a worm whose tail blossomed into a branch, and other marvels. When he could not obtain actual prodigies, live or preserved, Rudolf got drawings of them to make his collection as complete as possible. Among the most remarkable of these representations was the portrait of Pedro Gonzales and his children.

Gonzales, born in 1544 on Tenerife in the Canary Islands, was afflicted with hirsutism, the congenital occurrence of abnormal hair growth over one's entire body. Deemed "a miraculous work of nature," he was shipped as a baby to France, to the court of King Henry II. Educated by the king and "rejecting the customs of his native land" (his barbaric ways, presumably), Gonzales studied fine arts and Latin and became a man of letters. After his royal patron died, Gonzales moved to the Netherlands, where around 1563 he married a perfectly normal woman — a rather attractive Dutch girl. The couple had four children; three of them inherited their father's hirsutism.

Because of their marvelous appearance, the Gonzales family became international celebrities and were painted by several artists for princely collectors. In these portraits Pedro and his hairy children were depicted as nobility — dressed in opulent aristocratic garments — but with furry, animal-like faces. The little girl in particular looked like a pretty cat decked out in human clothing. The strangeness of these people — the wondrous way in which they combined a cultured European spirit with animal-like bodies — was heightened by the inclusion in some of the portraits of their mother, a pleasant smooth-skinned woman in simpler attire.*

As the naturalists of their day saw it, Gonzales and his children were the epitome of divine creativity. By adding their portrait to his collection of fauna, Rudolf augmented its encyclopedic scope. And although he did not keep people in cages, in this peculiar case

---

*The portraits usually showed only two of the hairy children. Perhaps the third one did not survive and the fourth, normal-looking one was too unremarkable to depict or also died.

he seems to have had no qualms about blurring the line between fantastic animals and people. As Carolus Clusius wrote in his *Ten Books of Exotica*, "I hear that in these foreign things of his, His Majesty is greatly delighted by the thought of all the miracles of Nature."

All of this collecting provided Rudolf with an escape from his political woes. Nothing illustrates this better than his long pursuit of a rhinoceros. Instrumental to this wild goose chase was his ambassador to the Spanish court, Hans Khevenhüller. Given the fraught relations between Rudolf and Philip II, Khevenhüller had his hands full with all kinds of diplomatic matters. It is astonishing, then, how much time and energy he devoted — or, depending on one's point of view, wasted — in tracking down the rare creature for his lord.

In September 1577 a rhinoceros arrived in Portugal from India. This massive beast, with a deeply creased hide that looks like armor plates, has an unpredictable character and can be dangerous when threatened, charging its potential enemy with its horn lowered and ready to strike. Few wished to risk their lives capturing and transporting live rhinoceroses, so the appearance of such a creature in Lisbon made international news. As soon as it reached Rudolf, he apparently instructed Khevenhüller to secure the marvelous beast for him.

Unfortunately, there were other contenders, including Francesco I de' Medici, the grand duke of Tuscany — another avid student of nature — and Pope Gregory XIII. But Khevenhüller was not easily discouraged. He began by ordering a portrait of the rhinoceros, which he dispatched to Prague as a kind of promissory note, as well as a piece for Rudolf's collection of illustrations. Khevenhüller's plan was to wait until King Sebastian of Portugal presented the animal to the king of Spain. He was reasonably sure that he would then be able to secure it for Rudolf since, "as Your Majesty knows, the king [Philip II] is not so keen on such things."

Frustratingly, however, Khevenhüller's initial negotiations were annulled when, in August 1578, King Sebastian fell in a bloody battle in North Africa between the Portuguese and the Moors. Sebastian's old uncle Henry, who had been a cardinal, stepped in to take the throne. Khevenhüller dispatched servants and diplomats to get the beast from Henry, offering to pay the cost of transporting the cumbersome and foul-tempered creature to Madrid and then on to Prague. But King Henry had different plans. He needed to persuade the pope to relieve him of the vow of celibacy he had taken as part of his previous ecclesiastical career and which, in his present position, was quite a burden. The gift of an astonishing animal seemed to him a perfect offering to gain the pontiff's favor.

On January 31, 1580, Henry died without having dispatched the rhinoceros to Rome. After several months of uncertainty and a struggle for succession, Philip II invaded Portugal and claimed the throne, in the process wreaking great bloodshed and destruction on Lisbon. Under the circumstances, the rhinoceros faded from view for some time.

In August 1582 Khevenhüller seemed to be getting closer to obtaining the beast. He was pondering how to send it to Prague. It was a ferocious animal, he reported to Rudolf, and its transport would cause great difficulties. "Even though its horn has been cut down, it does not cease to kick and maltreat people around it. Recently it even killed a royal servant. It is a dangerous animal. And blind in one eye, and they think it does not see much out of the other."

As it turned out, Khevenhüller had been wrong to get his hopes up. At the beginning of 1583, once Philip II had stabilized his affairs in Portugal enough to be able to return home, he decided to keep the rhinoceros for himself. Transporting it to Spain, along with an elephant that had arrived from India in 1581, he proceeded to send the two animals on a tour around the country to be shown to the marveling populace. Even three years later the animals were still bringing profit, both material and political, to Philip. In November of 1584 they were put on display in Madrid to impress the first Japanese delegation ever to come to Europe.

Since there was no love lost between Philip and Rudolf, the Spanish king obviously was not in a rush to cede his valuable animal to his Protestant-sympathizing, rebel-shielding nephew.

At last, in 1603, Rudolf received word that the rhinoceros had died. But the demise of an animal did not dissuade the emperor from trying to add it to his encyclopedic collection. In 1605 he would gladly buy from Emanuel Swerts of Amsterdam, a merchant who regularly supplied the court, a stuffed sloth that had expired en route from America. Rudolf also possessed the skin of a pangolin (a scaly mammal that dwells in Africa and Asia), three preserved South American iguanas, four armadillos, two chameleons, two Indian crawfish, and some blowfish and sea horses, among others.

Even in death, however, the rhinoceros, or what remained of it, proved elusive. After many months of inquiries and pleas, Khevenhüller was told that its hide was no longer available. It had been poorly prepared and was spoiled and full of worms. Still, the tenacious Khevenhüller and his lord were determined, after all this time, to get some piece of the beast. At last, in December 1603, Khevenhüller laid his hands on the animal's horn and some bones. He dispatched them to Prague with what must have been an audible sigh of relief. It had taken nearly three decades of intense diplomatic efforts to add this creature to the emperor's scientific menagerie. Though far from a complete specimen, it was, by the standards of the day, a valuable stand-in for the whole beast. The rhinoceros turned out to be a perfect symbol of Rudolf's intrinsic impotence to master his political world. Instead of pursuing diplomacy that might get him out of his bind with his family, with the Ottomans, and with his other rivals and critics, he spent his ambassador's time chasing after a rhino — and then the rhino's carcass.

JUST AS RUDOLF'S animal collecting was gaining momentum, his political situation worsened alarmingly, together with his mental state. In 1600 he suffered his second and more dramatic breakdown, caving in under a combination of pressures, disappointments, and fears that had been eating away at him for a decade. The final straw was his intense anxiety about the turn of the seventeenth century. Rudolf was highly superstitious by nature; now he was gripped by the fear that he would die before the age of fifty, like his father, and, worse, fall victim to an assassination. Around the year 1600 the court astronomer Tycho Brahe had drawn up the emperor's astrological chart and prophesied that he would be plotted against by members of his own family — certainly a very plausible scenario, which would indeed come true — and perhaps be stabbed to death. As a consequence, Rudolf began to fear audiences and to avoid appearing in public. Yet he refused to delegate authority and insisted on continuing to make important decisions himself. Predictably, his ability to govern in this agitated condition suffered, and his grip on political power deteriorated.

In the next few months, feeling cornered, Rudolf lashed out in all directions, insulting, dismissing, and imprisoning his ministers and even his trusted associates. In a fit of uncontrollable rage, he banished from his court two of his closest advisers, Wolfgang Rumpf and Paul Sixt Trautson. He faulted Rumpf for his close links with Spain and his pressure on Rudolf to settle the issue of succession. Rudolf was in the grip of the most severe depression he had ever experienced. He spoke of abdication and apparently attempted suicide more than once. As confusion in his court worsened, Rudolf retreated from the world and remained out of view for two years. Many thought that he had died.

This new breakdown only gave ammunition to Rudolf's family and enemies, who had long been harping that his hatred of the Church and his dabbling in alchemy had made the emperor unfit to rule. They voiced their growing conviction that he was both a madman and a damned soul and schemed to depose him on the grounds of lack of succession and insanity. But it seems that

Rudolf thought he was actually healing his soul by shunning the world and spending his time in the company of artists, scholars, alchemists, and animals. The more he sank into melancholy, the more he apparently hoped that being surrounded by his exotic and marvelous pets and his natural history collection would ease his mental anguish. Through his menagerie and his *Kunstkammer,* Rudolf tried to create an alternate world where he could be well.

His other fellows in this private kingdom were, in fact, men who shared the emperor's interests in nature, science, and the occult. Rudolf's family was indignant that, hidden in the recesses of his palace, "His Majesty is interested only in wizards, alchemists, kabbalists and the like, sparing no expense to find all kinds of treasures, learn secrets and use scandalous ways of harming his enemies. . . . He also has a whole library of magical books. He strives all the time to eliminate God completely so that he may in future serve a different master." This was not how the Holy Roman Emperor was expected to behave. But while his critics were correct that Rudolf immersed himself in occult studies, this was not a sign of madness so much as a logical extension of his pursuit of natural history.

In this period of political and religious upheaval, alchemy had reached the height of its popularity. (The second half of the sixteenth century is considered "the golden age of alchemy.") In his treatise *Philosophical Colloquium* (1597), Alexander Lauterwald argued that the alchemist's true purpose was to heal all bodies, "human, animal and metallic," of the worldly corruption that followed the fall of Adam and Eve. So at its purest, alchemy was the sacred work of curing underlying spiritual ills. No wonder Rudolf pursued alchemy with such keenness that his court became an internationally renowned and preeminent center for magic and occult studies.

Alchemy also claimed to offer health benefits. When Lorenzo de' Medici's health was declining in 1492, his physicians treated him with a potion composed of ground gems (by today's standards not the best therapy for the gout that eventually killed him). Lorenzo's court philosopher, Marsilio Ficino, explained that gems and precious metals could call down the favorable influences of the planets, for each celestial body was attracted to and acted through terrestrial matter. In his *Three Books on Life* (1489), Ficino outlined an entire program of mineralogical and astrological medicine best suited for the health of an intellectual and prescribed gold, gems, and other ingredients as potent curatives.

> If you want your body and spirit to receive power from some member of the cosmos, say from the Sun, seek the things which above all are most Solar among metals and gems, still more among plants, and more yet among animals, especially human beings. . . . These must both be brought to bear externally and, so far as possible, taken internally, especially in the day and the hour of the Sun and while the Sun is dominant in a theme of heavens. Solar things are: all those gems and flowers which are called heliotrope because they turn towards the sun, likewise gold, chrysolite, carbuncle, myrrh, frankincense, musk, amber, balsam, yellow honey, sweet calamus, saffron, spikenard, cinnamon, aloe-wood and the rest of the spices; the ram, the hawk, the cock, the swan, the lion, the scarab beetle, the crocodile, and people who are blond, curly-haired, prone to baldness, and magnanimous.

Rudolf obsessively worried about his health (he suffered from digestive as well as mental problems) and about his longevity, so he looked to alchemy's medical promises with great hope.

Alchemy also had more tangible material applications. Much of Rudolf's wealth depended on the mineral riches of his territories. Bohemia, for example, was especially abundant in silver, tin, lead, and semiprecious stones. But the demands of courtly splendor and Rudolf's obsession with acquiring exotic animals were depleting his coffers. At the same time, over the course of the previous century, the production of central Europe's mines had begun to stagnate. Because of the production slump, German and Bohemian rulers in particular sought ways to improve mining in their lands — their major source of income. Alchemical expertise could help extract precious metals from ores and increase yields. Besides, alchemists promised to multiply existing precious metals and to turn metals of lesser quality into gold or silver. Rudolf hoped to profit from this magic. He founded a new mining town named after himself (Rudolfov), fostered mining explorations, and supported the work of Lazarus Ercker, his main adviser on the exploitation of minerals. Ercker's treatise on assaying and smelting methods, published in Prague in 1574, became a landmark work on the subject.

So while the emperor seemed to his family to be wasting time and resources on useless indulgences, he believed that he was advancing science and industry in his realm, in part by personally engaging in scientific studies — apparently he invented a mechanical chart for travelers, actuated from beneath by a compass — but largely by sponsoring such investigations at his court. The same was true of the money and efforts he expended on building his menagerie and his *Kunstkammer*. By gathering examples of every kind of creation — *naturalia* (nature's inventions), *artificialia* (objects made by man), and *scientifica* (instruments of human knowledge) — Rudolf assembled the universe in microcosm, a theater of the world, as contemporaries called it.

According to theories of the time, there existed magical links between the microcosm and the macrocosm. Through the study of this variety of creation and of alchemy, Rudolf aspired to grasp the underlying unity, which could serve as a "key" to the harmony of the universe, much as physicists today continue to look for a "theory of everything." In a more personal sense, the objects and creatures Rudolf gathered were talismans that promised to strengthen his control over the greater world, which was so precipitously slipping through his fingers.

At the same time, Rudolf turned his collection into a hands-on scientific laboratory for specialists invited to his court. Alsemus Boethius de Boodt, one of Rudolf's doctors and also his chief lapidary, wrote his book *Gemmarum et Lapidum Historia* (A History of Gems and Stones) (1609), largely based on his study of minerals in Rudolf's *Kunstkammer*. This book, considered to be "the most important lapidary of the seventeenth century" and reissued in some ten editions, covered 647 minerals. It offered a complete reclassification of stones, discussed the location of their deposits, treated their morphological characteristics, examined their virtues and powers, and addressed their medical applications. In the book's dedication, de Boodt praised Rudolf as a lover of stones "not simply in order that he may thereby augment his dignity and majesty . . . but so that in them the excellence of God may be contemplated, the ineffable might of Him Who is seen to press the beauty of the whole world into such exiguous bodies and include in them the powers of all other created things."

De Boodt also helped found the Bohemian crystal industry, worked on alchemical transmutations, studied botany and zoology, and produced a splendid album of drawings depicting birds and plants, again using Rudolf's collection. Among the creatures de Boodt illustrated (some of them wearing collars and thus presumably alive rather than stuffed) were a skunk, a coatimundi, and a llama — all New World pets in Rudolf's menagerie.

Rudolf's chief botanist, Carolus Clusius,* also studied the emperor's collection of preserved animals and birds. Through careful observation he became the first to grasp the truth behind birds of paradise. These birds, with slender bodies and exquisite trailing plumes, were first discovered by the Spanish in the Spice Islands in 1519. They at once captured Europeans' imaginations,

---

*He is credited with introducing the potato to Europe.

in part because they were said to live always in the air, for they had no feet. This is how they got their name, which referred to the heavens rather than to the birds' tropical origins. This unlikely notion had arisen because for much of the sixteenth century, birds of paradise reached Europe as preserved, and modified, specimens. When in 1594 Clusius looked closely at the samples assembled by Rudolf, he realized that native traders had altered the beautiful birds by removing their feet and wings, presumably to give them a more striking and aerodynamic appearance.

Despite their spirit of scientific inquiry, Rudolf's scientists were sometimes misled by the more fabulous creatures in his collection. De Boodt described one illustration of a specimen from the *Kunstkammer* as "a Dragon which the Emperor Rudolf II has; dried it is this exact size, where it is preserved." Yet Rudolf and de Boodt were by no means out of step with developments in natural history in gathering and studying dragons. Gesner and Aldrovandi devoted lengthy discussions to their anatomical, etymological, and moral significance and distinguished between real and fake ones. Gesner described how certain apothecaries made fraudulent dragons from rays: "They bend the body, distort the head and mouth, and cut into and cut away other parts. They raise up the parts that remain and simulate wings, and invent other parts as well." De Boodt was not always so credulous. Examining the unicorn's horn in Rudolf's *Kunstkammer,* he concluded that the legendary unicorn did not exist, since the "unicorn horn" clearly came from a narwhal.

Rudolf promoted such research and engaged in it himself. "When our arduous tasks of government permit," he wrote to the Italian polymath Giovanni Battista della Porta, author of *Natural Magic* (which included observations on geology, optics, medicines, poisons, cooking, metallurgy, magnetism, perfumes, gunpowder, and invisible writing — a range of interests consonant with those of Rudolf), "we enjoy the subtle knowledge of natural and artificial things in which you excel." A Tuscan ambassador commented disapprovingly that "he himself [Rudolf] tries alchemical experiments, and he himself is busily engaged in making clocks, which is against the decorum of a prince. He had transferred his seat from the imperial throne to the workshop stool."

Although Rudolf was usually reclusive, he was always glad to display his collection to interested visitors and foreign dignitaries. When Cardinal Alessandro d'Este and Archduke Maximilian III came to Prague in 1604, the emperor eagerly took them on a tour of his menagerie, stables, and garden. During the visit of Elector Christian II of Saxony in July 1607, the only private audience he had with the emperor was spent visiting his collections. And the Venetian ambassador noted that because of Rudolf's interest in "the secrets of natural matter, as of artificial . . . he who has the chance to treat of these things will always find the ears of the emperor ready."

RUDOLF'S DARKEST YEARS as a ruler proved his most productive as a devotee of nature, alchemy, and science. His intellectual inquisitiveness and religious tolerance made Prague a beacon for scientists, scholars, and craftsmen. Karel van Mander, a Dutch painter and theorist who visited Prague in 1604 to study the emperor's superb art holdings, wrote admiringly, "Whosoever aspires today to do anything great need only come (if he can) to Prague, to the greatest patron of the contemporary world, the Emperor Rudolf II; he will see there, in the imperial residence . . . an extraordinary number of excellent and precious things, special, unusual and beyond price."

Among those who accepted Rudolf's invitation was Tycho Brahe, a renowned astronomer whose colorful personality rivaled Rudolf's own. Like Rudolf, Tycho was an animal lover. His pet of choice (before he came to Prague) was a moose that used to follow him around like a dog. One day it followed its master into a dining hall during a dinner party. Whether upon the urging of the amused company or out of its own sense of mischief, the moose got its muzzle into a vat of beer. Unfortunately, it drank so much that on exiting the banquet, it fell down the stairs, broke a leg, and died from complications shortly thereafter.

Tycho had another unusual attribute: a false nose. As a twenty-year-old student at the University of Rostock in Germany, he had quarreled with another Danish nobleman at a dancing party at his professor's house. The two young men parted in anger at the end of the evening and picked up their fight again a few days later, deciding to settle their differences in a duel. Tycho's opponent turned out to be the better swordsman, and in one successful swipe sliced off much of Tycho's nose. Tycho, whose talents lay outside swordsmanship, drew on his alchemical skills to fashion a prosthesis from an alloy of gold, silver, and copper — probably to match the color of his flesh. He made and attached his new nose so skillfully that it looked nearly real, although he always carried around a small box of paste or glue to reattach it if it popped off.

It was for Tycho's scientific gifts, however, that Rudolf invited him to Prague. Tycho brought with him an array of instruments and records on celestial bodies, for he believed that the advancement of astronomy hinged on accurate observations. He not only designed and built his own equipment but regularly checked and calibrated it for precision, thus revolutionizing astronomical instrumentation. He also changed observational practice. Earlier astronomers had been content to view the positions of the planets and the moon only at certain important points of their orbits, but Tycho studied them throughout their orbits and made explicit a number of orbital anomalies never noticed before. He was also the first astronomer to make corrections for atmospheric refraction. Even more impressive was the fact that he accomplished all this before the invention of the telescope, relying only on rulers, quadrants, sextants, and armillary spheres.

Tycho came to Prague in 1599, at a time when the emperor was sliding into one of his worst depressions. Although the troubled ruler shunned most other visitors, he greeted Tycho with open arms and bare head, as if the scientist were a fellow king. He offered the astronomer a salary of three thousand ducats per year, the largest at court, and put at his disposal the castle of Benatek, on the outskirts of Prague, to set up an observatory there. Rudolf also gave Tycho the Belvedere in the Royal Garden as his workspace so as to be able to visit the astronomer as often as he wished, ask Tycho to explain his instruments, and discuss experiments with him.

Rudolf was enthralled by Tycho's science and did not care in the least that he was a Protestant. But the Catholic faction at court viewed the astronomer as the emperor's "evil genius." So they may have gotten their wish when two years later, on October 13, 1601, Tycho attended a banquet at the house of a leading Bohemian nobleman. Tycho spent the evening eating and drinking heartily, but when nature called, he decided it would be impolite to leave the table to empty his bladder; he would wait until the dinner was over. Unfortunately, when he finally got home, he was unable to pass water. After five sleepless, agonizing nights, he finally produced bloody urine. Then followed more insomnia and fever. On the morning of October 24 he died after hours of delirium, during which he muttered, in Latin, "Ne frustra vixisse videar" (May I not seem to have lived in vain).

After Tycho's death, rumors began to circulate that he had been poisoned, given that both the Catholic council and the nobility had resented his influence over Rudolf. When an analysis of the astronomer's beard was conducted in the 1990s (his tomb had first been opened in 1901, revealing a male corpse with a nose opening rimmed with traces of copper), it showed that Tycho was, indeed, poisoned — but the poison was probably self-administered. As a practitioner of medical alchemy, Tycho concocted various drugs, including ones containing mercury, a common ingredient in curative potions in those days. Traces of mercury in Tycho's beard suggest that shortly before attending the banquet, he probably took pills containing mercury to treat his enlarged prostate and the resultant urinary problems. It was the combination of mercury poisoning and uremia that killed him within those few miserable days.

Soon thereafter Rudolf appointed Tycho's assistant, Johannes Kepler, as imperial mathematician, the most prestigious mathematics position in Europe. For the next eleven years, until Rudolf's death, Kepler thrived under the emperor's patronage. In 1604 he published *Astronomia pars Optica* (The Optical Part of Astronomy), in which he discussed atmospheric refraction and lenses and gave the explanation still accepted today for the workings of the eye. Two years later he produced *De Stella Nova,* describing a new star, actually a supernova, that had appeared in 1604.

In 1609 Kepler's *Astronomia Nova* (New Astronomy) came out, introducing his first two laws: first, that planets move in elliptical orbits with the sun as one of the foci (a thesis he was able to demonstrate thanks to Tycho's accurate observations); second, that a planet sweeps out equal areas of an ellipse during equal intervals of time, meaning that the closer a planet comes to the sun, the faster it moves. Kepler's *Tabulae Rudolphinae* (Rudolfine Tables) — which used Tycho's observations on the planets and stars to catalog the positions of 1,005 stars and offered tables of refraction values — was published in 1627 and posthumously paid homage to the emperor's enlightened support. Perhaps only someone like Rudolf — only a patron who was literally crazy about science — could have provided the means for all of these discoveries and momentous advances in knowledge. By giving his scientists free rein to pursue their research, Rudolf fostered a remarkably creative environment at his court and turned Prague into the intellectual capital of Europe.

When, in 1610, Kepler received news of Galileo's newly devised telescope, Rudolf wanted to learn all about the Italian astronomer's findings: irregularities on the surface of the moon, numerous new stars, and the satellites of Jupiter. It was another sign of the emperor's religious tolerance and broader vision that he embraced the work of Galileo despite the fact that the astronomer was condemned by the Catholic Church. Rudolf suggested that Kepler use instruments from his *Kunstkammer* to take these investigations further. Meanwhile, Galileo sent one of his telescopes to Prague. Thanks to these instruments and Rudolf's benefaction, Kepler published *Narratio de Observatis Quatuor Jovis Satellitibus* (Narration About Four Satellites of Jupiter Observed). Rudolf, Kepler wrote appreciatively, was endowed with the same restless spirit of seeking out nature that Galileo possessed.

The English philosopher Francis Bacon suggested in his *Gesta Grayorum,* presented at the English court during the twelve days of Christmas in 1594, that to achieve greatness, a ruler must engage in the conquest of nature, "the searching out, inventing, and discovering of all whatsoever is hid and secret in the world."

Those kingdoms were accounted most happy, that had rulers most addicted to philosophy. . . . And to this purpose I will commend to Your Highness [the English king] four principal works and monuments to yourself: First, the collecting of a most perfect and general library. . . . Next, a spacious, wonderful garden, wherein whatsoever plant the sun of divers climates, out of the earth of divers molds, either wild or by culture of man brought forth. . . . This garden to be built about with rooms to stable in all rare beasts and to cage in all rare birds; with two lakes adjoining, the one of fresh water the other of salt, for like variety of fishes. And so you may have in small compass a model of universal nature made private. The third, a goodly huge cabinet, wherein whatsoever the hand of man by exquisite art or engine hath made rare in stuff, form, or motion; whatsoever singularity chance and the shuffle of things hath produced; whatsoever Nature hath wrought in things that want life and may be kept; shall be sorted and included. The fourth such a still-house, so furnished with mills, instruments, furnaces, and vessels, as may be a palace fit for a philosopher's stone.

Although Rudolf had already put into effect just such an all-encompassing program, it seemed to rob him of his rule rather than enhance it. The protracted and indecisive Ottoman war had drained his finances and prompted his Hungarian subjects, who bore the brunt of the conflict, to revolt in 1604. The next year Rudolf's family stepped in and forced him to cede Hungarian affairs to his ambitious younger brother Matthias, who had become the candidate for succession after Ernest died in 1595.

There was little affection between the two siblings. Matthias, unlike Rudolf, had not been sent to Spain and had grown into a decisive, ambitious, and manipulative man who schemed for years to unseat his older brother and take his place on the imperial throne. Matthias was also politically savvy and saw that bringing the Ottoman and Hungarian conflicts to a close would help consolidate his power. In 1606, accomplishing what Rudolf had not been able to do, he laboriously concluded peace first with the Hungarian rebels and then with the Turks. At the same time, alarmed by Rudolf's growing detachment and incompetence, as well as his failure to guarantee succession, Rudolf's brothers and cousins began to speak about deposing him. On April 25, 1606, they met secretly in Vienna and recognized Matthias as the de facto head of the house of Habsburg.

Even as Matthias was moving to seize power, Rudolf, trapped in the enormous gap between the glorious ideal of his title and the sordid reality of family rivalries, was plunged into another depression and again disappeared from public view. Seemingly lost to the world, he focused more than ever on his natural history collection and on giving his *Kunstkammer* a new splendid shape. Up to now his specimens, instruments, and artifacts had been spread throughout the palace, but in 1605 Rudolf began to move them into a newly constructed series of rooms consisting of three vaulted antechambers, each measuring 65 by 18 feet, and a main hall some 98 by 18 feet.

The rooms were illuminated by large windows on their western sides and crowded everywhere else with cupboards, chests, and tables. Globes and clocks, sculptures and precious vessels, antlers and stuffed animals congregated on every available surface. The cupboards contained the embalmed, dried, and partial specimens of animals, birds, insects, and crustaceans, as well as shells, pieces of corals, and minerals. Chests housed the emperor's scientific instruments and clever mechanical toys — such as a peacock that walked, turned around, and fanned its tail made of real feathers, and a large gold spider that could be wound up and sent scurrying across the table. Small statuettes, works in gold and silver, carved gems, and ivories rested in their own cabinets, as did Rudolf's books and illustrations of fauna and flora.

In the middle of the main hall of the *Kunstkammer* stood a long table covered with green cloth on which were disposed various natural history objects and instruments. Here Rudolf would sit and study for hours. As the ambassador of the Duke of Savoy, Carlo Francesco Manfredi, reported home, Rudolf spent "two and a half hours sitting motionless, looking at the painting of fruit and fish markets sent by Your Highness." Were Rudolf's relatives right, and was he indeed mad to stare at one image for so long? Or was such focus a sign of passionate absorption in objects that brought him knowledge and joy? His collection, both inside the *Kunstkammer* and outside in his menagerie and aviaries, was his refuge and a source of unceasing pleasure, the one kingdom that never disappointed or failed him.

Outside the *Kunstkammer* and the Royal Garden, however, Rudolf's world continued to disintegrate. Appalled by Matthias's negotiations with the Ottomans, the emperor wanted to renew the Turkish war. Matthias moved faster. Rallying support among the disaffected Hungarians, and promising religious and political concessions to them as well as to the emperor's subjects in Austria and Moravia, Matthias received their assistance and marched on Prague at the head of a large army in the summer of 1608. Rudolf, cornered, was forced to cede Austria, Hungary, and Moravia to his hated brother. He was left only Bohemia, Tyrol, and the increasingly meaningless imperial title.

At least for the time being, his Bohemian subjects remained loyal, though for a price. Taking advantage of the emperor's political and mental weakness, they compelled him to issue, on July 9, 1609, a "Letter of Majesty" that gave the Protestants official permission to freely exercise their religion, construct churches and schools, control the university, and compose a constitution governing their rights. Although Rudolf had been a tolerant ruler, he had so far done his best to walk a middle road between the Catholics and Protestants, and this dispensation, larger than he felt comfortable with, underscored his decline.

In 1611 Rudolf attempted one last time to regain his power. He urged his chosen successor, his cousin Archduke Leopold V, bishop of Passau, to come to Prague with an army to restore his authority and oust Matthias, who had confined him to the city. Leopold complied, but as he marched through southern Bohemia, his army pillaged the countryside. And when his forces reached Prague, they devastated the New City but failed to turn out Matthias. This botched intervention only further discredited Rudolf. His Bohemian subjects now appealed to Matthias to defend them, and he was pleased to oblige. Taking Rudolf as a virtual prisoner, he forced him to yield the crown of Bohemia in May 1611. For the next nine months, the last of his life, Rudolf dwelled as a ghost in his own home. A contemporary portrait shows the pudgy emperor with a bushy beard concealing the Habsburg jaw and bags under his deep-set eyes, which look wearily and sadly out of the darkness of the picture. His personal physician, Johannes Pistorius, commented that the emperor was melancholic and that there were many malevolent types around him taking advantage of his condition to make things worse. Even in these last miserable years, when he was widely reputed to be mentally imbalanced and unapproachable, apathetic yet extremely stubborn, Rudolf continued to win over visitors to his court. Daniel Eremita, who came to Prague as part of the Tuscan embassy in 1609, was irritated by the delay before the reclusive emperor would receive even such a high-ranking delegation and remarked on his evidently failing powers. But he wrote admiringly that "the Emperor's amazing knowledge of all things, his ripe judgment, and skill have made him famous, while his friendliness, steadfastness in religion, and moral integrity have won him popularity; these were the principles of his outstanding and remarkable reign which gained the plaudits of the whole world."

In the opinion of his detractors, Rudolf had ruined everything by taking up the study of arts and nature with such a lack of moderation that he deserted the affairs of state for alchemists' laboratories, painters' studios, clockmakers' workshops, and animal enclosures. "Disturbed in his mind by some ailment of melancholy, he had begun to love solitude and shut himself off in his Palace as if behind the bars of a prison," lamented Eremita. The result was administrative chaos. Yet when Rudolf died from edema on January 20, 1612, the people of Prague mourned "der gute Herr" (the good lord), whose reign had brought to Prague a golden age. While Rudolf's temporal reign fell far short of success, his intellectual pursuits lived up to a princely ideal that few rulers managed to attain.

SHORTLY BEFORE HIS final showdown with Matthias, Rudolf began to inventory his vast holdings of *naturalia, artificialia,* and *scientifica.* This process, which started in 1607, continued for four years because his *Kunstkammer* was so huge in scope, variety, and importance. Truly it was the entire world in one place.

The richest and most significant portion of the collection were his specimens of *naturalia* (and the inventory did not even include the live beasts). In addition to the more familiar animals and those already mentioned, there were stuffed lorises (lemur-like animals from Asia) and various African and South American monkeys, including the first (dead) colobus brought to Europe from Ethiopia. A black-crowned crane from South Africa looked very elegant with its white-tipped wings and a golden crown of feathers atop its head. The splendid red-billed toucan — a black bird with a white throat and a massive red bill with black and yellow stripes at its base — was represented by six beaks. The stuffed African penguin, about 27½ inches long and weighing from 4½ to 6½ pounds, came from South Africa, where its habitat coincided with the cold, nutrient-rich Benguela Current. The inventory described it as "skin of duck of Magellan which walks upright on two feet like a man; the bird is black and white and has very curious wings, without true plumage."

Rudolf's marine specimens encompassed red and black coral, various shells, crabs and lobsters, blowfish, Norwegian basket stars (starfish with heavily branched arms that look like intricate tree roots), walking batfish from off the coasts of Brazil and Florida, and flying fish with enlarged winglike fins used for brief gliding flights several feet above the water.* And then there were marvelous insects, including a leaf insect from Southeast Asia, which has the color and shape of an old leaf with slightly browning and curling edges, and a South American cricket with jasper wings.

Rudolf also had an extensive collection of ethnographic arti-

---

*A Fugger agent sailing from Lisbon to India recorded that "I have seen many kinds of fish, whereof there would be much to write, especially of those that fly above the sea and have wings. This many will not wish to believe, but I have seen them a thousand times fly as near as the musket will carry."

facts from China, India, Siam (Thailand), Persia, Turkey, Egypt, and the New World (including Mexican feather pictures depicting Christian saints). And there was a section devoted to weapons, from superbly wrought Turkish swords captured in battle with the Ottomans to a dagger that supposedly was the one used to murder Julius Caesar in 44 BC. The inventory of the *Kunstkammer* described these objects with much care, giving their dimensions and explaining the techniques of their manufacture and decoration.

With Rudolf's demise, his collection quickly scattered. Just prior to his end, when he had lost his power and apparently his ability to care properly for his animals, the inventory of live beasts in the Lion's Court listed only one lion, two tigers, one bear, and two wildcats. There may have been some other creatures left elsewhere in the Royal Garden and the aviaries, but the menagerie was clearly at its nadir. Meanwhile, Matthias secretly began to move to Vienna the most valuable items from his brother's collection — primarily artwork and objects made from precious materials. (The Venetian envoy Girolamo Soranzo estimated that there were more than three thousand paintings alone. The other treasures were valued at seventeen million ducats — more than the entire Spanish royal budget in 1628.)

The Bohemian estates clamored for part of these assets, since they had helped pay for them, and a great deal more was dispersed when Prague was invaded by Swedish troops in 1648 at the end of the Thirty Years' War.* Ironically, this war, which would rage throughout Europe for a generation, was sparked on the very grounds of the Prague Castle on May 23, 1618. On that day the Catholic lieutenant governors serving the new Habsburg king, Ferdinand II (Matthias's successor) were hurled out of the windows

---

*This conflict swept central Europe from 1618 to 1648, pitting the German Protestant princes and a number of foreign powers against the Holy Roman Empire and its Catholic allies, and causing massive death and destruction.

of their offices by Protestant Bohemian nobles. The religious tolerance and peace that Rudolf had tried to preserve during his reign came to naught shortly after his death.

The surviving inventory of the *Kunstkammer* is the only testament to the once astonishing, marvelous, and inspiring world that Rudolf had created in Prague. Alas, the hundreds of lines of German script give us some idea of the *Kunstkammer* but do not bring it to life. There remains, however, one piece of the emperor's collection that still seems to breathe: the *Museum of Rudolf II.*

As if sensing that his *Kunstkammer* would vanish with his death, Rudolf ordered his court artists to produce a pictorial record of his beloved creatures, both live and preserved. The *Museum* consists of two large volumes, measuring more than 16 by 12 inches and containing 179 illustrated parchment folios. On their pages passes a parade of Rudolf's mammals and birds, reptiles and fish, insects and corals, and noteworthy animal parts. Here is the horn of the rhinoceros that Hans Khevenhüller spent almost thirty years trying to procure for the emperor; the tusk that de Boodt correctly identified as belonging to a narwhal rather than a unicorn; the skin of a hippopotamus with its head and teeth attached, draped over a dowel on which it hung from the ceiling of the *Kunstkammer.* Aside from these fragments, redolent with history, most of the other animals appear still alive and full of spirit. They are as mesmerizing now as they were to Rudolf when he strolled past their enclosures in the Royal Garden or pored over their remains in the *Kunstkammer.* And something of the emperor's own spirit lingers in the few images of *naturalia* arranged on the green cloth table at which Rudolf spent his days seeking to unlock the mysteries of the universe.

LES CORVETTES LE GÉOGRAPHE LE NATURALISTE
ET LA GOËLETTE LE CASUARINA.

SIX

THE BLACK SWANS
OF MALMAISON

Malmaison . . . was empty. Josephine was dead. . . .
Already, for want of attention, the exotic trees were
pining away; the black Australian swans no longer
glided along the canals; the cages no longer held the
tropical birds prisoners: they had flown away to await
their host in their native land.

FRANÇOIS-RENÉ CHATEAUBRIAND,
The Memoirs of Chateaubriand

During the eighteenth century, the sciences assumed increasing importance not only for professional natural
historians and a few curious rulers but also for larger society.
They came to be seen as useful for national industry and agriculture, general education and the improvement of the population.
In France, both in Paris and in the provinces, classes on natural
history, experimental physics, chemistry, and mathematics drew
lay audiences. Scientific societies sprang up across the country
like mushrooms after rain. Books on scientific topics came out in
multiple editions, and collecting natural specimens in an enlightened manner became a mark of taste.

Among the greatest fans of the sciences were women. Nikolai
Karamzin, a Russian historian and writer who visited Paris in the
late 1780s, noted in his *Letters of a Russian Traveler* that the chemist

Antoine-Laurent Lavoisier turned so many women on to science that "for some years young beauties have loved to explain the tender agitations of their hearts in terms of chemical process." Some contemporaries claimed that husbands were infuriated that their marriage beds were deserted as their wives spent night after night studying the stars and comets through telescopes.

One of these eager daughters of the Enlightenment was Josephine Bonaparte, the wife of the "liberator of Europe." A canny woman, she had risen to the height of power in the face of numerous adversities. Yet even as Napoleon's consort, her position remained insecure. For her, collecting exotic plants and animals was not merely a charming hobby. All her life she had tried to attain status and security through influential men. The natural sciences seemed to offer her an opportunity to stake out her own territory independent of her husband and to become a woman with power over her own life. The Australian voyage of Captain Nicolas Baudin would be the key to her venture, as well as its undoing.

CAPTAIN NICOLAS BAUDIN was at the height of his fame on the rainy morning of July 27, 1798, as a magnificent procession wound through the Left Bank of Paris, honoring the Fêtes de la Liberté. This holiday was established after the Revolution to celebrate the birth of the republic and its achievements. Starting at nine in the morning in front of the Museum of Natural History, the parade streamed all day along major boulevards, culminating in the Champ de Mars. The pageant opened with a prancing cavalry detachment. Behind it a military band played patriotic tunes. Leading artists, literati, scientists, and government officials marched in groups ordered by profession. At the heart of the spectacle was a convoy of carts bearing the fruits of France's glory: works of art and natural specimens brought back from lands conquered militarily by Napoleon and scientifically by French explorers. (Napoleon himself was at that moment in Egypt, fighting against the British and investigating the natural and manmade treasures of that land.)

The previous year Napoleon had conducted a brilliant war against the Austrians in Italy. In the process of "liberating" the peninsula he had carried off its greatest masterpieces. The French, he claimed, would take better care of them. As a lieutenant of the Hussars who had escorted a collection of artworks from an earlier campaign in Belgium reported to the government, "These immortal works are no longer on foreign soil. They are brought to the homeland of arts and genius, to the homeland of liberty and sacred equality, the French Republic." Now the spectators lining the parade route marveled at the sight of carts groaning under the weight of the ancient bronze horses stripped from the facade of the Basilica of San Marco in Venice; the dramatic marble group, removed from the Vatican, of Laocoön and his sons struggling in the deadly embrace of two giant snakes; the *Apollo Belvedere, Discobolos, Dying Gaul, Capitoline Venus,* and countless other ancient sculptures, as well as paintings by Raphael, Giulio Romano, Titian, and Veronese.

More astonishing still was the display of plants, animals, and minerals French voyagers and naturalists had brought home from across Europe and from faraway lands. Pride of place in the procession was occupied by the banana tree, the palm, the coconut, and the papaya, just delivered from Puerto Rico by Baudin. Under their canopies — however insufficient against the drizzle — rode lions from Africa, a bear from Bern, a pair of camels, and a couple of dromedaries (one-humped camels). "In this manner," the official program stated, "all parts of the world will have contributed to the enrichment of the most beautiful of our celebrations and rendered it as magnificent as the ancient Roman triumphs."

Josephine, as Napoleon's wife, likely watched this mesmerizing procession up close, and it may have given her the idea of assembling a menagerie of her own.

BORN IN 1763 on the French island of Martinique, in the West Indies, Josephine was christened Marie Joseph Rose de Tascher de la Pagerie. For much of her life she was called Rose, until Napoleon decided that she should have a loftier name. Her father's family was descended from country gentry in the Loire Valley, her mother from Martinique plantation elite. Rose was the oldest of their five children, and her childhood was relatively cheerful and carefree. While her impoverished and impractical father drank rum, gambled, and pursued amorous liaisons, and her mother languished in dispirited indolence, Rose was left largely to her own devices and to the care of her nurse, Marion. Indulged and spoiled by her nanny, Rose grew up untroubled by discipline or serious education.

She was not especially bright or outstandingly beautiful, but she did possess an ineffable allure. Of medium height, with dark blue eyes fringed by thick long lashes, and with light brown silky hair that complemented her pale olive skin, she began to beguile men as a teenage girl (as long as she kept her lips sealed, for she had blackened teeth as a result of the sugar-saturated diet of Martinique). In 1777 a French officer stationed on Martinique, the Comte de Montgaillard, mused, "Mlle de la Pagerie was noted for her charm, for an expression against which it was difficult to defend oneself . . . of a voluptuous and indefinable grace in her manner; it caressed, it went straight to the heart, it spoke especially to the senses. Her form was that of the nymphs; her entire person bore the mark of a vivacity, a softness, an abandon which belonged only to the Créole women." Three years later, on the strength of these virtues, Rose was married by proxy to Alexandre de Beauharnais, a young viscount who was distantly related to her family and had lived with them on Martinique as a boy. Alexandre, now a member of a fashionable aristocratic circle in Paris, had not seen Rose since they were children, but he was eager to come into his inheritance, and for this he needed to marry. The two families saw the match as mutually advantageous.

Alas, the urbane nineteen-year-old viscount, "a handsomely built man and the first [best] dancer in Paris," failed to be charmed by his sixteen-year-old "Bird of the Islands" when she arrived in Paris. He was annoyed by her inadequate education and child-ishness and chafed at her provincial ways. In his social circle, ladies were expected to trade clever quips and play the harp with elegance. Rose could only strum the guitar and prattle on excit-edly about the pretty clothes and jewels she loved to wear. She eventually improved on the harp but apparently always played the same tune.

Alexandre found his silly wife too embarrassing to accompany him to the salons. As he wrote to his former tutor,

> At the sight of Mlle de la Pagerie I felt I could live happily with her; I at once devised a plan to reform her education and zeal-ously to make good omissions of those first fifteen years of her life that had been so neglected. . . . Instead of spending a large part of my time at home with someone who has nothing to say to me, I frequently go out, more than I had planned to do, and have taken up some of my former life as a bachelor.

To be more precise, Alexandre returned to pursuing amorous affairs.

After only three years of marriage, even this arrangement grew tiresome to Alexandre. Under the influence of his mistress, Laure de Longpré, a distant relative of Rose's, he accused his wife, quite unjustly at that point, of immoral behavior on Martinique before their marriage and in France afterward. Despite the fact that by now they had two small children, Alexandre demanded a separation. In November 1783 the twenty-year-old Rose was shipped off to the convent of Pentemont in Paris, an establishment for disgraced ladies "of the first distinction." Rose took her son with her, leaving her baby daughter with relatives.

Rose's stay at Pentemont proved very useful. She resolved to transform herself from a provincial girl who could be disdained into an enchanting exotic belle. In that cooped-up setting, "the little American," as she was called, rapidly mastered the intricacies of being a fine Parisian lady. She learned the social subtleties expected of an aristocrat and developed a fine taste in personal and interior decoration, for which she would become famous. These would be her tools for surviving in the capital and climbing up the social ladder.

As Rose attempted to regain control of her life, an even greater upheaval erupted. These were the days of the French Revolution. Rose still bore her husband's name — although she was legally separated from him, she needed his financial assistance to support herself and their two children. When, in March 1794, Alexandre was arrested as a prominent member of the aristocracy, Rose was also dispatched to the prison that had been set up in the Carmelite convent in Paris. There seven hundred men and women were holed up around open latrines in corridors crawling with rats, mice, and other vermin. Rose spent three and a half harrowing months in those overcrowded and filthy conditions. Then, on July 24, Alexandre was guillotined. Rose was spared and soon freed on the grounds that no incriminating evidence could be found against her. Her gift of charming people (except, unfortunately, her husband) and of making powerful friends had stood her in good stead. In this case she was saved by members of the Committee of Public Safety, a branch of the revolutionary government responsible for the arrests and trials of counterrevolutionaries. She had known these powerful men before the Revolution.

Although Rose was admired by many for her unaffected grace

and generosity (Napoleon would later chide her, "Look after your affairs and stop giving to everyone who asks for something"), she was also shrewd about the ways of the world. Within a few months of her liberation from prison, in August 1794, she deployed her charms to become mistress to Paul Barras, one of five members of the Directorate that now ruled France.

In October 1795 Rose met Bonaparte. He was then only a young, though very promising, general. Coming from the provincial aristocracy, Bonaparte was looking for an advantageous match to solidify his position and ensure his rise through the ranks in the status-conscious military. By that time Rose had many important connections, and she put on an aristocratic Parisian persona so convincingly that Bonaparte assumed her to be much richer and nobler than she was. Her caressing Creole intonations and expressive face, the halo of wayward curls framing her brow, her smooth, radiant skin, and her deep blue eyes also captivated the general. In December he wrote, apparently after a rendezvous, "At seven in the morning I am awake, full of you. Your portrait, and the memory of the intoxicating evening of yesterday leave my senses no rest. Sweet and incomparable Josephine, what strange power do you have over my heart?"

By early 1796 Bonaparte proposed, but Rose was not convinced. He was clearly on the rise, but not an obvious step up from Barras, nor was he much to look at. Still, Bonaparte did not give up easily. He continued to pressure her in person and in a barrage of passionate letters. At last she agreed. Barras was powerful but unreliable. A hedonist, he had no intention of tying himself down. On March 9, 1796, Rose married Bonaparte in a modest civil ceremony. Their honeymoon lasted two days and was spent in her house. Bonaparte was getting ready for a campaign in Italy and passed most of the time poring over maps and plans. When he at last joined his new wife in the bedroom, her pug Fortuné bit his leg. And with that Bonaparte was off to war.

From Italy he wrote her ardent letters: "I have not spent a night without holding you in my arms [in my dreams]. . . . In the middle of business, at the head of the troops, inspecting the camps, only my adorable Josephine is in my heart, occupies my mind, absorbs my thoughts." He pleaded for her to write to him: "There is no greater torment than not to have a letter from *mio dolce amor*. . . . They gave me a great fête here; five or six hundred elegant and beautiful women sought to please me; none had that sweet and music-like countenance which I have engraved on my heart. I saw only you, I thought only of you!"

Despite his begging for her to join him, Rose stalled. Almost as soon as Bonaparte had left Paris, she had fallen in love with a dashing officer of the hussars, Hippolyte Charles. The young, dapper, olive-skinned and black-haired Captain Charles was a great wit, entertaining his social circle with endless quips and pranks. One time he glued the saber of Bonaparte's general Junot in its scabbard. On another occasion he showed up at Rose's salon wearing a Creole costume (a full, bright-colored skirt over a white cotton chemise and a matching headscarf). The heart of every party, he would put everyone into a state of utter hilarity, and Rose, too, would laugh and laugh, hiding her ugly teeth behind her handkerchief. Having just entered into a passionate affair with Charles (which would last for more than three years), she was not eager to hurry to her husband.

When she could delay no longer and finally joined Bonaparte in Italy, however, she had nothing but kind words for him. As she wrote to her aunt, "I have the best husband in the world. I never lack anything, for he always anticipates my wishes. All day long he adores me, as if I were a goddess. He couldn't possibly be a better husband." Yet she was not enjoying her new political role as his consort. Although "feted wherever I have gone, given receptions by all the princes of Italy . . . I would prefer to be an ordinary individual in France. I don't like the honors of this country, and I am often bored."

*　　*　　*

THREE YEARS LATER, in the spring of 1799, Napoleon was stranded in Egypt, where he had gone to wrest control of the Indian empire from the British, only to be crushingly defeated and to have his route home cut off by Admiral Nelson. Meanwhile, Josephine devoted her attention to acquiring the château of Malmaison, some eight miles west of central Paris. She had had her eye on this run-down estate, encompassed by sixty hectares of meadows and woods, for some time. Now that it had come up for sale, Josephine could not pass it up. She purchased it without telling her husband and threw a great deal of energy and borrowed money into restoring and embellishing her new abode. Napoleon was furious when he found out, but when he got home and saw Malmaison and his wife's improvements, he was charmed. He paid the bills, and the estate became the family's favorite retreat.

Here Napoleon, Josephine, and her children from her first marriage, Eugène and Hortense, whom Napoleon adored, relaxed and lived informally away from the strict protocols of the Tuileries. Hortense called Malmaison "a delicious spot." Louis-Antoine de Bourrienne, Napoleon's friend and private secretary, recalled that "nowhere, except on the field of battle, did I ever see Bonaparte more happy than in the gardens of Malmaison." Madame Junot, Josephine's lady-in-waiting, wrote in her *Mémoires Historiques* that

> Bonaparte loved Malmaison and liked the company to feel at ease there, although he worked continually, rising at six each morning, and not appearing until the evening. . . . On warm summer evenings Bonaparte would order dinner to be served outside on the lawns beneath the trees. On some days hunts were organized, and the youthful company would at times, when Bonaparte felt in the mood, play games like *barres* which

he vastly enjoyed, taking off his coat and running like a hare, or rather, like the gazelle he fed with all the tobacco from his pouch, encouraging it to run at us, and the horrid animal tore our dresses and often our legs.

The foreign minister Talleyrand also commented on this rustic spirit: "I arrived at Malmaison and do you know what I did, and where the First Consul had established his work-room? On one of the bowling greens! They were all seated on the grass. It was nothing to him, in his camp habits, his riding boots, and his leather breeches. But I, in my silk breeches and silk stockings! Can you see me sitting on that lawn? I'm crippled with rheumatism. What a man! He always thinks he is camping out."

But Josephine had her mind on more than a country haven for her family. She wanted to turn Malmaison into a natural history laboratory, "the most beautiful and curious garden in Europe, a model of good cultivation." Another part of this "laboratory" would be a menagerie of exotic animals that could be studied for their potential usefulness rather than for mere curiosity. Having grown up amid the lush flora and fauna of the Caribbean, Josephine missed them since moving to France. She had also become swept up in the Enlightenment excitement about exotic plants and animals, and Malmaison unleashed her inner naturalist. Through the patronage and cultivation of the natural sciences, Josephine hoped to stake out her own place in her turbulent world.

Even as Napoleon's wife, her position was vulnerable. She was in her late thirties, and she had failed so far to produce an heir for her ambitious husband. She worried that, though he loved her passionately, he might at any time decide that he needed a more fertile wife. Josephine also remained insecure about her provincial background and modest education. By choosing to cultivate the natural sciences at Malmaison, she was claiming male prerogatives, since scientific endeavor and animal collecting had thus far been the preserves of men. Malmaison would be her private kingdom, the source of her own authority and stature, and it would remain hers even if her marriage were to end.

These calculations aside, Josephine was also genuinely passionate about the natural sciences, and while her tastes in fashion or interior decorating could be capricious, she pursued botany, in particular, with remarkable tenacity. As one visitor to Malmaison noted, "In her dressing room were 4 or 5 books on botany: the only ones I saw in the house." Josephine's position and connections made it easy for her to collect plants. Ambassadors and travelers from abroad were encouraged to send her plant samples, and even in the midst of the Franco-British war, she received such gifts from England. She threw herself into gathering and cultivating flora with the same zeal she had brought to remodeling the château and its grounds, so that the richness of her gardens would impress her contemporaries for years. And she took into her service distinguished botanists, who, thanks to her sponsorship, made substantial contributions to their field.

In postrevolutionary France, applied natural sciences were promoted as a means of building national wealth and prosperity. In contrast to serving merely as private delights of the nobility, exotic plants and animals were now to be cultivated for their utility to the country. Josephine echoed these aspirations: "I wish that Malmaison may soon become the source of riches for all the departments [counties of France]. . . . For this reason I have planted a large number of trees and shrubs from Australia and North America. In ten years' time I would like each department to own a collection of rare plants from my nurseries."

In 1800 Josephine built a heated orangery that housed three hundred pineapple trees, and in 1805 she constructed a vast and magnificent greenhouse for the tropical plants she had loved as a child on Martinique. The greenhouse was a marvel of technology: the tender vegetation was warmed by the sun filtering through the glass panes above and by a dozen coal-burning stoves set up in the basement. Dinner guests at Malmaison were served compotes of the fresh pineapples, mangoes, and bananas grown on the estate. Between 1803, when her botanical efforts really took off, and her death in 1814, Josephine cultivated nearly two hundred new plants in France for the first time, among them camellias, dahlias, purple magnolias, and shrub peonies. Her favorites, however, were roses — a passion that resonated with her name and became something of her symbol. She grew some 250 varieties of roses, popularizing this flower in France.

Etienne Pierre Ventenat, the botanist at the Museum of Natural History in Paris, the leading scientific institution of the day, wrote in the foreword to *Jardin de la Malmaison* (1803) this account of Josephine's plant collection:

> You have gathered around you the rarest plants growing on French soil. Some, indeed, which have never before left the deserts of Arabia or the burning sands of Egypt have been domesticated through your care. Now, regularly classified, they offer to us as we inspect them in the beautiful gardens of Malmaison, an impressive reminder of the conquests of your illustrious husband and the most pleasant evidence of the studies you have pursued in your leisure hours.

Perhaps to compensate for her inadequate learning in other areas, Josephine was eager to communicate all that she knew about botany to her visitors. With the fervor of the manic collector, she recited endless specialized details — her plants' scientific names, their origins and traits — often to the point of boring her listeners. Georgette Ducrest, another of Josephine's ladies-in-waiting, wrote in her *Memoirs of the Empress Josephine* that

> when the weather was fine, the green-houses were inspected; the same walk was taken every day, on the way to that spot the same subjects were talked over; the conversation generally

turned on botany, upon her Majesty's taste for that interesting science, her wonderful memory which enabled her to name every plant; in short, the same phrases were generally repeated over and over again, and at the same time, circumstances well calculated to render those promenades exceedingly tedious and fatiguing. I no sooner stepped onto that delightful walk, which I had so much admired when I first saw it, than I was seized with an immoderate fit of yawning.

After botany, Josephine's second love was animals and birds. They were, of course, more costly and logistically tricky to collect and keep, but they would make her botanical garden still more spectacular. Napoleon, also a keen patron of the sciences, supported his wife's endeavors. After all, when he had gone to Egypt, he had brought along 143 specialists to explore local zoology, botany, mineralogy, and archaeology. And he declared, "The real conquests, the only unregretted ones, are those against ignorance. The worthiest and most significant occupation for nations is to enlarge the frontiers of human knowledge."

Soon those eager to please Napoleon and Josephine and to court their favor began to dispatch birds and beasts to Malmaison. At first Josephine's animals came to her a few at a time, mostly as diplomatic gifts. The king of Spain sent her a flock of merino sheep. The bey of Tunis presented her with lions, gazelles, and ostriches. She spent five hundred francs to transport a chamois (a goatlike antelope) from Switzerland and nearly three hundred francs to get a seal from the coast.

Josephine preferred animals that could be allowed to live at Malmaison freely and peacefully, grazing picturesquely in her meadows, drinking from the meandering streams and lily-strewn ponds. She gave the more aggressive beasts she received to the Museum of Natural History. Before long, exotic animals spread across the estate, with gazelles, antelopes, chamois, and llamas gracing the lawns. And in the château's main hall, a vast Roman-style atrium supported by four massive columns, the cages of rare birds alternated with antique busts.

The first lady constantly wrote to government officials, overseers of foreign provinces, nursery owners, and others who might help her obtain rare specimens. Though an amateur herself, she strove to advance zoological knowledge by nurturing scientific research at Malmaison. She granted pensions and favors to scientists, invited them to study her collections, and sponsored their publications. And she maintained a close rapport with the Museum of Natural History, with which she exchanged animals — wilder beasts for tamer ones — and to which she sent her deceased creatures for study and display.

One of those that ended up as a stuffed specimen at the Museum was a female orangutan from Borneo, presented to Josephine by General Charles Decaen, governor of Ile de France (Mauritius). The ape — whose name, alas, is not recorded — was remarkably well trained. When a visitor approached the chair on which the orangutan liked to sit, she would put on a dignified mien, pull over her thighs the long frock she wore, and rise to greet the guest while holding her dress decorously closed, just as a well-brought-up lady would do. She ate at the table with a knife and fork, more properly — wrote Bonaparte's valet, Constant — than many a child who passes for being well behaved.

The orangutan was, however, crazy about turnips. Once, when a lady-in-waiting brought her this vegetable, the ape began to run around, cavort, and somersault in glee, forgetting all the lessons in modesty and decency she'd been taught. Josephine was charmed by these antics. For her the orangutan was less an animal than an adorable, savage little girl, perhaps a bit like herself when she first came to France.

Unfortunately, within a year of the orangutan's arrival at Malmaison, she developed an intestinal inflammation. Whether it was this illness that killed her or another, the ape died before long. No doubt Josephine grieved. Then she gave the little body to the Museum of Natural History, to make it useful to science. Frédéric Cuvier, the keeper of the Museum's menagerie, devoted an entire volume, *Description of an Orangutan and Observation of Its Intellectual Faculties,* to his studies of Josephine's pet in life and death. Meanwhile, the minister of the interior, Jean-Antoine Chaptal, a scientist by training, wrote — partly in flattery, partly in appreciation — "May I congratulate you, Madame, for your taste in the natural sciences. You are contributing to their progress, and we thank you in the name of the naturalists."

In the aftermath of the Revolution, Josephine was careful to show that she was not just indulging in a frivolous royal pastime, nor was she merely playing a little shepherdess, as Marie Antoinette had done with her flocks of sheep. Utility being the catchword, Josephine aspired to make her activities at Malmaison practically beneficial. Thus she developed a model farm there, including a herd of Swiss cows, attended by herders from Bern, to furnish the estate with milk, butter, and cream. She delighted in visiting her dairy, her pheasantry, as well as her sheepfold, where she kept five hundred merino sheep, whose wool and offspring provided steady revenue to Malmaison.

Josephine also wanted to import and acclimae more exotic species to France in order to advance domestic zoology. This was a highly fashionable ideal of the age, and a justification for bringing to Europe all sorts of foreign creatures from distant, and hopefully newly conquered, territories. Georges-Louis Leclerc de Buffon's immensely popular forty-four-volume *Histoire Naturelle* helped promote the view that exotic beasts were economically viable commodities. Louis-Jean-Marie Daubenton, one of Buffon's assistants in preparing the massive anthology, advocated importing not only merino sheep but also peccaries, tapirs, and zebras. Josephine was eager to follow this trend, and a whole new opportunity to expand her collection and make it more scientifically important was about to arise. The explorer Nicolas Baudin had just proposed to the Museum of Natural History and to Napoleon, who had become First Consul, a voyage of discovery to Australia. This was Josephine's ticket — an exceptional chance to acquire from a new continent a set of animals that would make her reputation and secure her private world.

THE AUSTRALIAN VOYAGE was not Captain Nicolas Baudin's first venture. In 1798 he had returned to France from the West Indies to great acclaim and with many new specimens, including the exotic trees that opened the Fêtes de la Liberté. But the new venture he proposed was even more ambitious.

The eighteenth century was the second great age of European overseas exploration, and particularly of the investigation of the South Pacific. The French competed with the British in these voyages of discovery and strove to outpace them in the search for the southern continent — *terra australis*. This as yet uncharted territory was thought to counterbalance the vast landmasses of the Northern Hemisphere and to contain even greater wealth than the Americas or the Spice Islands of the East Indies. Captain James Cook's journeys on the *Endeavour* and *Resolution* in the 1770s clarified the position of Australia, but the continent remained a mysterious place. Most of its coast was still unexplored. Nothing was known about its interior or its inhabitants, human or animal. Both France and England wanted to claim this land and to corner the rich Pacific trade. Baudin's voyage would be part of that race.

Nicolas Baudin was born in 1754 on the Ile de Ré, off the Atlantic coast of France near La Rochelle. He was the third of thirteen children of a local merchant. Given his birthplace, his modest origins, and his large family, it is not surprising that he opted to make a living at sea. At age fifteen Baudin began working as a cabin boy on a coastal vessel — a thankless job, but it gave him a chance at maritime apprenticeship. Next he volunteered as a cadet at the naval depot in his hometown. Then he enrolled in the French India Company's regiment stationed at Pondicherry. After spending five years in the East Indies, he served in 1779 and 1780 in the West Indies, fighting in the American Revolutionary War on the frigate *Minerve*.

Baudin stumbled into natural history quite by chance. In the 1780s, while operating as a merchant mariner, he happened to transport Franz Boos, the head gardener of the Austrian emperor Joseph II. The emperor was a passionate collector of *naturalia* and was assembling a vast array of exotic plants and animals at his Schönbrunn Palace. Boos had gone out on a collecting expedition for the emperor and was now bringing back the living plants, birds, and mammals he had gathered. Baudin's sensitive and able handling of this precious cargo on the long journey from the Cape of Good Hope to Trieste, and the strong mutual regard he and Boos developed during the weeks at sea, recommended him to the emperor. Joseph soon engaged Baudin to go on collecting expeditions directly for him.

Baudin's enthusiasm for this new vocation was certainly spurred by the romance and glory of such voyages in this era, by the accounts of the journeys of Cook and Vancouver, La Pérouse and d'Entrecasteaux, and by the prospect of truly momentous discoveries, both geographic and naturalistic. The excitement generated by these expeditions was not unlike that provoked in our day by the dawn of the space age. Baudin was, of course, on a very mundane level also just trying to make a living. But he was genuinely fired up by the prospect of great overseas finds and eager to make his mark. Alas, the three naturalist voyages Baudin undertook for his new patron — to China, the Cape of Good Hope, and the East Indies — all ended in shipwrecks. None of the specimens made it to Schönbrunn.

Despite these failed missions, Baudin formulated a new plan. The last collection he had assembled actually did survive the shipwreck, and Baudin managed to deposit it with a friend in

Trinidad. By 1796, however, France was at war with Austria. So Baudin approached Antoine-Laurent de Jussieu, director of the Museum of Natural History in Paris, and proposed that if the Museum were to finance his journey to the West Indies, he would bring to France this splendid collection, "rich in madrepores, petrifications, insects, shells, mollusks, fish, and the skins and skeletons of birds and quadruped animals, . . . around 70 living birds, . . . [and] a large number of living plants and trees taken on the coasts of Malabar and Coromandel in China, in the straights of Malacca, at the Cape of Good Hope and in America." The Museum jumped at the idea of this scientific booty and persuaded the Directorate, the postrevolutionary government of France, to back the voyage. Its case was made easier by the fact that the Directorate was keen on instructing the public in the practical applications of formerly elite disciplines. The government also hoped to put the natural resources of foreign lands to use in rejuvenating France's agriculture and industry, which had been hurt by the Revolution. And so within six months of his petition to Jussieu, Baudin set sail from Le Havre on the *Belle-Angélique*.

The beginning of the voyage seemed to prophesy another disaster. Only three weeks after its departure, the *Belle-Angélique* was damaged beyond repair by a hurricane. Remarkably, Baudin managed to get the crippled ship — without a rudder, almost without masts, and with gaping holes fore and aft — to Tenerife, in the Canary Islands (west of Morocco). There he replaced it with a much smaller American brig, the *Fanny*. While he was refitting, his scientists — the zoologist René Maugé, the botanist André-Pierre Ledru, the gardener Anselm Riedlé, and three amateur naturalists who assisted them — went out gathering a wealth of specimens. Baudin loaded up these treasures and with renewed optimism continued on to Trinidad. He arrived to a rude shock: only a few weeks earlier the island had been taken by the British.

This was the time of the ongoing Franco-British war, which raged from 1792 to 1815 and was spurred by the French Revolution.

Both sides fought for what they saw as an ideal system of government, yet also at stake were economic considerations, with Britain seeking to achieve worldwide trade and commercial domination, and France striving to create a French empire in Europe. The war thus spilled well beyond the confines of the two countries and affected such far-flung territories as the West Indies. The British conquered Trinidad, a Spanish colony with a large French population, in February 1797. When Baudin arrived on the island, its new governor, Thomas Picton, dismissed Baudin's safe-conduct as a ruse by the French government to retake Trinidad and ordered him to leave at once. He also forbade Baudin from taking possession of the natural history specimens for which he had come.

Baudin cut his losses and came up with yet another creative solution. He took the *Fanny* to St. Thomas, in the Virgin Islands, a Danish possession. There his scientists proceeded to assemble "a most complete collection, and of a new kind," as Baudin would describe it to his superiors. While they hunted and gathered, Baudin replaced the too-small *Fanny* with a bigger and more suitable frigate, the *Triomphe,* recently captured from the British by the French. On this new ship he and his scientists sailed to Spanish-held Puerto Rico, where they remained for nine months. That stay and its extraordinary fruits — paraded with such pride during the Fêtes de la Liberté — made Baudin's reputation and paved the way for his next voyage, an expedition that would prove as ruinous to him as the West Indies sojourn had been triumphant.

THE WEST INDIES expedition made Baudin such a star that when he proposed another voyage around the world soon after his return home it became the talk of the town. Scores of young men clamored to sign on, including the celebrated twenty-nine-year-old German naturalist Alexander von Humboldt. "The voyage of Captain Baudin," Humboldt wrote, "has so filled my imagination that I see and think of nothing else." Unfortunately, Baudin's trip kept being postponed, and Humboldt went to South America instead. But when, two years later, in Havana, he read a report in an American newspaper that Baudin had finally set sail from France and would be in Lima within a year, Humboldt immediately embarked on an arduous eight-month trek by canoe and mule train, crossing the Andes to meet up with him. Only upon arriving in Lima did Humboldt discover that the report had been false.

Baudin's projected voyage around the world was, for political and economic reasons, scaled down to an exploration of the coasts of Australia, then called New Holland. Captain Cook had traced its east coast and claimed it for Britain. Baudin's expedition would take the investigation further. Napoleon, who had a weakness for Australia, readily approved the venture. While a pupil in military school, having avidly read about Cook's voyages, he had applied to join La Pérouse's ill-fated 1785 expedition to Australia and the South Pacific. One of Bonaparte's school friends, Alexandre Jean des Mazis, recounted that "Bonaparte would have liked the opportunity of displaying his energy in such a fine enterprise as an assistant astronomer." Luckily for him, he was not selected, and instead went back to concentrating on his military career. La Pérouse's team never returned, having perished on their voyage, and only traces of the expedition were finally found in 1827. Napoleon, however, remained fascinated by Australia and enthusiastically supported Baudin's plan as a way to extend the French empire and to supersede British activities in that strategically promising part of the world.

The British were sailing neck and neck with the French. Even as Baudin was setting off for Australia in *Le Géographe,* his British counterpart, Matthew Flinders, was planning a journey there on Britain's behalf. Appealing for support to Sir Joseph Banks, the president of the Royal Society of London, Flinders declared, "The interests of geography and natural history in general, and of the British nation in particular, seem to require that this only remaining considerable part of the globe should be thoroughly explored." Banks had served as a botanist on Cook's *Endeavour* and through his work had spurred a new enthusiasm for Australian natural history. While Flinders was awaiting his official benediction, the Admiralty got wind of Baudin's expedition. It promptly equipped a ship called the *Investigator* and put Flinders in command. In addition to the scientific benefits of exploration, both countries hoped to gain control over the lucrative Pacific trade. Thus part of Baudin's mandate was to examine the character and customs of the local people and to "give them an idea of French arts and manufacturers in order to foster among them a need for French products." He was also to bring back animals, plants, and minerals useful "for the nation's commercial advantage."

Since Britain and France were at war, Flinders and Baudin were expected to spy on each other when the opportunity arose. Yet British and French naval officers were remarkably cordial to one another when they actually met en route. As soon as Baudin set sail for Australia, for example, he was intercepted by a British frigate. Baudin boarded the enemy vessel and showed his passport to its captain, after which they spent half an hour drinking to the success of the French expedition. Then the British captain paid a visit to the French ship and received a present of a commemorative medal of the voyage and some fresh vegetables.

Baudin's encounters with the British in Australia were similarly pleasant. When *Le Géographe* met the *Investigator* off the south coast on April 8, 1802, Baudin shared his geographical, anthropological, and naturalistic discoveries with Flinders. The Englishman reciprocated by describing his findings, including the fact that Australia was indeed one continent with no north-south strait. Flinders also revealed to Baudin various features of New Holland's coastline that he had been able to chart. Still, both sides strove to be the first to claim new territories, as the war between France and Britain was conducted as much on the scientific as on the military plane. Flinders and Baudin were charged with "advancing the limits of science" and bringing back collections of flora and fauna that would give their nations a scientific and commercial edge.

According to his orders from the Institute of France, which played an important part in the organization of the expedition, Baudin was to examine in detail

> the south-west, west, north-west and north coasts of New Holland, some of which are still entirely unknown, while others are known only imperfectly . . . to determine precisely the geographical position of the principal points along the coasts that he will visit and to chart them exactly, so as to study the inhabitants, animals and natural products of the countries in which he will land. With regard to the products, he will give his attention to collecting those which appear capable of being preserved, and he will apply himself principally to procuring the useful animals and plants which, unknown in our climate, could be introduced here.

The specific instruction to bring back live animals was a new development. Collecting and transporting home live creatures was such a cumbersome and uncertain proposition that most eighteenth-century voyages returned primarily with stuffed or dried specimens. The live ones that made it to Europe were brought a few at a time. Baudin's Australian expedition would be the first to focus on fetching a significant sample of live exotic fauna.

To this Napoleon added the directive that Baudin should give careful attention to assembling a special collection for Madame Bonaparte. "You will make up this collection of living animals of all kinds, insects, and especially birds with beautiful plumage. As regards animals, I don't need to tell you how to choose them between those intended for the menageries and those for a collection of pure pleasure." At this stage Napoleon was still fully supportive of his wife's development of a menagerie at Malmaison, as he felt that besides making her happy, it also brought honor to him.

The wording of Bonaparte's order, however, is somewhat patronizing. Of course Josephine, like many collectors before her, was seduced by the sheer beauty and curiosity of exotic creatures and the thrill of acquiring them. But her menagerie was also a significant endeavor for her, one that she hoped would give her intellectual weight to counterbalance her image as a fashionable but shallow woman and provide her with personal prestige and security separate from that of her eminent husband. Being a woman, however, Josephine was not in a position to make her own demands on Baudin's expedition. She had to act through men — her husband, the director of the Museum of Natural History, and others — to assemble and shape her collection.

THE NAMES OF the two corvettes that Baudin took to Australia summed up his mission. *Le Géographe* and *Le Naturaliste* set sail from Le Havre on October 19, 1800, to great fanfare. A medal had been struck to commemorate the departure. The shore was crowded with government officials, elegantly dressed ladies, stately gentlemen, and children. A band merrily played a variety of uplifting tunes, including "What better place to be than with one's family?" — though this was perhaps not what men leaving their loved ones for several years of rough sea voyaging needed to hear. As the two ships made their way past Le Havre's fort, they were saluted by cannon salvos, and a train of small craft accompanied the expedition's ships out to sea.

Le Géographe, led by Baudin, was a 350-ton vessel measuring 124 by 30 feet and carrying 118 men. *Le Naturaliste,* headed by Captain Emmanuel Hamelin, Baudin's second in command, was of similar dimensions, with 120 people aboard. But being a storeship, it moved much more slowly, which caused Baudin endless aggravation and anxiety as they tried, and often failed, to stay together through storms, contrary currents, and unknown waters. Other difficulties would arise from the fact that the crews were larger than Baudin had intended. For example, fifteen midshipmen Baudin had not asked for were assigned to the expedition as excitement about it mounted and young officers begged for posts.

Each ship had its own supply of plants and animals on board. The gardener Riedlé, who sailed on *Le Géographe,* busily tended plum, apple, apricot, pear, olive, nut, and chestnut trees — some of them intended to be harvested en route, others to be shared, on Bonaparte's orders, with foreign peoples on distant shores. Riedlé also cultivated plots of lettuce, radishes, and watercress for the officers' table. For meat the corvettes carried live pigs, goats, sheep, and fowl. There were also cats for catching mice and rats, and five large dogs that would help hunt exotic animals in Australia. For now they annoyed the crew by running around the ship and relieving themselves frequently on the quarterdeck, usually on coils of rope.

To make room for all the animals, plants, and crew, the number of guns carried on board was reduced from thirty on *Le Géographe* and twenty on *Le Naturaliste* to six on each corvette. Additional decks were built on each vessel. Still, space was perpetually tight. After months at sea, cramped quarters would augment fatigue and tensions, particularly between Baudin and his crew.

The expedition had twenty-two men on its scientific staff: five zoologists, three botanists, five gardeners, two mineralogists, two astronomers, two hydrologists, and three artists charged with keeping a visual record of the animals, plants, and native peoples they would encounter. The scientists brought along a host of equipment, from chronometers to flowerpots and insect boxes, from a variety of scalpels and pincers to different kinds of paper and colored pens.

These voyages of discovery were an ongoing experiment in

themselves, with captains learning as much about how to plan and carry out the expeditions as about the foreign territories they visited. One may wonder how well considered this venture was. How wise was it to remove cannons during wartime, when piracy was rampant and the ships were sailing to unknown lands? How farsighted to fill the corvettes instead with too many men and goods, as well as with hundreds of books? Baudin himself brought along a personal library of some 1,200 volumes, including 392 on history, 139 memoirs and biographies, 175 dictionaries and encyclopedias, and 177 works of various authors, from French and Greek classics to Shakespeare and Sterne.

The first leg of the journey, to Tenerife, where the ships were to add to their stock of wine and fresh provisions, took two weeks and passed fairly smoothly, although *Le Géographe* moved faster than *Le Naturaliste,* and the rough waters made many of the scientists seasick. The astronomer Bernier and the zoologist Dumont d'Urville, their shipmate recorded, spent two days splayed out senseless under a table and did not even have the strength to cry out when someone accidentally stepped on their faces. Many men were already homesick and missing their families. But when the seas calmed down, the scientists emerged on deck to delight in the view of the high peak of Grand Canary. Baudin noted in his diary that "they behaved like madmen. . . . Pandemonium reigned on board. . . . Fore and aft there was not a soul to be seen not busy sketching."

Within two weeks of leaving France, Baudin realized that these men of knowledge were going to be his major headache. "Those captains who have scientists, or who may some day have them aboard their ships, must, upon departure, take a good supply of patience. I admit that although I have no lack of it, the scientists have frequently driven me to the end of my tether and forced me to retire testily to my room. However, since they are not familiar with our practices, their conduct must be excused."

Baudin was suffering from his own success in the West

Indies. His accomplishments had generated such enthusiasm that researchers rushed to sign up for the even more promising Australian expedition. As a result, his voyage became the most scientifically weighted one to date. Baudin's predecessor La Pérouse had had only five naturalists aboard, and d'Entrecasteaux, who was sent in search of La Pérouse, six. Baudin himself wanted no more than sixteen, but the Museum of Natural History and the Institute of France had a more ambitious vision. Ironically, the great number of scientists would ultimately undermine the expedition rather than aid in its success.

The problem was not so much in the numbers as in the clash of mentalities between scientists and seamen. Baudin was not the first captain to butt his head against this problem. D'Entrecasteaux had had similar troubles with his naturalists, and so had Cook, Vancouver, and La Pérouse. D'Entrecasteaux wrote, "One cannot overstress the advantage in all these kinds of expeditions of employing only people attached to the navy, for these people, being better judges of what is possible in all circumstances, do not make foolish demands, and would not take the refusal of impracticable requests as a sign of unwarranted ill will."

It was not simply a question of naval discipline, but one of class. Although these were postrevolutionary years and everyone on board was addressed as Citizen, Baudin was an officer risen through the ranks, whereas many of the scientists came from aristocratic families and had little respect for the orders of a self-made sailor. An independent observer of Baudin's troubles — John Turnbull, who met the French expedition in Australia while conducting his own voyage around the world — lay the blame on revolutionary politics. "The real difficulty of the voyage, as a voyage of discovery," he wrote, "was much augmented by a general want of discipline which pervaded the whole body of the officers, and which took its origin from the leveling principles at that time predominant in France." Baudin, the commoner, was struggling to impose naval hierarchy and control over a team of higher-born and free-spirited laymen come to do lofty scientific work. Even worse for him, he did not have the personality to carry it off gracefully.

Although Baudin would show himself to be a decent and humane man, he was not smooth, not good at mediating conflict or relating easily across class barriers. In this he was the opposite of Josephine. Both had come from modest beginnings, and both sought to improve their positions through this voyage to Australia, but Josephine was much more adept at establishing an easy rapport with all kinds of people. After all, she had charmed her way out of the guillotine and into the graces of the most powerful men in France. "I win wars," Napoleon said. "Josephine wins hearts." Baudin could adapt to difficulties presented by the sea, but he could not cope with those caused by human frictions. As a result, he lost the affection and trust of his crew almost as soon as he walked into their midst.

Charles Baudin (no relation), who enlisted for the Australian voyage as a sixteen-year-old midshipman, recalled in his memoirs that because of the last-minute delay in the departure of the expedition, all the men got to know each other before sailing.

> The greatest cordiality was established from the outset among all the members of the expedition, without distinction of rank or age. . . . All went wonderfully well, and in the most friendly free-and-easiness, until the arrival of the commandant, who proved a real wet blanket. Everyone tried at first to jump on his shoulder and eat out of his hand, but Captain Nicolas Baudin did not take to such courtesies, and was determined to establish discipline and hierarchy on a proper basis. He soon became the *bête noire*. . . . He began to detest cordially the scientists, the officers and the midshipmen. The midshipmen, the officers and the scientists reciprocated with all their heart. It must be

said also that, if we were all tolerably unreasonable, he for his part totally lacked the kindliness of character and style which is necessary in leaders in order to win respect for their authority.

These tensions continued throughout the voyage, as the two ships left Tenerife, rounded the Cape of Good Hope — which took a tediously long time because of the becalmed sea along the west coast of Africa — and made a stop at Ile de France.

Not that Nicolas Baudin was incapable of close and respectful relationships with his travel companions. He remained on the best of terms with the scientists who had previously sailed with him to the West Indies on the *Belle-Angélique*. But then they were fewer in number and felt themselves to be part of Baudin's team, rather than his opponents. The zoologists Maugé and Levillain and the gardener Riedlé had clearly become fond enough of their captain to sign up for the Australian voyage, and Baudin had nothing but praise for them. In the course of *Le Géographe*'s exploration of Cape Barren Island in July 1801, he noted in his journal:

Our head gardener, Riedlé, for whom every moment is precious, found on this small island seventy specimens of plants, most of which will, no doubt, be unknown to botanists. Maugé, the zoologist, occupied solely with Natural History and anxious to do his work well, collected ten species of birds which he believes to be new. The others hunted kangaroos and a few lizards. Amongst the latter, we found two which were undoubtedly the same as the ones Dampier speaks of by the name of guanas [iguanas], and they are really very hideous. But we caught two of another species which had extremely pretty coloring and were very large. . . .

An observation that I have made, which is not, perhaps, without interest, is that none of the animals that we found seemed savage. The lizards, although so ugly, allowed themselves to be picked up without trying to run away or defend themselves. . . . The wounded kangaroos that were caught still alive did not make any attempt to bite, and a little one that was caught unharmed immediately began to lick its captor's hand.

Although his crew continued to complain about their treatment under Baudin, the captain was in fact a passionate and outspoken advocate of the humane treatment of both native peoples and animals. As he sent ashore exploratory parties, he gave stern instructions to his officers:

> There is no need for me to recommend you to be constantly on alert for the safety of the longboat and all those accompanying you. But if you should meet any natives, which is very likely, you are absolutely forbidden to commit a single act of hostility towards them, unless the safety of anyone in particular, or all in general, is at stake. According to what is known of their character, the people of this country do not appear to be savage, except when provoked. Therefore, you must influence them in our favor by kind deeds and presents.

Baudin expressed similar concern for the welfare of Australian animals, presaging the modern-day calls of environmentalists. One of the expedition's naturalists, François Péron, was very impressed with the profit the British were deriving from the enormous seals and sea elephants crowding the shore of King Island. The largest of these animals measured 30 feet long and yielded up to 1,650 pounds of oil. Péron thought the French should get involved in sealing as well. Baudin, however, warned his friend Philip Gidley King, governor of Port Jackson (the British military colony at Sydney):

> There is every sign that in a short time your sealers will have drained the island of its resources through the hunting of the fur seals and the sea elephants. Both will soon abandon their

territory to you, if they are not allowed time to replenish the losses they suffer daily from the destructive war carried on against them. They are already beginning to be much scarcer than at first and in a little while you will hear that they have entirely disappeared, if you do nothing to put matters in order.

Baudin also was ahead of his time in calling for the colonial powers to treat native peoples more justly. In a letter to Governor King, Baudin responded fervently to British claims on the land of Tasmanian Aborigines.

To my way of thinking, I have never been able to conceive that there was justice or even fairness on the part of Europeans in seizing, in the name of their governments, a land seen for the first time, when it is inhabited by men who have not always deserved the title savages or cannibals that has been freely given them; whereas they were still only children of nature and just as little civilized as your Scotch Highlanders or our Breton peasants, etc., who, if they do not eat their fellow-men, are nevertheless just as objectionable. From this it appears to me that it would be infinitely more glorious for your nation, as for mine, to mould for society the inhabitants of its own country over whom it has rights, rather than wishing to occupy itself with the improvement of those who are very far removed from it by beginning with seizing the soil which belongs to them and which saw their birth. These remarks are no doubt impolitic, but at least they are reasonable from the facts; and had this principle been generally adopted you would not have been obliged to form a colony by means of men branded by the law and made criminals by the fault of a government which has neglected them and abandoned them to themselves.

It was an astonishing plea, given the time, when such ideas were not widely accepted. It may also have signaled a personal transformation in a man who had transported slaves in his merchant marine days.

How tragic that for all his humanity, Baudin lacked the personal touch that would have inspired affection or at least sympathy in his crew. Captain Hamelin, by contrast, clearly possessed this quality. The astronomer Bernier, who sailed under him, noted in his journal, "We [scientists and officers] recollected how frequently M. Hamelin took a pride in us, whereas M. Baudin, solemn and solitary, repulsed everybody by his brusque and rude manners — he had already made his authority felt by provocations and many people made plans to abandon the expedition. . . . M. Hamelin's conduct was quite the opposite of M. Baudin's." Hamelin himself was kinder toward his commander. In December 1802, when he would take leave of *Le Géographe* to sail *Le Naturaliste,* loaded with specimens, back to France, Hamelin would show "much sorrow" at parting from Baudin and praise the "unselfishness" and "goodness of heart that were typical of him." Unfortunately, Baudin's staff saw none of it. And none loathed him more heartily than the naturalist François Péron, who would prove decisive in discrediting Baudin's voyage and all but erasing it from history.

The twenty-five-year-old Péron had joined the expedition at the last minute, filling the position of a "trainee zoologist, especially charged with comparative anatomy," after another scientist dropped out. One wonders how differently Baudin's legacy might have been shaped had Péron not come on board. Péron was a fiery man, tireless in his passion for natural history, often to the point of carelessness for his own and others' safety. Many times during the voyage he would go ashore to explore and lose track of time and place. At one point, as he recalled in his *Voyage of Discovery to the Southern Hemisphere,* "I decided to explore a dangerous reef hoping to find living shellfish. I found them in abundance, but, while absorbed in separating them from the rocks, a mountainous wave broke over the reef with such force as to pick me up and throw me across the shell-infested rocks. My clothes were torn to pieces and I was covered in cuts and blood." On another occasion he allowed himself and his companions to be stranded on an unfamiliar coast without food or shelter, their shipmates desperately worried about their fate.

Péron was not blind to his faults. Just before joining the expedition, he drew up in his journal a kind of balance sheet of his qualities: "Inconsequent, thoughtless, quarrelsome, indiscreet, too obstinate in my opinions, incapable of yielding to any motive of expediency, I can make enemies and alienate my best friends. These faults are the result of my education and the independence in which I have lived. . . . [They] are redeemed by qualities of heart; kind, sympathetic, generous, I would not knowingly hurt anyone."

It would seem that Baudin did not experience much of Péron's kindness, sympathy, or generosity, but the zoologist's other qualities were clearly in evidence. On November 27, 1800, Baudin recorded a vignette from a day on the ship.

At about eleven o'clock we caught a fairly large shark and it was a great distraction, particularly for the scientists who were seeing one alive for the first time. Little accustomed to such a sight, they all wanted to get close to it. But when it had thrashed its tail from side to side a few times, they were less eager to go near. . . . Citizen Péron and Lharidon, the surgeon, however, were less eagerly discouraged than the others, and when the sailor had tied the shark down firmly, they both set to work upon it. I was far from foreseeing that this poor creature would become the cause of a very serious dispute between the two anatomists, each of whom wanted the glory of dissecting it. But finally, as I was strolling around the quarter deck, I saw Citizen Péron coming to me, dripping all over with blood, to complain that Mr. Lharidon had snatched the shark's heart from him. He would not go on dissecting after such behavior.

I did my best not to laugh at the complaint, which Doctor Péron considered very grave. But to console him, I promised him that the next one we caught should be his alone and that he could depend upon it that no one should touch it except with his permission. Doctor Péron was comforted by this promise and surgeon Lharidon was left the undisturbed possessor of the shark's heart.

One cannot help sympathizing with Baudin for having to adjudicate such schoolboyish disputes in addition to his other troubles with his staff, and for having to forge forward with scientific work against the background of such petty rivalries.

Baudin's troubles came to a head when, after five months of sailing, *Le Géographe* and *Le Naturaliste* stopped at Ile de France, the French base in the Indian Ocean, to resupply before the long haul to Australia. As soon as they docked, a large number of crew asked for permission to go to the hospital on shore for various ailments. A month later, as Baudin was getting ready to sail on, he noted in his journal:

> In the morning I went to the hospital to make a thorough inspection of our sick and their situation. I was not surprised to find neither officers nor naturalists, for they went there only when they were not on some outing, or dining elsewhere. But I was surprised indeed to learn that eight of my best mariners had deserted over the walls during the night. I pretended to believe this statement, but from more accurate information learnt that, far from climbing over the walls, they had gone out through the main gate, with their luggage, on a permit from the commissioner.

Baudin lost forty of his crew and nine of the expedition's scientific staff: two zoologists, two botanists, two gardeners, an astronomer, and two artists. Why did they decide to jump ship?

Partly they were so fed up with Baudin after five months of sailing that they preferred to give up whatever rewards Australia held rather than to continue under him. Many of Baudin's crewmen got offers of better employment on other vessels. For the scientists in particular, Ile de France — with its pure warm air, green forests and hills, beckoning cascades, and famous Gardens of Pamplemousses — exercised too seductive a pull. After the privations of shipboard life, to which most of them were unaccustomed, the prospect of many more months of sailing seemed too much to bear. Some of these men seized opportunities on the island. Baudin reported that "among the scientists who remained three are to become schoolmasters and are to teach drawing and mathematics. One has married." The zoologist Dumont d'Urville became a local doctor. As Charles Baudin later recalled, "There was not one of us who did not receive the most attractive offers, and many could not resist." There were also a few who just wanted to return home, to which they carried the first damning reports of Nicolas Baudin.

Baudin himself had little choice but to go on. He managed to replace most of the departed crew and set sail again for the Australian coast. As for the deserters, he was better off without them, he grumbled in his journal: "I was not very sorry about the officers and scientists who had abandoned the expedition." But what about the scientific cost to his enterprise? He would soon have cause for worry as the number of scientists dwindled further.

IF DEALING WITH scientists and crew was challenging when they were in reasonably good health and only feigning illness, it became almost unbearable when they really got sick. In mid-August 1801, after several months of exploring the west coast of New Holland, recording its soil and vegetation, watercourses and geographical features, animal and marine life, and charting the coastline, the expedition staggered to Timor in dire need of re-stocking and rest.

Investigating the unknown coast had been arduous and uncertain work. Small parties of scientists and sailors set out from the main ships in little dinghies and longboats, but landing was often difficult due to the rocky shoreline and heavy sea. The land frequently appeared ugly and sterile, and the explorers were apprehensive about local conditions and the hostile natives they might encounter. When rough weather set in, *Le Géographe* lost sight of *Le Naturaliste.* They would not come together again for three months. Meanwhile, supplies of firewood and food dwindled, and by the time Baudin arrived at Timor, his men had not had fresh meat or produce for a month. Ten crew members were in the first stages of scurvy. And the scientists were getting restless from being unable to explore as much as they had hoped due to bad weather and the unwelcoming coastal terrain.

At first the island appeared to be pure paradise. Their anchorage "seemed in the middle of a beautiful lake, on every side clothed with the richest colors," Baudin wrote. The island's "beautiful vegetation pleasantly refreshed our eyes, tired by the sad spectacle they had endured for three months, of the arid and desolate coasts of New Holland." Water and fresh food were plentiful. Men killed a buffalo every two days and bought goats, fowl, fish, eggs, rice, and vegetables. The inhabitants of Kupang could not have been more charming and welcoming. The Dutch governor kept sending Baudin and his men gifts of pigs, deer, sheep, and produce. Meanwhile, the wealthiest landowner on the island, Madame van Esten, the widow of a former governor, entertained the bedraggled Frenchmen in the most elegant style. Dozens of beautifully dressed female and male slaves ceremoniously waited on her guests, offering them tea, pastries, sweetmeats, and fruits. The women moved so gracefully as to remind the Frenchmen of "the beautiful scene of the toilet of Venus in the ballet in Paris." When in the evening it was time to leave, Péron recalled, "slaves in red cloaks appeared, each with a long torch made of the leaves of a certain tree, which spread a great light like so many flambeaux [to illuminate the way to the ship]. We might at the time have fancied ourselves with Orpheus in his descent to the infernal regions for our conductors, with their torches, their costume, and their color, resembled the devils of their opera."

But all was not a magical dream. The exploration of Timor's fauna did not proceed smoothly. Péron recounted how September 12 had nearly proved a fatal day for his assistant Charles Lesueur, who had started the voyage as a gunner but had become an artist and zoologist's assistant when the expedition's original artists defected at Ile de France.

> While he was in pursuit of a troop of monkeys among the rocks which obstruct the course of the river of Kupang, a venomous reptile bit him on the heel. Soon after he felt a sort of numbness in the whole of his leg, which made him but too well guess what he had to fear from this bite. Mr. Lesueur hastened back to the town, but before he could get there his leg was stiff and much swelled, and he could scarcely bend his knee.
>
> To retard the action of the venom, he bound his thigh tight round above the knee, but this ligature had little effect; the thigh itself swelled to such a degree, that it was as much as my poor friend could do to reach the house. As soon as M. Lesueur got there he laid himself down on his bed, overcome by fatigue and pain, and already experiencing all the symptoms of a violent fever. . . . Our doctor, M. L'Haridon, hastened to him, and without delay cauterized the bite of the reptile very deeply; and applying to the part a compress, wetted with ammoniac, he then gave a strong dose of the same drug to the sick man, recommending him to keep perfectly still and quiet. He was soon in a profuse sweat, and the pain abated; and in a few days M. Lesueur felt no more of the wound, except a stiffness and difficulty of bending his knee, which remained a long

time, and which he still feels at times, particularly in the variations of the weather.

While Lesueur recovered, debilitating illness began to attack other men. Scurvy had abated as soon as they got some fresh fruit, but the sickness that overcame them now was far worse. Within three or four weeks, eight men developed a high fever and another six dysentery. Baudin himself was down with a fever for ten of the twelve weeks *Le Géographe* spent at Kupang. He barely pulled through, and the fever left his legs weak and numb for the rest of the voyage.

Then, the botanist Riedlé, Baudin's old friend, expired from dysentery on October 21, after weeks of suffering. Baudin was shaken. "Nobody knows how much I love him, how attached I am to him," he lamented as Riedlé lay dying. "I feel in advance how much the expedition will lose." He ordered for his friend a most dignified funeral, which he himself was too ill to attend. For a man as resolute and stoical as Baudin, his illness must have been utterly debilitating to keep him in bed on such a day. From his bed Baudin commanded that the ships' yards be crossed and their colors lowered. A cannon was to be fired every half hour for six hours. Twelve Dutch soldiers carried Riedlé's coffin to the Timor cemetery. Two officers and two naturalists bore the pall over it. The governor, Captain Hamelin, and all the expedition's men fit to walk followed the coffin to its resting place. The grave was dug beside that of David Nelson, the botanist from the famous *Bounty,* who had died of inflammatory fever — "a burning in the bowels, loss of sight, and inability to walk" — when the *Bounty* launch docked on Timor in 1789. On the tomb erected over the two botanists, Baudin had inscribed that Riedlé had died as a result of "his zeal, his activity, and his labors."

By the time the two corvettes left Timor in mid-November 1801, six people had died of dysentery, and those who survived remained in danger of recurrence. Fifteen men were sick aboard *Le*

Géographe, including two other companions of Baudin's from the *Belle-Angélique* days, Maugé and Levillain, and at least a dozen on *Le Naturaliste.* Three, and probably more, had venereal disease, likely picked up as a result of the habit of poorer Malay husbands to prostitute their wives in return for "European bagatelle." Sublieutenant St. Cricq confessed in his journal that "some of us did not refuse their caresses."

Dysentery continued to hang like a dark cloud over the ships for weeks. Baudin was horrified by its torments:

> The symptoms of this terrible disease are so frightening that the moment one is struck down by it one feels dead already, and this contributes in no small way to the aggravation of the condition. . . . Three days before his death Mantel [a gunner] wanted to drown himself and would have done so, had he not been promptly rescued. When he was lifted back on board he said to us with great calmness: "You have done me a grave disservice, for I know well that I shan't recover from my illness. In this way you are only prolonging my suffering for a few more days."

When Baudin's friend Levillain finally succumbed a month after leaving Timor, Baudin grieved in his journal: "It seems I am destined on this expedition to be parted from my best friends, and to have not only the pain of seeing them die, but also my own reproaches, since it is only through friendship for me, and in order to accompany me, that they have joined it."

Then Maugé died, too. He had been ill for weeks but, despite Baudin's protests, continued to go ashore while *Le Géographe* was examining Van Diemen's Land (Tasmania) and to push himself past discomfort and fatigue to conduct his zoological research. In the last two weeks of his illness, when the doctors had given up on him, Baudin visited Maugé every two hours. But he could do little to console his friend, who "spoke of nothing but his imminent death and his regrets for the friends whose advice he had disregarded by undertaking the voyage." Baudin confided in his journal, "His dying words filled me with sorrow. A few moments before the end he said to me: 'I am dying because I was too devoted to you and scorned my friends' advice. But at least remember me for the sacrifice I have made for you.'" For Baudin, a man of so few but such deeply felt connections, the loss of his faithful companions in this terrible way was a huge blow.

With the death of his friends, Baudin became even more isolated from his shipmates. He strove to do the right thing, to push on with their exploration in the face of constant hardships — defections, deaths, ostracism, loneliness, foul weather, navigational troubles, and his own failing health. Yet the more doggedly he pursued his goals, the more he antagonized his crew. Instead of trying to reach out, he turned more in upon himself. He expected and obtained little from his depleted and demoralized staff, and spent many nights on deck, in inclement weather, while the officers slept in their cabins below. Baudin poured his grief and grievances into his private journal, which proved less private than he thought. His men apparently read it when he was not looking and grew more resentful for the words they found about themselves.

How much worse could it get? In late May 1802, three months after Maugé's death, when *Le Géographe* was studying the coast of Van Diemen's Land, twenty out of the remaining seventy-five men on board were again suffering from scurvy. They blamed it on Baudin. "Most of the sick men were complaining loudly that by not seeking rest in some place where they could find relief, I wanted to bring about their death at sea," Baudin wrote. Was he really the monster they painted him to be? He continued, "Since we had almost no fresh food left and since, fortunately for them, I had economized on the little that I still had from the time of my last illness, I gave them one of my three remaining pigs, which I had gone without in order to be of help to anyone who should fall sick." He got no credit for that.

Baudin did not know that the human body can store vitamin C for only sixty to seventy days. They had been at sea for more than one hundred days on each of the legs from Ile de France to Timor, from Timor to Tasmania, and while charting the southeast coast of Australia. As exigent of his men as he was of himself, Baudin did push the expedition beyond the point of safety, but not out of personal whim. His sailing instructions prescribed a rigid schedule that took into account his supplies and seasonal weather — including monsoons — in the area he was charting that would affect his progress. To avoid these hazards, Baudin was forced to subject his men to others. And because of natural and man-made setbacks, he was already very much behind schedule. The shape of Australia's coast made keeping his men healthy all the more difficult. It had very few inlets, so vessels had to stay at sea longer than they would on voyages to other countries. Even when they could get to shore, it was difficult to replenish dwindling supplies of food and water, since rivers on the continent are few and far between and much of the vegetation was unfamiliar. In fact, scurvy and water shortage plagued all early voyages to Australia, not just Baudin's.

Of course, this was hardly consolation to the captain and his undernourished crew. As Charles Baudin recalled, it is "hard to give an idea of the state of dilapidation and general deprivation to which we were reduced." In June 1802 *Le Géographe* limped into Port Jackson after being at sea for 110 days. By then four seamen had died of scurvy and thirty-one were close to death. The rest had stiff joints and shrunken flexors that bowed their limbs. Their complexions were leaden, and their gums so swollen that they protruded from their mouths and had either ulcerated or had lost all feeling and gave off a fetid stench. Only four crewmen were fit to work the corvette. For three days they struggled outside the port, unable to guide *Le Géographe* through the Heads (the promontories framing the harbor). Finally, the governor of

Port Jackson sent out a party of British seamen to help bring the French ship to shore. At this point it was unclear whether the French sailors would even survive the expedition, much less bring home the marvelous Australian plants and animals expected by the Museum of Natural History and Josephine.

BACK IN FRANCE, Josephine, too, was at a crisis point. Outwardly her life seemed to be shaping up gloriously. In August 1802 Napoleon was voted Consul for Life. In 1804 he had himself proclaimed emperor of the French, the highest title he could ascend to (although as the First Consul his powers had already been nearly absolute). By controlling the government, establishing a hierarchy of imperial offices, and reconstituting the ministry of police to crack down on any opposition, he had essentially returned the country to monarchy. To make his position fully official, he began to prepare for his and Josephine's coronation at the end of that year. Yet Napoleon's ascent was, for Josephine, a dangerous turn. She was forty years old, no longer young by the standards of the time, and ever less likely to produce an heir for her husband, who now needed one most urgently, having secured the right to make his imperial dignity hereditary. How could Josephine keep Napoleon from divorcing her to marry a more fertile wife? And if she could not stop this from happening, what would become of her?

The Bonaparte clan was contributing to Josephine's anxiety. They had never been well-disposed toward her, resenting her for diverting Napoleon's affection and loyalty from his family. Now, with the upcoming coronation, they begrudged her growing rank over them. Napoleon had little patience for their jealousies. "My wife is a good woman," he said, "who does them [my family] no harm. She is willing to play the empress up to a point, and to have diamonds and fine clothes — the trifles of her age! I have never loved her blindly, yet if I have made her empress it is out of justice. . . . If I had been thrown into prison instead of ascending a throne, she would have shared my misfortune. It is right for her to share my grandeur."

Preparations for the coronation made Napoleon's family only more hostile. Much of the bickering had to do with titles. Napoleon informed his brothers Joseph and Louis that they would appear at the ceremony as "Grand Dignitaries of the Empire," but they wanted to be called princes. Otherwise their wives would not consent to carry Josephine's train. After a period of angry outbursts, pouting, and deadlock, Napoleon finally gave in. The matter of Josephine's train was also refined to soothe everyone's ruffled feelings. The "princesses" would "hold up the robe" rather than "carry the train," a subtle distinction, but obviously crucial to the truce between the parties. Still, the formidable Madame Mère, Napoleon's mother, refused to suppress her aversion to her daughter-in-law and would not attend the coronation at all (although she was inserted into Jacques-Louis David's official painting commemorating the event). Small wonder that a visitor calling upon Josephine shortly before the great day found her in tears.

The Bonaparte family and advisers also nagged Napoleon continually to divorce his infertile wife as soon as possible. Now that he was becoming emperor, he could no longer put off the matter of his succession. On the eve of the coronation Josephine tried to shore up her marriage by asking for a private interview with Pope Pius VII, who had arrived to anoint the new emperor as tradition demanded. During their conversation she revealed to him a weighty "secret." The bonds uniting the imperial couple were merely those of a civil ceremony. She begged the pontiff to marry them in a more binding religious rite. This would not necessarily prevent a divorce, but it would make it politically more difficult for Napoleon to obtain one. Josephine's charm worked yet again. Pius VII promised that he would insist on the religious marriage ceremony as a condition of his taking part in the coronation.

Though reluctant to be painted into a corner, Napoleon agreed. On December 1, the day before the great event, the religious marriage was solemnized in a small private service.

As Josephine worried, Malmaison and its menagerie became all the more crucial to her. Even if her husband divorced her, this estate — her only property — would remain her possession and refuge. Its natural history collections would continue to bestow dignity and importance on Josephine whether she was with Napoleon or not. But at the moment she could not devote much time to this cherished project. The coronation preparations were all-consuming.

The ceremony was to take place in the Cathedral of Notre Dame. To plan all the details, the painter Jean-Baptiste Isabey was ordered to prepare seven detailed drawings, each with more than a hundred figures, that would map out all the stages of the event. Despairing of completing all the designs in the eight days he had for the task, Isabey ransacked the shops of Paris and bought every toy figure he could find. He dressed them up in appropriate costumes (made of paper, one presumes) and placed them in a large model of the interior of Notre Dame. With these figures, more convenient than the drawings anyway, Napoleon and his officials proceeded to perfect every detail of the elaborate ceremony.

Meanwhile, Jacques-Louis David was charged with transforming the cathedral interior into a vast theatrical set. He removed the choir screen and two subsidiary altars and built sloping tiers of wooden seats, covered with silk and velvet, on either side of the nave. He hung the walls with gold-fringed crimson cloths of silk and velvet and suspended twenty-four huge crystal chandeliers from the vaulted ceiling. On a platform to the left of the high altar, David placed a canopied throne for the pope, and directly facing it, on an elevated dais, two chairs of state for Napoleon and Josephine.

December 2 turned out to be a freezing winter day under overcast skies. Flurries swirled in the air and left white powder on the icy streets. Participants in the event began to groom and dress long before daylight. The first guests were admitted into the chilly interior of Notre Dame at seven in the morning. At that same hour the great officials set out on foot from the Palais de Justice to march in a slow and dignified procession toward the cathedral along streets decorated with red, white, and blue bunting, tapestries, and artificial and fresh flowers. At nine in the morning the pope, clad in white, took his place in a state carriage drawn by eight horses. By custom the carriage was preceded by a papal chamberlain riding astride a humble mule and carrying a large wooden cross. The contrast between the unglamorous beast and the surrounding splendor provoked much joking from the less devout Parisians who crowded the route.

Napoleon and Josephine were meant to leave the Tuileries at ten but were running late. In the last frantic minutes of preparation, the near-emperor was still dashing around his chambers, scrambling to assemble his complicated garb. For the procession to the cathedral, he wore silk stockings and breeches, half boots of white velvet with gold embroidery and gold buckles, a crimson velvet jacket, a short velvet cloak lined with white satin and held on one shoulder with a diamond clasp, and a black velvet cap with two plumes. He looked like a Renaissance prince. Josephine wore a dress and train of silver brocade scattered with gold bees. (Napoleon adopted bees, a sign of industry, to link himself with the earliest kings of France, who had used this emblem.) Josephine's gold bracelets, clasps, and necklace were set with jewels and antique cameos, and on her chestnut hair, coiffed into a mass of tiny curls, sat a diadem of four rows of pearls interlaced with diamond leaves. Her face was so well made-up that she looked twenty-four, onlookers remarked.

For the actual coronation Napoleon put on a long satin gown embroidered with gold and reaching to his ankles, and over it the imperial mantle of crimson velvet lined with ermine and strewn with gold bees. It weighed more than eighty pounds and required four dignitaries to help carry it. The train of Josephine's mantle, also of crimson velvet with gold bees, was borne by five princesses — Napoleon's three reluctant sisters, his sister-in-law, and Josephine's daughter, Hortense. After the coronation, as the imperial couple moved solemnly to the western end of the nave to ascend the dais and mount the thrones waiting for them, the five princesses bickered over the proper way to carry the empress's robe. Their altercation ended only after brusque orders from Napoleon. His attendants, meanwhile, were so clumsy in bearing the great weight of his garment that he almost fell backward as he began to climb the steps.

In the aftermath of the coronation Josephine's life became even more glorious in public but quite trying in private. Napoleon now insisted on strict protocols that regulated every activity: her movements through the Tuileries palace, her interactions with various visitors, and, of course, conduct at state events. The new rules were codified in *The Etiquette of the Imperial Palace,* a substantial volume prepared on Napoleon's orders and a throwback to the rigid etiquette of Louis XIV's day. Rule 40, for example, gives some of the flavor of Josephine's new life: "When Her Majesty is present in her Interior Apartments the chamberlain of the day may traverse the Apartment of Honor in order to take his orders; he must scratch lightly on the door of the bedroom, where one of the ladies of Her Majesty must always be in attendance and seek permission to introduce into her presence the chamberlain of the day."

In a letter to Hortense, Josephine confided, "I feel that I am not made for so much grandeur. I would be happier in some retreat, surrounded by the objects of my affection." She may have enjoyed the glamour of her position: the clothes and jewels, the adulation and outward respect. But affairs of the throne were overwhelming her other pleasures and pastimes, including her botanical and zoological pursuits, without giving her the security she wanted. Having produced no heir, she continued to live under the shadow of divorce. Napoleon may have loved her, but his carping clan urged him ever more insistently to leave Josephine and take a more suitable wife. He was also getting more tyrannical in his conduct toward her, causing her many tears and discomforts that she tried to hide so as not to antagonize him.

Among other things, he was carrying on affairs with other women, prompting Josephine to write to a friend, "I am very unhappy. . . . Every day Bonaparte makes scenes without giving any explanation. This is no way to live. I have tried to find out what could be the reason and I have learned that for the past eight days La Grassini [a young prima donna from La Scala with whom Napoleon was involved] has been in Paris." No wonder Malmaison gave Josephine some of her happiest hours. In this private realm she could recuperate from her mounting pressures and focus on searching out and collecting new animals and plants.

IN AUSTRALIA BAUDIN'S public anxieties were also mediated by moments of private happiness. Port Jackson provided a desperately needed respite for the French expedition. While his crew continued to blame Baudin for their bedraggled state, he made a new and valuable friend: the British governor of Port Jackson, Philip Gidley King. It was to King that Baudin would write some of his most stirring letters about the treatment of native peoples and animals.

King was a naval officer of similar age, rank, and humble social background as Baudin. He, too, had stumbled into natural history by way of a naval career. Years earlier he had been dispatched to Norfolk Island, off Australia's northeast coast, to establish a settlement and to cultivate New Zealand flax and tall Norfolk pines, which the British navy hoped to use for shipbuilding. From there King had ferried a cargo of live plants for Sir Joseph Banks and since then had maintained an ongoing correspondence with the eminent botanist.

Despite their countries' enmity, Baudin and King developed a genuine affection for each other. And just as Baudin and Flinders had treated each other with great cordiality (in fact, it was Flinders who had invited the Frenchmen to take a respite at Port Jackson), King offered the French expedition prompt and spontaneous hospitality. "I obtained from Mr. King . . . all that I could wish for," Baudin reported to Denis Decrès, the minister of the marine, "and from that moment he has not ceased to load us with kindness, furnishing us with provisions, all the things needed to cure our sick and make our stay useful by contributing to the increase of our collection." Baudin and King's mutual sympathy was bolstered by the fact that they had compatible personalities and were both lonely in their positions of power. King was serving as a naval governor over an isolated penal colony. Baudin was an outcast on his own expedition. During his four-month stay at Port Jackson, Baudin saw King every day, sometimes for business but often for the pure pleasure of his company.

While recovering at Port Jackson, Baudin also pored over travel narratives he had brought from France and realized that he had been staying at sea for too long. He figured out the body's limitations on storing vitamin C and its need to be replenished every sixty days or so. After that he never again remained away from the coast for more than two months and was able to keep his men in much better shape.

At the same time, he carried on with natural history work. In a letter to Jussieu, Baudin extolled the natural bounties of Port Jackson and the beauty of the plants and flowers he was getting ready to send back to France. After leaving Timor the expedition had been collecting animal, plant, and mineral specimens along the west and south coasts of Australia. Among the most fruitful surveys was that of Van Diemen's Land, where they had obtained examples of various live birds, Tasmanian echidnas (spiny anteaters), Tasmanian wombats, and diverse plants. They also had met and observed the Aborigines, who were for the most part very curious and rather friendly toward the Europeans. By the time Baudin reached Port Jackson and reunited with *Le Naturaliste,* he decided it was time for that ship to return home with the first installment of Australian animals and vegetation.

Among the new creatures *Le Naturaliste* would ferry back to France were black swans. The birds, native only to Australia, were first discovered by the Dutch navigator Willem de Vlaming in 1697. He named the place where he found them Swan River (it is located on the west coast of the continent). The lovely birds had totally black plumage, except for their white quill feathers, and a striking red beak. Slightly north of the swan habitat, the French scientists came across large sandbanks covered with turtles. "Invited by the facility with which they could be taken," Péron recounted, "our party procured in less than three hours fifteen turtles, some of which weighed from 122 to 147 kilograms [250 to 300 pounds]." These, too, would be shipped back to France and be claimed by Josephine for her zoological collection. In addition, in the course of their stay at Port Jackson, Péron and his assistant Lesueur "killed and prepared [stuffed] no less than 200 birds, and had amassed in our repositories 68 quadrupeds [also mostly stuffed]."

Péron, the only remaining zoologist on the expedition, spent three weeks getting the natural history collection ready for stowage on *Le Naturaliste.* "We arranged in the most methodical manner 40,000 creatures of all sorts and descriptions, filling 33 large packing cases," Péron wrote. In addition, Lesueur produced a great number of sketches and paintings of Australian flora and fauna. Hamelin also loaded *Le Naturaliste* with seventy tubs of live plants, including pines from Norfolk Island. Belowdecks he installed the animals: two black swans, two dingoes, four kangaroos, several emus (which would turn out to be less charming than they seemed at first sight), a goose from Waterhouse Island, a snake-headed tortoise, and a number of parrots. Midshipman Bougainville complained in his journal that all these animals, cramped into close quarters, emitted an overpowering stench.

Baudin, anxious for the well-being of the specimens, came aboard *Le Naturaliste* to inspect all the arrangements. He was mostly pleased with what he saw. The animals, birds, and plants looked healthy and ready for the journey. Baudin furnished Hamelin with elaborate instructions on how to care for his charges at sea and with adequate provisions for them (to be replenished during stops en route). He warned Hamelin to water the plants "with the same amount each time, once every ten days in temperate zones, twice in tropical . . . and those to whom you are entrusting this work must merit your confidence. . . . What happened to me on my last voyage could also happen to you. Among the disgruntled . . . there are some who are quite capable of substituting salt water for fresh. Watch carefully and taste the water yourself." As a parting gift Baudin presented his colleague with "an extraordinarily large wombat" that he himself had received as a gift from an English captain he had met at Port Jackson. And with that, in November 1802, *Le Naturaliste* sailed off toward home. Its voyage back to France was mostly uneventful, and after stops at Ile de France and the Cape of Good Hope, the ship reached Le Havre on June 7, 1803.

Le Géographe stayed behind to finish charting the south coast of Australia and to collect further flora and fauna for the Museum and Josephine. To make this work easier, prior to leaving Port Jackson in November 1802, Baudin had bought a schooner, *Le Casuarina*. Weighing thirty tons and measuring twenty-nine feet long, it was much better suited than the large *Géographe* to approaching harbors and inlets and conducting detailed surveys of the shore.

Baudin's zeal to gather and bring back to France a great assembly of novel plants and animals that would put his nation ahead of all others was now colored by a personal urgency. He began to suffer from increasingly more troubling symptoms of tuberculosis, which he had either picked up along the way or had prior to the journey but saw growing worse after all the physical strains of the voyage. Would he be able to complete his mission before the disease consumed him? Even if he did, this was likely his final expedition and his last chance to make his reputation.

At least Baudin must have been pleased with the animal collecting on King and Kangaroo islands off the south coast of Australia. Here the dogs that had been running around *Le Géographe* and soiling it since France (and surprisingly surviving the trip thus far without falling sick or getting eaten) got to earn their keep. On Kangaroo Island Baudin and his men came across very large kangaroos that grazed in flocks, like sheep, and were just as tame.

> During the day, with the help of the dogs, [Baudin wrote] the hunters caught twelve giant kangaroos of various sizes. Seven of them were taken alive and were put in pens aboard the ship to be kept. Amongst these ones that we hope to carry back to our country are three females which have offspring and may prosper. I shall try, before leaving, to obtain a full twenty live ones, so that we shall have better hope of keeping some throughout the voyage.

A month later they were still hunting: "I also brought back [to the ship] three live kangaroos which were put in pens like the others, and of which I am taking the greatest care. There were two males and one female, and the three of them were caught unharmed by our dogs. One tried to escape by throwing himself into the water, but fell into our hands after putting up magnificent resistance."

The dogs were also helpful in catching emus. Because these birds are very aggressive and can kick another animal to death, the dogs had to attack them from the front, grab them by the neck, and bend them down so as to avoid being pecked. Baudin was especially lucky to see and collect the dwarf emus that dwelled exclusively on King Island. They went extinct soon after his visit, eaten by the English sealers whom Péron so admired and Baudin so despised.

Baudin took great pains to keep his animals alive and well. Before leaving Kangaroo Island he tried to stock up on appropriate food for the kangaroos. One day he gathered branches of white casuarina trees, another he sent a little boat ashore "to obtain grass for our kangaroos, which are all in very good condition, with a healthy appetite; but what was brought back did not suit them at all and none of them would touch it. As they are beginning to get used to maize, I am hoping that I shall soon be able to feed them entirely on that."

Unfortunately, a few days after their departure from Kangaroo Island,

> at daybreak we found two of our kangaroos dead in their pens. I had no doubt at all of the bad weather being responsible, for they were completely soaked with the rain and the continuous mist that we had had for the past three days, in spite of our having been very careful to cover their pens well with good tarpaulins. This accident decided me to keep them no longer on the gangways, where they were housed. But in order to find them another suitable place, I had to create two malcontents.

Baudin dismantled the cabins of the botanist Leschenault de la Tour and the midshipman Ransonnet to make quarters for "the seven kangaroos that were exposed to the elements on our gangways." When one of the displaced men complained, Baudin reprimanded him for "preferring your own comfort and a few temporary advantages to the greater success of the expedition and whatever may serve our country." Not surprisingly, the captain's priorities did not win him any more fans among his crew.

By late June 1803, after four months of endless easterlies, squalls, drenching rains, and heavy swells that buffeted the ship as it continued its coastal survey, the captured animals were not doing well. "During the morning I was told that several of our quadrupeds and emus were very sick," Baudin noted with concern.

> We could only attribute this to the violent and incessant move-ment of the heavy sea, which left them not a moment's peace. This news was particularly unpleasant, as I saw myself on the brink of losing them after giving them such attention as should have secured them a happier fate. Since the emus refused to eat, we fed them by force, opening their beaks and introducing pellets of rice mash into their stomachs. We gave them, and the sick kangaroos likewise, wine and sugar; and although I was very short of these same things for myself, I shall be very happy to have gone without them for their sake if they can help in restoring them to health.

This was true dedication to the mission. But then Baudin, like Josephine, needed these animals alive and thriving to ensure his triumph in the face of so much adversity and to secure his legacy.

Baudin, however, was running out of time. His illness was get-ting worse. As he recorded in his diary, "During the night I was taken with a fit of spitting blood, similar to those that I had already had on two different occasions, and the sputum that I brought up was so thick, that one would have said that it was pieces of lung coming away from my body." Yet he worried about his creatures as much as or more than about himself. They were to be his legacy, and he was ready to terminate the expedition and fail to complete his mission of charting the Australian coast if he could salvage his glory by delivering these animals to France. "If the weather does not turn fine after the full moon," he lamented in his journal, "I have decided to make for Ile de France [the direction of home] rather than lose them all."

On July 7, 1803, seeing that the weather and the animals' con-dition had not improved, Baudin issued the order to stop explor-ing and turn homeward.

It is not without regret that I decided upon this step. A thousand reasons should have made me take it even earlier; but without listing them all, I shall limit myself to saying that we no longer had anything more than a month's supply of biscuits, at the rate of six ounces per man, and two months' of water, as a result of the amount consumed by the birds and quadrupeds. Twenty men were ill, several with dysentery, the others unfit for duty because of serious venereal diseases contracted at Timor. Nobody to replace me.

He was coughing and hemorrhaging so severely now, his tuberculosis eating away at his lungs, that all too frequently he had to take to his bed. And he had lost 10 out of the 20 kangaroos, 2 wombats, 4 emus, and 50 smaller birds out of the original 150. The cost of gathering and delivering these novel Australian creatures to the Museum of Natural History and to Malmaison was proving immense — in the crew's hardships, illnesses, and deaths; in the mental toll on the survivors; and in the suffering of the animals plucked from their natural habitats, stuffed into tiny quarters or cages on a constantly rocking ship, and fed inappropriate food. It is a miracle that any of them survived the months-long voyage.

Baudin's men were jubilant at the news of heading home. Charles Baudin remembered how "one night, at nine o'clock [the captain] came on deck and ordered the officer of the watch to steer a course for Ile de France. . . . In an instant the news spread throughout the ship. The half of the crew asleep below sprang up in a transport of joy, congratulating and hugging each other, and everybody spent the night on deck dancing and singing."

By the time *Le Géographe* reached Ile de France on August 7, 1803, two more emus had died, and Nicolas Baudin was on his last legs. At least Hamelin had left him some good news: all of his animals were in good health, with only one death — a Samoan turtle — and he had added two gazelles for Josephine to his floating menagerie. Baudin would have been delighted to learn (alas he did not) that *Le Naturaliste* had already reached Le Havre two months earlier and had delivered its living cargo of animals and plants in remarkably good condition — perhaps because Hamelin had not encountered the bad weather off the coast of Australia that had traumatized Baudin's creatures, and so had completed his return in less time.

Unfortunately, Baudin's own luck had run out. Six weeks after *Le Géographe* arrived at Ile de France, on September 16, 1803, Baudin died of pulmonary tuberculosis. Charles Baudin recalled with pathos: "His funeral was nothing less than dismal: he was universally detested. He had shown great strength of spirit in his last days. He had collected in a jar of spirits the lungs [*sic*] he had brought up in the course of his untold suffering, and he showed them to everyone who came to visit him. 'Are the lungs indispensable to life?' he would say. 'You see I no longer have any, yet I still exist.'"

After Nicolas Baudin's death, Pierre-Bernard Milius, who had served as a lieutenant aboard *Le Naturaliste* on the outbound journey, assumed leadership of *Le Géographe*. It took him three months to sail from Ile de France home, including a three-week stopover at the Dutch colony on the Cape of Good Hope. There he took on thirty more live animals and birds, some purchased, others presented by the governor of the colony to the Museum and to Madame Bonaparte. Among them were two lions, two panthers, a gnu, a zebra, and three ostriches. Milius installed them alongside the Australian animals and six others, including a "black tiger" and a panther, received at Ile de France as a gift to Josephine from its captain-general.

Despite the unpopularity it had caused his predecessor, Milius went even further than Baudin in turning the officers' quarters into housing for animals. All of the officers were now lodged in the great cabin or in the gun room, a change "not to everyone's taste." But at least they were going home. At last, on March 24,

1804, three years and five months after first setting sail, *Le Géographe* dropped anchor at the port of Lorient.

As soon as *Le Géographe* docked, François Péron, Baudin's most vehement enemy, moved to shape his own and the voyage's legacy. Within two days of arriving, he wrote a long letter to Decrès, the minister of the marine, ostensibly seeking official permission to oversee the unloading of the natural history collection. In packing it for the journey home, he had correlated the descriptions of the thousands of nonlive specimens to the crates in which they were stored. Now he worried that if the crates were mixed up, the journals in which he described the specimens, and all his efforts, would become obsolete. (He had also taken unprecedented care to identify precisely where he had collected each animal, recognizing that different species were restricted to different ranges.)

Péron also had a larger agenda. He wanted to secure his own reputation by claiming full credit for the acquisition of the collection and the success of the expedition. There were few to challenge him. With the death of Maugé and Levillain, he remained the only zoologist. (Deaths and desertion had reduced the overall number of naturalists from twenty-two to three. It was not an unusual rate of demise in those days, yet Baudin was especially blamed for it.) Péron also wanted revenge on the hated captain. In the letter to Decrès he hinted that Baudin had tried to sabotage the collection by selling off parts of it at Ile de France — an entirely false charge that contradicted Baudin's abiding concern to get all the specimens home safely. But Baudin was dead and could not defend himself, and those scientists who had jumped ship at Ile de France at the beginning of the voyage had already begun to darken his name.

Without waiting for a reply from Decrès, and with Captain Milius ill with fever at Lorient, Péron next set off for Paris, to be the first man from *Le Géographe* to present himself at the Ministry of the Marine and the Museum of Natural History. Péron wanted to publish the official account of the expedition and to collect a stipend for it. He would spend the next two years cajoling and begging the Museum, the government, and Josephine to sponsor his writing. In August 1806 Napoleon finally issued a decree charging Péron to produce the account of the voyage at government expense. By that time Péron had so besmirched Baudin's character and conduct that the captain's name did not even appear on Napoleon's order for the publication. According to Péron's biographer, Louis Audiat, Napoleon said that "Baudin did well to die. If he did not, on his return I would have had him hanged."

With the actual text of his *Voyage of Discovery to the Southern Hemisphere,* Péron finally put the nail in Baudin's coffin. He criticized Baudin's naval abilities, his navigational decision making, and his style of command. In describing the desertions at Ile de France on the outbound journey, Péron declared that "a great number of officers, naturalists and artists belonging to our two ships, already wearied by the ill usage they had experienced from our commander, or justly alarmed for the future, chose to remain in the colony." He painted Baudin as capricious and tyrannical, willing to abandon his people on barren foreign shores and indifferent to their well-being aboard ship. The captain's ban on "all wine, bread and fresh meat for the duration of the voyage [a misrepresentation of attempts to ration dwindling supplies] was . . . a sentence of death" for many of the naturalists. In the entire text of the *Voyage,* Péron referred to Baudin only as "our commander," erasing the captain's very name from the record of the expedition he had initiated. He mentioned it only once, in a sentence he must have very much enjoyed writing: "At last the moment arrived, and on September 16, 1803, around noon, Mr. Baudin ceased to exist."

Baudin's reputation may have survived Péron's assault had the political climate been different, but times had changed between 1800 and 1804. When Baudin set off for Australia, France and its

First Consul were feeling optimistic, hopeful of rebuilding the nation's navy after the losses inflicted by Admiral Nelson in Egypt and of expanding the French sphere of influence overseas. But in May 1803 Britain broke the Treaty of Amiens, and France plunged back into a war that would drag on for eleven more years. In January 1804 the police uncovered an assassination plot against Napoleon, which precipitated purges and political tensions within the country. (Josephine, whom old friends and those in dire circumstances beseeched for help, pleaded on behalf of a number of men implicated in the conspiracy and succeeded in saving their lives.)

Napoleon proclaimed his empire in May 1804, but this declaration did not reflect France's international strength. French ships were bottled up in European ports by the British fleet, which had firm control over the seas. Europe, which Napoleon had undertaken to free from tyranny by his conquests, was ungratefully restless: his allies kept rising against him, and new opposition was breaking out. Napoleon's expansion was hitting a wall. Understanding that the sea would never be his element, he was in no mood to welcome back the tainted expedition. Australia and the South Pacific were no longer promising frontiers, but rather reminders of the demise of his dream of an overseas empire — a dream that had been so alluring only four years earlier. How much easier to accept the story that these great plans had failed because of the incompetence and venality of Captain Nicolas Baudin. This time there was no triumphant parade of natural specimens. Whatever their scientific value, to Napoleon they were the fruits of failure.

As for Péron, ironically his efforts to claim full credit for the expedition's scientific accomplishments ended up casting the whole orphaned Australian venture into obscurity for more than a century. Not only were Baudin's labors deliberately forgotten, but his natural history finds were never properly recorded. As Georges Cuvier, one of the most influential figures in science during the early nineteenth century (and the older brother of Frédéric Cuvier, the head keeper of the Museum's menagerie), wrote in 1825,

The Baudin expedition to New Holland, where Mssrs. Péron and Lesueur made immense collections . . . did not give us, for science proper, fruits proportional to the rich materials it procured. . . . The late M. Péron [who died in 1810 of tuberculosis at age thirty-five], a man with a vast capacity and an industry astonishing in such a weak body, made an infinity of searching observations, and accumulated the most valuable and the most thorough detailed notes. . . . But in a most natural desire to assure for himself the sole glory for his discoveries . . . he kept carefully to himself all the manuscripts, and even all the pictures accompanying them, though he could not claim they were his own work; and since his death, no one knows where all his precious compilations have gone.

In the 1800s, as now, to ensure the recognition of new species, naturalists had to do more than just amass specimens and make a claim. Their finds had to be fully published, preferably in a monograph or an established scientific journal, and made available to the scholarly community. Péron and his assistant Lesueur, who remained faithful to the naturalist and worked and lived with him in a small apartment near the Museum, held on so tightly to their descriptions and drawings of Australian flora and fauna that most of these did not see the light of day.

Their behavior echoed the practices of the Museum professors. Accumulating specimens and tightly controlling access to them — regulating who could inventory, classify, dissect, store, display, and speak authoritatively about them — was a complicated game played by the savants to gain power and build careers. As a result, a major part of the thousands of new Australian zoological species and the hundreds of botanical ones failed to be acknowledged as new discoveries, and the scientific significance of the expedition was nearly squandered.

What a tremendous loss, given that *Le Géographe* alone brought back 180,000 dried and preserved specimens of animals, insects, shells, plants, and minerals — more than had been gathered by any previous voyage. As the Museum professors wrote to the minister of the interior, based on Péron's report, more than 2,500 species were new to science — ten times more than Cook had brought back from his famous second voyage to Australia — which more than doubled those of the known world. Seventy-three live animals survived the journey on *Le Géographe* and dozens more on *Le Naturaliste.* They not only enriched the Museum of Natural History but also transformed Josephine's modest menagerie into a unique and valuable collection of exotic beasts scarcely known in Europe until then.

When Péron published the *Atlas of the Voyage to Australian Lands,* he paid tribute to Josephine's enthusiasm, support, and efforts at acclimating the Australian animals and plants to France. The frontispiece of the volume shows the château of Malmaison in the background, with kangaroos, emus, and black swans arrayed on the front lawn. This was not mere flattery. Aside from the Museum professors, Josephine seemed to be the only grateful recipient of the fruits of the expedition's labors, and the only one eager to make something worthwhile out of them.

WHEN JOSEPHINE FIRST conceived of her menagerie, she had a novel idea: she would have a zoo without cages. Her animals would inhabit the Malmaison grounds as if they were in Eden — living free and rambling among the trees, shrubs, and flowers from their native lands. It was an original concept, presaging such modern sanctuaries as the San Diego Wild Animal Park by nearly two centuries. Josephine recognized that to create such a paradise, she had to be careful in her selection of animals. But, of course, as empress, she got first choice of what came off *Le Géographe* and *Le Naturaliste*.

As *Le Géographe* docked at Lorient, it was met by the Museum's celebrated zoology professor, Etienne Geoffroy Saint-Hilaire, and by Josephine's representative. Months earlier, when *Le Naturaliste* had returned, the professors of the Museum had been "invited" by the minister of the interior to defer to the desires of Madame Bonaparte.

I have authorized you, citizens, to deliver . . . for the gardens of Madame Bonaparte all that is not essentially necessary to the establishment. . . . You know as I do the success with which Madame Bonaparte looks after the cultivation of plants and the acclimatization of rare animals. It is in the interest of Science and the glory of France to encourage her distinguished taste and I invite you to back her vision and mine by all the means that you have in your power.

A letter from the minister of the marine to the director of the Museum reiterated this directive upon the arrival of *Le Géographe*: "Under the terms of the particular instructions that the deceased Baudin had received, a part of the collection . . . and living animals . . . are allocated to the gardens of Malmaison."

Under the eyes of Geoffroy Saint-Hilaire and Josephine's agent, the live animals, plants, and preserved samples were loaded on carriages without any pomp. Geoffroy Saint-Hilaire reported sixty-seven crates of zoological specimens.* Of the live beasts, there were two kangaroos, two emus, and five king parrots from Australia; one cassowary from the Moluccas; and two lions, four panthers,

---

*Péron stated that there were fifty-four. The discrepancy was probably due to some repacking of the crates for their transport to Paris.

two monkeys, two mongooses, one ostrich, one hyena, one jackal, one zebra, and one gnu from the Cape of Good Hope.* The origin of some of the other animals is less clear. The six unspecified birds and thirty-two tortoises likely came from Australia and Africa. The single civet cat, two deer, five lemurs, and two porcupines were probably loaded at Ile de France, where they had been brought by other captains sailing from distant regions. Baudin would have been distressed to learn that, despite his painstaking care, since Timor six kangaroos, two emus, two wombats, and forty-five birds died before reaching France.

For the journey to the capital, the animal cages were mounted on nine carts, marked A or B to distinguish those intended for Malmaison from those for the Museum. Josephine graciously let the Museum have the lions, panthers, and hyena. Although some of them had been specifically meant as presents for her, she could not have them roam freely in her park. But she was delighted with the kangaroos and black swans, and she gladly took the cassowary, the gnu, the crowned pigeons, a pair of lemurs, the secretary bird from the Cape of Good Hope, eleven tortoises, and the water cocks. In the end, of the seventy-three live animals brought back by *Le Géographe,* only twenty-three ended up at the Museum; the rest were claimed by Josephine.

The cortege left Lorient on April 11. A naval clerk directed the convoy, and four experienced men from *Le Géographe,* led by Lesueur, attended to the animals. Four gendarmes made sure that everything stayed in order. The modest procession was nothing like the triumphal parade of *naturalia* at the Fêtes de la Liberté in 1798. Nor did the journey proceed entirely smoothly. One giant

---

*Josephine probably never learned that Captain Milius got one mongoose for himself and kept it as a pet for many years. The little animal loved to chase and scare away cats, to sit on its owner's back when he was writing at his desk, to meet him along his route home after he had been away from the house, to steal food from plates during dinner, hiding pieces of meat in Milius's bed, and to sit up warming itself by the fireplace in the winter.

kangaroo and sixteen tortoises expired between Lorient and Paris, and at one point the jackal escaped and terrorized the surrounding neighborhood. Lesueur eventually recaptured it and lured it back into its cage with pieces of meat. On April 29 the carts arrived at Versailles, where they were handed off to the next set of officials. Botanist Charles-François Brisseau de Mirbel, superintendent of the Malmaison estate, came to take charge of Josephine's portion. Frédéric Cuvier received the rest for the Museum.

The Museum, although it obtained less than it had hoped, was very pleased with its share. Jussieu, reporting to the ministers of the marine and the interior as well as to Josephine, extolled the specimens and the work of the expedition's naturalists. Of all the collections from distant lands that had ever reached France, he wrote, this was the largest, especially in the animal realm, which had been neglected by the British. Referring to the account Péron hoped to write, he observed, "It will be glorious for France to forestall, by the publication of this voyage, a nation which despite its settlements and resources in this new region has published nothing that approaches the work of our naturalists."

Jussieu also discoursed on the utility of Australian birds and animals. The "smallest species of kangaroo," for example, possessed fine fur and meat. Péron had reported that "the flesh of this animal much resembles that of the wild rabbit . . . but [is] more aromatic, which is probably occasioned by the peculiar property of plants it feeds on, and which are almost all odoriferous. It certainly was by much the finest flavored flesh of the kangaroo that we ever tasted, and therefore this species would be a valuable acquisition to European countries." Péron also had suggested that the "giant kangaroo" could found a livestock industry, wombats would be good to eat and easily domesticated, the emu's flesh was comparable to turkey or milk-fed pork, the black swan's meat was tender and its down very fine, and the lyrebird had the potential to rival the peacock in France (it would seem he meant as food, rather than for its decorative display). Perhaps it is odd to hear that Jussieu, being the director of the Museum of Natural History, also rhapsodized about eating his specimens. But in extolling the practical benefits of exotic Australian animals, he was providing justification for a four-year expedition at the public's expense.

Josephine, in her turn, was delighted with her exotic acquisitions. It is hard for us to appreciate the novelty of Australian animals because we are now so familiar with them through zoos, books, and television programs. But imagine encountering for the first time birds whose tails are shaped like lyres and mammals that lay eggs or carry babies in pouches. At the turn of the nineteenth century kangaroos, wombats, black swans, and emus were like nothing Europeans had encountered before. The first European description of a kangaroo — by a seaman who had sailed with Captain Cook — reflected his bafflement: "as large as a greyhound, of a mouse color and very swift." Even Sir Joseph Banks was stumped: "To compare it to any European animal would be impossible as it has not the least resemblance to any one I have seen." No wonder these creatures became Malmaison's most remarkable inhabitants.

The dwarf emus proved to be Josephine's least favorite creatures. Emus are squat-bodied birds with short, thick legs ending in three fingers and with a call resembling a deep rumble. The full-size birds we know today (they stand 5 to 7 feet tall and weigh some 110 pounds) dwell in thick forests and are easily frightened. As they flee, they trot very fast, keeping their bodies horizontal and sticking their tail feathers up in the air, which makes them look taller in the back than in the front. They can also leap up to nearly five feet high as they try to escape. When threatened and feeling cornered, they attack animals and people, jumping on them to inflict damage with their beaks and sharp nails. With a kick they can easily shatter a man's leg. Since it takes nothing to spook an emu, the birds must be treated with extreme care, and some zookeepers are more afraid of them, with their mercurial temperaments, than of the big cats, whose moods are easier to gauge and do not shift so suddenly. In captivity emus eat not only bread, seeds, and apples but also little chicks or baby ducks that wander by.

It is likely that dwarf emus had similar natures. Once Josephine figured out what she had on her hands, she decided that these disagreeable birds were not right for her little paradise and passed them back to the Museum. What she did not know was that dwarf emus would soon go extinct and that her two birds would turn out to be great treasures. Josephine's emus, also unaware of the rest of their species' fate, spent the remainder of their lives at the Museum, outliving her by eight years.

Far more endearing to Josephine were the kangaroos. Visitors to Malmaison marveled at their strange movements — the way they hopped forward heavily, putting down their short front paws, then pulling up their hind legs while balancing with their muscled tails. They also looked adorable as they ate, seated on hind legs and tails as on a tripod and constantly twitching their ears (hearing is their keenest sense). But, being less intelligent than sheep, they did not perform any clever tricks and had a hard time learning to recognize their keepers. They jumped away at any perceived danger, covering as much as ten feet in a single leap — a marvelous sight in itself.

Josephine had rosy hopes for her kangaroos. She was eager to breed them as a scientific pursuit, as well as, eventually, for their fur and tasty meat. The task seemed promising at first as the kangaroos appeared to be content and ate heartily. Josephine waited for them to start reproducing, but the kangaroos would not oblige. She appealed for help to the Museum, graciously sending it two precious gifts — her zebra and her gnu. The professors were quick to express their gratitude and to reciprocate with two kangaroos. They believed, they wrote, that the animals' stay at Malmaison "would render them infinitely more interesting for natural history than the place where they were living until now. For that they need nothing more than the greater space and more tranquility."

The Museum's kangaroos arrived at Malmaison and were introduced to the resident animals. Still no issue materialized.

Soon afterward Josephine was in Germany, awaiting Napoleon's
return from the brilliant campaign that would culminate at
Austerlitz and attending the wedding of her son, Eugène, to
Princess Auguste of Bavaria. During her travels, the prince-elect,
Friedrich of Württemberg, gave her a lavish welcome in his capital, Stuttgart. The giant and obese Friedrich was also passionate
about nature. Between 1812 and 1816 he would create in his royal
domain of Stockach, between Stuttgart and Berg, the most important menagerie in Germany. He already had a zoo of sorts in
Stuttgart, which he proudly showed off to Josephine. Several weeks
later he followed up on her visit: "Your Imperial Majesty during
your visit to Stuttgart seemed to me to desire the Kangaroos for
your menagerie at Malmaison. I will hasten to dispatch a pair to
you." His animals had probably come through England, brought
there by British ships that had been exploring or sealing in
Australia.

Josephine continued her efforts to breed kangaroos for some
time, but with disappointing results. The one pregnancy achieved
ended in the death of both the baby and the mother. Knowledge
about these animals was still scant, and even today scientists
have trouble breeding some exotic animals in captivity. Kangaroos
in general breed weakly and rarely have more than one offspring
at a time. Perhaps some combination of the foreign setting and a
not quite correct diet kept Josephine's animals from increasing
their numbers. By the time she died in 1814, only one kangaroo
remained at Malmaison.

The black swans, however, became Josephine's success story.
They had been known to Europeans since the end of the seventeenth century, when explorers had first begun visiting Australia.
The handsome birds commonly dwell along the lakes, ponds, and
rivers of Australia and Tasmania, as well as in the interior of the
continent. They are not hard to capture, as they are noisy and not

at all timid. Especially during the mating period, their strange call, which resembles a deep trumpeting sound, gives away their location. They can well tolerate the harsh European winter and are not picky about their diet, making them easy to keep. And they breed yearly, producing six to eight eggs at a time. Josephine was, however, the first to acclimate them to France and to breed them in captivity. They flourished at Malmaison.

A male and a female swan arrived aboard *Le Naturaliste* in 1803, intended expressly for Josephine. The black beauties were apparently quite happy with their new home and produced more than fifty cygnets. Swans mate for life and are tender toward their young. The mother often carries them on her back and at night puts them under her wing. The father protects the female, staying near her to make sure no danger threatens her or his brood. Clever and highly adaptable, young swans readily bond with their human owners.

Josephine was delighted with her swan family. Within a few years she had enough of them to promise a few to the Museum (although she never delivered). One of her ladies-in-waiting, Mademoiselle Avrillion, recalled in her memoirs how the swans "had just given birth to cygnets, when the approach of the Allies forced the Empress to leave Malmaison.* She was greatly alarmed that the soldiers would kill the birds, but happily they were left undisturbed," as Josephine discovered when she returned to her estate.

Josephine's magnificent Australian birds impressed every visitor to the château. The savant Alexandre de Laborde wrote in his 1808 *Description of the New Gardens of France and Its Ancient Castles*: "The park of Malmaison is embellished with a quantity of exotic animals of the most beautiful species; instead of being assembled in a menagerie or a cramped enclosure, they wander freely over the settings that suit them best. The banks of the river

---

*The coalition of Austria, Britain, Prussia, Russia, Sweden, and several German states entered France in March 1814.

nourish swans of several species, among which are two black ones recently brought from New Holland." Black swans soon became sought after throughout Europe as live adornments for noble gardens and as ornamental motifs in Empire furniture, chandeliers, and clocks. After Josephine's death and Napoleon's exile, Chateaubriand gave them literary fame by evoking them in his *Memoirs.*

BAUDIN'S AUSTRALIAN VOYAGE at once made Josephine's menagerie and spelled its demise. By the time the Australian animals arrived at Malmaison, Napoleon was no longer interested in them. Thus in January 1805, when he went over Josephine's accounts, he was infuriated at the enormity of her expenditures. He severely admonished the superintendent of her estate, Mirbel, and ordered Josephine to scale down her animal collection. The following month Mirbel wrote to the director of the Museum, "Their Majesties, desiring to give pleasure to the public by the sight of several rare animals that form part of the Menagerie of Malmaison, gave me the order to have them transported to the Museum of Natural History." The magnanimous gift included a pelican, three ostriches, a cassowary, and the two dwarf emus Josephine had found so disappointing. Of course Mirbel was putting the best public face on Napoleon's curtailing of Josephine's passion and dream. As her peccary (an American piglike animal), llamas, secretary bird, axis deer, Malbrouk (vervet) monkeys, chamois, and mouflons (wild mountain sheep of Sardinia and Corsica) died, she did not replace them, nor did she go on to acquire new animals.

She was still permitted to buy birds and plants. Along with daily floral arrangements, aviaries adorned Malmaison's halls and vestibules, bringing the jungle into the palace and sustaining Josephine's enlightened impulses. In April 1808 she wrote to Victor Hughes, the commissioner in Guyana. She was most grateful for his gift of a remarkable bird that was so domesticated that it could distinguish strangers from her personnel. Alas, the bird had died. "I would be charmed if you could replace it, and at the same time send me other live birds."

But even such acquisitions were diminishing in number. Meanwhile, the divorce that Josephine had been dreading for years was fast approaching. The problem of succession loomed large over Napoleon, and given his lofty position yet modest roots, he craved to take his place among royalty by marrying into one of the historical dynasties of Europe. By 1807 one of Napoleon's advisers told Josephine directly that her divorce was essential to the welfare of France. Josephine was finding the mounting pressure increasingly difficult to bear. She told her children, "You know that I aspire for nothing but his love. If they should succeed in separating me from him, it is not the loss of rank that I should regret."

The following year she confided to her son, "You can easily guess that I have had much cause for unhappiness. . . . Well, I entrust myself to Providence and the Emperor's will; my only defense is my conduct which I shall try to make blameless. . . . How unhappy do thrones make people, dear Eugène! I would resign mine tomorrow without any regret. For me the affection of the Emperor is everything. If I should lose that I would have few regrets about anything else." And when Madame Junot paid a visit to Josephine with her little daughter, Josephine broke down: "I felt as if a deadly poison were creeping through my veins when I have looked upon the fresh and rosy cheeks of a beautiful child, the joy of its mother, but above all, the hope of its father! And I! struck with barrenness, shall be driven in disgrace from the bed of him who has given me a crown! Yet God is my witness that I love him more than my life, and much more than that throne which he has given me."

At last the inevitable came to pass. On December 14, 1809, Josephine and her children, the Bonaparte family decked out in full court dress and glittering jewels, and important state officials gathered in the throne room of the Tuileries palace. There, in a solemn ceremony, Napoleon read the statement of divorce. He declared that the good of the state and the need of an heir had prompted him to take this step and that he was sacrificing "the one who has adorned fifteen years of my life" and whose "memory will always be engraved on my heart." Josephine was to retain her title of empress and receive generous financial support. Josephine began to read her reply, prepared by Napoleon: "I declare that having no further hope of children who would satisfy the needs of his policy and the interest of France, I am pleased to offer him the greatest proof of attachment and devotion that could be given." At this point she choked and broke into sobs, passing the paper to the secretary of state to finish reading her "consent to end a marriage which henceforth is an obstacle to the well-being of France." Afterward, under pouring rain, she departed miserably to Malmaison, accompanied by her remaining possessions from the Tuileries palace: her clothes, some furniture, a parrot, and her two favorite mongrels, each with its litter of puppies. Only three months later, on March 11, 1810, Napoleon married Marie-Louise, daughter of Francis I of Austria. A year after that, on March 20, 1811, Marie-Louise gave birth to a boy, who was given the lofty name Napoleon François Joseph Charles Bonaparte.

After the divorce Josephine continued to live at Malmaison. It was now her home and refuge, and her chief solace. Although her importance declined, Josephine's legendary glamour, the reputation of Malmaison, and continuing curiosity about her plants, birds, and few surviving exotic animals still drew visitors to her. In June 1813 she wrote to her son, "My garden is more frequented by the Parisians than my Salon. As I am writing, I am told that there are at least 30 people walking there." In the spring of 1814 — though by this time Napoleon was defeated and Josephine's status was minimal — Tsar Alexander I paid her several visits, as did the king of Prussia, the grand duke of Baden, the Prince of

Bavaria, and some distinguished English guests. Thus Malmaison achieved what Josephine had wanted. Even after her official relationship with Napoleon was over, her natural history collection helped her uphold a widely recognized public image.

Josephine and Napoleon remained in touch, and their affection for each other emerged in the letters and occasional visits they exchanged. When, in June 1810, Napoleon stopped by Malmaison to see Josephine, his footman observed that "one could see the tears of joy flowing down the cheeks of one as much as the other." After their hour-and-a-half meeting Josephine wrote to her daughter, "I have had a day of happiness. The Emperor came to see me. His presence made me happy, even though it renewed my sorrows. . . . While he was with me I was strong enough to keep back the tears which were ready to flow, but after he left I could no longer restrain them and I felt very miserable. He was good and kindly to me, as he usually is, and I hope that he read in my heart all the tenderness and devotion I have for him."

After Napoleon's disastrous invasion of Russia in 1812, when his triumph at taking Moscow was literally turned to ashes as the city was razed by its citizens and the French army's homeward march through one of the coldest winters on record cost a huge number of lives, Napoleon's fortune turned. His former allies formed a coalition against him, defeating him at Leipzig in mid-October 1813. The allies took Paris on March 31, 1814. Napoleon abdicated his imperial crown a few days later and was exiled to Elba.

Josephine retained her concern and fondness for Napoleon as he suffered his military and political defeats. She told her lady-in-waiting that she felt depressed thinking about the lonely Napoleon on Elba. "How I have suffered at the way in which they have treated the Emperor!" Josephine wrote to her son. Napoleon, too, continued to think warmly of his former wife. When he attempted suicide shortly after his abdication, he instructed his servant to tell Josephine "that she has been very much in my thoughts." And he concluded his last letter to her, on April 16,

1814, with the words, "Adieu, my dear Josephine. Resign yourself, as I am doing, and never lose the memory of one who has never forgotten you, and never will forget you." When he heard of her death in May 1814, one of his companions at Elba recorded that "he appeared profoundly afflicted; he shut himself up within, and would see no one but his grand marshal."

Josephine's little empire at Malmaison also came to a sad end, her enlightened animal collecting proving as fleeting as her power and security. At her death all that remained at Malmaison were four hinds, a deer, a lonely kangaroo, a ruffled lemur, a llama, a sheep from the Cape of Good Hope, and seven goats. (Friedrich of Württemberg, who was still actively shopping for his menagerie, bought a number of these animals.) Some forty gold and silver pheasants were living out their days in her beloved pheasantry. About eighty birds dwelled in the park, and a few others chirped in large cages in the château's echoing entrance hall. And of course a number of her creatures ended up in the Museum, preserved as stuffed specimens to this day. After all of Josephine's efforts, her menagerie ended up as mere dusty taxidermy concealing, beneath matted feathers and fur, not only a significant episode in her life but also Baudin's heroic and fateful expedition.

Only the majestic black swans endured as a lasting product of Josephine's and Baudin's labors. The descendants of Malmaison's first swan couple outlived the empress and the captain and became so commonplace throughout the world that their origin is all but forgotten, as are the passions and travails of the woman and man who brought them to France.

SEVEN

BEYOND PRIVATE DELIGHT

Hearst was most interesting to meet, and I got to like him — a grave simple child . . . playing with the most costly toys. A vast income always overspent: Ceaseless building and collecting . . . complete indifference to public opinion, a strong liberal and democratic outlook, a 15 million daily circulation, oriental hospitalities, extreme personal courtesy . . . and the appearance of a Quaker elder.

WINSTON CHURCHILL to his wife, Clementine,
September 29, 1929

Hearst Castle — the magnificent, art-filled residence built by the American newspaper tycoon William Randolph Hearst — floats like a fairy-tale apparition in the hills high above the Pacific Ocean, halfway between Los Angeles and San Francisco. Hayes Perkins, who came here to work in May 1928, marveled:

The vista from the hill top is one of surpassing loveliness. From this view point one has a vast expanse of ocean at his feet, while up and down the coast for many miles is a jumble of grassy hills with clumps of oak and pepperwood and forest in the valleys. These latter trees stand out on knobs here and there and in the background to the east are higher ranges, the Santa Lucias. . . . There are orchards set out on the hills, and half way down are some 2,000 acres of pasture set aside for wild animals where many species of hoofed animals are enclosed, and where the road winds through this setting among the game herds. . . . There are hundreds of deer of several species, many antelopes, kangaroos, large flightless birds and even giraffes. There are herds of elk and bison wandering about at will. . . . Only a wealthy man could afford such a palace and estate, the world has hardly seen its like in history.

There is a large zoo here where carnivorous animals are held in steel barred cages. Lions, leopards, a tiger, many bears of different species, coyotes, coons, wildcats, a cheetah, chimpanzees, a few monkeys and many, many birds.

Most people see the creator of this fantastic mini-kingdom through the lens of Orson Welles's brilliant and vicious film *Citizen Kane*. Charles Foster Kane is an arrogant, brash, though charismatic young man who grows into a megalomaniacal media mogul. Forsaking his youthful ideals and friendships in pursuit of power, he deservedly ends up joyless and all but alone in his gloomy, echoing castle, amid countless art treasures.

The real Hearst Castle was very different from Kane's Xanadu. It was cozy despite its size and lively with frequent guests. Glamorous Hollywood stars — Gary Cooper, Douglas Fairbanks, Clark Gable, Cary Grant, Joan Crawford, Jean Harlow, Greta Garbo — and other distinguished visitors gathered here for elaborate costume parties, their host bringing truckloads of outfits from Los Angeles for these occasions. Many came for leisurely weekends — to splash in the exquisite outdoor Neptune Pool rimmed by Roman-style colonnades, to go horseback riding, and to dine in the Refectory, a majestic hall made warm by dark wooden Gothic choir stalls, lush tapestries lining the walls, and festive

Siena Palio banners suspended overhead. And everyone was fascinated by the antics of the hundreds of exotic animals and birds inhabiting Hearst's private zoo.

The lord of this enchanted realm was, of course, the immensely rich and influential owner of a vast media empire that included twenty-six newspapers; scores of magazines and newsreels; serial, feature, and animated films; and radio and wire services. But Hearst was a far more winning and generous man than Charlie Kane. As one of his zookeepers noted, "He has a lot more good in him than bad." And Alice Head, who ran Hearst's newspapers and magazines in England, wrote:

> He is a man of profound learning and an absolutely first-class brain but with a number of engaging boyish characteristics. He is the soul of courtesy, . . . he is quixotically generous, and he has a gay and responsive sense of humor. . . . He is genuinely shy with strangers, but anyone who treats him as an ordinary human being and is not afraid of him will find him a most interesting and entertaining companion. No one with his love for children and animals could have anything but a kind heart. His shyness puzzles me as it seems to proceed from some sort of inferiority complex produced in his youth. . . . He must always have had a better than normal intelligence, he has been good to look upon at all ages, and he has never been poor. Such people usually have an instinct for facing the world and their fellow creatures with supreme confidence, but William Randolph Hearst usually wears a gentle and disarming air of diffidence which is natural and not assumed.

It was, to a large degree, this insecurity and the need to prove himself that propelled not only Hearst's publishing and political careers but also, more unusually for his time, the creation of a vast menagerie at his dream home at San Simeon.

*   *   *

WILLIAM RANDOLPH HEARST was the only child of George Hearst, a farmer from Franklin County, Missouri, who went to California in 1850 in search of gold and became a millionaire and a U.S. senator. George was virtually unschooled and was called by a contemporary "an assassin of grammar." But he had a gift for mining and would make a fabulous fortune on the ore deposits in the Sierra Nevada, Utah, the Dakotas, Montana, and Mexico.

Having laid the foundation of his future success in his first ten years of prospecting, George went back home to care for his ailing mother and to find a wife. His eye fell on a young schoolteacher (a distant relative) named Phoebe Apperson, a girl with a resolute streak beneath her innocent facade. George was forty-one years old, tall, muscular, and ruggedly handsome, with a full blond beard and large, deep-set eyes. As his grandson would later write, "He cussed at times and drank his share of rotgut whiskey. . . . He was not a big talker. . . . A lot of folks saw him as a soft touch."

Phoebe was nineteen, small and delicate, with intent grayish blue eyes and a fair, oval face. Her intellectual curiosity and ladylike southern manners contrasted with George's uncouth, loud conduct and dogged preoccupation with mining. She would have to remind him to change his clothes regularly, to trim his bushy beard, and not to spit tobacco juice in public. Still, she saw romance and adventure in a future with George. She told her grandson Bill Jr. that "she also was lured by the prospect of a faraway land with a golden rainbow . . . [and] saw George as a handsome dreamer who would find gold." And so, on June 15, 1862, they eloped to Steadman, Missouri — probably because her parents were not thrilled with the notion of their daughter moving to the distant West with a man more than twice her age — and immediately left for California.

George settled his wife in San Francisco and departed for his mining camps across the mountains. On April 29, 1863, while he was away — as he would be for most of their marriage — Phoebe gave birth to their robust baby son. Though George affectionately called his baby Sonny, and later Billy Buster, he spent most of his time at his mines and seldom saw his boy. Phoebe, lonely in California, channeled all her affection and attention into her only child. Little Willie slept in his mother's bed and "was very much put out when his Papa came home because he could not sleep with me," Phoebe wrote to a friend. "I told him when his Papa went away again he could sleep with me. He said, well, he wished he would go."

George bought his young wife and son an elegant house in San Francisco on Chestnut Street, north of Russian Hill, overlooking San Francisco Bay. He also helped Phoebe move her parents from Missouri to California and settled them on a farm in Santa Clara, south of the city. But much of the time Phoebe lived on her own, learning to make all the practical decisions, run the household, and raise her child. She had always been interested in the arts and humanities, and now, with little Willie as her partner, she frequented museums and theaters in San Francisco, studied French, and invited Bay Area artists and writers to tea. With time she would become a patron of educational institutions and a champion of women's rights.

Though doted on and spoiled by his mother, Willie was, as his biographer David Nasaw writes, "a small boy trying desperately to call attention to himself." Dragged around on adults' errands and pastimes, he often misbehaved. After George Hearst entered politics and was elected to the California State Assembly in 1865, Phoebe and Willie went to visit him in Sacramento. "He misses his big playroom and many toys," Phoebe noted in her diary. One evening, as she was getting ready to attend a stately function with her husband, Willie poured castor oil on her antique moiré dress, "so I had to dress twice."

Another time the Hearsts were staying with friends while their house was being remodeled. "On the whole Willie was painfully and portentously well behaved," Hearst would recollect about himself in a newspaper column many decades later, "until the First of April came along. Then Willie felt that something ought to be done to relieve the monotony of this serene household and to prevent himself from degenerating into a sissy."*

He waited until the adults fell asleep. Then he lit half a dozen Bengal lights — the kind that flare up in a bright red flame — in pie tins obtained from the family cook. He opened his door, shrieked "Fire! Fire!" down the silent corridors, and promptly locked himself in his room to await his parents' response. As smoke filled the hallway and red light glinted in the crevices above and below the door, Phoebe and George frantically tried to break into their son's room — without success. The servants called in the firemen, who rushed in through the window and turned on the water hose.

To the boy's disappointment, "Willie's Mama was so pleased to find her darling boy alive that she did not say much of anything," and "with all his pretense of severity, Willie's Papa never did warm [spank] Willie as he deserved." Getting his father's attention would be Willie's perpetually unfulfilled desire and being a mama's boy his frustration. As he reflected in adulthood, "Sometimes boys are bad just because they do not want to be considered sissies." Phoebe would mother Willie and keep him on a leash, which he would chafe against but fail to escape from, until she died.

While adept at navigating and manipulating the world of adults, Willie delighted in the uncomplicated company of animals. In their presence he could be just a little boy, whether he puttered around his home with his two black dogs, Caesar and

---

*Curious as it seems, Hearst would often tell stories about himself in the third person, making them into moral tales, mythologizing his life, and distancing himself from his readers.

Pompey, or went to Meiggs' Wharf, down the hill from Chestnut Street, to gaze in wonder at the strange birds and beasts brought by sailors from all over the world. At his grandparents' farm he listened with delight to the canaries singing in the courtyard, watched Grandpa Apperson's pet squirrels, and walked everywhere in the company of the Newfoundland called Prince. During one visit to Santa Clara, Phoebe wrote to a friend that Willie got "a little rat terrier. He is a dear little puppy. . . . Grandma has several little kittens. She has given us one. We will take it when we go home. Willie kisses the dogs and cats all over." This fondness for and fascination with animals would run as a thread through Hearst's life.

Though privileged, Hearst's childhood was constantly disrupted, which was Phoebe's doing. Treating him like her partner rather than her child, she kept removing him from school so that he could accompany her on her travels, including an eighteen-month sojourn in Europe, on which they embarked in the spring of 1873, when he was ten. They visited every important museum, palace, and church in England and on the continent. To many boys his age, this would have seemed an ordeal, but Phoebe had been instilling a love of art in Willie since early childhood, and he greatly enjoyed all the sightseeing. In Paris he was so fascinated by the Louvre that he asked his mother to buy it for him. But he also showed his kind and generous side. In Dublin, deeply affected by the sight of poverty, he "wanted to give away all his money and clothes, too." This first European trip laid the foundation for Willie's passion for art, history, and culture, and it triggered his obsession with collecting.

The psychologist Werner Muensterberger, in his book *Collecting: An Unruly Passion,* argues that the urge to collect often stems from some childhood trauma. The absence or disappearance of parents or a child's perceived inferiorities lead him to turn to objects to quell his feelings of vulnerability. Objects "serve as powerful help in keeping anxiety or uncertainty under control" and give a child — and later an adult — a sense of permanence, affirmation, or security otherwise missing from his life.

Willie's father was nearly always absent, and his mother would from time to time disappear on long trips. In the spring of 1866 she sailed to Hawaii for a month, depositing Willie with his grandparents, and in September she left for another month to visit George in Idaho. When she returned, she told a friend that Willie "does not want to go to his grandma's again, seems to be afraid all the time I will go away and leave him again." During that first trip to Europe, Willie had already begun acquiring stamps, coins, beer steins, and porcelains, and as Phoebe wrote to George, he developed "a mania for antiquities." In London he tried to persuade her to buy him the four specially bred white horses that pulled the English royal carriage. Phoebe tried to curb his acquisitiveness, but he "gets so fascinated, his reason and judgment forsake him."

Willie and his mother returned from Europe to more disruptions. While they were away, America had undergone a financial crisis in which eighteen hundred American banks folded. George lost most of his assets, and Phoebe was forced to curtail expenses and sell their San Francisco house to raise money. For the rest of his childhood Willie would move from one rented home to another, from school to school. There would be no place he could call his own, no constancy of friends. Small wonder that he grew shy with strangers and that he would dream for years of building his own home in the one place where he returned regularly and felt happy — the family ranch and vacation spot at San Simeon.

Willie's coddled yet disjointed childhood, his mother's smothering and controlling affection, and his father's absence and lack of approval made him a complicated young man: at once cocky and childish, diffident yet keen on splashy pranks and showmanship. Phoebe thought him brilliant and believed he could succeed at anything. George, observing his boyish conduct and immoderate spending habits, was skeptical that he would amount to much. It was not an easy set of expectations to balance.

In 1882 the nineteen-year-old Will entered Harvard University. George Hearst had restored and multiplied his fortune in recent years by acquiring shares in a series of mines. Now that George was fabulously rich (much more so than before), Phoebe had decided that her boy must go to the best school in the country. And so the tall, thin, handsome Californian with short sandy hair and intense blue eyes arrived at the most class-conscious of colleges. An outsider with no connections in Boston or Cambridge and no pedigree, Will set out to conquer this world on his own terms.

He moved into 46 Matthews Hall, a suite of rooms in a Gothic building in Harvard Yard. Phoebe decorated his apartment, bought him a library of books, and hired a maid and a valet to look after her boy. With the help of his enormous allowance, Will gave lavish dinners and parties in his suite and at restaurants around town, unabashedly buying himself popularity with the classmates who could get him into Harvard's top social clubs. Deep pockets were crucial to his success, but he also possessed genuine charisma, an ability to rally people behind him, and an immense drive. In less than two years he was elected to the most prestigious clubs, among them the Porcellian, whose former members included Oliver Wendell Holmes and Theodore Roosevelt, and Med. Facs. — an even more secret and esteemed society — the major activity of which seems to have been stealing and defacing Harvard statues and plaques.

Recognizing that he would never be accepted by the New England aristocracy, Will instead chose the route of eccentricity to attract attention, awe, and admiration. Not only did he dress like a dandy, sporting splendidly tailored suits and loud ties, but he impressed and amused his fellow students by keeping a live alligator in his suite. The animal took an active part in Will's festivities, acquiring the name Champagne Charlie for avidly guzzling

free-flowing spirits. When drunk, the alligator twitched errati-
cally and rolled its eyes, which greatly entertained Will's classmates. Alas, the jolly collegiate lifestyle did not agree with
Charlie, nor did Will have a clue as to how to care for the animal
properly. After a year of riotous living, the alligator expired. "Be
sure to send 'Charley' to be embalmed," Phoebe wrote to her son
in April 1885. "He will decay & cause illness if left in the house."
Will agreed and sent his pet by express delivery to C. I. Goodale,
Taxidermist and Naturalist, in Boston, to be stuffed for $6.40.

Despite his social achievements, Will was still viewed by many
of his classmates as an arriviste who spent too openly and exu-
berantly to earn a place in society. George Santayana noted in his
memoirs that Hearst "was little esteemed in college." But Will
didn't have much use for the pretensions of high society. Rather
than ingratiate himself with Boston Brahmins, he passed his
evenings at comedy theaters and after-hours clubs.

As Will's social life blossomed, his academic performance declined. He was certainly smart, and he had done well enough as
a freshman, but by his second year his energies were diverted into
his new passion — publishing. He had been elected business manager of the *Harvard Lampoon* and set out to turn the struggling
humor magazine into a thriving enterprise, a performance he
would later repeat with newspapers across the country. Departing
from the usual strategy of *Lampoon* business managers, who were
elected for their wealth and expected to subsidize the magazine,
Will undertook an aggressive advertising and marketing campaign. In a short time the *Lampoon* became self-sufficient and
profitable.

This venture may have been spurred by Will's desire to impress
his father. In 1880, after more than a decade's hiatus, George had
decided to return to politics. Since in those days newspapers
were the chief means of connecting with the electorate, George
acquired the *Examiner,* the only Democratic paper in San Francisco, to curry the favor of Democratic leaders and voters.

In 1884 George ran for the U.S. Senate. At the same time, following his father's cue, Will campaigned with great flair for Grover Cleveland, a Democratic presidential nominee. Harvard was then a predominantly Republican campus, and of the more than two hundred members of Will's class, only twenty-eight declared themselves Democrats. Undaunted, Will organized a huge rally in Harvard Yard with a great flag raising, a bonfire, and a parade. The event was so boisterous and conspicuous that, in his own words, "everyone saw it and heard it — and everyone complained about it." George lost his race, but Cleveland won. Politics would become Will's second passion after publishing.

Meanwhile, dreaming of the chance to one day run the *San Francisco Examiner,* Will hoped that his success at the *Lampoon* would prove to George that he was up to the task. Yet his attempts to connect with his father through these mutual interests remained frustrated. That same year Will began to describe to George in long and detailed letters his visions for improving the *Examiner,* which was struggling. George would not reply. Will grumbled,

> I wrote you not long ago and inserted in my letter a mild request for an answer, but the answer never came. I stated a few business points that I thought might be of interest and gave you some ideas on the way to conduct your private affairs and yet you did not respond. Will you kindly take some slight notice of your only son? Will you be so good as to answer his letters and let him know that you at least appreciate his kindness in allowing you to draw upon his large experience and gigantic intellect?

Will's tone was jocular, but he was pained by George's silence. Meanwhile, Phoebe barraged her boy with complaints about his inattention to her and her queries. "It grieves me deeply that you *never* regard any promises made to your mother. If you ever realize how I feel about it, I cannot understand how it is possible for you to be so utterly indifferent to my wishes. I am mortified and grieved beyond your comprehension."

Will's overactive social and political life on campus — "he majored in jokes, pranks and sociability," Hearst's official biographer Cora Older wrote — began to have unwelcome consequences in his sophomore year. Fed up with his tricks (on one occasion he delivered to his professors customized chamber pots with the recipients' names embossed on the inside bottom) and his indifferent scholarly performance, the administration "rusticated" (temporarily suspended) Will and placed him on academic probation. When in his junior year he still did not improve his grades, he was asked to leave Harvard.

Will was not at all sorry. He had never felt at home in Cambridge and missed California. "I am beginning to get awfully tired of this place," he wrote to his mother, "and I long to get out West somewhere where I can stretch myself without coming into contact with the narrow walls with which the prejudice of the bean-eaters has surrounded us. . . . I long to see our own woods, the jagged rocks and towering mountains, the majestic pines, the grand impressive scenery of the 'far West.' I shall never live anywhere but in California." But most of all, he wanted to be in San Francisco running the *Examiner*.

It took Will two years to cajole his father into letting him take over the newspaper, which was competing poorly against others in the city and losing money. Will looked to Joseph Pulitzer's enormously successful *New York World* as a model: "It would be well to make the paper as far as possible original," he wrote to George in 1885, "to clip only some such leading journal as the *New York World* which is undoubtedly the best paper of that class to which the *Examiner* belongs — that class which appeals to people and which depends for its success upon enterprise, energy and a certain startling originality." After a great deal of lobbying, George relented, but it might have had to do more with Phoebe's persuasiveness than with Will's.

The previous year Will had proposed to Eleanor Calhoun, an aspiring actress who had been Phoebe's protégée and even had accompanied her on a trip to Europe. "He wooed her with flowers, gifts and ardent devotion," Cora Older wrote, "but no wooing was necessary. Eleanor Calhoun was as rapturously devoted to him as he was to her. They had like tastes, a romantic love of the theater and literature. Both were young and handsome." Despite her previous mentoring of Eleanor, Phoebe embarked on a campaign to break them up. She thought actresses were women of loose morals, in no way suitable for her son, and she decided that Eleanor was a fortune hunter, out to snare innocent Will. She wrote to a friend:

> Will is a brilliant fellow, has improved wonderfully in many respects, has not bad habits, given up the foolishness and carelessness of a great part of his college life, and is immensely interested in business. . . . You will wonder how it is with all this that I am so unhappy about my boy. You will understand when I tell you that he is *desperately* in love with Miss Calhoun, the *actress*. He has simply gone mad about her, and she is quite willing for she wants to marry a man who has money. . . . Oh! Dear! If I could tell you half of all I have gone through in connection with his affair, you would be astonished. . . . I feel that it will ruin my boy's life to marry such a designing woman.

After much effort, conniving, and bullying, Phoebe succeeded in forcing Will to drop Eleanor. Part of his consolation prize was the editorship of the *Examiner*.

Phoebe would continue to try to micromanage her son's affairs all her life. As Will's son Bill Jr. commented, "Grandma knew precisely what her place was and what ours were — and ran her roost with a velvet voice and a withering look of disapproval. I believe she was the only person on earth who ever scared my father." Through family friends and accountants, newspaper employees, and personal interventions, Phoebe kept her son under constant surveillance. Will, in his turn, learned to charm and coax his mother into giving him money and other rewards. And so, on March 4, 1887, the same day George Hearst took the oath of office as a U.S. senator from California, "W. R. Hearst, Proprietor" appeared on the masthead of the *San Francisco Examiner* for the first time. Will was twenty-four years old and, as Florence Finch Kelly, the wife of his city editor at the *Examiner* remembered, "tall, slender, good-looking, very blond, with a pink and white complexion and a little golden moustache, boyish and slightly diffident in manner and still a bit under the influence of the impish high spirits of youth."

With boundless energy, dedication, and creativity, Will plunged into remaking and improving the *Examiner*. He turned the sleepy and parochial paper into a cosmopolitan publication by contracting with other newspapers in the country to run their cabled articles, including those published in Europe, and thus offering his readers more national and international news. He hired the best journalists around, such as Ambrose Bierce, a popular writer of caustic editorials and short comic pieces for San Francisco weeklies. As Bierce recalled of their first interview, when Will showed up at his door, "his appearance, his attitude, his manner, his entire personality suggested extreme diffidence. . . . 'I am from the San Francisco *Examiner*,' he explained in a voice like the fragrance of violets made audible [Will had a high, feminine voice]. . . . 'O,' I said, 'you come from Mr. Hearst.' Then that unearthly child lifted its blue eyes and cooed; 'I am Mr. Hearst.'" Despite his boyish demeanor, Will shrewdly offered Bierce a combination of journalistic freedom and more money than he had ever earned to become his editorial writer. Bierce accepted at once.

Will proceeded to attract more talent in a similar manner, so that, in the words of Winifred Black, who also came on board, the *Examiner* became "a place full of geniuses. Nowhere was there ever a more brilliant and more outrageous, incredible, ridiculous, glorious set of typical newspaper people than there was in that shabby old newspaper office."

In addition to making the content of his paper more engaging through better, or more sensational, writing (which resembled short stories in pace and coloring), Will also overhauled the *Examiner*'s appearance. He reduced the number of columns per page, doubled the size of the headlines, and added large line drawings, which, along with more dramatic narratives, helped the stories come to life. As he told his father, illustrations not only "embellish a page, [they] attract the eye and stimulate the imagination of the lower classes and materially aid the comprehension of an unaccustomed reader and thus are of particular importance to that class of people which the *Examiner* claims to address." He was not targeting one type of audience, however. He wanted every resident of the city to find something of interest in the *Examiner*, whether he or she was concerned with sports or crime, local politics or international developments, serialized novels or salacious gossip about naked ladies and adulterers.

Will also mastered the technical aspects of newspaper publishing. To make his papers look good, and thus sell well, he upgraded his printing equipment to the finest machinery available, despite the high costs. To reach a greater number of readers, he began delivering the *Examiner* by railway to Sacramento in the north and Santa Cruz and San Jose in the south. By June 1887 the *Journalist,* the chief trade journal of newspaper publishers, commenting on the *Examiner*'s quality and sophistication, announced that it had become California's first truly metropolitan daily.

Under Will's stewardship the *Examiner*'s circulation doubled in its first year. By 1890 it drew even with its chief competitor, the *Chronicle,* and became self-supporting. Though according to his cousin Anne Apperson Flint, Will had the "flabbiest handshake of anyone," he ran his paper with bravado and determined decisively what was printed in it and how. He also got results by being generous and encouraging to his employees. Alice Head wrote of "the joy that I have always found in working for him. He is so human in all his reactions — quick to feel pleasure or indignation, yet controlled and reasonable. Even if he disagrees with you, he is always willing to listen to your point of view and to give your plans a trial. He is Olympian in his attitude towards big things, yet can be as pleased as a small boy over simple pleasures."

Even after he proved himself a successful publisher, however, Will's parents continued to treat him like a child. Will would report to Phoebe on his activities in affectionate and wry letters and wait in vain for his father's consideration. As he concluded in one letter to George, "I have given up all hope of having you write to me, so I suppose I must just scratch along and trust to hearing of you through the newspapers."

When George Hearst died on February 28, 1891, he left his only child not one penny nor one acre of his vast landholdings. The entire estate, including the *Examiner*, went to Phoebe, who was to "make suitable provisions" for their son. Despite Will's accomplishments in turning the *Examiner* into a thriving paper, his father did not trust him to own it or anything else. Now nearly thirty years old, Will remained under his mother's control.

The one area where he seemed to take the lead in their relationship and enjoy some autonomy from his mother was collecting. Having gone to Europe in early 1889 to recover from the exhaustion of running the *Examiner*, Will wrote to Phoebe from Rome that he had been struck by the

art fever terribly. . . . I never thought I would get it this way. I never miss a gallery now and I go and mosey about the pictures and statuary and admire them and wish they were mine. . . . I want some of these fine things and I want you to have some of these things and do you know, my beloved mother, there is a way in which you might get them. If, instead of buying a half a dozen fairly nice things, you would wait and buy one fine thing, all would be well. . . . I for my small part am not going to buy any more trinkets.

Although he did begin to buy more discriminatingly, the pace of Hearst's collecting accelerated exponentially. He shipped loads of artwork from Europe. This was in part because he was genuinely fond of them and loved living among them, but also because he was used to giving in to momentary whims, just as his parents had given in to most of his childhood requests. With such a prodigious rate of acquisition, it was small wonder that countless crates full of treasures remained unopened in his warehouses. Will was always keen to move on to something new.

FIVE MONTHS AFTER his father's death, Will decided to try to break into the New York newspaper market and began to look for a suitable vehicle. But to be able to buy a paper in that city, he needed a loan or a gift from Phoebe. The price again came to a sacrifice of his love. When Will was still at Harvard, and before he fell in love with Eleanor, he had had a relationship with a young woman named Tessie Powers, a waitress who, in Bill Hearst Jr.'s words, "was pretty and fun, and adored Willie." After Phoebe forced him to break up with Eleanor Calhoun, Will brought Tessie to San Francisco. They lived, traveled to Europe, and entertained friends together — all to Phoebe's fury. As long as Will remained with Tessie, Phoebe would not give him the money to buy a New York paper. Meanwhile, she threatened Tessie with criminal action if she remained in San Francisco and promised to buy her off if she left. Eventually Phoebe got her way: Tessie departed in 1893, after a ten-year relationship. Now Will wanted his reward.

In a letter to his mother he requested a change in the terms of his allowance and salary from the *Examiner*. Instead of having to go to Irwin Stump, the family business manager, for money to pay his every bill, Will asked Phoebe to deposit to his "credit at any bank on the first of each month a definite sum of $2,500," which he could spend as he saw fit — not an unreasonable request for a man of thirty running a major newspaper. "As long as I come to ask him [Stump] for an extra thousand dollars here and there," Will wrote, "he will treat me as a child, asking 10 cents for soda water. . . . You have always been most kind and generous to me and given me extra money whenever I asked for it but don't you think it would be better for me if I didn't ask for it so often, if I were put now on a more independent and manly footing?"

Phoebe would not agree to this change of status. But she did give him $150,000 in 1895 to buy New York's *Morning Journal* and the German-language daily *Morgen Journal,* plus $250,000 to bring these papers "up to Will's standard."

Just as he had done at the *Examiner,* Will made these papers successful in a short time. His pro-labor, pro-immigrant, and anti-Republican stance helped attract a wide Democratic readership in New York. Not content to rise to the top of the city's dailies, Will decided to break into the lucrative Sunday editions as well. In a brash gesture typical of him, instead of building up his staff piece by piece, he lured over Joseph Pulitzer's brilliant editor, Morrill Goddard, who had made the *New York World*'s Sunday paper prosper. And when Goddard hesitated, worried about running Hearst's paper without his old staff, Will brought (or bought) them as well by offering them much bigger salaries and greater freedom to exercise their abilities, as long as they increased his circulation. "Pulitzer was left with an empty office and one stenographer," writes David Nasaw. "Even the office cat, it was reported, had defected to Hearst." Many of these reporters would remain with Hearst's papers for decades.

Over the following years Will would expand his newspaper

empire across the country, in part to conquer new challenges, in part to build his political base once he began running for office. As Bill Jr. noted, "He carried an excitement about news and public issues in his bones." Will's love for publishing and his tremendous gift for it would turn him into a national media mogul.

But even as he matured into a powerful figure, Will retained his boyishness. James L. Ford, the theater columnist for the *New York Journal,* recalled in his autobiography that it was hard to take his boss seriously. "He reminded me of a kindly child, thoroughly undisciplined and possessed of a destructive tendency that might lead him to set fire to a house in order to see the engines play water on the flames." In his publishing work, this quality expressed itself in Hearst's strident backing of controversial or unpopular causes when he felt strongly about them. He often spoke up for the underdog: defending immigrants, supporting Irish independence, reporting on pogroms against Jews in Russia. And at a time when it was not a widely admired or accepted attitude, he also urgently advocated opposition to vivisection — a position stemming from his love of animals and especially from his childhood bond with dogs.

CONCERN FOR THE well-being of animals and their treatment — not as useful beasts for science and industry or merely as diverting pets, but as sentient beings with a right to dignity — entered public debate in the eighteenth century. In 1789 the British lawyer and moral philosopher Jeremy Bentham posed his famous challenge: "The question is not, can they reason? nor can they talk? but can they suffer?" Bentham likened the position of animals to that of African slaves and looked forward to the day when "the rest of animal creation may acquire those rights which never could have been withholden from them but by the hand of tyranny."

In 1824 animal defenders in Britain formed the Royal Society for the Prevention of Cruelty to Animals (RSPCA), the first such group, which led the way for others in the United States and Canada. The goal of the RSPCA and its followers was to educate the public about the maltreatment of animals and to introduce and enforce legislation that would protect them from further abuses. Charles Darwin's *Origin of Species*, which appeared in 1859, also helped change the perception of animals by suggesting, as a corollary to his theory, that there was greater continuity between humans and nonhumans than previously thought, and that animals were, in essence, conscious, thinking beings. "The difference in mind between man and the higher animals, great as it is, certainly is one of degree and not of kind," Darwin wrote. "The senses and intuitions, the various emotions and faculties, such as love, memory, attention, curiosity, imitation, reason, etc., of which man boasts, may be found in an incipient, or even sometimes in a well-developed condition, in the lower animals." The defense of animal rights formed part of a continuum of battles waged at this time over the rights of the oppressed of all kinds, including the struggle for woman suffrage and the abolition of slavery.

Yet, at the same time, scientists were increasing their use of animals for medical research. In opposition, a number of antivivisection societies sprang up. In Britain in 1876 antivivisectionists persuaded Parliament to pass the Cruelty to Animals Act, which strove to limit, however modestly, experimentation on animals. The act restricted painful tests and required those performing studies on live creatures to obtain a yearly license through the Home Office.

American advocates of the humane treatment of animals followed the British lead. Henry Bergh, a diplomat to the Russian court of Tsar Alexander II, founded the American Society for the Prevention of Cruelty to Animals (ASPCA) in 1866. Bergh spoke ardently against the mistreatment of horses, "these mute servants of mankind," and condemned Spanish bullfights, American cockfights, and the horrors of slaughterhouses. "This is a matter purely of conscience," he argued; "it has no perplexing side issues. No; it is a moral question in all its aspects."

The American Anti-Vivisection Society was formed in Philadelphia in 1883, and other such regional organizations followed. The New England Anti-Vivisection Society, established in 1895, declared that its goal was "to expose and oppose secret and painful experiments upon living animals, lunatics, paupers or criminals." Members hoped that once people learned about such practices, they would demand legislation to regulate and then prohibit vivisection.

Such defenders of animals were, however, a minority, often regarded with disdain, especially by the medical establishment. So when Hearst began to speak emphatically against the abuses of animals, not just in scientific laboratories but in other contexts as well, he was not doing so out of any calculation that it would increase the circulation of his papers or advance his political career. On May 31, 1909, his *Los Angeles Examiner* ran an editorial titled "The Prize Ring and the Bull Fight."

Respectful objection may be taken . . . to the position maintained by one Professor Monaghan of Chicago, who proclaims bull fighting as "a splendid spectacle" enjoyed by "every American or Englishman," while the prizefight is "the most brutal, disgusting spectacle."

Is that a "splendid spectacle" where an animal, goaded to desperation, is compelled to fight with not more than one chance in 500 for his life? Or where poor, starved, miserable horses are gored to death in a fight not of their choosing? . . .

No intelligent person will argue for the necessity or morality of the so-called prize-fighting. But it is infinitely more reasonable, more humane, more defensible, in its presentation of the self-elected contest of two trained athletes than the wanton and cruel torture and killing of animals in the Spanish bull fight.

On August 15, 1909, Hearst's papers published an illustrated feature on the killing of birds for their feathers, used to decorate ladies' hats. The article was titled "Stamping Out the Cruelest Fashion: The Struggle to Save the Great White Heron, Whose Maternity Plumage Gives the Coveted Aigrette — and Whose Beauty Has Nearly Caused Its Extinction." "The aigrette [a tuft of long plumes attached to a hat]," the article declared, "is as flagrant an example of the cruelty or thoughtlessness of the fashionable woman as was the baby lamb coat." It went on to explain that the aigrette appears on the white heron only at breeding time, so when the mother heron is killed for its prized feather, its chicks are left to starve in their nest, further decimating the bird population. Hearst would reprise this subject in a December 8, 1940, article, "Proud of Your Feathers? Maybe You Ought to Be Ashamed," which emphasized in large print that "after 30 years of comparative peace and in defiance of humane laws for their protection, the wild birds are once more being massacred for fashion."

Hearst was as forceful in addressing the subject of vivisection. An editorial in his *New York American* on April 26, 1916, called for strict legislation regulating this practice.

> We suppose that 99 per cent of these cruel experiments are useless and resultless. Of course, a small proportion may result in increased knowledge, but we are pretty sure the same knowledge could be gained by dissecting dead bodies.
>
> A strong objection to vivisection is that it develops in the vivisectors a callousness to human suffering and stimulates the mania for operating, which is the curse of modern surgery.
>
> Furthermore, it is always the weak and the helpless that are subjected to the torture of vivisection. Dumb animals, wards of the State, like the insane, the poor in hospitals — these are the victims.

It is time that this disposition to cruelly cut up living animals and human beings to satisfy the experimental mania of surgeons and students should be stopped. The best way to stop it or to limit it within reason is to make it necessary to secure the approval of the government for every individual case of proposed vivisection, and to make it obligatory on the vivisector to state in his written application exactly what vivisection experiment he purposes making and what he hopes to accomplish by it.

Hearst was part of a passionate minority of animal rights defenders. Antivivisection societies across the country fought to institute regulations on the use of animals in medical research. In January 1908, in response to the recent establishment in New York of the Rockefeller Institute for Medical Research as a center for vivisection, the local society introduced two bills in the state legislature seeking to curb animal experimentation. Hearst's *New York Herald* actively supported the president of the New York Anti-Vivisection Society in rousing public opinion against the Institute and its practices. The paper sent a reporter to investigate charges of cruelty to animals on a New Jersey farm set up by the Rockefeller Institute to raise laboratory animals. And in December 1909 Hearst published the affidavit of an employee of the Institute describing numerous cruelties to animals there.

Unfortunately, the bills seeking to curtail vivisection mostly failed. In 1915 the California Anti-Vivisection Society introduced a bill before the state legislature which called, in somewhat convoluted language, for "creating and establishing a commission for the investigating and gathering of data and statistics concerning the use of live animals for experimental purposes." The bill intended to make transparent the activities taking place in the vivisection laboratories and to awaken public opposition to them. The state senate voted 30 to 1 and the Assembly 47 to 3 in favor of the bill, but Governor Hiram W. Johnson vetoed it.

Antivivisectionists were vehemently countered by the medical establishment, which denied charges of cruelty, stressed the benefits of medical research, and accused opponents of inaccuracies and ignorance. In 1909, at the height of the controversy, the eminent American neurologist Charles Loomis Dana gave vivisectionists new ammunition. He proclaimed that heightened concern for animals was a form of mental illness, which he termed "zoophil-psychosis." He categorized it as a kind of obsessive insanity. Because most antivivisectionists were women, neurologists also charged them with "hysteria" (although among the famous antivivisectionists were not only Queen Victoria but also George Bernard Shaw, who wrote ardently and repeatedly on the subject, and Hearst himself).

Hearst's rival the *New York Times* applauded Dr. Dana's diagnosis of zoophil-psychosis and praised the neurologist for showing how little antivivisectionists cared for human suffering: "This is because animals make a small and strictly limited demand for affection and care, and therefore are favorite objects of those with little to bestow." This charge could hardly be applied to Hearst.

HEARST WAS A champion of the powerless, be they animals, immigrants, or laborers. His advocacy of the rights of workers, in particular, permeated not only his papers but also his political campaigns.

Running New York papers provided Hearst with a stepping-stone to electoral politics. His father, he thought, had waited too long to enter the fray and died only a senator. Will, keen to prove his worth, intended to surpass his father and end up in the White House. He began his political climb in November 1902, when at age thirty-nine he was elected to Congress. Two days after his victory he proclaimed that the Democratic Party would, in the future, triumph only by associating itself "intimately and sincerely with the working people of this country."

In 1904 Hearst declared his candidacy for the presidency, running on a pro-labor platform. Without labor unions fighting for higher wages, Hearst argued, America could well move in the direction of "China and India where rich mandarins and rajahs lord it over starving populations." Besides, he asserted in his papers, unions were good for the well-being of the whole nation, because they increased the purchasing power of the masses and thus benefited all manner of business.

> Poverty-stricken people do not eat beef or mutton; they do not buy woolen clothes in profusion. They have not enough for life's real necessities; nothing at all for the books, the travel, the pleasures that should accompany genuine national prosperity. Wide and equitable distribution of wealth is essential to a nation's prosperous growth and intellectual development, and that distribution is brought about by the labor union more than any other agency of our civilization.

It was easy for Hearst to take this stance when his industry did not rely on the kinds of workers who unionized at this time. Later, when the unionization of newspaper employees would be proposed, Hearst would vehemently oppose it. But his political opinions did shift to the right over time, and he was a man of contradictions. In 1904 his pro-labor platform seems to have been genuine, and his support of the unions and attempts to bring together rural populists with urban workers were incendiary to party leaders and the business community.

Realizing the danger of Hearst's candidacy, his opponents unleashed a barrage of personal attacks, dredging up his youthful relationship with Tessie Powers and maligning his motivations. An editorial in the *New York Evening Post* titled "The Unthinkable Hearst" called him "a low voluptuary trying to sting his jaded senses to a fresh thrill by turning from private to public corruption." And a *New York Times* editorial asserted that "he makes his appeal solely to restlessness and discontent. . . . He represents the sterile policy of agitation, nothing more. That is to say, Mr. Hearst stands for absolutely nothing but the arraying of class against class in the United States." When the Democrats met in St. Louis the week of July 4, they nominated the conservative Judge Alton B. Parker. In November Republican Party candidate Theodore Roosevelt won the presidency. Disappointed but not defeated, Hearst accepted the nomination for a second term in Congress and was reelected in November 1904. He would attempt to rise to the top in the next round.

In the meantime, in 1905 Hearst ran for mayor of New York, declaring that if elected, he would institute municipal control and ownership of public services and exclude the trusts (the term of disapproval used to describe the corporate monopolies of the day) from supplying and overcharging the city for water, transportation, gas, electricity, ice, milk, and other necessities. He also pledged to end the corruption of Tammany Hall (the Democratic political machine that dominated New York City politics) and return city government to the people. The popular support for Hearst's candidacy was fervent, but Tammany Hall politicians stole the election by leaving ballot boxes unopened and uncounted and dumping some of them into the East River. They also chased away and beat poll watchers, flooded the polls with repeat voters, and delayed reporting returns. By the end of Election Day the incumbent mayor George McClellan was said to have outpolled Hearst by several thousand votes. Although Hearst, "pale with anger," demanded a recount, nothing was done to right the fraud. He was too much of a menace to the New York establishment.

In 1906 Hearst ran once more, this time for governor of New York — a step toward the presidency. As his popularity rose, his opponents again began circulating rumors of his immorality and slammed him for what they considered to be his unsuitable marriage.

In late April 1903, at the age of forty, Hearst had married Millicent Willson, a twenty-one-year-old former chorus girl whom he had been dating for five years. Millie was tall and beautiful, with a round face, pale skin, dark hair, and large dark eyes. Hearst himself still looked youthful, his long face clean-shaven and distinguished, his hair cut short and parted in the middle. Eager to project gravitas commensurate with his political ambitions, he had by now exchanged his loud collegiate ties and checkered jackets for dark three-piece suits, long, black, double-breasted coats, and soft, broad-brimmed, black hats. With his pale face and forceful blue-eyed stare, he looked to the outside world like an undertaker. But though Hearst appeared stern in official photographs, in person he smiled often and had a charming and courtly manner.

Phoebe was, of course, "terribly upset" at Will's consorting with yet another inappropriate woman, but this time she failed to break them up. She refused to attend the wedding, sending only a telegram and an emerald brooch, for which Will and Millie thanked her effusively and repeatedly. But soon Millie's devotion to Will and her sweet and solicitous conduct toward her mother-in-law won even Phoebe's heart. A year after the wedding Phoebe wrote to a friend, "Will is very happy and Millicent is a good wife." She would improve her estimation further when Millie produced five sons.

Millie's wifely and maternal virtues were not, however, credited by Hearst's opponents. As he proceeded to campaign for the gubernatorial seat, he was pounded for both his politics and his personal life. President Theodore Roosevelt, "horrified at . . . Hearst's strength on the East Side among laborers and even among farmers," told Congressman James Sherman, chairman of the Republican Congressional Committee, "We must win by a savage and aggressive fight against Hearstism." Roosevelt's negative campaigning included attacks on Hearst's marriage: "Hearst's private life had been disreputable. His wife was a chorus girl or something like that. . . . It is not the kind of family which people who believe that sound home relations form the basis of national citizenship would be glad to see in the Executive Mansion in Albany, and still less in the White House." The decisive blow came less than a week before the election. Roosevelt accused Hearst of complicity in the assassination of President William McKinley in 1901. He claimed that the "reckless utterances" against McKinley in the Hearst papers had incited the assassin to his bloody deed. So late in the race, Hearst did not have enough time to shake this accusation. He lost the election by a margin of only 4 percent.

"I was pretty much tired out and discouraged and disgusted with everything," Will confessed to his mother. To recover, he, Millie, and their sons retreated to the family ranch at San Simeon. George Hearst had purchased this 60,000-acre estate spread over the undulating hills overlooking the Pacific Ocean in 1865 and had built a modest family vacation home there. Will had adored it since his childhood. "I love this ranch," he wrote to Phoebe, "I love the sea and I love the mountains and the hollows in the hills and the shady places in the creeks and the fine old oaks and even the hot brushy hillsides — full of quail — and the canyons full of deer. It's a wonderful place. I would rather spend a month here than any place in the world."

But he had not yet given up his hopes of attaining the highest office in the country. During the 1912 election he had little chance of being nominated directly by the Democratic Party, having criticized in his papers and speeches the corruption and incompetence of many Democratic politicians. But he hoped that the convention would deadlock and nominate him as an alternative. Unfortunately for him, that did not happen, and the candidate Hearst backed, Champ Clark, was defeated by Woodrow Wilson.

In 1922 Hearst ran for governor of New York once more. Again his denunciation of corporate power, the trusts, and the corrupt elected officials who refused to take them on were too much for political and business leaders. In July 1922 the *New York Times* reported that the Democratic convention struck "a death blow to the political hopes of William R. Hearst by eliminating him as a candidate for any place on the ticket and virtually reading him out of the party."

This final crushing of his electoral hopes, his failure to become even as successful in this arena as his father had been, and changes in his personal life spurred Hearst to rechannel his energies and passions. He would turn to the creation of his own kingdom and, at last, his own home at San Simeon, where he could stay out of the public light and enjoy the company of a new love.

In 1915 W.R., as he was now called by those close to him, met another show girl, Marion Davies. He fell head over heels in love, although she was only eighteen at the time and he was fifty-two. Marion was a slight blonde with wavy hair, blue eyes, a Cupid's bow mouth, and an endearing stutter. Vivacious and funny, she was utterly unpretentious and extremely kind. Alice Head recorded in her memoirs that

> there is the side of her that all the world knows, the gay, beautiful, gaminesque star of the films, and then there is the side of her that is only known to her friends, who will all without exception confirm the statement that she has the kindest heart and most generous disposition in the world. Marion is that *rara avis*, a genuinely unselfish person. . . . Her wit and gaiety have the same bubbling quality as champagne. She is . . . an inspired mimic, but wholly without malice.

Hearst loved to laugh — one of his employees at San Simeon commented that he "has a decided streak of humor in his makeup, and has one of the most infectious grins I have ever seen on a human face." Marion made W.R. feel cheerful and lighthearted.

He also saw her as a potential star for a movie studio he wanted to set up and hoped to make her into another Mary Pickford. In 1916 Hearst added feature film production to his International Film Service, which had been making serial films and weekly episodes, and he offered Marion a contract for five hundred dollars a week, a tenfold increase from her stage salary. By her own admission, Marion began their relationship as a gold digger, but she ended up deeply in love with him. "Most of the time Hearst and Marion are like two sixteen-year-olds," remarked one observer. "Arms about waists, a gentle slap on the cheek, Hearst holding her tightly in his capacious arms murmuring sweet nothings."

By the time Hearst met Marion, he had been together with Millicent for almost twenty years, and they had grown apart. Millie wanted to be part of high society — she dressed her servants in liveries and preferred to live in New York. W.R. detested society's pretensions, had his chauffeur wear a plain business suit, and yearned to spend more time in California. For a while Hearst maintained parallel lives — one with his wife and five sons, another with his mistress. At one point Millicent asked him to choose between her and Marion, but neither of them really wanted a divorce, which would drag their names through the mud and tarnish their reputations. For Millicent there was an advantage to being supported by her husband and bearing the name Mrs. Hearst. And W.R. was loath to cede to her half of his assets, especially as his incurable spending habits always put his finances in a precarious position. Nor was W.R. prepared to give up Marion. So while Millie lived mostly on the East Coast, W.R. spent increasingly more time in California. He and Millie remained on good terms and communicated regularly by letter and telephone. She and the boys went west for vacations, while W.R. went to New York for business and important family occasions. But his life now centered on San Simeon, where Marion presided as the princess of his new kingdom.

What made this possible was Phoebe's death in 1919, from the influenza epidemic that raged around the globe at the end of World War I. With his mother's demise, Hearst finally came into possession of the family real estate, stocks, and bonds, the total value of which was about $7.5 million, an immense fortune at the time. For the first time in his life he was financially independent and free from his mother's scrutiny. He was fifty-six years old.

Part of his inheritance was his favorite spot in the world: the ranch at San Simeon. Hearst had long dreamt of building a larger, more comfortable house on the property, but Phoebe had never given him the money for it. Now he was in a position to do as he wished. The new complex would also allow him to compensate for his insecurities by impressing his guests with its many delights, from lavish interior decorations to outdoor vistas and pastimes.

Frances Marion, a screenwriter who worked for Hearst, detected the vulnerability behind his imposing facade, which clearly spurred his creation of the Enchanted Hill, as he called the complex he constructed at San Simeon.

> Most people thought Mr. Hearst possessed everything a human being could ever dream about. . . . [He] had fame, power, enormous wealth, friends that catered to him, lauded him, and gazed at him with the fervor the Incas had for their ancient gods. I saw him as a frustrated and lonely man. He was frustrated over losing his bids for the presidency of the U.S. He was unhappy about his inability to become the most potent motion picture producer of the time. He was sad when Marion did not become the star to outshine all other stars. He loved and yet envied [President Calvin] Coolidge and Louis B. Mayer their positions, which he thought that he should have had.

Hearst coped with these disappointments by transferring his drive, vision, enthusiasm, and affection to the building project.

George Hearst had constructed a two-story Italianate vacation house for the family close to the shore. But Will found it much more fun to "rough it" on the hill above. Camp Hill, as he called it, was an oval ridge 1,600 feet above sea level overlooking a spectacular panorama of the ocean, rolling hills, and mountains. When Will came here with his family, he would pitch Venetian-style brightly colored tents the size of cottages — with Oriental rugs thrown over wooden floors — and indulge in a feast of outdoor activities. "I can take long rides over these beautiful hills," he wrote to Phoebe, "I can camp out in the pretty spots beside the creeks, in the valley, or in the little hollows on the mountain tops; I can go fishing in the streams, or fishing and boating on the sea. It seems to me that anything that can be done anywhere is all assembled and ready to be done on the ranch."

In the spring of 1919 Hearst went to visit the architect Julia Morgan in her San Francisco office to discuss building a permanent house at Camp Hill. It was the beginning of a remarkable partnership that would last some twenty years. Morgan would say that "Mr. Hearst and I are fellow architects. He supplies vision, critical judgment. I give technical knowledge and building experience. He loves architecting. If he had chosen that career he would have been a great architect. San Simeon *is* Mr. Hearst." Frances Marion recalled that "Mr. Hearst spent a great deal of his time at San Simeon with Miss Morgan, either in that little shack in back of the building, or up in his library. He was never happier than when he was planning new additions to his fantastic home."

The work of realizing Hearst's dream proved as monumental as the final result. (George Bernard Shaw quipped that San Simeon was what God would have built if he had had the money.) All building materials had to be shipped by water from San Francisco or Los Angeles, then driven up the hill along a winding, unpaved road five miles long. It was very difficult to retain workmen, as the location was so remote and isolated that they did not want to stay. Some did not even unpack their bags before turning around and leaving.

The hilltop was steep, rugged, and very rocky, with laurel trees and oaks dotting it here and there. W.R. wanted his new home surrounded by lush gardens, but for that the ridge had to be entirely regraded and terraced. All the topsoil had to be trucked up the hill and water piped down from natural springs. Where the ground was too rocky to plant, workmen hacked crevices with pickaxes, inserted sticks of dynamite, blew apart the rock, and filled the new openings with soil. Then plants, shrubs, trees, and flowers were driven up the hill and planted in profusion. (Some 500,000 to 700,000 annuals would be grown in the gardens every year.) As Nigel Keep, Hearst's chief gardener, proudly said, "I took bare grounds and rocks and rattlesnakes and made a beautiful place."

Hearst himself was also a challenge. He always paid his bills late and had to be nudged repeatedly, and he incessantly requested changes to designs and already completed work, ever striving for something more novel and exciting. He asked Morgan to redo the outdoor Neptune Pool three times before he was satisfied with it. He was also an exacting master. Maurice McClure, the construction superintendent at San Simeon, said that Hearst "was a very difficult man to work for. He could not understand an error. He would fire a man on the spot for little or nothing."

Other employees, however, found Hearst kind and considerate, and many stayed with him for years. Norman Rotanzi, the groundskeeper, recalled that "you really felt at ease around him. He knew all the names of the plants and most of the pests we have to deal with. The gardeners were sort of his pets. He would like to come out and stroll around and talk to everybody. And it didn't make any difference who he had with him — Winston Churchill, or the president of U.S. Steel, or whoever else it was, he would always introduce you to these people."

Even when annoyed, Hearst remained polite and even humorous in his requests. In February 1927, when he returned to the ranch after a month's absence, the hill was buffeted by a ferocious storm. Hearst wrote to Camille Rossi, Morgan's construction supervisor (he often communicated with his employees by letter), asking for immediate weatherproofing improvements: "We are drowned, blown and frozen out. . . . Everybody has a cold. . . . Of course the houses are wonderful to look at but one cannot live on looks alone. . . . Let's make what we have built practical, comfortable and beautiful. If we can't do that we might as well change the names of the [guest] houses to pneumonia house, diphtheria house and influenza bungalow. The main house we can call the clinic."

The emphasis on the comfort and livability of the ranch was palpable throughout the Casa Grande — the main building — and the three guest cottages. The rooms, despite being stuffed full of artwork — imported Renaissance and Baroque ceilings and fireplaces, antique furniture and tapestries, sculptures and paintings — felt cozy rather than forbidding. Each window gave onto a beautiful and restful view of the ocean, hills, or mountains. One could readily see that Hearst enjoyed living here, surrounded by his possessions.

These continued to accrue at an astronomical rate. A 1921 letter from Morgan conveys the pace and scope of Hearst's acquisitions:

> So far we have received from him, to incorporate in the new buildings, some twelve or thirteen carloads of antiques, brought from the ends of the earth and from prehistoric down to late Empire in period. . . .
>
> They comprise vast quantities of tables, beds, armoires, secretaries, all kinds of cabinets, polychrome church statuary, columns, door frames, carved doors in all stages of repair and disrepair, over-altars, reliquaries, lanterns, iron-grille doors, window grilles, votive candle-sticks, all kinds of chairs in quantity, and six or seven well heads.

From the mid-1920s on, W.R. would spend the greatest portion of his time and his corporation's money at San Simeon, which became his main home and business headquarters. As Alice Head recorded, when visiting Hearst at San Simeon, she would sit down with him to discuss business in "a quiet spot, in the garden," only to see "other Hearst executives lurking in the bushes, awaiting their turn. . . . One scribe, after his first visit to the ranch, wrote as follows: 'The place is full of worried editors dodging the kangaroos.'"

HEARST BEGAN COLLECTING animals in 1924, five years into the construction of his dream home. His propensity to follow his whims and to make a grand impression transformed a boyish fancy into a princely menagerie. Hearst's first idea at San Simeon was to assemble species that could roam freely on the hills and meadows of the estate: elk, white fallow deer, and bison. In October 1925 Morgan reported on the delivery of a group of reindeer. The man who brought them said they needed "Iceland moss and careful feeding and watching until used to new food. Iceland moss supply used up enroute, more should be sent for." In March 1926 Morgan wrote that, "the buffalos have been put in the larger enclosure and looked very pretty browsing in the green grass."

Guests arriving at San Simeon by the winding road from the ocean were startled and awed by the sight of the water buffalo and American buffalo grazing in the first pasture, closest to the coast; llamas, emus, ibex, and camels dwelling farther up the hill; and elk and zebras roaming the distant slopes. The spectacle of the animals was no less striking at night. Brayton Laird, who worked for Hearst in the orchards, recorded sometime later, when Hearst's collection expanded further, how driving along the road in the evening he came across "a big herd of buffalo . . . then . . . a whole herd of elk. . . . There [were] water buffalo, wildebeest, kangaroos running around, little kangaroos jumping in and out of the pouch and they looked like a bunch of rabbits. . . . There must have been five hundred animals like in [the]

African plains there. . . . Your headlights would light the eyes of those animals up. They'd all be looking at you and it was just like the lights of a distant city."

Hearst wanted the ranch to be full of delights for himself and his guests, especially the young Hollywood actors and actresses — Marion's colleagues and friends — who came here for the weekends. He put at their disposal the outdoor Neptune Pool, with a Roman temple facade on one long side and curving colonnades on the short ends. Or, if they preferred, they could take a salt-water swim in the indoor Roman Pool, inlaid floor to ceiling with blue and gold mosaics. They could play tennis against each other or against champions invited by their host. Hearst led horseback expeditions, from which he would return smiling and invigorated, whereas his guests, half his age and size (he got portly with time), would be utterly worn-out. But the most unusual pastime the ranch offered was the chance to observe his wild and rare animals. Davies wrote in her memoirs that "W.R. wanted the animals around because it was picturesque. And he thought the zoo might entertain his guests." That was certainly the case. But, still a boy at heart, as well as an incorrigible collector, Hearst also indulged a childish impulse to collect all the animals he could get.

In 1927 W.R. decided that he should have more striking beasts than just the ruminants in his pastures. He hired Richard Addison, formerly of the San Diego Zoo, to serve as his zookeeper and dispatched him to Boston and New York to acquire exotic creatures arriving on ships from Africa, India, Tibet, Australia, New Guinea, and other parts of the world. Once purchased, the beasts and birds were loaded onto private express railway cars and transported across the country. Unloaded at San Luis Obispo, they were put on trucks and driven up to the Enchanted Hill. On July 22, 1927, Morgan wrote to Hearst about the latest shipment: "The animals arrived in beautiful shape. I had to rub my eyes last night when out of the semi-darkness staring at the lights were grouped three ostriches, five zebras, five white deer, two with big horns, a llama, and some speckled deer. All in a group!"

Hearst newspaper employees were also enlisted in their boss's hunt for rare beasts. Alice Head recalled that

> one of the most interesting cables I ever received from Mr. Hearst read approximately as follows: *Go to number —— Tottenham Court Road and inspect the giraffes for age size sex quality and price.*
>
> I went to —— Tottenham Court Road, which turned out to be a parrot and cockatoo shop, and demanded to see the giraffes. The gentleman who had stepped forward to serve me regarded me with pitying surprise. "You surely know we are not allowed to land animals of that sort except for the Zoo," he said. And then looking at me more closely, he said, "Where do you come from?" I told him I was the representative of William Randolph Hearst. And suddenly a great light dawned on him and he disappeared into the dark recesses of the shop, returning with a printed pamphlet, which advertised the fact that he was an agent for procuring certain wild animals from South Africa. Hearing that Mr. Hearst had a private zoo he had dispatched one of these pamphlets, and my cable was the result. The next time I visited the Ranch Mr. Hearst said one afternoon: "I am going to take you [for] a little walk." We drifted down the mountainside and came to an enclosure. "And," said Mr. Hearst, "there are your giraffes."

The arrival of Hearst's giraffes in America made news. New Orleans newspapers reported on July 28, 1934, that three giraffes were disembarked in that city from the SS *Bilderdijk*. "William, whose head periscopes into the air 17 feet, is said to be the tallest giraffe ever to be brought to the United States," one paper declared. Along with him were two female giraffes. The exquisite animals arrived in New Orleans "from Rotterdam where they were transshipped following their arrival by steamer from East Africa where they were captured on February 13. They will be shipped by steamer from here to California, where two will be placed on the ranch of William Randolph Hearst."

Other animals were procured via dealers such as Horne's Zoological Arena Company of Kansas City. Mr. Horne wrote to Hearst in March 1931, confirming a large order for animals and birds from Africa, India, Asia, Europe, Japan, and the United States, and offering his further services:

> [If] you can see your way clear to make up an order of $150,000.00 or more of stock, the writer will make a special trip over to Africa and personally select for you the finest collection of African Antelope ever imported into this country, and many varieties of which have never been seen on the American continent or elsewhere outside Africa. I will have my keepers come back on the same boat that I return on so that I can personally supervise the handling of this stock enroute, and will make delivery at New York City with a guarantee of live arrival in perfect condition at San Luis Obispo, California on everything I sell you. In this manner you will get a quality of stock that you can obtain in no other way, and I am sure that you can have the most wonderful collection that has ever been assembled at anyone [sic] spot in the entire world outside of Africa.

Hearst's animal collection was, in fact, shaping up to be the largest such private gathering in his day. Although menageries had been the hobbies of rulers for centuries, with the decline of royalty and the establishment of public zoos in the nineteenth century, very few people found it feasible or expedient to keep their own assemblages of rare beasts. Of course some of the very rich and powerful would continue to acquire exotic animals for diversion and vanity well into the twentieth and twenty-first centuries. But it is still an unusual and rarefied pastime, and it was certainly a mark of Hearst's enormous wealth, extravagance, and uniqueness that he went to such lengths to set up his own animal kingdom at San Simeon.

When Hearst's zookeeper, Richard Addison, was asked why his boss collected such a variety of animals, he replied, "It was because of his fondness for them, maybe as a little boy's love for his pets. It wasn't just for show or part of the setting; he actually liked those creatures and was always concerned for their comfort." During their initial meeting, Addison recalled, "we discussed the types of animals which would or wouldn't thrive in the San Simeon climate and terrain, and I found that he knew quite a bit about wild animals, their natures, and the requirements for keeping them healthy and contented under semi-confinement."

Addison's job was to locate and buy the animals his boss desired. Thus Hearst wrote to Addison in June 1929, "I enclose herewith check for $4400.00 to pay for the white oryx and the Malayan Tapirs. The Tapirs will have to be put in a better place. As things are at present we might just as well not have any Tapirs. Nobody knows about them or sees them." In August 1929 he issued further instructions: "I will buy the elephant at $1650 IF YOU LIKE IT WHEN YOU SEE IT. Furthermore, I hope you will soon hear about the gorilla. . . . You can also get the pair of hog deer and the pair of anoas. You might also get the trio of sambar deer and the pair of grey rheas, if you can make a wholesale price for the lot."

Although Hearst's letter speaks of tapirs in the plural and suggests that there were already some at the ranch, it seems from later documents that only one such animal survived and thrived at his zoo. The tapir is a curious-looking creature with a piglike body supported by relatively slender legs, a flexible and trunklike snout, large, erect ears, and small, deep-set eyes. The Malayan tapir, the largest of the species, measures six to eight feet in length, weighs five hundred to more than one thousand pounds, and has a black coat with a white "saddle" — its body from the shoulder blades to the rump is white — which serves to camouflage it in the shady forest where it dwells. Hearst's tapir was named Squeaky (probably because tapirs produce loud birdlike chirps and squeals). Addison's successor, Carey Baldwin, recalled that she was "a gentle old lady that had come from Malaya and had spent several years in our zoo."

Squeaky was a dame of fine judgment and excellent taste. One summer day, Baldwin wrote, when all the vegetation stood dry and the temperature soared to 108°F, a harsh wind sprang up from the east and began one of those California wildfires that regularly ravage the region. The animal keepers rushed about opening enclosures so that their inhabitants could run away from the smoke and flames.

> Most of the wild creatures in the path of the fire did little to help themselves but dashed madly ahead of the blaze. The old tapir, however, . . . came deliberately out of her pen and started leisurely for the Castle area. She ambled up to the beautiful grounds and flower beds, sniffed about with her long nose, nibbling flavorful plants here and there, and headed for the magnificent outdoor swimming pool [Neptune Pool] that was intended only for special guests. Squeaky did not hesitate. She slipped quietly into the pool, and while men and animals ran for their lives, she dozed and swam contentedly about the pool, remaining there until evening.

Remarkably, only a few animals suffered serious injuries — some deer had bad enough burns on their feet that they could not be saved. But none weathered the disaster in such style as the tapir.

Squeaky lived at the hilltop, on a promontory behind the Casa Grande where Hearst kept his more high-maintenance beasts. In the beginning he was full of exciting plans for displaying his animals on the hill. On August 12, 1926, he wrote to Morgan:

How about a maze in connection with the zoo. I think getting lost in the maze and coming unexpectedly upon lions, tigers, pumas, panthers, wild cats, monkeys, macaws and cockatoos, etc. etc., would be a thrill even for the most blasé.

If the space is big enough — and we will make it big enough by cutting off more hill if necessary — we could have a great maze with all these "animiles" and birds and with a pretty pool in the middle, with cranes and flamingoes, etc., and a fountain and EVERYTHING.

Let's do this, I think it is a novel idea. If it should not prove practical we can make a maze in connection with the big pools on Chinese Hill, — but I kind of like the animal maze.

The maze was never built. Instead, Morgan designed a large polygonal structure with enclosures opening onto a central viewing and feeding area, where individual animals could be displayed to better advantage. Even so, guests were regularly startled by wild beasts. The actor Ralph Bellamy recalled how on his first visit to San Simeon he arrived late in the evening and was getting ready for bed. "When I came out of the bathroom, I found my wife petrified in the middle of the room saying, 'There's a lion outside that window!' And I said, 'Oh, come on, it's late. We had a drink or two. Go ahead and get your face washed and get to bed.' When we woke up the next morning and I went to the window, there was a lion!" In fact, the Bellamys were occupying the Doge's Suite, whose back windows faced the animal enclosures.

Charlie Chaplin, too, had vivid memories of scary animal sounds in the night. In his memoirs he described how one evening he took a walk about the grounds.

The château was drenched in moonlight, looking wondrous and ghostly against the wild setting of the seven mountaintops; the stars pierced an intensely clear sky. . . . From the zoo the occasional roar of a lion could be heard and the continual scream of an enormous orangutan, that echoed and bounced about the mountaintops. It was eerie and terrifying, for each evening at sundown the orangutan would start, quietly at first, then working up to horrific screaming, which lasted on into the night.

The lions had been among the first exotic animals to take up residence on the hill. On April 22, 1925, Julia Morgan, reporting to Hearst on the progress of work on the site, noted that "the lions are beauties — about the size of St. Bernards and as well kept and groomed as human babies. It seems incredible that any living creature could contain the resentment felt by those wild cats. They have not 'tamed' in the slightest." In 1928 Queenie, the lioness, gave birth to four cubs. Hayes Perkins, one of the animal keepers, observed her with fascination and respect.

Her eyes glow with a cold light, and it is easy to see the demons lurking in them when any one approaches. Yet she is as tender as any mother might be in caressing her young. She will turn her meat over to them until they have eaten their fill, then devour what is left. She is one of the most ferocious lions I have ever seen. When born these cubs were about two-thirds as large as common cats, but they grow very rapidly and are beginning to play about their den.

The chimpanzees Jimmy, Mary, and Jerry also lived in the hilltop complex. Jerry was the grumpiest of the three and liked to scoop up his waste and hurl it at the ogling Hollywood stars. In 1928 Mary and Jimmy produced a youngster. Hayes Perkins recorded with affection: "There is a small chimpanzee in the zoo, and I am its keeper. The chimp is intelligent, and is for all the world like a baby. It climbs up my leg and sits in the crook of my arm, its arms round my neck just as a small kid would do."

The little chimp was named Darwin, but unfortunately he died within a few months. In 1936 Mary and Jimmy had another baby, Darwina.

Some exotic animal pregnancies created consternation among the keepers. When one of Hearst's giraffes seemed to be expecting, Hearst brought out a woman veterinarian, Dr. Carpenter, to play midwife. Yet even she was stumped, as "there was no books on pregnant giraffes."* Carpenter estimated a due date, but the pregnancy dragged on for several weeks past that. When at last the baby was born, it was named Delayo.

Hearst also had a young Indian elephant, called Marianne after the title of Marion Davies' first talking picture. A year old or younger when she came to San Simeon, she had quirks of her own. Perkins noted in his diary that the elephant "becomes petulant at meal times. I was fixing its feed when Joan [Crawford] leaned idly against the screen [of the elephant house], her forehead on the wire. The elephant butted the other side, and she [Joan] wept because of the pain. The screen was imprinted on her face."

Other hilltop denizens included mountain lions, Bengal tigers, black and spotted leopards, jaguars, orangutans, spider and Java monkeys, South American coatimundis and kinkajous, African porcupines, a Galapagos tortoise, and several varieties of bears — sloth bears from India, polar bears, sun, brown, and American black bears, and grizzlies. In the heat of the summer W.R. had truckloads of ice brought up the hill for the polar bears.

By 1928 there were more than 300 animals on the Enchanted Hill, and by 1937 that number had doubled. There were also some 1,500 birds — cassowaries, rheas, emus, macaws, parakeets, cockatoos, pigeons, swans, a pelican, a stork, pheasants, curas-

---

*The baby giraffe story was recalled by Hearst's telegraph and telephone operator, Franklin Whitcomb, in the Hearst Castle Oral History Project, 1989.

sows, and guinea fowl — although tropical birds did not do very well in San Simeon's climate.

Hearst had an idea for housing some animals in the indoor pool behind the Casa Grande. He initially thought that the pool ought to be set into a hothouse with palms, ferns, and a profusion of orchids. "The temperature of the hothouse, and of the pool, too, would be warm on the coldest, bleakest winter day," he wrote to Morgan. "We would have the South Sea Island on the Hill. . . . The pool, of course, would be the main attraction, and we might put a turtle and a couple of sharks in to lend verisimilitude." Morgan was game: "I like your idea for the combination indoor pool and orchid green house. It should be very tropical and ex- otic. There could be a plate glass partition in the pool and the al- ligators, sharks, etc. could disport on one side of it and visitors could unsuspectingly dive toward it." Unfortunately, the shark idea was never realized — whether because of expense or im- practicality is difficult to know.

Hearst's letters to Morgan about the zoo — especially early on, when it was new and everything seemed possible — reveal his boyish exuberance and delight in animal collecting. At times he seemed genuinely concerned for the well-being of his creatures. On January 8, 1932, he wrote urgently to Morgan:

During the month of December we lost eleven of our best an- imals,
  2 Waterbucks
  1 Sable antelope
  1 Kudu
  1 Ibex
  2 Blesbok
  1 Sambar
  1 Blackbuck
  1 Oryx (baby)
  1 Nylgau

I would say they represent something like $8,000 or $10,000 in value. They were lost through exposure in heavy storms.

Mr. Baldwin said that these losses occurred in spite of the best efforts of himself and staff to save these animals and that others would have been lost except for vigorous efforts.

He said we need more shelters and some pens. . . .

If we are going to lose $10,000 worth of animals a winter — and we may lose more than that — we can well afford to put up more shelters and the kind which will protect the animals and keep them warm as well as dry.

I advise, therefore, first, that we alter our present shelters and make them larger and very much more protective.

Second, that we build about two more shelters for the smaller animals in the upper field and one in the lower field for the larger animals. . . .

I do not think we need any general heat, but I think that it would be well to have in connection with two or three of these shelters a room with a fireplace where sick animals could be taken and attended to.

Some of Hearst's worry may have stemmed from the financial toll of these losses, but his affection for animals could also be sentimental and even obsessively protective. Marion Davies recalled how once he went to extraordinary lengths to take care of a little mouse that had been discovered in a big iron flowerpot in the main living room of the Casa Grande. Arming himself with a big spoon, Hearst went into the garden, despite an impending storm, and when he returned half an hour later, Davies asked him what he had been up to. "I dug a little hole for the mouse and put leaves over it so the mouse will be warm," he replied. "The mouse is frightened. I don't want it to be around where Helena [his beloved dachshund] is, because Helena's a mouse-killer. Now nobody will find it." After dinner Hearst went to feed the mouse with some cheese, and during the night, which was stormy and windy, he kept worrying about the little creature. At some point he got up and went to check on it, returning content. "That mouse is fine. Nice and warm," he said. "That mouse was warm," Davies wrote, "because W.R. had taken a scissors and cut off part of the little blanket I had on my chaise lounge. He had ruined my lovely blanket just to keep that mouse warm. And the next day at luncheon he was very happy. The mouse was fine." For the next two days Hearst kept checking on his little pet.

> The third day W.R. wouldn't come to luncheon, and nobody knew where he was. I asked his valet to find him. Well, W.R. finally walked in, and you never saw such a gloomy face. He said, "The mouse is gone."
>
> I said, "Well, with all the food you've been feeding him, you kept him so full, he probably thought he'd like to go get a little fresh air and run around and see life."
>
> W.R. said, "I hope — I really and truly hope that's it."
>
> He really loved animals. I think it all started with the little white mouse that he had had as a pet when he was a child. He'd carry it around in his pocket.

On another occasion Nigel Keep, Hearst's head gardener, complained to the Chief, as Hearst was called by his staff, "You know, we're just getting wiped out by the quail." He had planted a profusion of flowers, and the quail had chewed them all up. "I guess we'll have to plant more flowers next time, won't we?" Hearst replied. "You're not going to shoot those quail." Norman Rotanzi recalled that Hearst "would carry wheat around in his coat pocket and feed the quail. There used to be huge flocks of quail."

Davies observed that "W.R. had an immense amount of feeling inside. He was very emotional, but not outwardly. Very few people understood this." To protect the animals grazing on the hill, he posted signs along the road declaring that "Animals Have the Right of Way" so motorists would drive slowly and watch out

for the beasts. Some animals took their owner's ideas to heart.
Carey Baldwin recounted that

> the pair of ostriches that hung around the road leading up to
> the hill to the Castle were real pests. . . . They considered all
> cars a personal affront, and humans were trespassers on their
> domain. . . . Cocoa [the female] would walk along the road,
> and when a car came along, she would stop and stare at it. She
> never seemed to realize that the road was meant to be a thor-
> oughfare, and she just wouldn't get out of the way as the other
> animals learned to do. . . . She would just stand there and stare
> at it. The driver would either have to honk his horn until she
> decided to walk away, or he would have to wait patiently until
> she decided to go elsewhere. Chocolate [the male], however,
> never failed to demonstrate chivalry in front of his mate, and
> he often charged the car. His great size and weight, together
> with a long toenail on each foot, could play havoc with the fin-
> ish on a shiny auto and put holes in the radiator.*

As troublesome as some of the animals were, no one was allowed to interfere with them. Even Winston Churchill was held
up for more than an hour by a stubborn, inquisitive giraffe that
refused to get out of his way.

Hearst worried not only about his animals being run over by
cars but also about their falling prey to coyotes. In April 1927 he
wrote to Morgan: "I am anxious to have all the fences [enclosing
the grazing areas] coyote proof — the outside as well as the inside fences — because in this way we have double protection for
the weaker animals. The gates should also be made coyote proof,

---

*One of Hearst's employees actually got severely injured by an ostrich and sued
him for forty thousand dollars. The man was working at the back of a truck
along the road when the ostrich came up behind him, knocked him down, and
trampled him with such ferocity as to cause a hernia, a concussion, and profound shock.

so that protection will be complete. The animals as now arranged are very interesting and scenically effective." To which Morgan replied the next day: "The animals do look very picturesque and interesting as seen unexpectedly grouped here and there. Now if you could come upon the lions for instance, as unexpectedly, it would produce a real thrill."

Anxious as he was for the well-being of his beasts, Hearst often seemed more concerned that they impress his guests than that they live in ways that were most comfortable for them. In October 1927 he wrote to Morgan:

> I think we must positively proceed immediately to build certain animal houses and shelters. I thought at one time that it was desirable to hide the houses in places where they would not be particularly conspicuous, but I find that the animals collect around such feeding places and shelter places, and that if we put the shelters in distant spots we would have our animals where they would never be seen.
>
> I would suggest, therefore, that we make these shelters exceedingly picturesque log houses and put them in certain picturesque locations not far from the main road. Watering troughs can be put adjacent and feeding rooms established in connection, so that the animals will congregate at places where they can be seen from the road. . . .
>
> I think the giraffes should be transferred from where they are. Nobody yet who has come to the ranch has seen the giraffes.

Hearst's guests did have ample opportunity to view the animals — sometimes even more than they would have liked. The movie director King Vidor recalled that "at feeding time at the zoo we'd follow along a two-wheeled cart with a man . . . going to feed the animals. And the lions would roar and get excited about the food." However, Vidor added, "Some people used to take walks and come back and complain about little animals with horns attacking them occasionally. Well, it's called an emu or ibis or something like that. Well, they'd . . . take a walk and go about a quarter of a mile away from the Castle and these little things would come at them. But they generally had a stick and they'd fend them off with a stick."

Hayes Perkins thought that it was the animals that were put out by the humans. The glamorous actors and actresses formed their own exotic menagerie, which did not mix harmoniously with the beasts. "I hope the old man keeps his harem away from my work," he grumbled about the parade of Hollywood guests to the zoo, "for the animals are scared of the bizarre coloring in the garments of the movie stars." Perkins was unimpressed by movie celebrities in general. He wrote in his diary:

> I see a lot of the Hollywood crowd. They are constantly attracted by the wild animals, and are about asking foolish questions. One wonders what the public can see in them, especially the stars among the women. Few of them are beautiful, and all use so much makeup their skins become tanned to the texture of hippo hide. . . . Most are affable enough, if they only wouldn't tease the animals.
>
> Chaplin is the most intelligent of the lot. He is one of the most despondent men I have ever seen. Energetic, ambitious, he rises early and comes down to the zoo in his gaudy pajamas. I am always up early too, cleaning out the cages and fixing feed before the crowd is about. He gives me a sort of "what do you want out of me" sort of look, glaring like a wild beast. I never trouble him, and he goes his own way. One fine thing, his face lights up when the animals notice him.

The animals had good reason to be wary of the humans. Marion Davies remembered that there were signs at the zoo: DO NOT TEASE THE ANIMALS. "Of course that was just the very thing we'd do. . . . Jerry [the chimpanzee] was enormous and quite a character. We used to throw stones at him, or we'd get a rope and give him one end and we'd all be at the other end. One jerk and we'd all go right down. Then he'd get mad and shake the bars, and we'd all run. All this was under the sign, DON'T TEASE."

Even the staff sometimes engaged in such games, as Norman Rotanzi recollected:

> We used to go over to the zoo every evening and have a tug-of-war with one of the big gorillas. We'd put a great big rope through the bars, and five of us would hang on to the rope and the gorilla would pull us right up to the bars. Then we'd pull him back. About the second time, we'd let go of the rope, he would fall on his back, and he'd climb up to the ceiling and make all kinds of noise. So Carey Baldwin caught us one night and put a stop to that. Dismissal if this continued.

W.R. did not pester his exotic pets, and he wished them well. But his animals suffered when his designs for them conflicted with his aesthetic vision for San Simeon. In September 1932, apparently worried about his menagerie and the competence of its keeper, Carey Baldwin, under whose watch he had lost a few giraffes, Hearst asked George Bistany of San Francisco's Fleishhacker Zoo to come to the ranch and evaluate his charges and their condition. Bistany examined everything carefully and wrote a four-page report. His impressions were not favorable.

> The situation, in my opinion, is quite deplorable. Mr. Hearst has a collection of rare and valuable animals, and certainly they should be given proper attention to keep them healthy and in good condition.
>
> There has been no regular cleaning or sanitation of the corrals or cages, and as a result the stock is sickly and ailing because of germs and disease. I understand that the Super-

intendent of the ranch is not interested in the care of wild animals, and that there are only three men taking care of the whole stock. The grounds are dry and the vegetation in the corrals exceedingly poor. All the animals have been watered at the same trough, which has not been cleaned or disinfected for some time. The feeding of the collection has been ignored and evidently no attention given to what should be fed the various species of animals and birds.

I am suggesting various changes which must be made in order to keep the stock in condition and free from disease.

The Buffaloes, now in a field together with the Elk and Zebras, should be separated from the other species and kept by themselves. These animals are at present badly fly-bitten and raw; something must be done for this condition, or the animals will die from the germs and destruction of skin: sheep-dip, animal-spray, or tar are excellent to keep the flies off the animals and give their hides a chance of improving.

The Elk should be kept in a separate corral.

The Zebra should be kept in a corral with the Brindled and White-tailed Gnu, the Springbok and Blesbok; these animals go in herds together in their native land, and so would go well together in captivity.

The Giant Elands will have to be given special care. These animals should be moved immediately to the location where the Giraffes used to be, and should be put together with the Beisa Oryx, and the White Oryx. . . .

The Elephant should have a large enclosure with a pool in which she can bathe. . . .

The two Chimpanzees should be kept together in one big cage, and be given some apparatus, swings, etc., with which to amuse themselves; these intelligent apes must be made as contented as possible in captivity. . . .

The arena where the Lions, Panthers, other cats, and Bears are kept is in poor condition: the animals are tearing up the floor, and I am afraid that soon they will have destroyed enough of the wood to enable them to escape. If Mr. Hearst wants to keep them where they are, he should have the inside of the cages repaired with iron-wood, and logs placed in each compartment so the animals can sharpen their claws on these instead of tearing up the building. . . .

The Polar Bears do not look well; they need a big pool in which to dive and swim. The place where they are now is not suitable for them. . . .

It will be necessary that the Kangaroo infected with an incurable and infectious jaw disease, be killed. There is no way of curing this trouble, and unless the animal is killed the germ will spread and cause further loss among the stock. . . .

A small hospital for sick animals is necessary so that the stock can be moved to this place for care. . . .

A store-room should be built, equipped with frigidaire, in which to keep the food-supplies; there should also be a kitchen where the keepers may prepare the food for the various animals. . . .

I understand from Mr. Baldwin that there are at present only three men caring for the stock on the ranch; it is impossible for three men to care for the entire collection as it should be cared for, and do all the work that involves. You will have to have at least three more men for this purpose.

Hearst read Bistany's report and cabled Morgan on October 14, 1932. He agreed with the

absolute necessity for more protection and care and hospital accommodations for animals, also possibly greater segregation. Yet main necessity must not be forgotten, that of riding through all enclosures and coming into immediate contact with all animals. I suggest complying in the main with recommendations of Bistany — including hiring additional animal keepers and constructing better shelters, food kitchens, and hospitals — but not going as far as supplying Frigidaires and other refinements. I would in fact prefer to eliminate animals which require these ultra-refinements and confine ourselves to animals which naturally do well on ranch.

By the end of the month his commitment to follow Bistany's recommendations seems to have waned. He wrote to Morgan:

I realize the necessity of improving the animal service. I do not want to divide the animals into groups, because I want the roads to go through all this variety of animals, and it would be inconvenient to have a number of parallel divisions, all separated by fences and gates, with the necessity of continually opening gates all the way up the hill.

Moreover, too many divisions, in addition to making an ugly effect, would deprive the situation of its naturalness and make you feel that you were driving through an artificial zoo, instead of through open fields in which these various animals were disporting themselves.

Mr. Bistany's whole idea is contrary to what I want to accomplish, and rather than adopt his idea I would abandon the whole animal proposition. What he will have to do is to find what animals can accommodate themselves to my idea and those that cannot do so we will get rid of. . . .

With regard to the hill, I think we could perfectly well get rid of all the meat eating animals and I think we could arrange the other animals, the bears, the elephants, giraffes and some interesting samples from our general collection, such as a pair of oryxes and a pair of sable antelope, a pair of riding camels, etc., in an interesting zoological park, which would also include your pink flamingos. . . . We can have a reasonable representation of amusing monkeys and I think it would be well to lay out the hill as a park, such as you suggest, rather than as a stiff and ugly zoo.

I think we need a man who knows about animals and Mr. Carey Baldwin really does not know, and his ignorance is very costly. The loss of our four beautiful giraffes was a calamity.

The superintendent of the ranch, George Loorz, defended Baldwin to the Chief: "I believe 95% of the 'lack of Care' to be due to a program of economy for which Mr. Parks [the game-keeper] is responsible only as the agent of those above him. I feel that Carey Baldwin did all that could be done with the limited supply of food and help provided for the care of the animals." But Hayes Perkins (privately, in his diary) faulted Parks for starving a number of animals to death by cutting down on their food so as to get himself a raise. And he blamed Baldwin, whom he despised, for murdering two giraffes, the tapir, a big sable, and other animals through starvation and ignorance.

Baldwin was not much liked by other ranch employees either. He was high-handed and had a volatile temper. Wilfred Lyons, who worked at San Simeon, recalled that

Carey Baldwin was a character. . . . He pulled some of the craziest things! For instance, we heard some shooting over by the zoo one Saturday afternoon. We went to see what it was, and Carey Baldwin had got mad at his radio and had it sitting out on a post and he was shooting at it with a 30/30 rifle. . . . [Some time later] I said to his wife: "Does Carey still lose his temper?" She said, "Lose his temper?! The other day he was writing and he got mad at his typewriter and he threw it in the swimming pool!"

Hearst spoke of dismissing Baldwin several times, but in the end kept him on for several more years. Nor did W.R.'s other plans for zoo improvements come to anything. Morgan drew up designs for a "chimp cage" with a pedestal, a trapeze, and a hanging ring for play, as well as plans for an animal complex with a pond and separate space for the elephant and enclosures for the remaining giraffes, camels, oryx, monkeys, birds, and other creatures. But neither these structures nor the animal hospital was ever built.

In a letter to Addison, written in November 1962, after the Chief's death, Baldwin reminisced, "In my time Hearst would not build an animal hospital and I was always careful how I reported deaths of animals as I was told he did not like the word death, so I reported 'Losses' of animals. As you know, he always wanted the animals free as much as possible. He was always greatly concerned that the animals be 'happy.' I believe he did think a lot of his animals and was essentially kind to them."

Hearst did care for his beasts, but in truth his zoo was less about the animals than about his own needs and dreams. Having begun to collect objects as a ten-year-old boy in search of security, he now gathered animals at San Simeon in part as a bulwark against disappointments and a means to make up for what he lacked. In some sense W.R. remained a child all his life, excited about his toys and impetuous when the game was not played as he wished. Charlie Chaplin recounted in his autobiography how during one of his stays at the ranch, the guests decided to play charades and divided into teams. Hearst complained that he was left out. "'Well,' said Jack Gilbert facetiously, 'we'll play a charade on our own, and act out the word "pillbox" — I'll be the box and you can be the pill.' But W.R. took it the wrong way; his voice quivered. 'I don't want to play your old charades,' he said, and with that he left the room, slamming the door behind him."

Hearst's love for animals was real, but it was as contradictory as other aspects of his character. He had enormous power and dignity, yet entertained childish delights and caprices. He disregarded societal pretensions and lived openly with his mistresses, yet insisted that there be no mingling between unmarried guests at the ranch. He spoke passionately against vivisection, yet raised an array of animals for food on the ranch: chickens, turkeys, pheasants, quail, ducks, geese, guinea hens, and cattle. He strictly curbed hunting on his property, yet paid rewards for killing pests. One time, at Wyntoon, his northern California estate, his and Marion's dachshunds, Helen and Gandhi, got into a fight with some porcupines and had a bunch of quills stuck in their noses. Hearst, very upset, put a bounty of five dollars on every porcupine that could be killed in the area. While fussing over individual pets, he failed to refurbish his zoo because it would interfere with his notion of natural scenery. Hearst's son Bill Jr. wrote with eloquence his father's baffling and fascinating qualities:

> He was a Caesar. He had an inferiority complex.
>
> He was a Charlemagne. He was shy and unassuming.
>
> He was a Napoleon. He was indecisive.
>
> He was a megalomaniac. He was a reserved, restrained, private man.
>
> He was ruthless, reckless, a rogue. He was a keen competitor but a man of principle . . . , demonstrably kind, a gentleman of impeccable manner and speech.
>
> He was one of the most hated men in America. He was a man of vision and greatness.
>
> He was a muckraking sensationalist, a terror in print. He was one of the greatest technical innovators and public crusaders in the history of American journalism.
>
> He was an enigma, two different men, a human contradiction. He was many things, but one for certain: a genius.

And Charlie Chaplin wrote in his memoirs:

> If I were asked what personality in my life has made the deepest impression on me, I would say the late William Randolph

Hearst. I should explain that the impression was not always a pleasant one — although he had commendable qualities. It was the enigma of his personality that fascinated me, his boyishness, his shrewdness, his kindness, his ruthlessness, his immense power and wealth, and above all this genuine naturalness.

In 1934, when much of the work on the Enchanted Hill was completed, the zoo housed hundreds of marvelous creatures, and the ranch drew distinguished guests. In addition to the movie stars, Winston Churchill, George Bernard Shaw, P. G. Wodehouse, Edwin Hubble (the creator of the telescope), Irving Berlin, and others came to visit. At this point Hearst did what royalty had been doing for centuries: he dispatched several of his animals as a memorable diplomatic gift.

The *American Weekly* announced the event in a splashy headline: "First Live Bison Ever Seen in Japan. Mr. Hearst Ships Three of the Huge, Shaggy Creatures from His Private 'Zoo' on His California Ranch to the Astonishment of the People of Tokyo and a Special 'Buffalo Week' Is Declared." The article went on to explain that Hearst had recently received an ancient samurai suit of armor from Matsutaro Shoriki, president of Tokyo's *Yomiuri Shimbun*, the largest newspaper in Japan. The gift followed an agreement for the exchange of news between the *Yomiuri Shimbun* and Hearst's papers. Hearst wanted to reciprocate with an equally old and interesting American gift and decided to send Shoriki a few of his bison — animals completely unknown in Japan.

A huge bull and two smaller females were loaded on a Japanese ship and dispatched over the Pacific. Their arrival caused both delight and anxiety in Japan. Shoriki contacted the head of Tokyo's Ueno Zoo, Tadamichi Koga, with a request to house the bison. Koga replied that he had very little free space but promised to make room, "no matter if some of the other animals had to sit in each other's laps." He then radioed the captain of the ship that was ferrying the bison from California to inquire about their diet. "Captain Okubo," the newspaper reported, "replied that they were rather seasick, showing little interest in their food, but nevertheless managed to take a little nourishment every day, averaging about 20 pounds of oats and a few bushels of wheat straw apiece. The bull washed this down with ten gallons of water daily while his consorts contented themselves with only seven and a half each."

Armed with this intelligence, Koga cast a critical eye over his zoo. The largest enclosure was occupied by three camels. "America, he knew, had just repudiated prohibition, therefore what could be more fitting than to oust these emblems of a lost cause in favor of that ten-gallon-a-day American drinker and his family?" The camels were moved out of their quarters, and the zookeepers began to stock up on oats and straw. Meanwhile, schoolchildren across the nation learned to draw the bison in anticipation of their arrival.

The landing of the much-awaited foreigners at the port of Yokohama was heralded on the front page of the *Yomiuri Shimbun*: "Wild Bison Landed on Japan's Soil for the First Time." As the honored guests journeyed from the port to Tokyo aboard a convoy of trucks, throngs of curious citizens flocked to gawk at them along the route, frequently holding up the motorcade. The bison were disembarked at the zoo without a glitch and were greeted in an official ceremony the following day. A small boy dressed in a sailor suit was chosen to present a bouquet to the exotic strangers, handing it to the male bison through the bars of his new home. The bull "showed that the flowers were accept-able by eating them. Perhaps it would have looked a little better if the bull had shared them with the lady bison, but he didn't." A week of celebrations followed, with countless visitors streaming into the zoo to marvel at the outlandish creatures sent to their country by what must have been the most powerful man in America.

*   *   *

HEARST WENT ON acquiring animals and artwork for San Simeon throughout the Depression, as if he were impervious to the economic hardships crippling the nation. George Loorz, Hearst's construction superintendent in the 1930s, wrote to Julia Morgan in October 1935:

> Mr. Hearst walked into the office in splendid spirits about five last night and we spent an hour of building and creating new projects. An airport on a hilltop above the fog was one. Oh boy, it would be an expensive project if it goes ahead. Sooner or later he will do something. In thirty minutes he moved the zoo, constructed new bear grottos and divided the present ones for cats. He leveled animal hill out here. We tore down the shop and lowered a dozen oak trees in groups of five, making tremendous concrete boxes, excavating under them and letting the trees right down into position. Moving one tree at a time is a big job, moving a close group of about five is still bigger. Anyway he laughed a lot and seemed happy so we will put it down as a successful interview.

But by 1936 Hearst's fortune took a plunge. The Depression was finally having an impact on his publishing empire. More damaging yet were his own actions. For the past few years he had been speaking out vehemently against Roosevelt, the New Deal, and communism, and it had damaged his image and the popularity of his newspapers. Hearst faulted Roosevelt for being an internationalist. (Hearst staunchly opposed America's involvement in European affairs.) He was incensed at the National Recovery Administration for wanting to raise the wages and reduce the working hours of newspaper employees. (Although he had defended such provisions for other sectors of labor, Hearst now saw their application by government to newspapers as a violation of the First Amendment.) He railed against New Dealers for "wasting people's money in futile and fantastic experiments," endangering free enterprise, and encouraging newspaper employees to unionize — which threatened his control over his papers and their content. He even compared the New Deal to European fascism.

All these declarations made him more than ever a figure of controversy and attack. Harold Ickes, FDR's secretary of the interior and head of the Public Works Administration, wrote in his diary on August 30, 1936, that there was "more widespread anti-Hearst feeling among the people than there has been for a great many years, if ever. I am told that when his name appears on the screen in some movie theaters, he is hissed, and there are anti-Hearst clubs being organized in some parts of the country."

The more Hearst propounded his views in his editorials and on the front page of his papers, the more he alienated readers who supported Roosevelt and the New Deal. The boycotts of Hearst publications by Communists, who organized the People's Committee Against Hearst, and by the American Newspaper Guild, which was infuriated at Hearst's opposition to newspaper unions, were joined by many people who had been buying his papers for decades. As a result, circulation and advertising plummeted, as did revenues. Yet W.R. continued to spend extravagantly on real estate, art, animals, and other luxuries. He was so used to indulging his zeal for collecting that he just could not stop.

In truth, Hearst had been on the brink of financial catastrophe for decades, his expenses always far outpacing his income. But thus far he had managed to fund his old debts by raising new capital through bonds and stock issued by the Hearst publishing corporation. Now his magazines and papers did not generate enough income to pay off the interest on his loans and the dividends on his stocks and bonds. And banks were no longer willing to lend to him because of his papers' financial losses and his deteriorating reputation.

In 1937 a crisis hit. Hearst and his corporation were $88 million in debt, of which $39 million was scheduled for repayment within a year. There was no money to settle these bills. The first payment, of a million dollars, was due immediately. As soon as Marion Davies heard about it, she called her business manager and begged, "Get me a million dollars right away. I want to sell everything I've got — everything." He sold off her real estate and jewelry and raised the required sum. Of course W.R. refused to take it, although Marion eventually persuaded him. Still, it was just a tiny portion of what he needed. On May 25 Hearst and Davies boarded a train to New York to meet with his advisers and determine how to keep his empire from ruin.

As David Nasaw writes,

> The unthinkable had come to pass. For fifty years, Hearst had ruled his empire as autocratically as his heroes Julius Caesar and Napoleon Bonaparte had theirs. He had trusted no one, rejected suggestions that he share power or delegate decision-making, and refused to name a successor. At age seventy-four, he was as hearty as ever and convinced that if left alone he could once again pull off a miracle. But no one, with the possible exception of Marion, believed him capable of making the tough decisions that were necessary and cutting back on personal and corporate spending. The Chief was a builder, not a wrecker; an accumulator, not a liquidator.

Hearst's board of advisers resolved that they would now manage the Chief's affairs. Following their meeting in New York, they devised a salvage plan: Hearst would drastically cut his personal expenses, dispose of losing papers, sell off his overmortgaged real estate, and put part of his art collection up for sale. It was all incredibly painful and humiliating, but there was no choice. Hearst returned to San Simeon "a pathetic, broken man" and ordered Julia Morgan "to stop work entirely." Morgan relayed to the ranch manager that "Mr. Hearst today instructed me to tell you to close up the Hilltop, dispensing with the services of everyone who is not actually required to keep the interior of the castle and house in clean condition and prevent unnecessary deterioration." Half the gardeners and most of the household staff and other ranch employees were let go. The zoo animals were to be sold or given away. "I guess I'm through," Hearst told Davies.

Too numerous for any single recipient, the animals had to be distributed among several zoos. The Fleishhacker Zoo took the chimpanzees, one rhesus monkey, two sloth bears (Gooloff and Gooluff), four black leopards, three coatimundis, and eleven white fallow deer. Edmund Heller, director of the zoo, expressed special delight with the chimpanzee family because they are "more vivacious and alert than any of the other apes. The baby [Darwina] is the first chimpanzee to be born on the Pacific Coast and from a Zoological, as well as an exhibition standpoint, is of much value. The Sloth Bears are new to our collection and are very distinctive in appearance due to their long fox-like muzzles and long shaggy hair."

The California Zoological Society in Los Angeles got a pair of spider monkeys, a male sun bear, a male Russian bear, two Sumatran tigers, two jaguars, one tortoise, three African porcupines, and the elephant Marianne. The vice president of the society assured Hearst that "suitable credit plates bearing the words 'Donated to the children of Los Angeles by Mr. William Randolph Hearst' will, of course, be placed on each and every den and cage in which those things Mr. Hearst has donated are housed. . . . The Elephant, Mary Ann [sic], has been going through her daily training routine, and while she was quite tricky in the beginning, she is a very apt scholar, and before many months will be carrying children on her back."

Two lions, one pair of spotted leopards, and one California mountain lion were dispatched to the San Antonio Zoo. The San Diego Zoo was the recipient of one black leopard and two emus.

And the Central Park Menagerie in New York took delivery of one American black bear, two female lions, one pair of kinkajous, and three spotted leopards.

Of course, being who he was, Hearst could not part with all of his pets. He insisted on retaining the "field and forest" animals that could largely sustain themselves by grazing on the hillsides of the ranch (although in dry weather they still had to be supplied with feed). His reduced menagerie consisted of 8 nilgais, 10 oryx, 6 waterbucks, 2 gnus, 2 blesboks, 56 blackbucks, 89 axis deer, 320 white deer, 70 elk, 2 barasingha deer, 24 bison, 14 kangaroos, 18 tahr goats, 15 ibex, 19 llamas, 3 giraffes, 5 yaks, 24 sambar deer, 10 zebras, 7 camels, 4 ostriches, 3 cassowaries, 30 emus, 5 rheas, 3 elands, 4 water buffalo, 3 polar bears, 2 American black bears, 2 eagles, and 6 grizzlies.

Even after dispersing most of his hilltop menagerie, W.R. could not quite give up acquiring rare beasts. In March 1938 he telegrammed the animal dealer Louis Ruhe in New York: "Do you know where we could get a pair of pandas? Please reply collect care Los Angeles Examiner." He never got them, probably much to his advisers' relief.

THE CURTAILING OF the zoo did not mean the end of Hearst's involvement with animals. In fact, bereft of his menagerie, he resumed with great energy his crusade on behalf of abused animals, publishing more articles about them than ever. Still in control of the content of his newspapers, W.R. reviewed the text of every editorial and major article before it went into print, and on March 10, 1940, he began to write his own column, called "In the News," which appeared on the front page of his papers several times a week. He turned frequently to the subject of cruelty to animals.

The defeat of a number of antivivisection bills in the 1910s and 1920s had sent the movement into decline, but with the expansion of medical research during and after World War II, the demand for animals soared and stirred a resurgence of antivivisection activity. Hearst took up this cause with vigor, condemning in particular the use of dogs for medical experiments.

The love of dogs had been a constant throughout Hearst's life. It had begun with his childhood pals Pompey, Caesar, and Prince. While at Harvard he had worried about the dogs on his father's ranch: "Dear Papa, I can never rest easy as long as I remember that those beautiful dogs are free to hang, drown, or otherwise put an end to themselves. I shall never be happy until I see them all safely housed in a healthy and commodious kennel and carefully cared for by a competent man whose sole business it shall be to take care of them." Hearst's antivivisection position was inspired by this affection and by his outrage that stray as well as pet dogs were abducted and sold to medical labs.

"Are we the nation of sentimentalists or Sadists?" he asked in his "In the News" column on February 20, 1941.

Why do we allow them [dogs] to be vivisected in awful agony by hordes of sadistic medical students and by almost any idle experimenter, amateur or professional, who wants to learn something useful or else just to find out how good and faithful and devoted and trustful animals can be under torture?

Mind you, your columnist is not opposed to vivisection where it is necessary.

But why allow promiscuous vivisection, and why vivisect man's most devoted friend?

Are there not rats and rabbits and goats and guinea pigs enough in the world?

Why not vivisect the pests? . . .

And why vivisect promiscuously anyhow?

We are the only highly civilized nation in the world that allows it. . . . Even in far less (presumably) civilized countries than our own you cannot go in and gather up a pound full of dogs, some of them lost pets, and carry them off to be stretched on racks and cut up alive and sliced apart in every quivering muscle and nerve to make a hideous, harrowing holiday, and to teach the young [the] idea [of] not helpful surgery but vicious cruelty.

Sympathetic readers sent Hearst glowing letters. Mrs. L. L. Kelsey of Kirkland, Washington, wrote that his column

was a terrible shock to me. I presume that many people, like myself, have not known that dogs are used for vivisection. All experiments that we see illustrated in papers and magazines are made with rats or mice or guinea pigs. It is horrible. . . .

With your great influence and wide publications, I am sure you can arouse public feeling to such an extent that the public would back a law prohibiting the vivisection of dogs and cats.

Hearst's efforts were, in fact, yielding some results by effecting the passage or defeat of bills regarding vivisection. Members of the Washington Anti-Vivisection Society wrote enthusiastically:

We, who have been fighting for years for just common justice and humaneness for animals, can never adequately express our appreciation of the stand you took, in your paper, in the matter of vivisection of dogs. The reaction on the public was so tremendous that I am sure this was a big factor in the defeat of that terrible bill in your state, designed to send all impounded dogs to the laboratories.

Hearst also received letters of appreciation for his defense of other animals, especially those sacrificed in the making of films. "Dear Mr. Hearst," wrote one reader in January 1941, "I agree with you 99% of the time and applaud your crusades against cruelty to horses in the movies."

Hearst continued to speak on behalf of animals through the

1940s, when the war led to an increase in vivisections.* "Noted Churchmen Brand Vivisection Anti-Christian, Sadistic Cruelty" proclaimed a Hearst newspaper editorial on March 21, 1946. The column published statements by two cardinals, a professor of theology at the University of Graz in Austria, and a reverend from Nottingham, England. "Pets Sold for Torture at Night Auction" read the headline over a spread of photographs showing animals on their way to vivisectors in the papers on Sunday, March 2, 1947. An image of a tall stack of cages containing dogs was captioned: "Doomed to Torture, these terrified dogs await buyer at night auction of potential vivisection victims. The cruel bartering took place at Lancaster, Pa., and was only one of several such sales last week. Pets thus sold were later traced to big city laboratories where their lives will end on a torture table." Another caption declared: "Jammed into Cages, these abused pets await their turn to be sold. The frightful facts behind this cruel traffic are revealed for the first time today as a result of an investigation conducted by the Baltimore American and News-Post, Hearst newspapers."

AMERICA'S ENTRY INTO World War II, which Hearst vehemently opposed, saved his publishing empire. As people looked hungrily for news from Europe, the circulation of Hearst's papers increased, as did advertising. At the same time, the Hearst corporation began to license its comic characters — especially Popeye and Blondie — for radio, animation, children's books, and knickknacks. By early 1945 W.R. had regained control of his finances and presided over an empire of seventeen daily papers, four radio stations, nine American and three English magazines, a wire service, a feature service, and a Sunday supplement. He resumed construction at San Simeon, and although he had stopped ac-

*Not that he was unconcerned with people; at the onset of the war he had personally spoken to Hitler in the hope of halting his anti-Semitic policies, an effort as commendable as it was ineffectual.

quiring exotic animals, he kept dozens of dogs in his kennel, including seventy-three dachshunds.

Hearst's affection for dogs mushroomed in the same way his collecting of other animals and works of art had. He loved dachshunds the most, but also kept Great Danes, Russian wolfhounds, greyhounds, Kerry blue terriers, and Boston bull terriers. The breeds were housed separately, so as not to mix their genes. All received balanced, cooked meals of meat and vegetables. And they inhabited clean, well-ventilated quarters — much better maintained than Hearst's zoo had been. Dr. Charles White, who visited Hearst's kennel in May 1941 to examine and vaccinate its inhabitants, wrote an enthusiastic report: "The floors and woodwork were immaculate and the runs freshly raked. It is a real pleasure to see dogs living in such conditions."

While most of Hearst's dogs dwelled in this communal heaven, W.R. and Marion's favorite short-haired dachshunds, Helen and Gandhi, had the run of the castle. During dinners in the Refectory they sat on velvet cushions in the choir stalls that stood along the walls. And when Hearst, Davies, and their guests proceeded to watch movies in the plush, red-upholstered theater off the billiard room, the dogs perched next to their masters. Hearst was brokenhearted when Helen died and honored their bond in his "In the News" column.

A boy and his dog are no more inseparable companions than an old fellow and his dog. To his dog he is just as good as he ever was — maybe better because he is more appreciative of the dog's devotion. Anyhow, the dog and the old guy understand each other and get along "just swell." So I do miss Helen. I was very fond of her.

She always slept in a big chair in my room and her solicitous gaze followed me to bed at night and was the first thing to greet me when I woke in the morning. Then when I arose she begged me for the special distinction of being put in my bed, and there she lay in luxurious enjoyment of the proud privilege until I was ready to leave. . . .

Aldous Huxley says: "Every dog thinks its master Napoleon, hence the popularity of dogs." That is not the strict truth. Every dog adores its master notwithstanding the master's imperfections, of which it is probably acutely aware . . . because love creates love, devotion inspires devotion, unselfishness begets unselfishness and self-sacrifice, and that fact is more than a commendable quality in the animal kingdom. It is the eventual hope of humanity.

Helen died in my bed and in my arms. I have buried her on the hillside overlooking the green lawn — where she used to run — and surrounded by the flowers. I will not need a monument to remember her. But I am placing over her little grave a stone with the inscription — "Here lies dearest Helen — my devoted friend."

Age caught up with Hearst as well. In early 1947, when he was almost eighty-four, he developed a dangerously irregular heartbeat and possibly suffered a mild heart attack. His doctors ordered him to stop working and move from the remote San Simeon to Los Angeles, where he could get prompt medical help in case of further trouble.

On May 2, 1947, W.R. and Marion descended the Enchanted Hill for the last time. As their car wound its way past the slopes and meadows of the ranch, tears streamed down W.R.'s face. Marion leaned over to wipe them away. "We'll come back, W.R., you'll see." But it was the last time he would see his dream home — the haven where he had lived as he pleased, free from parental supervision and political disappointment and surrounded by nature, art, and the animals he loved.

As Frances Marion recalled of this complex and captivating man,

I have heard people say that Mr. Hearst was cold and unfeeling; he may have been to some, but he never was with me. . . . He seemed to be suspicious of strangers and did not meet people well. When you got to know him, however, you found a very warm and personable individual with a good sense of humor. Mr. Hearst always had a lot on his mind, when you talked to him, he might be half listening to you while also thinking about the press room. This would give an impression of him being distant and cool and aloof. . . . But Mr. Hearst was not aloof. He was always concerned about the "little man" and was always very kind and generous to his friends and his employees.

This generosity was apparent in his reception of his guests at San Simeon, his defense of abused animals, and his random acts of kindness, noted by those close to him. As Marion Davies recalled:

Once we were driving in France. There were about twelve cars. W.R. had a chauffeur named Hall who got a little drunk that day over the wine at lunch. We were passing through a small out-of-the-way village near the coastline when he hit a goose.

Mr. Hearst said, "You're fired. But first take the goose and go back to the house and say that it was killed. Then I'll drive." Well, I would rather drive with Hall drunk than W.R. sober, because W.R. was a wild driver. But we waited and watched, and when a woman answered the door of the farmhouse, W.R. got out of the car and went over. . . .

When they came back, Hall rode in another car, and W.R. drove to Bordeaux. I did not find out until we got back to Paris that W.R. had arranged for that woman to have a new car, a Renault. He had it delivered to her with a goose inside.

EPILOGUE:

LITTLE PEOPLE IN FURRY SUITS

In 1938, when William Randolph Hearst unsuccessfully sought to obtain giant pandas, they were great rarities. The first panda to reach the West had been brought to the Museum of Natural History in Paris in 1869 by the French missionary Père Armand David. Though only a stuffed specimen, this strange and beautiful animal was a revelation to the Europeans, and it prompted a wave of hunts for more such beasts. But giant pandas are reclusive and hard to find, and the few that Westerners stumbled upon in the late nineteenth and early twentieth centuries were shot as trophies of sport and science. The sons of President Theodore Roosevelt, Theodore Jr. and Kermit, gained the dubious distinction of being the first Americans to kill a giant panda in the wild in 1929.

The credit for bringing the first live panda to the West was claimed by a thirty-five-year-old New York socialite named Ruth Harkness. Her globe-trotting adventurer husband, William — who had captured Komodo dragons in the Dutch East Indies — went to China in search of a live panda two weeks after their wedding in 1934. William died of an illness in February 1936, in Shanghai, before ever reaching the panda region. Before long his intrepid and flamboyant wife resolutely picked up where he left off — even retailoring his expedition clothes so they would fit her. She engaged an American-born Chinese hunter, Quentin

Young (Yang Tilin), as her partner (they actually became lovers) and set off in search of the elusive animals.

Braving physical danger and hardship, hiking in unmapped and trackless terrain, crawling on hands and knees through water-saturated bamboo thickets, Ruth Harkness was rewarded for her efforts. On November 9, 1936, her small expedition stumbled upon a baby panda, a mere three-pound black-and-white fuzz ball. Harkness had had the perspicacity to bring along baby bottles and milk, and thanks to these supplies, she managed to nurse her prize and keep it alive and well. Ecstatic, she boarded the liner *President McKinley* in Shanghai on December 2 and arrived triumphant in San Francisco on December 18, with baby Su Lin (mistakenly identified as a female) cradled in her arms. The adorable cub created a sensation — "Panda-monium," the headlines screamed — and was covered rapturously by newspapers across America. Huge crowds assembled everywhere Harkness appeared, eager to see her feed the baby bear from a bottle and carry it around like a child. Little wonder that Hearst was so interested in getting a panda for San Simeon.

Su Lin, who ended up at Chicago's Brookfield Zoo, so enchanted Americans and Europeans that he was credited with ending the killing of giant pandas for sport and spurring the desire to obtain more live pandas for Western zoos. Between 1937 and 1946 fourteen live animals made it to Europe and America. A number of others probably died en route. But because few survived long in captivity and none of them mated, these early ambassadors soon died out. Then civil war and the formation of the People's Republic of China in 1949 put an end to imports for more than twenty years.

The story goes that at a state dinner during President Richard Nixon's historic visit to China in February 1972, First Lady Pat Nixon picked up a cigarette holder decorated with pictures of pandas and commented on how much she loved these animals. In that case, Chairman Mao Zedong replied magnanimously, he would give her some. Shortly thereafter Hsing-Hsing ("Shining Star") and Ling-Ling ("Darling Little Girl") were sent to the National Zoo in Washington, D.C., as symbols of the renewed friendship between the two nations. In a gesture of reciprocity the United States dispatched to China a pair of Alaskan musk oxen named Milton and Matilda. Exotic animals clearly had not lost their potency as agents of international diplomacy.

Hsing-Hsing and Ling-Ling, protected by armed guards, arrived at the National Zoo on a breezy April day in 1972. As U.S. and Chinese officials looked on, the two panda cubs emerged from their green-lacquered crates. Ling-Ling, described by the keepers as "the rough-and-ready type," charmed viewers immediately by batting her paws, rolling over, and jumping up and down on the pile of logs in her new home. More than twenty thousand people visited the pandas during their first day on exhibit, and millions more followed in the years to come.

The pandas became ambassadors for two causes: they sealed a major political breakthrough and came to symbolize all endangered animals, helping to introduce millions of people to the issue of wildlife conservation. In fact, a key purpose of bringing the pandas to the National Zoo was to try to mate them so as to augment their rapidly shrinking population in the wild — a mere one thousand at the time.

The pair's first reproductive attempts in the mid-1970s were something of a comic opera. Hsing-Hsing, it seemed, was unclear on female anatomy, and so Ling-Ling's ear flap, wrist, and right foot all served as targets of his amorous attempts. "Ling-Ling tolerated this for a while under the optimistic impression that it could be classified as foreplay," wrote Judith Martin in the *Washington Post* in 1977 (before she became the nationally syndicated etiquette columnist Miss Manners). "Then she did what any normal, healthy woman would do — she hauled off and swatted him one." As time went on, Ling-Ling and Hsing-Hsing did manage to produce five offspring, a great coup given pandas' exceedingly tricky reproductive behavior (female pandas ovulate only once a year and are interested in mating for only two or three days per cycle), but none of these cubs lived longer than a few hours. In those days breeding pandas in captivity had proved successful only in China and Mexico, where a modern zoo had been set up in 1923 on the site of Montezuma's menagerie.

Despite their reproductive difficulties, Ling-Ling and Hsing-Hsing enjoyed a long and pampered life in Washington. But with time they inevitably declined. Ling-Ling died of heart failure in late December 1992 at the age of twenty-three (a panda's life span can range from about fifteen to thirty years). She received almost as much coverage in the media as the legendary ballet dancer Rudolf Nureyev, who died the following week. Five years later Hsing-Hsing was diagnosed with testicular cancer. Surgery was successful, but the twenty-six-year-old panda steadily weakened. He suffered from arthritis, and by May 1999 had developed a fatal kidney disease. Lethargic and listless, everyone's favorite "teddy bear" would no longer eat and soon lost fifty pounds. Worried zookeepers tempted him with Starbucks blueberry muffins — he would have no other — in which his medicine was concealed. Some days they closed the Panda House to allow Hsing-Hsing to rest or receive treatment, posting a sign to inform disappointed visitors that Hsing-Hsing was "not feeling very well."

As his condition worsened, animal lovers and schoolchildren from across the country flooded the zoo with messages, many of them addressed directly to the panda. On Friday, June 4, 1999, the *Washington Post* printed several of them under the rubric "To the Most Noble Creature in D.C."

Dear Hsing-Hsing,

You will never know how much I love you. Even though you are a wild animal and never would be able to return my affections physically, emotionally you have brought more joy to me than you will ever know. Ever since your arrival when I was a little boy in second grade, I have visited you at least once every year. I hope you get better soon, and if not, I hope you have a quick and painless death. Shih shih for everything, Bright Star. — Chris, Washington, D.C.

Dear Hsing-Hsing,

I love you very much. When my kidneys hurt, I drink tons of cranberry juice. This always helps — I do not know why. Tell the zoo keepers that you need several glasses a day.

I hope you feel better soon. All my love, — Cathy

My prayers go out for Hsing-Hsing. I know he must be lonely as he has no companion, in addition to experiencing the discomfort that he is going through with his illness. Tears came to my eyes as I was reading the article. I cried when Ling-Ling lost her newborn cubs. And of course I cried when she passed a few years ago. I have shed more tears over the life of Hsing-Hsing and Ling-Ling than I've shed over family members. As all animals are God's creatures, Hsing-Hsing too is in His hands. My prayers also go out to those employees who are responsible for his daily well-being. I know his illness is having a profound affect [sic] on them also. — Linda Smith

Like Ling-Ling's death in 1992, Hsing-Hsing's passing in 1999 (he was euthanized on November 28) unleashed a torrent of grief across the United States and abroad. Thousands of cards, letters, drawings, mementos, and e-mail messages poured into the zoo, and flowers piled up in front of the pandas' empty enclosure.

In an article titled "The Panda Puzzle," published in the *Washington Post* on December 1, 1999, David Ignatius asked, "How to account for the outpouring of public grief over the death of Hsing-Hsing?" He went on to reflect that "part of our feeling for Hsing-

Hsing must be anthropomorphism. We endow Panda bears with quasi-human qualities." Of course Hsing-Hsing was also a celebrity. "He was undisputably the most famous animal in the world," Albert J. from Washington observed in an e-mail message to washingtonpost.com. Ignatius continued:

Perhaps we grieved for him the way we grieved for JFK Jr. or Diana — celebrities we felt as if we knew but didn't. Indeed, it was the not knowing — the perfect, media-framed portrait — that allowed the tears to flow so easily for many of us. . . . The danger of our media-saturated environment is that it leads us to confuse . . . sentimentality and real grief — and to imagine that they're the same. My friend Garrett Epps, a law professor and sometime novelist, recalled this week the story in the papers a few years ago about a blind man and his seeing-eye dog, who were both injured by a runaway taxicab in New York City. The dog, Smokey, got hundreds of get-well cards from strangers. The blind man received just four. It made people feel good to love the animal, not so the ordinary man.

In our modern, prosperous, but emotionally needy society, we often make animals into our children or closest friends — we think of them as little people in furry suits. Ling-Ling and Hsing-Hsing, in particular, seemed so sweet and cuddly that they became everyone's pets. As the director of the National Zoo, Michael H. Robinson, mused:

Perhaps the appeal results from the animal's baby-like appearance: the round, snub-nosed face; the domed head; rounded, upright ears; soulful, black eye-patches. Add to this the fact that giant pandas sit upright and erect on their haunches with their short legs jutting out . . . [and] grasp bamboo stalks with a front paw that looks like a child's hand in a mitten. . . . Add all these physical traits together and the panda becomes the cuddly bear of human fables and folklore. Adorable! Charming! Beguiling! Mysterious!

In fact, giant pandas are wild and dangerous animals. Ling-Ling, for example, once mauled a keeper who startled her in her cage.

Given the tremendous appeal of pandas in general, and in the wake of Ling-Ling's and Hsing-Hsing's popularity in particular, numerous zoos sought to procure their own Chinese bears. But in the 1980s China stopped sending them out as gifts. Instead, it began to "lease" them for short periods, charging $100,000 per animal per month. The price did not deter many zoos, for they could recoup the steep fee through admission tickets, so more and more zoos, as well as Disney World and the Michigan State Fair, clamored for rentals. In 1988, however, the U.S. Fish and Wildlife Service decided to ban panda imports, arguing that such commercial use of these highly endangered animals hampered efforts to conserve and breed them.

In 1998, just as Hsing-Hsing was experiencing his final decline, the moratorium was lifted. As the aged veteran of cold war diplomacy neared the end of his life, the National Zoo began quiet negotiations with Chinese authorities to secure new giant pandas. In addition to an import permit from the U.S. Fish and Wildlife Service, a panda loan required approval by senior Chinese officials. The animals were so rare, valuable, and politically visible that their movements were a matter of national interest — especially when they were intended for a zoo in the U.S. capital.

The negotiations were hampered by various impediments. By 1998 the Chinese were requesting $10 million for a ten-year loan of two pandas to the National Zoo. Being a public institution, the National Zoo does not charge admission and it balked at the price. For a while the two sides haggled over money. Then, in July 1999, during the Serbian war, the Americans mistakenly bombed the Chinese embassy in Belgrade. The same year a scientist at the Los Alamos National Laboratory in New Mexico was accused of sharing U.S. nuclear secrets with China. A Chinese embassy spokesman declared that reaching a panda agreement with Washington would be helpful, given the strained relations between the two countries.

In 2000, as the National Zoo was finally filing a permit application for the pandas, Congress had begun to debate whether to renew China's most favored nation trade status or to deny it because of the regime's dismal record on human rights. It was a tense period, and the general downturn in Sino-American relations threatened to scuttle a panda deal. "Pandas are China's national symbols. They are tokens of friendship, and are themselves priceless," said Wang Weiming, head of the panda department at the Beijing Zoo. "The most important thing is to see the American government's attitude."

In May 2000, despite the ongoing controversy over human rights abuses, President Bill Clinton granted China permanent most favored nation status. The National Zoo raised the $10 million for the panda loan through donations from corporations and private sponsors, and an accord with the Chinese was reached. In October the U.S. Fish and Wildlife Service issued the National Zoo a panda import permit, and on December 6 two cubs arrived in Washington, D.C. Liu Xiaoming, chargé d'affaires of the Chinese embassy in the United States, called them "VIPs — Very Important Pandas — who have brought our two great nations closer together once again."

The female, Mei Xiang ("Beautiful Fragrance"), and the male, Tian Tian ("More and More"), were both born at the China Research and Conservation Center for the Giant Panda in Wolong, Sichuan province. They flew to the United States on a FedEx jet named *PandaOne*. Their debut in Washington was featured live on all the major television networks, and the frisky youngsters instantly captivated the public. The day after the panda exhibit opened, the *Washington Post* published an eight-page supplement on the animals, including a plan of their enclosure and copious details about their diet and habits. Using banner headlines such as "Pandamonium" and "Pandamania," television stations gave hourly updates on the progress of the adorable cubs. And President Clinton honored them with their first official visit, peppering keepers with questions and expressing a particular interest in their food and appetites.

A ten-person team was assigned to care for the two bears, the National Zoo having committed to a long-term research and conservation program designed to enhance the survival of giant pandas. The new panda enclosure, refurbished for $1.8 million, was planted with Sichuan firs and Chinese red cedars and bathed in fog and mist to replicate the animals' natural habitat. Rocks and pools were provided for the pandas' pleasure, and a pair of air-conditioned caves gave the cold-loving bears a refuge from Washington's stifling summer heat. Not a bad life, as captivity goes.

The pandas sleep in separate quarters, but their bedrooms are unlocked at 7:00 A.M. In the early days at the zoo, Mei Xiang liked to sleep in; Tian Tian tended to be bouncy and full of energy. Some mornings, growing impatient, Tian Tian would roll on Mei Xiang or step all over her to initiate play. Lest the pandas grow bored with each other, the zoo staff offers them additional stimulation, called "enrichment." To supplement their regular feedings, they get high-fiber biscuits, boxes stuffed with hay, and tubs of water filled with apples and carrots. Tian Tian dives right in; Mei Xiang, ladylike, quietly eats one piece at a time. No other animals have such a lavish lifestyle or receive so much attention to satisfy their every need.

As much as the pandas have captured people's hearts, they are, like all other exotic animals, more than mere receptacles for our own feelings or substitutes for human connections. "The panda has not evolved to amuse humankind," wrote panda scientist George Schaller. They are a discrete species with a physiology and behavior of their own, which we need to understand better if we are to safeguard them and continue to enjoy them as part of our world. The sense of wonder that compelled past generations to collect and display exotic animals now inspires us to save them from the edge of extinction — a state to which we have driven them. Hearteningly, the magnetic appeal of pandas — which has been the linchpin of their survival — seems to be leading us to extend similar care to other, less glamorous beasts.

The saga of the giant pandas, like the stories of the other animals in this book, provides a mirror of our times. As mascots for the World Wildlife Fund, pandas have become symbols of our concern with the preservation of endangered species and ecological systems. At the same time, the great attention devoted to both sets of pandas demonstrates that rare animals still serve as effective pawns in international politics. We have come a long way from treating wild beasts as war machines, slaughtering them by the hundreds for entertainment, and collecting them in the course of empire building. Our terror and awe of exotic animals have diminished as a result of familiarity. But our fascination with them remains. Perhaps we sense that our fates are inextricably intertwined — that without them there would be no us.

ACKNOWLEDGMENTS

I t has been a delight to write this book, all the more so be-cause so many people have offered me their generous help and enthusiastic support as I searched for menageries through the ages and tried to understand cultures and eras often foreign to me.

From the beginning of this project, when it was a mere embryo, and in the course of its evolution and maturity, my agent, Rob McQuilkin, has been a tireless champion and enthusiastic cheer-leader. I am deeply grateful to him for believing in this book and for making it happen. My editor, Asya Muchnick, fell in love with the idea and through her meticulous, intelligent, creative, and con-siderate critique made the final product immeasurably better. The copyeditor, Barb Jatkola, polished the manuscript with admirable thoroughness. My unofficial editors — Harold Freiman, Lorna Bieber, my parents, Alex and Irene Belozersky, and especially Audra Crane — strengthened individual chapters through their thought-ful reading and astute suggestions. So did my long-term editor and most loyal, patient, and affectionate supporter, Ken Lapatin.

The chapters on Ptolemy Philadelphos and Pompey the Great also benefited greatly from discussions with and advice from Kathleen Coleman, Erich Gruen, Lucy Blue, Liliane Bodson, Claire Calcagno, and Adrienne Mayor. In writing about Lorenzo de' Medici and the Mamluks, I profited from the generosity of Barry Flood, Avinoam Shalom, Sylvia Auld, Carl Petry, and William Wallace. Aztec culture and history became clearer to me thanks to Patricia McAnany, Donald Altschiller, Patricia Anawalt, and Alistair Cochran, who enlightened me on the medical practicalities of ripping a living heart out of a human body. Amara Solari kindly shared with me her master's thesis on Montezuma's menagerie. Mark Meadow and Jeffrey Chips Smith answered my queries about Rudolf. Gail Feigenbaum led me to Josephine's menagerie by mentioning the black swans at Malmaison. And once I began to look into how these Australian birds first came to France, Kate Akerman, Diana Jones, and Peta Osborne at the Western Australian Museum offered great assistance. In working on Hearst's zoo, I was most fortunate to receive a gracious welcome and unstinting help from Keri Collins, Hoyt Fileds, Victoria Kastner, and Jana Seely at the Hearst Castle; Nancy Loe and Ken Kenyon at the Kennedy Library at California Polytechnic University; and David Kessler at the Bancroft Library at the University of California at Berkeley. Mary Levkoff also kindly shared her extensive knowledge of Hearst with me. And Annie Hall helped me with archival materials at the New England Anti-Vivisection Society.

It is also my great pleasure to acknowledge Rita Brock, former director of the Bunting Institute at Harvard University, and Lyn O'Conor, coordinator of its Publications Day, for supporting my work and first introducing my book idea to the publishing world. A Bogliasco Foundation fellowship provided the most inspiring setting for writing the first chapter. Charles Cohen, John Hand, Peter Hawkins, Rachel Jacoff, and Irene Winter kindly wrote letters of recommendation that made these fellowships possible.

Rory Browne, Vickie Garagliano, Susan Haskell, Marvin Jones, Alexander Kruglov, Brian Little, Alane Mason, Robin Ray, Bruce Redford, Nigel Rothfels, Zainab Zakari, and Boyd Zenner provided help or advice at various stages of this project. My warmest thanks to Shellburne Thurber for the beautiful author photo.

Finally, the debt I am happy to repay with boundless affection and many yummy treats is to my own exotic beast, my gorgeous and goofy vizsla, Audrey, who curled up by my side as I wrote this book and provided both inspiration and much-needed walk breaks. She has taught me a great deal about human interactions with animals.

COPYRIGHT ACKNOWLEDGMENTS

Kennedy Library, California Polytechnic State University, San Luis Obispo.

Permission from the executor of Frank Horner's estate to quote material from *The French Reconnaissance: Baudin in Australia, 1801–1803* is gratefully acknowledged.

From *The Broken Spears* by Miguel Leon-Portilla. Copyright © 1962, 1990 by Miguel Leon-Portilla. Expanded and Updated Edition © 1992 by Miguel Leon-Portilla. Reprinted by permission of Beacon Press.

From *Plutarch*. Reprinted by permission of the publishers and the Trustees of the Loeb Classical Library from *Plutarch*: Vol. V, Loeb Classical Library Vol. 87, translated by B. Perrin, Cambridge, Mass.: Harvard University Press, © 1917, by the President and Fellows of Harvard College. The Loeb Classical Library® is a registered trademark of the President and Fellows of Harvard College.

From *Diodorus Siculus*. Reprinted by permission of the publishers and the Trustees of the Loeb Classical Library from *Diodorus Siculus*: Vols. I and II, Loeb Classical Library Vols. 279 and 303, translated by C. H. Oldfather, Cambridge, Mass.: Harvard University Press, © 1933 and 1935, by the President and Fellows of Harvard College. The Loeb Classical Library® is a registered trademark of the President and Fellows of Harvard College.

From *Strabo: Geography*. Reprinted by permission of the publishers and the Trustees of the Loeb Classical Library from *Strabo: Geography*: Vols. VII and VIII, Loeb Classical Library Vols. 241 and 267, translated by Horace L. Jones, Cambridge, Mass.: Harvard University Press, © 1933 and 1932, by the President and Fellows of Harvard College. The Loeb Classical Library® is a registered trademark of the President and Fellows of Harvard College.

The copyright holder to the excerpt from *A Florentine Diary from 1450 to 1516* by Luca Landucci, translated by Alice De Rosen Jervis and published by JM Dent in 1927, could not be located.

Every effort has been made to secure permission to reprint the materials included in this book. If for any reason permission has not been given or has been given in error, please contact the publisher and amendments will be made in a future edition.

SOURCES

Introduction
Bedini, Silvio A. *The Pope's Elephant.* Nashville, TN: J. S. Sanders, 1998.
Loisel, Gustav. *Histoire des ménageries de l'antiquité a nos jours.* 3 vols. Paris: Octave Doin et Fils and Henri Laurens, 1912.

One: Elephants for a Kingdom
Agatharchides. *On the Erythraean Sea.* Translated and edited by Stanley M. Burstein. London: Hakluyt Society, 1989.
Athenaeus. *The Deipnosophists.* Book 5. Translated by Charles Burton Gulick. Volume II. Cambridge: Harvard University Press, 1928.
Diodorus of Sicily. *Library of History.* Books 1 and 3. Translated by Charles Henry Oldfather. Volumes I and II. Cambridge: Harvard University Press, 1933, 1935.
Diodorus Siculus. *Historical Library.* Translated by Edwin Murphy. Book 1: *Diodorus on Egypt.* Jefferson, North Carolina: McFarland, 1985.
Pliny. *Natural History.* Books 8, 12, 13. Translated by Harris Rackham. Volumes III and IV. Cambridge: Harvard University Press, 1940, 1945.
Strabo. *Geography.* Books 16 and 17. *The Geography of Strabo.* Translated by Horace Leonard Jones. Volumes VII and VIII. Cambridge: Harvard University Press, 1930, 1932.

Bodson, Liliane, ed. *Les animaux exotiques dans les relations internationals: espèces, functions, significations.* Liège: Université de Liège, 1998.
———. "A Python (*Python sebae* Gmelin) for the King." *Museum Helveticum* 60 (2003): 22–38.
Casson, Lionel. "Ptolemy II and the Hunting of African Elephants." *Transactions of the American Philological Association* 123 (1993): 247–60.
Coarelli, Filippo. "La *pompé* di Tolomeo Filadelfo e il mosaico nilotico di Palestrina." *Ktema* 15 (1990): 225–51.
Coleman, Kathleen M. "Ptolemy Philadelphus and the Roman Amphitheater." In *Roman Theater and Society,* edited by William J. Slater, 49–68. Ann Arbor: University of Michigan Press, 1996.

Desanges, Jehan. *Recherches sur l'activité des méditerranéens aux confins de l'Afrique VIe siècle avant J.-C.-IVe siècle après J.-C.* Rome: Ecole français de Rome, 1978.

Dunand, Françoise. "Fête et propagande à Alexandria sous le Lagides." In *La Fête, pratique et discours. Annales littéraires de l'Université de Besançon* 262 (1981): 11–40.

Erskine, Andrew. "Culture and Power in Ptolemaic Egypt: The Museum and Library of Alexandria." *Greece & Rome* 42 (1995): 38–48.

Foertmeyer, Victoria. "The Dating of the *Pompe* of Ptolemy II Philadelphus." *Historia* 37 (1988): 90–104.

Fraser, Peter Marshall. *Ptolemaic Alexandria.* 3 vols. Oxford: Clarendon Press, 1972.

Hölbl, Günter. *A History of the Ptolemaic Empire.* London: Routledge, 2001.

Hubbell, Harry M. "Ptolemy's Zoo." *Classical Journal* 31 (1935): 68–76.

Meyboom, P. G. P. *The Nile Mosaic of Palestrina: Early Evidence of Egyptian Religion in Italy.* Leiden: E. J. Brill, 1995.

Murray, G. W. "Trogotitica: The Red Sea Littoral in Ptolemaic Times." *Geographical Journal* 133 (1967): 24–33.

Parker, Anthony John. *Ancient Shipwrecks of the Mediterranean and Roman Provinces.* Oxford: Tempus Reparatum, 1992.

Raïos-Chouliara, H. "La chasse et les animaux sauvages d'apres les papyrus Grecs." *Anagennesis* (1981): 45–88, 267–93.

Rice, E. E. *The Grand Procession of Ptolemy Philadelphus.* Oxford: Oxford University Press, 1983.

Scullard, Howard Hayes. *The Elephant in the Greek and Roman World.* London: Thames & Hudson, 1974.

Sly, Dorothy I. *Philo's Alexandria.* London: Routledge, 1996.

Wendrich, Willemina, and Steven Sidebotham. "Port of Elephants and Pearls." *Egypt Today* 16, no. 12 (1995): 144–45.

Two: Controlling Nature in the Roman Arena

Appian. *The Mithradatic Wars.* Book 12 in *Appian's Roman History.* Translated by Horace White. Volume II. Cambridge: Harvard University Press, 1912.

Augustus. *Res Gestae Divi Augusti. The Acts of Augustus.* Translated by Frederick W. Shipley. Cambridge: Harvard University Press, 1924.

Cicero. *Letters to Atticus.* 2.19, 5.21, 6.1. Translated by Eric Otto Winstedt. Volume I. Cambridge: Harvard University Press, 1912.

———. *Letters to His Friends.* 2.11, 7.1, 8.2, 8.4, 8.6, 8.9. Translated by W. Glynn Williams. Volumes I and II. Cambridge: Harvard University Press, 1921, 1929.

Dio Cassius. *Roman History.* Books 37, 39, 43. *Dio's Roman History.* Translated by Earnest Cary. Volumes III and IV. Cambridge: Harvard University Press, 1914, 1916.

Martial. *De Spectaculus Liber (On the Spectacles)* 21. Translated by K. Coleman, "Fatal Charades," p. 62.

Pliny. *Natural History.* Books 8, 12, 13. Translated by Harris Rackham. Volumes III and IV. Cambridge: Harvard University Press, 1940, 1945.

Plutarch. Lives of *Crassus, Pompey,* and *Caesar. Plutarch's Lives.* Translated by Bernadotte Perrin. Volumes III, V, and VII. Cambridge: Harvard University Press, 1916, 1917, 1919.

Seneca. *Ad Lucilium Epistulae Morales. Epistles* 7. Translated by K. Coleman, "Fatal Charades," p. 55.

———. *De Brevitate Vitae (On the Shortness of Life). Moral Essays* 13. Translated by John W. Basore. Volume II. Cambridge: Harvard University Press, 1932.

Strabo. *Geography.* Book 6.273. Translated by K. Coleman, "Fatal Charades," p. 53.

Velleius Paterculus. *Compendium of Roman History.* Book 2. Translated by Frederick W. Shipley. Cambridge: Harvard University Press, 1924.

Baldson, John Percy Vyvian Dacre. *Life and Leisure in Ancient Rome.* New York: McGraw-Hill, 1969.

Coleman, Kathleen. "'The Contagion of the Throng': Absorbing Violence in the Roman World." *Hermathena* 164 (1998): 65–88.

———. "Entertaining Rome." In *Ancient Rome: The Archaeology of the Eternal City,* edited by Jon Coulston and Hazel Dodge, 210–58. Oxford: Oxford University School of Archaeology, 2000.

———. "Fatal Charades: Roman Executions Staged as Mythological Enactments." *Journal of Roman Studies* 80 (1990): 44–73.

Epplett, Christopher. "The Capture of Animals by the Roman Military." *Greece & Rome* 48 (2001): 210–22.

Evans, Richard J. *Questioning Reputations: Essays on Nine Roman Republican Politicians.* Pretoria: University of South Africa, 2003.

Frézouls, Edmond. "La Constructions du *theatrum lapideum* et son contexte politique." In *Théâtre et spectacles dans l'antiquité: Actes du Colloque de Strasbourg, 5–7 november 1981,* 193–214. Leiden: E. J. Brill, 1983.

Friedländer, Ludwig. *Roman Life and Manners Under the Early Empire.* London: George Routledge & Sons; New York, E. P. Dutton, [1908]–13.

Gleason, Kathryn L. "The Garden Portico of Pompey the Great." *Expedition* 32, no. 2 (1990): 4–13.

———. "Porticus Pompeiana: A New Perspective on the First Park of Ancient Rome." *Journal of Garden History* 14 (1994): 13–27.

Greenhalgh, Peter. *Pompey: The Republican Prince.* Columbia: University of Missouri Press, 1982.

———. *Pompey: The Roman Alexander.* Columbia: University of Missouri Press, 1981.

Holliday, Vivian L. *Pompey in Cicero's Correspondence and Lucan's Civil War.* The Hague: Mouton, 1969.

Jennison, George. *Animals for Show and Pleasure in Ancient Rome.* Manchester, Eng.: Manchester University Press, 1937.

Kyle, Donald G. *Spectacles of Death in Ancient Rome.* London: Routledge, 1998.

Leach, John. *Pompey the Great.* London: Croom Helm, 1978.

Seager, Robin. *Pompey the Great: A Political Biography.* 2nd ed. Oxford: Blackwell, 2002.

Shelton, Jo-Ann. "Elephants, Pompey, and the Reports of Popular Displeasure in 55 BC." In *Veritatis Amicitiaeque Causa: Essays in Honor of Anna Lydia Motto and John R. Clark,* edited by Shannon N. Byrne and Edmund P. Cueva, 231–71. Wauconda, IL: Bolchazy-Carducci, 1999.

Toynbee, Jocelyn M. C. *Animals in Roman Life and Art.* London: Thames & Hudson, 1973.

Veyne, Paul. *Bread and Circuses.* London: Harmondsworth, 1990.

Ville, Georges. *La gladiature en Occident des origines à la mort de Domitien.* Rome: Ecole française de Rome, 1981.

Three: How a Giraffe Turned a Merchant into a Prince

Dio Cassius. *Roman History.* Books 37, 39, 43. *Dio's Roman History.* Translated by Earnest Cary. Volumes III and IV. Cambridge: Harvard University Press, 1914, 1916.

Pliny. *Natural History.* Books 8, 12, 13. Translated by Harris Rackham. Volumes III and IV. Cambridge: Harvard University Press, 1940, 1945.

Amari, Michelle, trans. and ed. *I diplomi arabi del R. Archivio fiorentino.* 2 vols. Florence: Tipografia di Felice Le Monnier, 1863.

Ashtor, Eliyahu. *Levant Trade in the Late Middle Ages.* Princeton, NJ: Princeton University Press, 1983.

Behrens-Abouseif, Doris. *The Citadel of Cairo: Stage for Mamluk Ceremonial.* Cairo: Institut français d'archéologie orientale du Caire, 1988.

Bullard, Melissa Meriam. *Lorenzo Il Magnifico: Image and Anxiety, Politics and Finance.* Florence: Olschki, 1992.

Donati, Lamberto. "La Giraffa." *Maso Finiguerra* 3 (1938): 247–68.

Fabri, Felix. *Voyage en Égypte de Félix Fabri, 1483.* Translated and edited by Jacques Masson. Cairo: Institut français d'archéologie orientale du Caire, 1975.

Fisher, Sidney Nettleton. *The Foreign Relations of Turkey, 1481–1512.* Urbana: University of Illinois Press, 1948.

Ghistele, Joos van. *Voyage en Egypte de Joos van Ghistele, 1482–1483.* Translated and edited by Renée Bauwens-Préaux. Cairo: Institut française d'archéologie orientale du Caire, 1976.

Haarman, Ulrich. "The Mamluk System of Rule in the Eyes of Western Travelers." *Mamluk Studies Review* 5 (2001): 1–24.

Hale, John Rigby. *Florence and the Medici: The Pattern of Control.* New York: Thames & Hudson, 1978.

Harff, Arnold Ritter von. *The Pilgrimage of Arnold von Harff, Knight from Cologne, Through Italy, Syria, Egypt, Arabia, Ethiopia, Nubia, Palestine, Turkey, France and Spain, Which He Accomplished in the Years 1496 to 1499.* Translated and edited by Malcolm Letts. London: Hakluyt Society, 1946.

Hatfield, Rab. "Some Unknown Descriptions of the Medici Palace in 1459." *Art Bulletin* 52 (1970): 232–49.

Hattox, Ralph S. "Qaytbay's Diplomatic Dilemma Concerning the Flight of Cem Sultan (1481–82)." *Mamluk Studies Review* 6 (2002): 177–90.

Joost-Gaugier, Christiane L. "Lorenzo the Magnificent and the Giraffe as a Symbol of Power." *Artibus et Historiae* 8 (1987): 91–99.

Landucci, Luca. *Diario fiorentino dal 1450 al 1516 di Luca Landucci.* Florence: G. C. Sansoni, 1883. Translated by Alice de Rosen Jervis as *A Florentine Diary from 1450 to 1516* (London: J. M. Dent & Sons, 1927).

Laufer, Berthold. *The Giraffe in History and Art.* Chicago: Field Museum of Natural History, 1928.

Lloyd, Joan Barclay. *African Animals in Renaissance Literature and Art.* Oxford: Clarendon Press, 1971.

Mack, Rosamond E. *Bazaar to Piazza: Islamic Trade and Italian Art, 1300–1600.* Berkeley: University of California Press, 2002.

Mallett, Michael E. *The Florentine Galleys in the Fifteenth Century.* Oxford: Clarendon Press, 1967.

Martines, Lauro. *April Blood: Florence and the Plot Against the Medici.* Oxford: Oxford University Press, 2003.

Masi, Bartolomeo. *Ricordanze di Bartolomeo Masi, Caldelario Fiorentino, dal 1487 al 1526.* Edited by Gius. Odoardo Corazzini. Florence: G. C. Sansoni, 1906.

Natura viva in Casa Medici: Dipinti di animali dai depositi di Palazzo Pitti con esemplari del Museo zoologico "La Specola." An exhibition catalog, Palazzo Pitti. Florence: Centro Di, 1985.

Newhall, Amy Whittier. "The Patronage of the Mamluk Sultan Qa'it Bay, 872–901/1468–1496." PhD diss., Harvard University, 1987.

Petry, Carl F. "Holy War, Unholy Peace? Relations Between the Mamluk Sultanate and European States Prior to the Ottoman Conquest." In *The Jihad and Its Times,* edited by Hadia Dajani-Shakeel and Ronald A. Messier, 95–112. Ann Arbor: Center for Near Eastern and North African Studies, University of Michigan, 1991.

———. *Twilight of Majesty: The Reigns of the Mamluk Sultans al-Ashraf Qaytbay and Qansuh al-Ghawri in Egypt.* Seattle: University of Washington Press, 1993.

Rogers, J. Michael. "To and Fro: Aspects of Mediterranean Trade and Consumption in the 15th and 16th Centuries." *Revue du monde musulman et de la Méditerranée.* 55 (1990): 57–74.

Ross, Janet, trans. and ed. *Letters of the Early Medici as Told in Their Correspondence.* London: Chatto & Windus, 1910.

Tafur, Pero. *Travels and Adventures, 1435–1439.* Translated and edited by Malcolm Letts. London: George Routledge & Sons, 1926.

Thuasne, Louis. *Djem-Sultan, fils de Mohammed II, frère de Bayezid II (1459–1495).* Paris: Ernest Leroux, 1892.

Trexler, Richard C. *Public Life in Renaissance Florence.* New York: Academic Press, 1980.

Wansbrough, John. "A Mamluk Commercial Treaty Concluded with the Republic of Florence 894/1489." In *Documents from Islamic Chanceries,* edited by Samuel Miklos Stern, 37–79. Cambridge: Harvard University Press, 1965.

Four: Human Animals in the New World and Old

Anawalt, Patricia Rieff. "Understanding Aztec Human Sacrifice," *Archaeology* 35, no. 5 (1982): 38–45.

Berdan, Frances F., and Patricia Rieff Anawalt. *The Codex Mendoza.* Berkeley: University of California Press, 1992.

Campbell, Mary B. *The Witness and the Other World: Exotic European Travel Writing, 400–1600.* Ithaca, NY: Cornell University Press, 1988.

Chiappelli, Fredi, ed. *First Images of America: The Impact of the New World on the Old.* Vol. 1. Berkeley: University of California Press, 1976.

Cline, Howard F. "Hernando Cortés and the Aztec Indians in Spain." *Quarterly Journal of the Library of Congress* 26 (1969): 70–90.

Cortés, Hernán. *Letters from Mexico.* Translated and edited by Anthony Pagden. New Haven: Yale Nota Bene, 1986.

Díaz del Castillo, Bernal. *The Discovery and Conquest of Mexico, 1517–1521.* Edited by Genaro García, translated by A. P. Maudslay. New York: Farrar, Straus and Cadahy, 1956.

Durán, Fray Diego. *The History of the Indies of New Spain.* Translated and annotated by Doris Heyden. Norman: University of Oklahoma Press, 1994.

Evans, Susan Toby. "Aztec Royal Pleasure Parks: Conspicuous Consumption and Elite Status Rivalry." *Studies in the History of Gardens and Designed Landscapes* 20 (2000): 206–28.

Fuentes, Patricia de, trans. and ed. *The Conquistadors: First-Person Accounts of the Conquest of Mexico.* New York: Orion Press, 1963.

Gómara, Francisco López de. *Cortés: The Life of the Conqueror by His Secretary.* Translated and edited by Lesley Byrd Simpson. Berkeley: University of California Press, 1964.

Greenblatt, Stephen. *Marvelous Possessions: The Wonder of the New World.* Chicago: University of Chicago Press, 1991.

Hampe, Theodor. *Das Trachtenbuch des Christoph Weiditz.* Berlin: Verlag von Walter de Gruyter, 1927.

Hanke, Lewis. "Pope Paul III and the American Indians." *Harvard Theological Review* 30 (1937): 65–102.

Hassig, Ross. *Trade, Tribute, and Transportation: The Sixteenth-Century Political Economy of the Valley of Mexico.* Norman: University of Oklahoma Press, 1985.

Honour, Hugh. *The European Vision of America.* Cleveland: Cleveland Museum of Art, 1975.

———. *The New Golden Land: European Images of America from the Discoveries to the Present Time.* New York: Pantheon Books, 1975.

Keen, Benjamin. *The Aztec Image in Western Thought.* New Brunswick, NJ: Rutgers University Press, 1971.

Las Casas, Bartolomé de. *A Short Account of the Destruction of the Indies.* Translated and edited by Nigel Griffin. Harmondsworth: Penguin, 1992.

Leon-Portilla, Miguel, ed. *The Broken Spears: The Aztec Account of the Conquest of Mexico.* Boston: Beacon Press, 1992.

Nicholson, Henry B. "Montezuma's Zoo." *Pacific Discovery* 8, no. 4 (1955): 3–11.

Prescott, William H. *History of the Conquest of Mexico.* New York: Modern Library, 1998.

Riley, Michael G. "Fernando Cortés and the Cuernavaca Encomiendas, 1522–1547." *The Americas* 25 (1968): 3–24.

Rothfels, Nigel. *Savages and Beasts: The Birth of the Modern Zoo.* Baltimore: Johns Hopkins University Press, 2002.

Sahagún, Bernardino de. *Florentine Codex: General History of the Things of New Spain.* Translated by Arthur J. O. Anderson and Charles E. Dibble. Santa Fe, NM: School of American Research, 1970.

Smith, Michael E. *The Aztecs.* Oxford: Blackwell, 1996.

Solari, Amara L. "'Lords of All Created Things': Aztec Political Ideology in the Collections of Motecuhzoma II." Master's thesis, University of Santa Barbara, 2003.

Soustelle, Jacques. *Daily Life of the Aztecs.* New York: Dover, 1962.

Sturtevant, William C., and David B. Quinn. "This New Prey: Eskimos in Europe in 1567, 1576, and 1577." In *Indians and Europe,* edited by Christian F. Feest, 61–140. Aachen: Edition Herodot, 1987.

Thomas, Hugh. *Conquest: Montezuma, Cortés, and the Fall of Old Mexico.* New York: Simon & Schuster, 1993.

Townsend, Richard F. *The Aztecs.* London: Thames & Hudson, 1992.

Five: Rudolf II's Empire of Knowledge

Bacon, Francis. *Francis Bacon: The Major Works.* Edited by Brian Vickers. Oxford: Oxford University Press, 1996.

Bauer, Rotraud, and Herbert Haupt. "Das Kunstkammerinventar Kaiser Rudolfs II, 1607–1611." *Jahrbuch der Kunsthistorischen Sammlungen in Wien* 72 (1976).

Bennett, Jim, and Scott Mandelbrote, eds. *The Garden, the Ark, the Tower, the Temple: Biblical Metaphors of Knowledge in Early Modern Europe.* Oxford: Museum of the History of Science and Bodleian Library, 1998.

Charles, Prince of Schwarzenberg, et al. *The Prague Castle and Its Treasures.* New York: Vendome Press, 1994.

Evans, Robert John Weston. *Rudolf II and His World.* Oxford: Clarendon Press, 1973.

Faber Kolb, Arianne. *Jan Brueghel the Elder: The Entry of the Animals into Noah's Ark.* Los Angeles: J. Paul Getty Museum, 2004.

Findlen, Paula. *Possessing Nature.* Berkeley: University of California Press, 1994.

Fučíková, E. "The Collection of Rudolf II." In *The Origins of Museums: The Cabinet of Curiosities in Sixteenth- and Seventeenth-Century Europe*, edited by Oliver Impey and Neil MacGregor, 47–53. Oxford: Clarendon Press, 1985.

Fučíková, Eliska, ed., et al. *Rudolf II and Prague: The Court and the City*. Prague: Prague Castle Administration; London: Thames & Hudson, 1997.

Gorgas, Michael. "Animal Trade Between India and Western Eurasia in the Sixteenth Century — the Role of the Fuggers in Animal Trading." In *Indo-Portuguese Trade and the Fuggers of Germany: Sixteenth Century*, edited by Kuzhippalli Skaria Mathew, 195–225. New Delhi: Manohar, 1997.

Haupt, Herbert et al., eds. *Le Bestiaire de Rudolf II: Cod. Min. 129 et 130 de la Bibliothèque nationale d'Autriche*. Paris: Citadelle, 1990.

Hendrix, Lee. "Of Hirsutes and Insects: Joris Hoefnagel and the Art of the Wondrous." *Word & Image* 11 (1995): 373–90.

Hoeniger, F. David. "How Plants and Animals Were Studied in the Mid-Sixteenth Century." In *Science and the Arts in the Renaissance*, edited by John W. Shirley and F. David Hoeniger, 130–48. Washington, DC: Folger Shakespeare Library; London: Associated University Presses, 1985.

Kaufmann, Thomas DaCosta. *The Mastery of Nature: Aspects of Art, Science, and Humanism in the Renaissance*. Princeton, NJ: Princeton University Press, 1993.

———. "Remarks on the Collection of Rudolf II: The *Kunstkammer* as a Form of *Representatio*." *Art Journal* 38 (1978): 22–28.

———. "Variations on the Imperial Theme in the Age of Maximilian II and Rudolf II." PhD diss., Harvard University, 1977.

Kenseth, Joy, ed. *The Age of the Marvelous*. Hanover, NH: Hood Museum of Art, Dartmouth College, 1991.

Klarwill, Victor von, ed. *The Fugger Newsletters*. New York: G. P. Putnam's Sons, 1925.

Ley, Willy. *Dawn of Zoology*. Englewood Cliffs, NJ: Prentice Hall, 1968.

Maselis, Marie-Christiane et al., eds. *The Albums of Anselmus de Boodt (1550–1632): Natural History Painting at the Court of Rudolph II in Prague*. Tielt, Belg.: Lannoo, 1999.

Matthews, George T., ed. *News and Rumor in Renaissance Europe (The Fugger Newsletters)*. New York: Capricorn Books, 1959.

Moryson, Fynes. *An Itinerary Containing His Ten Yeeres Travell Through the Twelve Dominions of Germany, Bohmerland, Sweitzerland, Netherland, Denmarke, Poland, Italy, Turky, France, England, Scotland & Ireland*. Glasgow: J. MacLehose, 1907–8.

Prag um 1600: Kunst und Kultur am Hofe Rudolfs II. Freren, Germany: Luca Verlag, 1988.

Smith, Pamela H., and Paula Findlen, eds. *Merchants and Marvels: Commerce, Science, and Art in Early Modern Europe*. New York: Routledge, 2002.

Spicer-Durham, Joaneath Ann. "Drawings of Roelandt Savery." PhD diss., Yale University, 1979.

Six: The Black Swans of Malmaison

"Ancien Moniteur." *Réimpression de l'ancien Moniteur: depuis la réunion des Etats-généraux jusqu'au Consulat (mai 1789–novembre 1799).* Vol. 29. Paris: Au Nurau Central, 1843: 322–24.

Andia, Béatrice de, et al. *Fêtes et Révolution.* Paris: Imprimerie Alençonnaise, 1989.

Baudin, Nicolas. *The Journal of Post Captain Nicolas Baudin, Commander-in-Chief of the Corvettes Géographe and Naturaliste.* Translated by Christine Cornell. Adelaide: Libraries Board of Australia, 1974.

Bonnemains, Jacqueline. "Les artistes du 'Voyage aux Terres Australes' (1800–1804): Charles-Alexander Lesueur et Nicolas-Martin Petit." *Bulletin trimestriel de la Société Géologique de Normandie et des Amis du Muséum du Havre* 76 (1989): 9–55.

Bonnemains, Jacqueline, Elliott Forsyth, and Bernard Smith. *Baudin in Australian Waters: The Artwork of the French Voyage of Discovery to the Southern Lands, 1800–1804.* Melbourne: Oxford University Press, 1988.

Brown, Anthony J. *Ill-Starred Captains: Flinders and Baudin.* Adelaide: Crawford House Publishers, 2000.

Burkhardt, Richard W., Jr. "Unpacking Baudin: Models of Scientific Practice in the Age of Lamarck." In *Jean-Baptiste Lamarck, 1744–1829,* edited by Goulven Laurent, 497–513. Paris: Editions du CTHS, 1997.

Chateaubriand, François-René. *The Memoirs of Chateaubriand.* Translated by Robert Baldick. Harmondsworth: Penguin, 1965.

Chevallier, Bernard. "Malmaison: An Imperial Country House." *Antiques* 143/4 (1993): 572–83.

DeLorme, Eleanor P. *Joséphine: Napoléon's Incomparable Empress.* New York: Harry N. Abrams, 2002.

Guicheteau, Thierry, and Jean-Pierre Kernéis. "Medical Aspects of the Voyages of Exploration, with Particular Reference to Baudin's Expedition, 1800–1804." In *European Voyaging Toward Australia,* edited by John Hardy and Alan Frost, 67–69. Canberra: Highland Press and Australian Academy of the Humanities, 1990.

Henn, P. U. "French Exploration on the Western Australian Coast." *Journal and Proceedings of the Western Australian Historical Society* 2 (1934): 1–21.

Hoage, R. J., and William A. Deiss, eds. *New Worlds, New Animals: From Menagerie to Zoological Park in the Nineteenth Century.* Baltimore: Johns Hopkins University Press, 1996.

Horner, Frank. *The French Reconnaissance: Baudin in Australia, 1801–1803.* Victoria: Melbourne University Press, 1987.

Hubert, Gérard. *Malmaison, le château et son histoire, les appartements et collections, Bois-Préau.* Paris: Edition L'indispensable, 1997.

L'Impératrice Joséphine et les Sciences Naturelles. Paris: Réunion des Musées Nationaux, 1997.

Jill, Duchess of Hamilton. *Napoleon, the Empress and the Artist.* East Roseville, Australia: Kangaroo Press, 1999.

Jose, Arthur W., Francis J. Bayldon, and W. M. Dixon. "Nicolas Baudin." *Journal and Proceedings of the Western Australian Historical Society* 2 (1934): 337–96.

Joséphine, Impératrice. *Correspondance, 1782–1812*. Edited by Bernard Chevallier, Maurice Catinat, and Christophe Pincemaille. Paris: Payot, 1996.

Jouanin, Christian. "Les émues de l'expédition Baudin." *L'Oiseau et la Revue française d'ornithologie* 29 (1959): 169–203.

———. "Josephine and the Natural Sciences." *Apollo* 106 (1977): 50–59.

———. "Les premières tentatives d'acclimatisation du cygne noir en France." *L'Oiseau et la Revue française d'ornithologie* 30 (1960): 1–11.

Jouanin, Christian, and J.-C. Balouet. "Systématique et origine géographique des émues récoltés par l'expédition Baudin." *L'Oiseau et la Revue française d'ornithologie* 60 (1990): 314–18.

Knapton, Ernest John. *Empress Josephine*. Cambridge: Harvard University Press, 1964.

Milbert, Jacques. *Voyage pittoresque à l'Ile-de-France, au Cap de Bonne-Espérance et à l'Ile de Ténériffe*. Paris: A. Nepveu, 1812.

Osborne, Michael A. "Applied Natural History and Utilitarian Ideals: 'Jacobin Science' at the Muséum d'Histoire Naturelle, 1789–1870." In *Re-creating Authority in Revolutionary France*, edited by Bryant T. Ragan Jr. and Elizabeth A. Williams, 125–43. New Brunswick, NJ: Rutgers University Press, 1992.

Péron, François. *Voyage de découvertes aux Terres Australes, exécuté par ordre de Sa Majesté l'Empereur et Roi, sur les corvettes Le Géographe et le Naturaliste et la goëlette Le Casuarina, pendant les années 1800, 1801, 1802, 1803, et 1804*. Paris: De l'Impremerie impériale, 1807–16.

———. *Voyage of Discovery to the Southern Hemisphere, Performed by the Order of the Emperor Napoleon, During the Years 1801, 1802, 1803, and 1804*. London: McMillan, 1809.

Plomley, Norman James Brian. *The Baudin Expedition and the Tasmanian Aborigines, 1802*. Hobart, Australia: Blubber Head Press, 1983.

Quynn, Dorothy Mackay. "The Art Confiscations of the Napoleonic Wars." *American Historical Review* 50, no. 3 (1945): 437–60.

Raj, Kapil. "18th-Century Pacific Voyages of Discovery, 'Big Science,' and the Shaping of an European Scientific and Technological Culture." *History and Technology* 17 (2000): 79–98.

Robbins, Louise E. *Elephant Slaves and Pampered Parrots: Exotic Animals in Eighteenth-Century Paris*. Baltimore: Johns Hopkins University Press, 2002.

Seven: Beyond Private Delight

Addison Collection, Baldwin Collection, and Oral Histories. Hearst Castle Archives. Hearst San Simeon State Historical Monument/CA State Parks.

Hearst, William Randolph. "In the News." *San Francisco Examiner* and other Hearst papers.

———. Papers. Bancroft Library. University of California at Berkeley.

Morgan, Julia. Papers. Robert E. Kennedy Library. California Polytechnic State University at San Luis Obispo.

Aidala, Thomas R. *Hearst Castle: San Simeon.* New York: Hudson Hills Press, 1981.

Baldwin, Carey. *My Life with Animals.* Menlo Park, CA: Lane, 1964.

Boutelle, Sara Holmes. *Julia Morgan, Architect.* New York: Abbeville Press, 1988.

Buettinger, Craig. "Antivivisection and the Charge of Zoophil-psychosis in the Early Twentieth Century." *Historian* (Phi Alpha Theta, History Honor Society), Winter 1993.

Chaplin, Charles. *My Auto-Biography.* New York: Simon & Schuster, 1964.

Coblentz, Edmond D. *William Randolph Hearst: A Portrait in His Own Words.* New York: Simon & Schuster, 1952.

Coffman, Taylor. *Building for Hearst and Morgan: Voices from the George Loorz Papers.* Berkeley, CA: Berkeley Hills Books, 2003.

Davies, Marion. *The Times We Had: Life with William Randolph Hearst.* Indianapolis: Bobbs-Merrill, 1975.

Finsen, Lawrence, and Susan Finsen. *The Animal Rights Movement in America: From Compassion to Respect.* New York: Twayne, 1994.

Head, Alice. *It Could Never Have Happened.* London: W. Heinemann, 1939.

Hearst, William Randolph, Jr., with Jack Casserly. *The Hearsts: Father and Son.* Niwot, Colorado: Robert Rinehart, 1991.

Kastner, Victoria. *Hearst Castle: The Biography of a Country House.* New York: Harry N. Abrams, 2000.

Lederer, Susan E. "The Controversy over Animal Experimentation in America, 1880–1914." In *Vivisection in Historical Perspective,* edited by Nicolas A. Rupke, 236–58. London: Croom Helm, 1987.

Loe, Nancy E. *Hearst Castle: An Interpretive History of W. R. Hearst's San Simeon Estate.* Santa Barbara, CA: Companion Press, 1994.

Murray, Ken. *The Golden Days of San Simeon.* Los Angeles: MurMar, 1995.

Nasaw, David. *The Chief: The Life of William Randolph Hearst.* Boston: Houghton Mifflin, 2000.

New England Anti-Vivisection Society. *A History of Compassion.* Edited by Margaret Moreland Stathos. Boston: New England Anti-Vivisection Society, 2000.

Older, Cora. *William Randolph Hearst, American.* New York: D. Appleton-Century, 1936.

Perkins, Hayes. "Here and There." Unpublished manuscript, Robert E. Kennedy Library, California Polytechnic State University at San Luis Obispo.

Procter, Ben. *William Randolph Hearst: The Early Years, 1863–1910.* New York: Oxford University Press, 1998.

Soames, Mary, ed. *Winston and Clementine: The Personal Letters of the Churchills.* Boston: Houghton Mifflin, 1998.

Winslow, Carleton M., and Nickola L. Frye. *The Enchanted Hill: The Story of Hearst Castle at San Simeon.* Millbrae, CA: Celestial Arts, 1980.

Epilogue: Little People in Furry Suits

Cohn, D'Vera. "The Long-Running Panda Show." *Washington Post,* April 12, 1997, A1.

Cohn, D'Vera, and Michael Laris. "Ailing Panda Feeling Better, Officials Say." *Washington Post,* June 3, 1999, B1.

Croke, Vicki Constantine. "The Lady Panda." *Washington Post,* March 4, 2001, W14.

————. *The Lady and the Panda: The True Adventures of the First American Explorer to Bring Back China's Most Exotic Animal.* New York: Random House, 2005.

Grimaldi, James. "Starbucks Muffins Soothe Ailing Hsing-Hsing." *Seattle Times,* July 22, 1999.

Ignatius, David. "The Panda Puzzle." *Washington Post,* December 1, 1999, A43.

Lumpkin, Susan, and John Seidensticker. *Smithsonian Book of Giant Pandas.* Washington: Smithsonian Institution Press, 2002.

Shen, Fern. "Zoo Awaiting Word on Bid." *Washington Post,* July 10, 1999, B3.

"To the Most Noble Creature in D.C." *Washington Post,* June 4, 1999.

INDEX

ABOUT THE AUTHOR

MARINA BELOZERSKAYA was born in Moscow, USSR, and was an award-winning teacher at Harvard, Tufts, and Boston universities. She currently lives in Los Angeles with her husband, a curator at the J. Paul Getty Museum, and her own marvelous beast, a vizsla named Audrey.